International Community Development Practice

International Community Development Practice provides readers with practice-based examples of good community development, demonstrating its value for strengthening people power and improving the effectiveness of development agencies, whether these be governmental, non-governmental or private sector. The chapters focus upon the making of the community development profession and the eight core competences required of the professional practitioner, as outlined by the International Association for Community Development (IACD), whatever their job title or host agency, in order to be able to undertake community development. These are concerned with the ability of the practitioner to:

- Put ethics and values into practice
- Engage with communities
- Ensure participatory planning
- Organize for change
- Support learning for change
- Promote diversity and inclusion
- Build leadership and infrastructure
- Develop and improve policy and practice

From a policy perspective, the book will reassert the role of community development approaches as related to a wide variety of global challenges, including poverty amelioration, climate change, human rights, peace building and social, environmental, political and economic development. From a practice perspective, the book will reassert the importance of high levels of professional competence building upon decades of experience in the field around the world by development practitioners working in community work, social work, health, adult education, environmental protection, local economic development, urban design, cultural work and other disciplines concerned to support effective community development.

Charlie McConnell is a past President of IACD. He has been involved with community development for nearly five decades and has been one of the leading advocates for greater professionalization within the field nationally and internationally. He was the chair of the world's first national standards setting body and chaired the IACD working group that produced the International Standards for Community Development Practice. He has held director/CEO posts in government agencies, foundations and higher education. His publications include *The Making of an Empowering Profession* (3rd edition 2002).

Daniel Muia is a Sub Saharan Director of IACD and a member of the IACD Training, Publications and Professional Development Committee. He is a Senior Lecturer in the Department of Sociology at Kenyatta University, Kenya. He has published journal articles and book chapters on community empowerment processes. He is the Chair of the Association of Community Development Practitioners, Kenya and chaired the 2021 World Community Development Conference.

Anna Clarke is the President of IACD and a Director for Europe. She is Director for Communities at Prospect Awards, a community development learning social enterprise in Northern Ireland. She also contributes to the community development degree at Ulster University. She co-authored the 2009 and 2015 *UK Standards for Community Development*, authored the *Guide on Using Community Development Standards* (2011) and was a co-author of the *International Standards for Community Development Practice* (2018).

The Community Development Research and Practice Series

Series Editor: Rhonda G. Phillips Purdue University, USA

Editorial Board:
Mark Brennan Pennsylvania State University, USA
James Calvin Johns Hopkins University
Brian McGrath National University of Ireland
Norman Walzer Northern Illinois University, USA
Patricia A. Wilson University of Texas, Austin, USA

Emeritus Board:
Jan Flora Iowa State University, USA
Gary P. Green University of Wisconsin, USA

As the series continues to grow, it is our intent to continue to serve scholars, community developers, planners, public administrators and others involved in research, practice and policymaking in the realm of community development. The series strives to provide both timely and applied information for researchers, students and practitioners. Building on a long history since 1970 of publishing the Community Development Society's journal, *Community Development* (www.comm-dev.org), the book series contributes to a growing and rapidly changing knowledge base as a resource for practitioners and researchers alike. For additional information please see the series page at http://www.routledge.com/books/series/CDRP/.

The evolution of the field of community development continues. As reflected in both theory and practice, community development is at the forefront of change, which comes as no surprise to our communities and regions that constantly face challenges and opportunities. As a practice-focused discipline, change often seems to be the only constant in the community development realm. The need to integrate theory, practice, research, teaching and training is even more pressing now than ever, given rapidly transforming economic, social, environmental, political and cultural climates locally and globally. Current and applicable information and insights about effective research and practice are needed.

The Community Development Society, a non-profit association of those interested in pushing the discipline forward, is delighted to offer this book series in partnership with Routledge. The series is designed to integrate innovative thinking on tools, strategies and experiences as a resource especially well suited for bridging the gaps between theory, research and practice. The Community Development Society actively promotes continued advancement of the discipline and practice. Fundamental to this mission is adherence to the following core Principles of Good Practice. This book series is a reflection of many of these principles:

- Promote active and representative participation towards enabling all community members to meaningfully influence the decisions that affect their lives.
- Engage community members in learning about and understanding community issues, and the economic, social, environmental, political, psychological and other impacts associated with alternative courses of action.
- Incorporate the diverse interest and cultures of the community in the community development process; and disengage from support of any effort that is likely to adversely affect the disadvantaged members of a community.
- Work actively to enhance the leadership capacity of community members, leaders and groups within the community.
- Be open to using the full range of action strategies to work towards the long-term sustainability and well-being of the community.

We invite you to explore the series, and to continue to do so as new volumes are added. We hope you will find it a valuable resource for supporting community development research and practice.

Other books in the series:
Knowledge Partnering for Community Development
Robyn Eversole

Social Capital at the Community Level
An Applied Interdisciplinary Perspective
John M. Halstead and Steven C. Deller

Arts and Community Change
Exploring Cultural Development Policies, Practices and Dilemmas
Max O. Stephenson Jr. and Scott Tate

Community-Built
Art, Construction, Preservation, and Place
Katherine Melcher, Barry Stiefel and Kristin Faurest

Using Collective Impact to Bring Community Change
Norman Walzer and Liz Weaver

Addressing Climate Change at the Community Level in the United States
Paul R. Lachapelle and Don E. Albrecht

The Heart of Community Engagement
Practitioner Stories from Across the Globe
Patricia A. Wilson

Culture, Community, and Development
Rhonda Phillips, Mark A. Brennan, Tingxuan Li

Community Capacity and Resilience in Latin America
Paul Lachapelle, Isabel Gutierrez-Montes and Cornelia Butler Flora

50 Years of Community Development Vol I
Norman Walzer, Rhonda Phillips and Robert Blair

50 Years of Community Development Vol II
Norman Walzer, Rhonda Phillips and Robert Blair

Community Owned Businesses
International Entrepreneurship, Finance, and Economic Development
Norman Walzer

International Community Development Practice
Charlie McConnell, Daniel Muia and Anna Clarke

International Community Development Practice

Edited by Charlie McConnell, Daniel Muia and Anna Clarke

Routledge
Taylor & Francis Group

NEW YORK AND LONDON

First published 2022
by Routledge
605 Third Avenue, New York, NY 10158

and by Routledge
2 Park Square, Milton Park, Abingdon, Oxon, OX14 4RN

Routledge is an imprint of the Taylor & Francis Group, an informa business

Library of Congress Cataloging-in-Publication Data
A catalog record for this book has been requested

ISBN: 978-0-367-69124-0 (hbk)
ISBN: 978-0-367-69123-3 (pbk)
ISBN: 978-1-003-14049-8 (ebk)

DOI: 10.4324/9781003140498

Typeset in Univers
by Apex CoVantage, LLC

Contents

List of Figures		*xi*
List of Tables		*xiii*
List of Contributors		*xv*
Case Study Authors		*xix*
Foreword		*xxv*
Rhonda Phillips		
Preface		*xxvii*
Anna Clarke, President of IACD		

1 The Making of an Empowering Profession   1
Charlie McConnell

2 Putting Ethics and Values into Community Development Practice   29
Anna Clarke and Anastasia Crickley
Case Study 1 – India: Promoting Social Justice in Garment Work Districts
in Tamil Nadu   35
Pradeep Narayanan and Sarah Banks
Case Study 2 – Ireland and Scotland: Small Places Close to Home:
Housing Rights in Practice   39
Dessie Donnelly and Clare MacGillivray
Case Study 3 – Kenya: Case Study Life Bloom Services International   43
Catherine Wanjohi and Meriba Mwende
Case Study 4 – Australia: The Agunya Project   46
Anne Jennings and Andy Grieg, Australia
Case Study 5 – Scotland. UK: Developing a Code of Ethics   49
Maggie Paterson and Kirsty Gemmell

3 Engaging with Communities   55
Charlie McConnell, Anita Paul and Kalyan Paul
Case Study 1: India: The Grassroots Story   63
Anita Paul and Kalyan Paul

Contents

Case Study 2: Nicaragua: Hope and Clean Water   69
Anna C. Ortiz and Victorino Centeno

Case Study 3: Mongolia: Partnership for Organic Farming   72
Tsetsgee Gavaa

Case Study 4: Peru: Constructing a Metropolitan Green Belt   76
Anna Zucchetti, Taícia Marques and Yamile Sánchez

Case Study 5: Kenya: A Community-Based Approach to Tackling Violent
Extremism   80
Halimu Suleiman Shauri and Yusuf Lule Mwatsefu

4   Ensuring Participatory Planning   85
Dee Brooks, Huston Gibson, and Asnarulkhadi Abu Samah

Case Study 1 – Croatia: Putting the Pieces Back Together   93
Dragana Knezić, Ana Opačić, and Dijana Vuković

Case Study 2 – Hong Kong, China: Bottom-up Participatory Planning
on Wing Fong Street Market   97
Kenny Ng Kwan-lim

Case Study 3 – Global: A "Glocal" Assets- and Strengths-Based
(un)Conference: Co-Creating Our Stories of Hope and Action   101
Dee Brooks

Case Study 4 – New Zealand/UK: Engaging with the CHASE Model
to Enhance Community Wellbeing   105
Jean Ross, Keith Whiddon, Samuel Mann and Daphne Page

Case Study 5 – South Africa: Bafenyi ka Bakwena Community
Champions Project   109
Siena Shaker

5   How to Organize for Change   113
Daniel Muia and Charlie McConnell

Case Study 1 – Zimbabwe: Young People Organizing for
Community Transformation   120
Tatenda Nhapi and Bongani Madziwa

Case Study 2 – Peru: Sustainable Tourism in San Bartolo   124
Ursula Harman and Bernardo Alayza

Case Study 3 – Canada: Citizens Struggling Near the Lagoons of Mercier   127
*Jean-Denis Lefebvre, with input by Denis Bourque,
translation by Gilles Beauchamp.*

Case Study 4 – England: Anti Toxic Dump Campaign   130
Julia Wilton

Case Study 5 – Hungary: The Story of Ág   134
Kitti Boda

6   Learning for Change   138
Kwok-kin Fung, Suet-lin Hung and Colin Ross

Case Study 1 – Hong Kong: Together We Sew, Fighting the Virus!   147
Siu-wai Wong

Case Study 2 – Nepal: Facilitation for Empowerment and Social
Transformation (FEST)   150
Ammar Bahadur Air
Case Study 3 – Scotland: Health Issues in the Community   154
Kate McHendry
Case Study 4 – Mozambique: Preserving Through Change   158
Eduarda Cipriano
Case Study 5 – England/Canada: Building Relationships for Community
Development Practice Learning and Sharing   163
Jen Wingate

7   Promoting Diversity and Inclusion   169
    Maryam Ahmadian and Holly Scheib
    Case Study 1 – Ecuador: Promotion of an Affirmative Action Civic Law
    in the Town of Espíndola   176
    Karen Heinicke-Motsch and Olmedo Zambrano
    Case Study 2 – Georgia: Tackling Disability – The Inclusive Practices Network   180
    Anastasia Matvievskaya
    Case Study 3 – England. UK: Using Community Arts for Inclusion – Red
    Water Arts   184
    Sue and Mike Pemsel
    Case Study 4 – Zimbabwe: Taking Women Empowerment to a New Level
    in Hwange District   187
    Nyarai Sabeka and Yvonne Phiri
    Case Study 5 – Australia: Challenging Racism – The Case of Benarrawa
    Aboriginal and Torres Strait Islander Solidarity Group   190
    Tina Lathouras and Dyann Ross

8   Building Leadership and Infrastructure   194
    Michelle Dunscombe and Ron Hustedde
    Case Study 1 – Senegal: Grandmother Project – Change Through Culture   204
    Judi Aubel
    Case Study Two – USA: Kentucky Entrepreneurial Coaches Institute (KECI)   208
    Ron Hustedde
    Case Study Three – Australia: IndianCare   212
    Jaya Manchikanti
    Case Study 4 – Hong Kong, China: Tuen Mun District Council Yan Oi Tong
    Youth Space   215
    Kim Cheung
    Case Study 5 – Scotland, UK: Children's Parliament   220
    Katie Reid

9   Evaluating and Improving Policy and Practice   225
    Jo Ferrie and Paul Lachapelle

Contents

Case Study 1 – Scotland, UK: Supporting Best Practice
in Community Development   233
Alan Barr and Stuart Hashagen
Case Study 2 – USA: Critical Reflection of Community Philanthropy   237
Paul Lachapelle
Case Study 3 – Canada: Vibrant Communities   241
Tamarack Institute
Case Study 4 – Cameroon: Empowering Partnerships and Supporting
Communities in Francophone Africa   245
Moussa Bongoyok
Case Study 5 – Hong Kong, China: Evaluating Community Work
amid COVID-19   248
Kwok-kin Fung, Suet-lin Hung, King-lai Wong, Yu-cheung Chan, Juxiong Feng

10 The Way Forward   254
Charlie McConnell, Daniel Muia and Anna Clarke

*Appendix: Towards Shared International Standards for
Community Development Practice*   *262*
Index   *267*

Figures

1.1   The seventeen Sustainable Development Goals   20
2.1   Promoting social justice in garment work districts in Tamil Nadu, India   35
2.2   Leith, Scotland   39
2.3   Students receiving study materials for use during Covid-19 school
      closure – Kenya   43
2.4   End product – furniture from felled trees and recycled industrial
      material – Australia   46
2.5   Open space practice discussion – Scotland   49
3.1   The National Standards for Community Engagement   57
3.2   Typical monthly meeting of SHGs – the bedrock of sustainable change
      at the grassroots – India   63
3.3   Community member and community development practitioner open
      water nozzle at inauguration event for the water system – Nicaragua   68
3.4   Promoting diverse local food baskets – Mongolia   72
3.5   Tree-planting drive in Cerro Verde del Milagro, Peru   76
3.6   Reciprocity cycle related to methodological stages   78
3.7   HURIA Executive Director addressing community members in a
      community sensitization forum – Kenya   80
4.1   Sherry Arnstein's ladder of participation   87
4.2   City of Hrvatska Kostajnica and Una region, Croatia   93
4.3   Different stakeholders participated in "Our Kwai Fong Circuit" city
      planning workshop which was facilitated by city planners to discuss
      their expectation on Wing Fong Street Market and their community –
      Hong Kong   97
4.4   Graphic harvest of the ABCD (un)Conference   100
4.5   Food box – New Zealand and United Kingdom   105
4.6   Bakwena champions celebrating a successful ABCD course – South Africa   109
5.1   Equipping community leaders in Epworth, Zimbabwe   120
5.2   Food sharing at the Pachamama Mamacocha Ayni event in August 2019, Peru   124
5.3   Mercier Lagoon Community Action Campaign – Quebec   127
5.4   Campaign against Buckfastleigh anti toxic waste dump – England   130
5.5   A brainstorming session in Ag, Hungary   134
6.1   Together we sew – cloth face mask workshop – a community hub –
      Hong Kong   147
6.2   FEST – Constructing the community path – Nepal   150
6.3   Health Issues in the Community – Group in Douglas, Dundee,
      performing play – Scotland   154
6.4   Lucia Narito giving testimony of the impact of the project – Mozambique   158

Figures

6.5 Nguni Theory of Change   159
6.6 Illustration of the relationships built to share and learn about community development – Canada and England   163
6.7 An illustration of what was shared to named individuals by some community development practitioners in Canada who participated in the research   165
7.1 Promotion of an affirmative action civic law in the town of Espindola, Ecuador   176
7.2 Inclusive practices team – Georgia   180
7.3 Mural arts project inspired by architectural archways of our town. Ways of seeing, using photography – England   184
7.4 Northern Products detergent making graduation ceremony – Zimbabwe   187
7.5 Elders representing the Waka Waka, Yagarabul, Biggera, Kao and Wangan Jaoialunga countries gather to support Sorry Day – Australia   190
8.1 Grandmother leaders listening to adolescent girls   203
8.2 Crossing hands   208
8.3 Board members and General Manager of IndianCare – Australia   212
8.4 Tuenmununity formed by a group of youth leaders concerned with primary care of the elderly in Hong Kong. They establish close community relationships by organizing a weekly fitness class for the local elderly – Hong Kong   215
8.5 Members of Children's Parliament in Scotland celebrating 30 years of the United Nations Convention on the Rights of the Child (UNCRC)   220
9.1 The dynamic flow of activity and reflexivity toward community goals   229
9.2 Outcome-led participatory planning workshop in progress – Scotland   233
9.3 The ABCD model: a framework towards a healthy community   235
9.4 One Valley Community Foundation, Montana, USA   237
9.5 Evaluating Communities – Canada   241
9.6 Soulédé, a village in the Mayo-Tsanaga division in northern Cameroon   245
9.7 Sealing off residents of Hong Kong's Jordan neighborhood in January 2021 – Hong Kong   248

Tables

1.1 The eight core competencies required of all community development
    practitioners   24
9.1 Details of the evaluation work undertaken over the course of the
    Vibrant Communities project   243

Contributors

Maryam Ahmadian is the Middle East Director of IACD and a member of the IACD Training, Publications and Professional Development Committee. She is an Affiliate Faculty member in the Department of Women and Gender Studies at George Mason University. She completed her Ph.D., Postdoctoral and Research Fellowship in Community Development at the University of Putra Malaysia and her second Postdoctoral Fellowship in Women's Studies in Iran. She has authored several papers on Community Development in refereed journals.

Dee Brooks is the Oceania Director for IACD. Over twenty years, her work has inspired people at hundreds of events and workshops worldwide where she offers Community engagement and Development training and provides professional co-design, facilitation and keynote addresses for conferences, forums and events. Based on two decades of grassroots work, her specialism is in Asset-Based Community Development.

Anna Clarke is the current President of IACD and a Director for Europe. She is Director for Communities at Prospect Awards, a community development learning social enterprise in Northern Ireland. She also contributes to the community development degree at Ulster University. She co-authored the 2009 and 2015 *UK Standards for Community Development*, authored the *Guide on Using Community Development Standards* (2011) and was a co-author of the *International Standards for Community Development Practice* (2018).

Anastasia Crickley is a past Vice President of IACD and a Director for Europe. She has over forty years of community development experience, working for the rights of marginalized, minority and migrant communities and is Chairperson of the Irish Community Workers' Cooperative. She was Head of the Department of Applied Social Studies at NUI, Maynooth, the leading provider of Community Work education in Ireland where she pioneered access routes for minorities and marginalized groups. She is a past President of the UN Committee for the Elimination of Racial Discrimination.

Michelle Dunscombe is the IACD Country Correspondent for Australia. She is an Australia-based community development practitioner and trainer. She works across Australia and internationally with a focus on community-led development, community leadership and disaster recovery. She is the co-facilitator of ABCD Asia Pacific and chair of Firefoxes Australia.

Jo Ferrie is a Senior Lecturer in the School of Social and Political Sciences and Director of Q-Step at the University of Glasgow and Deputy-Director of the Scottish Graduate School of Social Sciences. An expert in methodology, Jo has worked closely with human rights frameworks to create participatory projects with impact.

Kwok-kin Fung is the East Asia Director for IACD. He is an associate professor of the Department of Social Work, Hong Kong Baptist University and International Advisory Board member of the Editorial Board of the *Community Development Journal* (Oxford University Press). His research interests include community development, financialization, neo-liberalization, gender and welfare regimes. He has written extensively for the *CDJ*.

Huston Gibson is an IACD Country Correspondent for the USA and a member of the IACD Training, Publications and Professional Development Committee. He is an associate professor & director of the Community Development academic program at Kansas State University, USA. His work and scholarship have centered around Community Development since 2000. In 2019, he edited a special issue of IACD's magazine focusing on Community Development Education around the world.

Suet-lin Hung is the IACD Country Correspondent for China. She is an associate professor and associate head of the Department of Social Work, Hong Kong Baptist University. She is a registered social worker, former chair of the Social Work Registration Board, and member of the Women's Commission, the Equal Opportunity Committee of the Hong Kong government. Her research interests include gender, divorce, single mothers, narrative practice and community development.

Ron Hustedde is a past Vice President of IACD and a member of the IACD Training, Publications and Professional Development Committee. He is professor of community and leadership development at the University of Kentucky. He is past President of the Community Development Society in the USA. He works as a practitioner in the areas of leadership development, public deliberation, public conflict and rural entrepreneurship and innovation. He has written numerous articles for the *CDS* journal.

Paul Lachapelle is a past President of IACD, Director for North America and co-chair of the IACD Training, Publications and Professional Development Committee. He is Professor in the Department of Political Science at Montana State University, Bozeman, USA. His publications include the edited book, *Addressing Climate Change at the Community Level* (2019).

Charlie McConnell is a past President of IACD. He has been involved with community development for nearly five decades and has been one of the leading advocates for greater professionalization within the field nationally and internationally. He was the chair of the world's first national standards setting body in the UK and chaired the IACD working group that produced the International Standards for Community Development Practice. He has held director/CEO posts in government agencies, foundations, think tanks and higher education. His publications include *The Making of an Empowering Profession* (3rd edition 2002).

Daniel Muia is a Sub Saharan Director of IACD and a member of the IACD Training, Publications and Professional Development Committee. He is a Senior Lecturer in the Department of Sociology at Kenyatta University, Kenya. He has published journal articles and book chapters on community empowerment processes. He is the Chair of the Association of Community Development Practitioners, Kenya.

Anita Paul is a past Vice President of IACD and the Director for South Asia. She is the co-founder of the Pan-Himalayan Grassroots Development Foundation and has been a community development practitioner, pursuing gender-inclusive sustainable development initiatives for forty years. She engages actively on issues of mountain ecosystems and small holder women farmers, including dialogues with policymakers and other stakeholders.

Kalyan Paul is co-founder of the Pan-Himalayan Grassroots Development Foundation and has been engaged with the conceptualization and implementation of community development programs in the Indian Himalayan Region since the 1980s, when he was also elected as an Ashoka Fellow. He believes in building upon the capacities of local people to bring forth sustainable change and development at the grassroots.

Colin Ross is the co-author of the International Standards for Community Development Practice and a member of the IACD Training, Publications and Professional Development Committee. He is Policy and Practice Development Officer with the Community Learning and Development Standards Council Scotland. Since 1979 he has worked as a community development practitioner and in policy development and practice support roles. He edited the reader *Influencing Change: Community Learning and Development in Scotland, 2001–2015* (2016).

Asnarulkhadi Abu Samah is the Southeast Asia Director of IACD. He is a Professor in the Department of Social and Development Sciences, Faculty of Human Ecology, University of Putra, Malaysia, and a past Director at the Institute for Social Science Studies. He has over twenty years of research and practice experience in the field of Community Development and has been actively involved in work around climate change and human adaptability and work with indigenous people.

Holly Scheib is a Director of IACD for North America. She has more than twenty years of experience in global health, social work and human rights, adapting scientific methodologies to fit the needs of complex communities. Her transformative evaluation and participatory methods are institutionalized within Federal Ministries in the Government of the Somalia and in the Tribal Law of Taos Pueblo, a Native American nation within the United States.

Case Study Authors

(in order of appearance)

Pradeep Narayanan facilitates participatory research programmes at Praxis Institute for Participatory Practices, New Delhi, India.

Sarah Banks is Professor in the Department of Sociology and Co-director of the Centre for Social Justice and Community Action, Durham University, England.

Dessie Donnelly is Director of Participation and the Practice of Rights organization based in Belfast, Northern Ireland.

Clare MacGillivray is the Interim Chief Executive of Making Rights Real in Scotland.

Catherine Wanjohi is Founder and Executive Director for Life Bloom Services International, Kenya.

Meriba Mwende Micheni is the Project Officer for Monitoring, Evaluation and Learning at Life Bloom Services International, Kenya.

Anne Jennings is a PhD candidate at the University of Notre Dame Australia, Broome, Western Australia.

Andy Grieg is the founder and Director of the social enterprise, Agunya Ltd, Broome, Western Australia.

Maggie Paterson is Development Officer (Approvals) at Community Learning and Development Standards Council Scotland, Glasgow, Scotland.

Kirsty Gemmell is Development Officer (Professional Learning) at Community Learning and Development Standards Council Scotland, Glasgow, Scotland.

Anita Paul is the founder and co-director of Grassroots, India.

Case Study Authors

Kalyan Paul is the founder and co-director of Grassroots, India.

Anna Carolina Ortiz is a public health advocate and International Program Director for Esperança.

Victorino Centeno is Executive Director of AVODEC and a community development practitioner.

Tsetsgee Gavaa is the Partnership for Organic Agriculture Project Manager, ADRA Mongolia.

Anna Zucchetti is a founding member of PERIFERIA and leads the national Platform of Sustainable and Resilient Cities in Peru.

Taícia Marques is an Associate Professor at the Universidad Nacional Agraria La Molina interested in green design in cities.

Yamile Sánchez is a forestry expert specializing in forest plantations, agroforestry and climate change.

Halimu Suleiman Shauri is a professor at Pwani University in Kenya and a board member of HURIA.

Yusuf Lule Mwatsefu is the executive director of HURIA, a Kenyan human rights advocacy NGO.

Dragana Knezić works at the Rehabilitation Center for Stress and Trauma, Zagreb, Croatia.

Ana Opačić works at the University of Zagreb, Faculty of Law, Department of Social Work, Croatia.

Dijana Vuković works at the Center for Social Welfare, Hrvatska Kostajnica, Croatia.

Kenny Ng Kwan-lim works at the Group & Community Work Unit at the Sheng Kung Hui Lady MacLehose Centre, Hong Kong, China.

Dee Brooks works as an ABCD Community Builder with the Jeder Institute, Australia.

Daphne Page is the founder of Little Woodbatch Market Garden, Bishop's Castle, Shropshire, England.

Samuel Mann is a Professor at Otago Polytechnic, New Zealand, leading on sustainability and community development.

Jean Ross is an Associate Professor at Otago Polytechnic, New Zealand and a community development practitioner.

Keith Whiddon is Chair of Bishop's Castle Community Partnership, Shropshire, England.

Siena Shaker is a social scientist and consultant with Zutari, South Africa.

Tatenda Nhapi is an independent Zimbabwean social work researcher.

Bongani Madziwa is a community development practitioner in Epworth, Zimbabwe.

Ursula Harman is a lecturer at the Pontificia Universidad Católica del Perú. She is also a District Councilor for the Municipal Council of San Bartolo in Peru.

Bernardo Alayza is a doctoral researcher at Pontifical Catholic University of Peru.

Jean-Denis Lefebvre is a community organizer at CSSS Jardins-Roussillon Montérégie, Quebec, Canada.

Denis Bourque works at the Université du Québec, Canada.

Julia Wilton is a teacher and was the co-chair of the Buckfastleigh Community Forum Anti-Toxic Waste Campaign, Devon, England.

Kitti Boda is a community development worker at the Hungarian Association of Community Development, based in Budapest, Hungary.

Siu-wai Wong is a Senior Social Work Supervisor in Caritas Hong Kong, Community Development Service.

Ammar Bahadur Air is the Executive Director of Sahakarmi Samaj in Nepal.

Kate McHendry is a Development Manager with the Scottish Community Development Centre.

Eduarda Cipriano was the Executive Director of the Associacao Nguni, Mozambique.

Jen Wingate is a community development and community engagement practitioner and teacher.

Karen Heinicke-Motsch is a Senior Global Adviser in Community-Based Inclusive Development at Christoffel-Blindenmission (CBM).

Olmedo Zambrano is a Latin America and Caribbean Community-Based Inclusive Development Adviser at CBM.

Anastasia Matvievskaya is the Director of the Inclusive Practices Network, Georgia.

Sue Pemsel was a founder and co-director of Red Water Arts, West Yorkshire, England.

Case Study Authors

Mike Pemsel was a founder and co-director of Red Water Arts, West Yorkshire, England.

Nyarai Sabeka is a part-time teaching assistant at Zimbabwe Open University, Faculty of Applied Social Sciences, Department of Development Studies.

Yvonne Phiri is a part-time teaching assistant at Zimbabwe Open University, Faculty of Applied Social Sciences, Department of Development Studies.

Tina Lathouras is a Senior Lecturer in Social Work, University of the Sunshine Coast, Queensland.

Dyann Ross lectures in social work at the University of the Sunshine Coast, Queensland.

Judi Aubel is a founder and Executive Director of Grandmother Project – Change Through Culture in Africa.

Ron Hustedde is Professor of Community & Leadership Development, University of Kentucky.

Jaya Manchikanti has worked as a community development practitioner in Melbourne, Australia for more than twenty years.

Kim Cheung works with the Tuen Mun District Council Yan Oi Tong Youth Space in Hong Kong, China.

Katie Reid is a social researcher and practitioner focused on children's human rights, with the Children's Parliament in Scotland.

Alan Barr was a co-director of the Scottish Community Development Centre, Scotland.

Stuart Hashagen was a co-director of the Scottish Community Development Centre, Scotland.

Paul Lachapelle is a Professor in the Department of Political Science at Montana State University, USA.

Alison Homer is Team Lead and Manger of Cities working with the Tamarack Institute's Vibrant Communities, tackling poverty across Canada.

Moussa Bongoyok is a Professor at William Carey International University, and President of Institut Universitaire de Développement International, Cameroons.

Kwok-kin Fung is Associate Professor and Programme Director in the Department of Social Work at Hong Kong Baptist University.

Suet-lin Hung is Professor of Social Work Practice and Head of the Mental Health Centre at Hong Kong Baptist University.

King-lai Wong is a Lecturer in the Department of Social Work at Hong Kong Baptist University.

Yu-cheung Chan is a PhD student based in the Department of Social Work at Hong Kong Baptist University.

Juxiong Feng is based in the Department of Social Work at Hong Kong Baptist University.

Foreword

Rhonda Phillips, Ph.D., FAICP, Purdue University

It does not happen as often as needed – a work is published that truly stands to not only transform but inspire for achievement of higher purpose and outcomes. This is one such work. In *International Community Development Practice*, Charlie McConnell, Anna Clarke and Daniel Muia present a range of work compiled by highly accomplished scholars and practitioners from around the globe for parsing through and pushing forward vital missions. Never before have we, as a global society, needed such guidance and inspiration during the pandemic that has decimated economies and societies, and ground progress and well-being grinds to a halt in numerous places across the world.

It may sound like an unobtainable goal to continually seek to improve conditions for all, in ways that dismantle inequalities while promoting social justice and desirable development outcomes. But this is the essence of what community development is. It is indeed a noble pursuit of these higher purposes and one that community development practitioners can help address. It is a unique profession, and demands oftentimes fearless pushing forward with ideas, plans and policies founded on participation by members of communities and in some cases aided by local, regional and global partnerships. We need more connection to each other in this demanding and vital journey of community development; it should be noted that the editors and contributing authors of this book are members of the International Association for Community Development (IACD) where support and connection can certainly be found. The book represents this clearly – colleagues from around the globe are sharing and learning from each other and all readers can benefit from it.

International Community Development Practice provides inspiring yet realistic information to aid any practitioner, scholar or community member to better understand "the way forward." Chapters are supported with numerous case studies that illustrate how community developers engage and move forward. The book is a global experience in itself with a panoply of insightful accounts and stories of how progress is gained. Beginning with empowering the profession in need of expanding its reach, chapters range from ethics and diversity, participatory planning, building support with leadership, to evaluation.

Mentioned earlier is the need for guidance in these unparalleled times. Using the IACD's International Standards for Community Development Practice, the editors and contributing chapter and case authors frame their work in these Standards. This is a major contribution to the knowledge base of the scholarship and practice of community development, bringing together direction and approaches for guiding towards goals and outcomes for the benefit of community members. In doing so, this book is clearly one that will impact at a scale that can help us all move forward. As noted by the editors, it has been six decades since the United Nations promoted community development use and practice. We have made significant progress over these years yet there is much more ahead to accomplish. *International Community Development Practice* can aid us all in facing this challenge.

Preface

Anna Clarke, President, International Association for Community Development

This book has been written by members of the International Association for Community Development (IACD). The book builds upon IACD's *International Standards for Community Development Practice*, published in 2018, and is intended to provide an accessible guide to support community development practice in all countries.

IACD is the only global association for those who work in the community development field, with a membership that ranges from grassroots practitioners to academics and policy influencers. It is accredited with the UN as an international, non-governmental organization. You can find out more about IACD at https://www.iacdglobal.org/.

IACD defines community development as a practice-based profession and an academic discipline that is concerned with the organization, education and empowerment of people within their communities. The eighteen contributing chapter authors to this book, together with the sixty-five case-study contributors come from every UN global region. They work in many and varied contexts with diverse communities in both urban and rural settings, employing a range of tools and methodologies to support their community development practice. You will notice this as you read the different chapters and case studies. What we share, in terms of our field of practice is a commitment to the purpose of community development, underpinned by a clear and explicit set of shared values.

There are four intended audiences for this book.

- The first are practitioners and managers in the field of community development as well as those working in other disciplines which adopt community development approaches. From a practice perspective, the book reasserts the importance of high levels of professional competence in practice and builds upon decades of experience. It presents examples of community development practice, demonstrating its added value in terms of promoting equality and social justice, strengthening community empowerment, collective action, problem resolution and impact effectiveness.
- The second are faculty teachers, researchers and students of professional community development education and training programs and those seeking a career in this field. It will also be of value to other faculties and students engaged in areas such as rural development, public health, environmental practice, public policy and administration, social work, community economic development, community arts, urban planning and design. The book is an ideal text for any course concerned with community development as it

is framed around and informed by agreed standards in the practice. From an educational perspective, the book provides a framework for the content and design of initial training and continuing professional development, alongside addressing the need for practitioners to have a strong foundation in social, political and ecological sciences.

- The third are community activists organizing either spatially, by identity or by interest. Across the globe, people in communities voluntarily come together, plan, organize and take collective action to bring about positive social change. This book will be of value to them as it offers international examples of communities working with practitioners and others to bring about meaningful change and beneficial outcomes.
- The fourth are policymakers/advisers and funders/investors in community development programs. From a policy perspective, the book reasserts the value of community development practice in addressing key concerns in communities such as poverty, racism, gender-based inequality, climate action, the promotion of human rights, participatory democracy, peace building and sustainable development. It is our hope this book will inform renewed interest in strategic support for community development programs locally, nationally and internationally to address these key themes over the next decade.

How you can use the book.

We encourage readers to dip into chapters as well as reading the whole book. Other than Chapter One which presents a review of the emergence of community development as a profession and Chapter Ten which presents pointers for the way ahead for community development practice, the book is based chapter by chapter around IACD's International Standards for Community Development Practice. Each chapter begins with an introductory essay that draws upon international literature and research that has informed the respective key areas of practice. Each essay is followed by five case studies drawn from around the world exploring examples of practice related to the chapter's key theme. The chapters are co-authored by highly regarded community development practitioners and academics.

I wish to express sincere thanks to my co-editors Charlie McConnell and Daniel Muia who have worked tirelessly to bring this book to fruition and to the team of chapter authors who willingly and eagerly agreed to take on the challenge. Special thanks are also due to each of our case-study contributors who generously contributed to bringing this book to life.

I would like to acknowledge the Board of IACD whose openness to exploring new opportunities and commitment to enabling the sharing of practice created the environment for the initial idea of the book to grow and flourish and for their ongoing support through the process. Also, huge appreciation to Meredith Greta, administrator at IACD for her superb work supporting the editors.

Finally, I say thank you to Rhonda Phillips and the editorial board of the Routledge Community Development Research and Practice series, and to Sean Speers and the team at Routledge for their advice and support in publishing the book. Routledge is recognized as the premier publisher in the community development field and we are delighted to have had the opportunity to partner with them to add to the community development canon of knowledge.

Disclaimer. Whilst the chapters in this book have been written by IACD members, other than sharing a commitment to the IACD Statement on Community Development and the International Standards for Community Development Practice, the content lies with the respective authors.

About the International Association for Community Development

Community development is a practice-based profession and an academic discipline concerned with the organisation, education and empowerment of people within their communities and the International Association for Community Development (IACD) is the only global multi-disciplinary network for those active and working in this field. Membership is open to all who share our commitment to the purpose and values of community development.

To find out more about IACD, please visit their website iacdglobal.org

Chapter 1

The Making of an Empowering Profession

Charlie McConnell

Part One: On Becoming a Community Development Practitioner

This book is about what professional community development practitioners currently do and have been doing around the world since the United Nations (UN) first promoted this work. It traces the making of this still relatively young field into the practice-based profession and academic discipline it is today. You may already be a community development practitioner or agency manager, someone who trains community development practitioners or a student seeking to enter a career in this field. You may be a development partner interested in or already funding community development programmes. Or you may be working for an international body such as the UN or one of its agencies, or for national or local government or a non-governmental organization (NGO) or a community-based organization (CBO) already supporting or interested in finding out more about what community development practitioners do. It is the story about the work of community development practitioners who, through education, organization and resources, support disadvantaged and vulnerable communities.

Community activists and community leaders are vital to the creation of stronger communities who through collective action stand a better chance at achieving changes people want to see. Being a community development practitioner is not however a synonym for being a community activist or community leader. The International Association for Community Development (IACD) sees the latter as volunteer active citizens, and the former primarily as trained professionals employed to support community action with technical expertise, funds and other assistance. The practitioner facilitates educational and

DOI: 10.4324/9781003140498-1

organizational support, with people power at the heart of the process. This is not to imply that community activists are not often highly skilled, nor that all communities need the support of community development practitioners. More affluent communities can pay for such expertise. But for disadvantaged or vulnerable communities, educational and organizational support can be invaluable. And at a time of limited finances, providing free community development support to disadvantaged and vulnerable communities must be the priority. This book therefore focusses upon such work.

The two words "**community**" and "**development**" are perhaps the least clear in the English language. Academics have spent years trying to define them.[1] So, let's keep it simple.

Community development agencies and practitioners use the word "**community**" in three interconnected ways.[2] Most community development agencies focus upon working within designated **communities of locality**, which can vary in geographic size and population. This means that you may be working at the level of villages, clusters of villages, towns or city neighbourhoods. There are also job opportunities for work with **communities of identity**, such as an ethnic or religious minority, people with disabilities, mental health problems or discriminated towards because of their sexual orientation. These jobs can be locality-based or involve working across a wider area. The third is working with **communities of interest**, which means supporting people who share a common concern such as poor housing and where the agency employing you focusses primarily upon that issue, perhaps with a peripatetic remit embracing a number of localities across a city or county. Community development agencies and practitioners use the word "**development**" also in three interconnected ways. It is used to mean facilitating socio-economic and environmental **improvement** in people's lives. It is also used to mean supporting people through deliberative and collective action to deal with and ideally to shape **change** in their lives. And it is used to promote **sustainability,** helping people to address the challenges impacting upon their lives without compromising future generations.

Human communities can be complex systems and any developmental intervention needs to be thought through carefully with both professional colleagues and the residents and members you will be working with. There will always be both intended and unintended consequences in any community development activity. Over the past five decades, we have learned much about how this process, at its best, works and what interventions can lead to more successful and sustainable outcomes in people's lives. Conversely, we have been able to observe poor practice and how by supporting colleagues through continuing professional development we can improve practice. The disadvantaged and vulnerable communities we work with are not apart from wider society and neither are the hugely complex interactions and power dynamics, positive and negative, this work creates. This is why, an understanding of the political, social and ecological sciences is so vital. As the great Beethoven said: "Don't only practice your art but force your way into its secrets ... "[3]

Usually as a community development practitioner you will find yourself working in a team within the agency that employs you. Sometimes jobs can be quite isolated, especially in rural areas. Most community development jobs involve working in and with disadvantaged or vulnerable communities. These are communities which are daily faced with some huge challenges and problems, whether it be poverty, unemployment or in some cases oppression and conflict, together with communities which may not be poor, but which are, for example, especially vulnerable to discrimination or climate change. Working with such people will be hugely transformative – for you, the practitioner. People who have to deal daily with debt, with the premature death of their children due to polluted water, who have to search day in and out for work, who have to walk miles to school barefoot, who risk sexual violence, who regularly face systemic discrimination, are the most entrepreneurial and caring people you will ever meet. Such communities often contain high levels of what Putnam calls social capital. People don't bowl alone.[4] They help and care for each other in ways that more affluent people, living materialistic and atomized lives have forgotten to do, or pay others to do for them. This is not to take a rose-tinted view of being disadvantaged or vulnerable. As Karl Popper observed, "All life is problem solving."[5] And the problems such communities face can sometimes be life-threatening. But it is to recognize what a privilege it is to be able to work with them to overcome or at least try to tackle some of the challenges they face.

To obtain a job as a community development practitioner these days you will probably need to be a graduate, with a relevant degree or diploma. Not all employers require this, especially smaller NGOs and CBOs. But being able to demonstrate knowledge of community development and, even more so, skills and experience will be an advantage. The main community development course providers, Higher Education Institutes (HEIs), generally encourage and support mature applicants with experience as a community activist or volunteer. In a few countries you may find linked work and training opportunities, where you are in effect an apprentice working with a community development organization and spending a few days a week at college acquiring your qualification part time or online. In some countries training providers recognize and accredit the prior experiential learning that comes from being a community activist; and some employers positively encourage opportunities for activists from indigenous and working-class communities to be employed as community development practitioners. There are a wide variety of community development courses available around the world. Most of these include community development as part of another qualification such as social work or health work.

Community development practice is a career with a myriad of job titles determined by the focus of the employing agency. You will find practitioners specializing in health work, environmental work, local economic development work, social work, urban planning and design, cultural work and so on. Community development has in effect become a hybrid profession, with practitioners often merging two (or more) professional identities. Community development practice has been greatly enriched by the number of disciplines that both use and shape its methods. By looking through the holistic prism of "community", traditional silos have cross-fertilized in hugely creative ways. Over the past decades thousands of people with community development expertise have moved through their careers into senior and more strategic posts in NGOs, local authorities and other public agencies, companies or government departments, hopefully taking with them these ways of working – looking at problems holistically and supporting people to work collaboratively to solve them.

Part Two: The Journey[6]

In 2018 IACD celebrated the sixty-fifth anniversary of the setting up of the association in the USA with a special issue of its magazine *Practice Insights*.[7] This profiled over sixty pioneers of community development from around the world who had shaped our practice and scholarship over the past six decades. It was noted in the magazine that community development had always been a politically contested practice, with both conservatives and radicals adopting the term. The UN started promoting community development in the 1950s as a way of reaching out with technical assistance on the ground locally to developing and low-income countries, promoting economic opportunity and building up social development infrastructure such as primary education, health facilities, clean water supply, affordable housing, or introducing new ideas for agricultural production. The term (or in translation) became more widely adopted around this time in many countries. The 1950s generation of community development practitioners had been influenced by the 1930s depression, by the rise and defeat of fascism in the Second World War, by a belief in planning and the positive role of the state, by national liberation movements and by the vision reflected in the existence of the UN and its agencies. It was the period of decolonization and the creation of around a hundred newly independent states across Asia, Africa, Oceania and the Caribbean. It was also the early days of the Cold War ideological rivalries between Western liberal democracies "led" by the USA and Eastern communist republics "led" by the USSR, together with the non-aligned group of countries, "led" by socialist India. But whatever the wider political and ideological context, the drive was generally similar – to develop undeveloped poorer communities.

The UN established a Regional and Community Development Division and a Community Development and Organization Section within its Division of Social Affairs to encourage the dissemination of lessons learned for both policy and practice. In some countries government departments were established specifically to promote community development. International development aid took off in the early 1960s, with the founding of the United Nations Development Programme (UNDP), USAID and the Peace Corps set up by the American government, the British government's Ministry of Overseas Development (later renamed Department for International Development), the French government's Agence Française de Développement and similar international development agencies in other developed countries, with philanthropic donors playing a complementary and increasingly important role in financing projects across Africa, Asia, the Pacific and Indian Ocean islands, Latin America and the Caribbean.

During the 1950s and 1960s the international development support provided by the USSR favoured large-scale economic development infrastructure projects, but was also an advocate for community-based primary health care programmes[8] In China the "Barefoot" movement was established by the communist government to promote health and education amongst poorer rural communities. In the Indian sub-continent community development projects were inspired by Gandhi's holistic development model with governments supporting rural community development programmes across the sub-continent. East Asian governments were supporters of community development type programmes such as the Saemaul Undong movement in South Korea and, in Southeast Asia, the Philippines Assistance on Community Development Programme. In Latin American countries there were initiatives in community education in poorer rural communities inspired by Cuba's impressive health and literacy programmes. Across Sub-Saharan Africa homegrown community development programmes proliferated, such as the Ujamaa movement in Tanzania. In Oceania, alongside state-funded programmes, indigenous community work around land rights took place. In Middle East and North African countries social Islam provided social welfare such as Jamiyyaat Khayriyya in Egypt. Israel was one of the few countries in the region where the government actively promoted community development programmes.

After the Second World War across Europe and East Asia, where there had been enormous war damage and forced movements of millions of people, governments (liberal and communist) generally adopted top-down reconstruction and development approaches within their countries. There was an urgency to re-build houses, transport infrastructure, to introduce social welfare systems and to create jobs. Consultation with residents on the design of rebuilt towns and cities was not given high priority. However, by the 1960s growing interest was taken by many Western governments in introducing community development programmes within their own countries focusing upon targeted disadvantaged urban and rural communities. Community development programmes were introduced to tackle poverty, with evidence that growing numbers of citizens were falling through the welfare net; to improve race relations in response to the civil rights movement and concerns about immigration and race relations; and as a process for consulting communities on urban regeneration planning proposals as inner-city working-class urban neighbourhoods were demolished, redeveloped and/or relocated. Most community development programmes and projects of this type were financed and managed by central and local governments, with NGOs and philanthropic donors (e.g. the Ford Foundation) playing an important role. These programmes reflected an "interventionist" role by the state among many governments.

By the late 1960s four people began to have a huge influence upon a new generation of community development scholarship and practice. The first was a powerful critique by Ivan Illich of "experts" in the development field who, he believed, had created a form of dependency amongst the poor towards development professionals.[9] Secondly, there was growing interest in the notion of citizen participation and the right of people to have more of a say over the policies and decisions that affected their day to day lives. Sherry Arnstein's ladder of citizen participation symbolized the aim of supporting greater community control of the development agenda.[10] The third was the inspiring community organizing work of Saul Alinsky with his Machiavellian primer for the "Have Nots," *Rules for Radicals*.[11] The fourth was Paulo Freire and his community education work in Brazil,[12] which introduced problem-posing educational methods, where the practitioner, working with disadvantaged people, helped them to more clearly understand the situation in which they lived, the reasons for this situation and the possible solutions.

A new generation, many also with experience of student politics, the totemic "summer of 1968", of volunteering overseas or domestically, became community development practitioners. This new generation brought into the field a passionate belief that community development practice should be seen as part of a radical social change movement. Some were opposed towards the whole idea of community development being seen as a profession. Others, also wanting to see more equitable social change, believed that the "movement or profession" polarization was unnecessary and worked to enhance the professionalism of community development practice and create an infrastructure of support for practitioners. David Thomas, one of the main architects of professional community development in the UK and Europe, argued that the extent of criticism by some of the former towards the British government's community development programmes[13] did however delay the creation of a stronger profession and the extent of state funding for subsequent programmes.[14] We shall return to this in Section Three.

Charlie McConnell

Two Employment Trends Appeared in the Early 1970s

The first trend was the influence that community development methodologies began to have upon several existing disciplines. The social work discipline became interested in complementing "individual" and "family" case work with a broader community development approach, adding skills in community work to social work training.[15] Health professionals were recognizing the value of working out in the field to provide basic healthcare, working with the local knowledge people had.[16] In adult education didactic teaching methods were seen as having "failed" many disadvantaged people, so rather than expecting them to come into an institutional setting, adult educators experimented with more informal outreach/extension work within local communities, linking this with social action.[17] Youth workers[18] and schoolteachers began engaging in community development, reflecting a growing interest amongst young people in social and environmental issues and as part of a movement to transform schools into community schools, available as a wider community resource.[19] In urban design and planning, reaction to vociferous community action campaigns against top-down planning and regeneration programmes, led to some planners and architects adopting public participation approaches, providing community technical assistance in the planning and design of the built environment to community groups in poorer urban communities.[20]

We saw some adopting job titles like community social worker, community health worker, community educator, youth and community worker and community architect. What we were seeing here was the emergence of a different type of professional, one who worked <u>with</u> local communities rather than top down. What this was also indicating was that a practitioner could be for example both a health professional <u>and</u> a community development professional. The second, smaller trend entailed moves in some countries from the 1970s to create a new discipline called community work.[21] This was where community workers, employed by both governmental and non-governmental organizations, had a more generic role that could range from running a community centre to providing outreach support for local groups. In some countries the terms community development and community work are used interchangeably, in others they mean completely different things. IACD has decided to use the term **community development practitioner** to embrace any practitioner in any discipline adopting community development approaches. By this IACD means engaging with communities in a sensitive and inclusive way, ensuring participatory co-design and co-planning of programmes, having expertise in community education and community organizing, promoting diversity and inclusion, building leadership and a support infrastructure (resources, money, etc) to sustain community action, and evaluating development projects and activities together with local communities.

It was and still is impossible to ascertain the size of the overall workforce embracing disciplines adopting community development approaches and methods during this period, or indeed in the 2020s, as we have no global labour market statistics. But we might conject that it currently runs into many tens of thousands worldwide. It is also difficult to indicate a typical salary level. Where the practice is part of an existing discipline, such as health or social work, the salary aligns to those professional disciplines in different countries. For time limited smaller projects run by CBOs, promotion opportunities tend to be limited, starting as a field practitioner, becoming a team leader and then perhaps an agency manager. When employed by a larger NGO or governmental type agency, there can be a longer career ladder, with some employees eventually becoming a department head with a strategic rather than fieldwork role. Community development practitioners often find themselves working for several employers during their career. For a few, this may include moving out of field practice to become community development educators and academics. For others it may involve becoming a freelance community development consultant. Some practitioners may move on to become policy advisers within large organizations, companies, or a government ministry.

As job opportunities grew there was a demand for community development practitioners to be trained. By the 1970s more HEIs in North America, Western Europe and Oceania began offering undergraduate and post-graduate community development type qualifications.[22] Some of these were purely academic degrees teaching about community development, others were more vocational qualifications that included practice-based placements where the student would practice how to do it. Most of these diplomas or degrees included community development type modules as part of another qualification such as social work or adult education. Others were generic community development degrees and para-professional courses for community support workers (these tended to be pre-degree certificate type programmes). Some courses focused more upon international development work, preparing students to work within a developing country. Others focused upon work within developed countries. There was considerable overlap in the use of course books and teaching and learning resources. Although the first course in Asia was established in the Philippines in the early 1970s, it was not until later in that decade that we saw a gradual and then rapid growth in the number of HEIs in Africa, Asia and Latin America offering community development type degrees.

As the employment market grew around the world, practitioners and community development educators began networking, with the first national professional association, the American Community Development Society being set up in 1967, followed by associations in the UK, Australia and many other countries. In all cases, these associations were open access only requiring members, who came from a wide range of disciplines, to agree to the aims and underlying principles of the organization and pay a membership fee (if there was one). Practitioners and academics also began to launch peer reviewed academic journals, the first being the Community Development Journal (CDJ), published by Oxford University Press in 1966. Again, the editorial boards of these journals, primarily academics who had worked in the field, came from a wide variety of disciplines and in the case of the CDJ balanced expertise in both international work and work within developed countries.

Well over a dozen national and discipline-specific journals (e.g. *Journal of Housing and Community Development*) began to be published and the growing canon of research papers, toolkits and books about community development was demonstrating the wealth of critical reflection in this field. Initially publications from the USA and the Commonwealth[23] dominated, due to the widespread use of the English language. From the mid-1970s other European, Latin American, Oceanic, Asian, and African writers were being translated and contributing towards community development scholarship and practice around the world. We also saw from this time, an increasing focus in the literature upon work around racism and upon work with women in the community.[24] The International Convention on the Elimination of All Forms of Racial Discrimination, adopted by the UN came into force in

1969. The 1979 UN Convention on the elimination of all forms discrimination against women led to a growing focus on programmes and scholarship supporting women in community leadership roles and upon addressing gender discrimination issues. Community development practice and scholarship was evolving in light of these trends. The field was becoming more eclectic drawing upon ideas and methods developed in other fields and experimenting with new approaches that in turn an increasing number of disciplines found worked and adopted. Community development conferences were attracting a much broader range of practitioners than in earlier days. While at the same time more specialist gatherings of practitioners were meeting, for example of black practitioners, women practitioners, practitioners working just in rural areas, or urban.

The world's first National Institute of Community Development was established in India in 1958. In Europe, it was the Dutch who took the lead. The idea of a national institute for community development was to establish a centre employing a team of experienced practitioners, researchers and educators to offer continuing professional development support to the field within the respective country, along with research, publications, conferences, library, and information facilities and sometimes to secure contracts for the management of demonstration projects. Some of these institutes obtained government or regional government core funding, as in the UK. In the late 1980s several national and regional institutes from across Europe created a combined European Bureau which worked to offer a policy and practice support role with respect to the European Union and its different development programmes and encouraged learning exchanges between practitioners in Western and Eastern Europe after the end of the Cold War. There are numerous institutes now supporting community development across the world. In the late 1970s IACD moved its HQ from the USA to Belgium, where it secured funding from the Hainault Regional Government and besides organizing international conferences, published a journal COMM, ran a clearing house providing information on community development undergraduate courses, and promoted demonstration projects, especially across Africa and South East Asia.

IACD, along with emerging national associations, academic journals, national support institutes, professional education and training programmes and investment in continuing professional development by employers and employees, are evidence of the increasing professionalization of the field from this period. Later this included interest in national and international standards for professional practice and even discussions about professional registration. This was an incremental and piecemeal picture, however. In some countries an emerging architecture of support secured governmental support and some governments, and other supporters of community development such as foundations, were highly pro-active. More often it was practitioners who took the initiative using their organizational expertise to create the support infrastructure they found most useful, unsurprisingly after extensive consultation and debates at local, national and international gatherings of practitioners.

Recognizing the Need for a Holistic and Integrated Approach

Through their work on the ground, practitioners were soon discovering what social science researchers were evidencing, that the challenges in disadvantaged people's lives – poverty, the poor quality of the surrounding environment, ill health, unemployment, illiteracy, discrimination, et al were interconnected. Researchers into the causes of poverty were able to map spatial and other concentrations of multiple disadvantages, with one problem overlapping another.[25] Poorer people had worse health, lower levels of education, higher levels of physical disability and mental health problems, higher unemployment, worse housing and in cities lived in more polluted environments, were more discriminated against and had a poverty of influence within the political system. What the research was also demonstrating was that the causes of these disadvantages were connected, structural and systemic and that this was a common trend across all countries. These problems were not being caused by disadvantaged and vulnerable people.

It was the structural inequalities in life chances within countries between richer and poorer people, together with governmental systems (the silo nature of bureaucracies and the discriminatory cultures within those systems, e.g. systemic racism) that were largely creating and certainly compounding the multiple disadvantages poorer and more vulnerable communities faced. However, the elites, unwilling to accept research that pointed to inequality, and popular opinion, influenced by media propaganda and conservative government policies, continued to portray a "blame the victim" picture of poor people and ethnic minorities as lazy and criminal. Amongst many in community development practice and scholarship, this meant moving beyond simply promoting social development projects, to a concern with promoting social justice and systems reform. One of the pioneers here was Gary Craig,[26] who became the world's first professor of social justice. A prolific writer on community development since the 1970s he became a President of IACD.

Some local authorities began to adopt *multi-discipline* community development strategies to tackle *multiply disadvantaged* communities.[27] Such programmes could be huge in scale, with multi-million-dollar investments, a recognition that "community" development programmes did not necessarily mean "small" development programmes. The various disciplines that were beginning to use community development approaches were encouraged to work collaboratively outside their discipline silos, whilst retaining their specialist expertise. By adopting a holistic community development approach, disciplines were making connections, so that what they first thought was, for example, a health problem, was seen also as a built environment problem and an economic problem. The results could be impressive. Poor neighbourhoods in some cities were being revitalized as they were redesigned in consultation with local communities. New affordable, higher quality resident-managed housing estates were being built in more disabled-friendly and eco-friendly ways, as architects, social workers, housing workers, health workers and local economic development workers collaborated and adopted more participatory ways of working with local communities. In Germany, there was a pioneering eco-architects movement working with communities to re-design and "green" disadvantaged neighbourhoods in such cities as Berlin.[28]

Priests, punjaris, nuns, imams, preachers, pastors and other faith leaders have long played a powerful role in shaping people's attitudes, opinions and behaviours. In the period covered, many religious leaders working with the poor were radicalized, even though the heads of their religions usually remained more conservative. Faith based foundations became significant players in national and international development programmes from the 1970s onwards and at times significant critics of governments' failures with regards to human rights abuses, inequality and poverty amelioration.[29] The Quakers for example set up

Oxfam. In some countries, priests were in effect community development practitioners, harnessing their local resources, facilities and members to support community action amongst the poor. Through their international networks they could have a powerful influence. In Latin America influenced by liberation theology, many Catholic priests adopted Paulo Freire's approach working within a context of largely military dictatorships and considerable personal danger.

Freire's approach led to considerable debate amongst community development practitioners and community development academics. Was it appropriate for practitioners to adopt such a politicizing role?[30] Clearly no community development practice is apolitical and practitioners working with disadvantaged communities felt empathy towards the people they were supporting. If they were activists, the choice would have been unequivocal. For professional practitioners, however, they also had accountability to their employing agency, and it was essential to ensure they endorsed this approach and would support the practitioner. One of the main reasons the US government under President Reagan left UNESCO, the UN agency responsible for promoting education, was because they saw it as too left wing, citing UNESCO's support for Cuba's programme to eradicate illiteracy. Similar to the ideas propounded by Freire, this saw education and literacy as a method for raising worker and peasant political consciousness.[31]

UNESCO was also an advocate of community arts programmes concerned with the heritage, arts and music of indigenous communities.[32] Community arts work (art, music, film and theatre) became an important feature of community development from the late 1960s, used in health and literacy education campaigns, and as a powerful way of giving a voice to poor communities. What the community arts movement brought into community development practice was not just the democratization and politicization of the arts. Artists working with community organizations were bringing colour into deprived urban neighbourhoods with wall murals, community and street theatre and festivals. Community singing was a powerful participatory and collective experience. Music had the power to move and change people and community action had the power to change artists. Community action inspired the Nueva Canción movement in Latin America, Reggae in the Caribbean and Mayibuye iAfrika in Southern Africa. And music had the power to reach and engage young people. A more politicized community theatre inspired by Augusto Boal and others brought participative plays into deprived communities. Community owned newspapers and radio were giving voice to communities taking on issues they felt aggrieved about or celebrating indigenous cultures and the growing multi-culturalism in many cities. Far from there being a culture of silence or deference, with the support of community cultural workers the voices were getting louder, more diverse and inclusive. The community arts movement contributed towards the 1960s/70s' cultural revolution, by adding the cutting edge of social action, protest, diversity and people participation.

The Contracting Role of the State

The reasons why neo-conservative (neo-con) governments were elected from the late 1970s need to be placed against the wider geo-political context of the time.[33] The unilateral decision by US President Nixon to break with the post Second World War Bretton Woods settlement at the beginning of the decade, together with the massive increase in oil prices by OPEC, the oil-producing countries' cartel, led to hyper-inflation and rapidly growing unemployment across many industrial countries at levels not seen since the 1930s. US power seemed to be in retreat after losing the Vietnam War. The USSR had successfully invaded Afghanistan. Cuba was aiding the liberation movements in Angola and Mozambique. The Western installed dictatorship in Iran, was replaced in a revolution by a radical anti-US Islamist government. Students and civil society within Western countries continued to be vociferous critics of their own governments. It was, the neo-cons argued, time to reverse all of this.

The neo-cons did not simply believe that free market capitalism was better than communism and social democracy, they had a political agenda to reverse the liberal and social democratic post Second World War settlement in the West, to reduce the regulatory roles of the state, to privatize state services and utilities and to roll back the cultural and social reforms that had taken place since the1960s. For thirty years the redistributive taxation policies of liberal and social democratic governments had reduced inequality. But for the rich this had meant higher taxation and, the left argued, such taxation needed to be increased in order to reduce rising poverty and unemployment in the 1970s and 80s. The rich proved far better organized and by way of conservative think tanks, lobbyists and the media, most of which they owned, political parties committed to neo-con policies started winning elections. But rather than adopting Keynesian interventionist policies to reduce hyper-inflation and unemployment, the role of the state began to contract as neo-con economics and social policies spread out from the USA and neo-con governments took power. Some services and utilities were taken away from public ownership, to be run by not-for-profit charities and for-profit companies. In some countries this included water, telecoms, electricity, public transport and even social service and public health systems, together with a considerable weakening of the development planning powers of local and state authorities. Privatization made joined-up approaches to tackling the multiple problems disadvantaged and vulnerable communities faced far more difficult and saw a significant cut in state-funded community development programmes.

The neo-con revolution also compounded the enormous levels of national debt amongst developing countries across the global south. Following independence many of these countries had turned to a form of socialism, but other than India most soon ceased to be democracies. The independence settlements had drawn artificial "lines in the sand" splitting indigenous communities and leading in many cases to civil wars as in Biafra and Bangladesh. Spending on arms and hugely expensive top-down development projects encouraged respectively by armament companies and international finance capitalism along with undemocratic local elites, led to a debt crisis. The IMF (International Monetary Fund) and the World Bank, also influenced by neo-con ideology, offered loans and advice to governments across the global south to help them manage their debts under the banner of structural adjustment. These Catch 22 loans were conditional upon governments cutting further public expenditure and privatizing national assets. Within a short period, many of these countries were spending more on debt interest payments than on poverty reduction, education and health programmes.[34]

With less community development practitioners employed by the state and less government grants available to NGOs and CBOs, practitioners and community organizations had to become ever more entrepreneurial and adept at repackaging their project proposals to a wider range of funders, highlighting such themes as job creation, economic development and social enterprise.[35] The role and influence of non-governmental grant-making trusts and philanthropic foundations grew in significance during the 1980s. The Ford Foundation had been the pioneer supporting urban community development. This was followed by many others, including the Charles Stewart Mott Foundation – community education, the Gulbenkian Foundation – community work and social change, the Carnegie Trust – rural community development, and the Tata Trusts – sustainable communities. They provided grants for local projects and staff, for research, commissions of inquiry and used their influence to make policy recommendations to governments.[36]

The Community Foundations movement took off worldwide and played an increasingly important role as a non-governmental funder of community development projects in many countries. Community Foundations covering a large geographic area, for example, the whole of Northern Ireland[37] were designed to pool philanthropic, private and corporate donations into a single co-ordinated investment tool for targeted community development in disadvantaged communities. A third type of foundation was also influential in supporting community development. These were independent foundations set up by governments, with grant-making and other support roles, including advising their respective governments on policy. Examples here include the British Community Development Foundation and the French Fondation de France. These three different types of foundations became increasingly pro-active players who aimed to influence the agenda and were not simply re-active cash machines.

With cuts in public investment new, or rather older forms of community support emerged with an emphasis upon self-help, and poorer communities being encouraged to use the assets they had more effectively. The Asset Based Community Development (ABCD) approach was a critique of earlier practice that had often started with "problems" rather than "assets".[38] ABCD proponents argued that community development practitioners should start by building upon a community's local assets and not its needs. They were correct that previous governmental community development programmes around the world had tended to designate areas and groups as being deprived and requiring positive discrimination measures. And the call by ABCD advocates to start with people's strengths did find traction and became a powerful addition to any practitioner's toolkit. But the limitation of the ABCD approach was that it underplayed the continuing need also for considerable inward investments of money and technical support for disadvantaged and vulnerable communities if they were really to be strengthened and have the opportunities richer communities had.

We also saw a re-emergence of consumer, community and worker owned co-operatives inspired by the likes of Mondragon in Spain,[39] the Grameen Bank micro-credit movement in Bangladesh[40] and national legislation such as President Carter's Community Reinvestment Act in the USA which made loans available to low-income communities.[41] Through such initiatives community economic development practitioners assisted communities to set up community-controlled not-for-profit income-earning and job-creating enterprises in areas of high unemployment. The business sector generally left the funding of community development projects to governments and foundations. As neo-con guru Milton Friedman said, "The business of business is business." However, some businesses did become more active players, for example assisting disadvantaged urban communities to form Community Development Corporations (CDCs).[42] CDCs focussed upon building affordable housing and other local economic development activities. The number of CDCs multiplied into thousands and can now be found around the world.[43]

Wider engagement by the private sector was also the result of the growing calls by civil society for greater corporate social responsibility. The lesson learned by more enlightened companies from the appalling 1984 disaster in Bhopal, India,[44] was that they either become responsible neighbours, or they would face opprobrium from consumer activists, international media and even shareholders. And from most business leaders' perspective it was better to respond voluntarily than face legislative regulation and higher corporation tax.[45] Their support ranged from giving money and equipment to seconding staff to provide pro bono business and financial management expertise to community development projects.[46] It is possible to see the motives behind the business sector's involvement in community development initiatives as "greenwash" and "redwash" giving the impression of being concerned about environmental or social issues. For most managers and staff involved there was good intent and a genuine desire to help.

Short-termism has been endemic in community development. And the reduction in state funding and in the number and scale of public sector community development programmes and jobs, significantly exacerbated the problem. Tackling deep structural and systemic inequalities became increasingly challenging in an era of short-term funding. Some disciplines using community development approaches, such as social workers and health workers, still employed by the state were able to plan longer term interventions. NGOs and CBOs were increasingly caught up in a never-ending round of grant applications, short-term staff contracts and the loss of experienced staff as projects had to close. Most international and national grant-making donors limited their funding to between three and five years, sometimes only annually and not necessarily renewed. This was one of the chief drivers behind projects establishing income-earning arms. Community Foundations became advocates for supporting community development projects that had potential for financial self-sustainability.

What all the above initiatives were demonstrating was that this was increasingly a world of public/private/NGO partnerships in the financing and delivery of community development programmes. Despite a reduction in the financial support from central and local government around the world, the new players on the bloc were bringing in significant funds (often in the form of loans rather than grants) and other resources. Community Foundations and CDCs might have funds running into many millions of dollars, even billions. There remained however an imbalance in terms of power between disadvantaged communities and this multiplicity of development agencies and funders. And unlike local government, which in democratic countries is accountable to a wide constituency of the electorate, the boards of businesses, foundations, CDCs and NGOs are not as widely accountable. This might lead these players to pursue their own development agendas, but it also meant they could target disadvantaged and vulnerable communities in ways that many local politicians might not because there were insufficient electoral votes to be had from poor communities. The World Bank became especially supportive of community-driven development, with funds going directly to local community development programmes and not via governments for fear of politicians syphoning off the funds.[47]

Funders increasingly wanted demonstrable value for money against performance targets. So, community development practitioners and agencies needed to become much more skilled at project evaluation and at the presentation of what their programme delivered to governments and grant-making donors if they were to secure further investment in a more competitive marketplace.[48] Community development practice is an art as much as a social science, with community development practitioners needing to become more skilled at the art of evaluation and presentation, to ensure the programme got noticed and funded.

Breaking Down Barriers

The end of the Cold War and globalization were seen by Western neo-con political leaders as the victory of capitalism over communism. Community development practitioners were less triumphalist and saw it as opening up new opportunities for learning and exchange between practitioners in Western and Eastern countries from the 1990s. An example of this is reflected in IACD's Budapest Declaration following its international conference in Hungary.[49] The fall of the Berlin Wall in 1989 saw the European Union and the Council of Europe[50] promoting community development policies and programmes across Europe, with particular traction amongst municipalities and regional authorities in the Nordic and Iberian countries, the UK, Netherlands, Ireland and Belgium. In 1992 the OECD (Organization for Economic Co-operation and Development) sponsored a conference on community development in Europe. And there was a proliferation of American and Western European donors funding projects in Eastern Europe and the former countries of the USSR, discovering also that a rich tradition of community action and non-governmental community development had existed in some of these countries under the radar during the Soviet period, despite that government's predilection for top-down planning.

Although responsibility for community development lay at national and local government level within the EU, the European Commission (the EU government) led by the French socialist Jacques Delors, made considerable funds available for community development type initiatives related to supporting Eastern Europe, for anti-poverty programmes and funding for less economically developed urban and rural regions across Europe. An opponent of the neo-con agenda that dominated under US President Regan, Delors was the European Commission President who changed the name of the European Community to European Union, extended its remit to embrace social and environmental policies and programmes, introduced the Single Market and prepared the way for the Euro currency and the Schengen Agreement, which removed border controls between member countries. Combined, the EU member countries became the world's largest funder of international development and aid programmes.

During USSR President Gorbachev's perestroika and glasnost reforms of the late 1980s there were experiments in greater decentralization with a growing number of co-operatives, tenants' associations and CBOs encouraging active participation by local residents in projects to improve their neighbourhoods.[51] While there was conflict between and within some of the Soviet republics after the collapse of the former USSR, it was the disintegration of centralized systems of social protection and the asset stripping of publicly owned resources by local oligarchs and Western multi-national companies that proved disastrous for more vulnerable communities. In China and the former Asian Soviet republics, the World

Bank and other donors started to finance community development programmes from the 1990s. Here, community development practitioners discovered a general lack of public awareness about the concept of public participation in decision-making in development programmes led by the state..[52] The end of the Cold War and the growth in community development type jobs in the former USSR countries and Eastern Europe, saw several HEIs in former European communist countries establishing community development training courses and there was a growth in national networks of community development practitioners across Eastern European countries.

Inter-communal and inter-racial/religious conflict and genocide led at this time to a growth in community-based peace and reconciliation projects in different parts of the world – from South Africa to Northern Ireland, Bosnia to Rwanda. Here integrated community development and conflict resolution strategies were recognized as helping to promote human rights and sustain peace in "post-settlement" contexts.[53] Community development projects in these countries began to specialize in peace and reconciliation work in part because of the availability of funds from governments and international donors concerned that such violence might spread. Across conflict riven communities, women played an increasingly higher profile in peacebuilding community development programmes.[54] Community-based approaches were adopted in various stages of a conflict, as a means of prevention, to build dialogue and reconciliation between groups and to prepare communities for peace processes and post-peace settlements.[55] The election of President Mandela in South Africa was hugely significant in this regard with his advocacy of truth and reconciliation work. His government invested in recruiting and training hundreds of community development practitioners as part of the post-apartheid Reconstruction and Development Programme.

Promotion of human rights increased as a focus for some community development programmes from the 1990s as minority communities of identity in war torn areas were attacked and evidence of human rights abuses were exposed by investigative journalists and local activists.[56] The civil war in Rwanda was the worst genocidal atrocity in the last half of the twentieth century. Minority communities across the world were facing growing discrimination under dictatorial and authoritarian regimes. The theme of IACD's 1997 conference held in South Africa included a focus upon work around human rights issues in conflict zones.

There was also from this time increased practice around the empowerment of children and young people influenced in part by the adoption by the UN of the Convention of the Rights of the Child in 1989.[57] One omission within the Convention was the right of children and young people to participate in decision-making and this became a focus of advocacy and community development practice in many countries. In 2006 the UN adopted its Convention on the Rights of Persons with Disabilities, which in turn stimulated funding for community development projects with people with disabilities. In contrast, this Convention called for the right for disabled people to be able to participate and have a say in decisions that affected their lives.[58] The UN has yet to adopt a Convention on LGBT rights with high levels of homophobic, biphobic and transphobic discrimination in many countries. Collective organizing by the LGBT community goes back to the late 1960s but only gradually received higher attention from community development projects supported by local authorities and NGOs.

Tackling social inequality also saw significant progress as a result of communities of identity organizing and campaigning for legislative and other social reforms. The various UN Conventions referred to did not come out of the ether or as a result of benign politicians, but because discriminated people organized and were assisted to organize to assert their rights. Tackling economic inequality however proved more challenging for community development projects. The impressive work of CDCs and community-controlled enterprises was putting real economic power into the hands of local communities, but social enterprises generally employed few people and co-ops often paid low wages. Projects that focussed upon land reform did put real economic assets into the hands of particularly indigenous and First Nation communities, but the land was often marginal.[59]

Into the New Millennium

In the six decades since community development was first promoted by the UN the global population tripled. More than half of the world's population now lived in urban areas. This presented massive challenges for community development work, especially in the many shanty towns that had grown up around cities in the global south and in the mega-cities from Mexico City to Mumbai, Sao Paulo to Shanghai. Developing countries were making the same mistakes as had occurred in nineteenth-century Europe and the USA as poor rural workers and immigrants moved to rapidly growing and increasingly polluted industrial cities searching for work, living in poor quality housing and unhealthy environments. There were dramatic increases in global migration flows caused by conflicts, resource shortage and climate change.

Profound environmental changes were impacting upon rural, desert, island, coastal and indigenous communities across the globe. The migration to cities of younger people to search for employment, the growth of industrial scale agriculture at the cost of smaller farms, the genetic modification of crops, biodiversity loss, deforestation, soil damage, rising sea levels and desertification meant profound, indeed existential change for hundreds of millions of people and for some areas irreversible environmental damage. Community development practitioners working in highland communities from the Himalayas to the Appalachians, forest communities from the Amazon to Borneo, desert communities from the Sahel to the Atacama, island and coastal communities from the Tuvalu to Bangladesh, sought to mitigate the worst of this by adopting community development approaches to environmental protection. These areas became a melting pot for some hugely creative initiatives that sought to build upon indigenous insights, along with the introduction of environmental education programmes, community reforestation projects and renewable energy initiatives.

Towards the end of the 1990s, the decision was made to move the IACD HQ to Scotland following its 1997 international conference in South Africa. Initially supported by the Scottish Community Education Council (SCEC), a government agency, IACD subsequently secured support from the City of Dundee Council, the Carnegie Trust, and an annual grant from the Scottish Government. The association was in effect re-launched. The move of IACD was the result of a split within the former Board as to its direction.[60] This together with new funding enabled the association to appoint new staff and a small secretariat. A new constitution, which encouraged membership from paid and unpaid practitioners, educators and students, was adopted and a far more diverse Board elected at the association's relaunch conference in Edinburgh. From the outset the new IACD ran regular international and global regional conferences in partnership with regional and national community development networks and, for the first time, developed partnership agreements, the first two being with the American Community Development Society and with the Community Development Journal (CDJ).

Over the following two decades, IACD partnered with community development networks on conferences in New Zealand, Israel, China, UK, Canada, USA, Hungary, Cameroons, Australia, Portugal, Nigeria, India, Philippines, Ireland, Georgia and Kenya. It ran an international professional development programme of study visits for practitioners and educators to Cuba, Chile, India, Ireland, Indonesia, Scotland and Nepal, and published its new magazine Practice Insights, together with special issues with the CDJ, particularly encouraging community development practitioners to share their work. And with the New Zealand network it launched an on-line resource bank called the Global Community Development Exchange, where practitioners and educators could share their teaching and learning resources. On the policy influencing front, IACD had accredited status with the UN and its representatives attended consultative meetings on UN initiatives. One of IACD's Vice Presidents, Anastasia Crickley, was appointed chair of the UN Committee for the Elimination of Racial Discrimination. The association published several global regional Declarations following international conferences, targeting policy recommendations at the UN, regional bodies such as the EU, national governments and the field.

IACD's first international conference in the new millennium was held in Rotorua, New Zealand with support from the government there. It was on the theme of community development in a globalized world. This was also the first IACD conference which sought to identify the common elements required in order to do community development, irrespective of the discipline or occupation involved or the country where it was practiced. This initiative ran alongside interest in some countries in producing occupational standards for the field. (This is picked up in more detail in section three). Following IACD's relaunch a working group convened by SCEC,[61] where IACD was now based, produced a set of core competencies for community development practice whatever the discipline using this approach, which was presented at the conference. The key themes identified were the ability:

- to undertake participative planning
- to consult and negotiate with participants
- to foster a partnership approach committed to inter-agency and inter-professional practice
- to manage conflict, diversity and change
- to develop and implement participative approaches to accessing and managing resources
- to devise policies, structures and programmes that promote social inclusion
- to provide and promote empowering leadership
- to foster a culture committed to organizational learning
- to employ participative evaluation to inform strategic and operational practice

In 2000 IACD co-chaired the session on strengthening the role of women in community development at the civil society gathering at the UN World Social Development Summit. This summit focused on achieving social development for all in a globalizing world. The UN adopted the Millennium Development Goals (MDGs) in 2000. These were intended to provide additional development assistance to the world's poorest countries. They included halving extreme poverty rates, halting the spread of HIV/AIDS, promoting gender equality, and providing universal primary education by 2015. The MDGs were a partnership between the UN, governments, the World Bank, NGOs and the business sector. The new millennium brought a growing awareness amongst social democratic governments around the world and by the communist government in China that the state needed to be more interventionist if poverty and related disadvantages were to be significantly reduced and other issues such as climate change and its impact upon vulnerable communities were to be addressed.

The poverty reduction figures coming out of China were impressive leading to interest in the international development community into learning how this had been achieved. China's approach was multi-disciplinary recognizing the inter-related disadvantages facing the rural and urban poor and it targeted designated communities, with the state and local authorities the main players. China was also experimenting with community-driven development and community development financing in some poor rural areas providing grants to farmers' mutual-help co-operatives supporting improved and diversified crop production, animal husbandry and other income generating activities.[62] There was a mushrooming of professional social work training courses across Chinese HEIs, and an interest in including community development within some courses, influenced by the more established positioning of community development in social work training in Hong Kong. China was also becoming a major player in international development aid across Africa, Asia and Latin America through its One Belt, One Road programme. Although these tended to be large capital and infrastructure projects rather than local community development programmes and they were investment loans rather than grants.[63]

Outside China, public/private/NGO funded partnerships remained necessary, but with local and central government in many countries once again beginning to take a more pro-active role to address socio-economic inequality and climate change and taking more of a lead in orchestrating such partnerships. The situation globally with regards to investment in development and poverty reduction appeared more optimistic. In 2005 under a deal brokered by British Prime Minister Blair at a meeting of the G8, (the world's eight wealthiest countries) the eighteen poorest countries had 100 per cent of their debt cancelled.

And then in 2008 the irresponsible behaviour of some of the world's banks, deregulated by neo-con governments in the 1980s, created a global financial crisis which governments had to bail out. In many countries, there was an immediate reduction in state funding upon domestic community development programmes with significant cuts in jobs alongside general cuts in public expenditure. The election of President Obama in 2008 in the USA (Obama had a background in community organizing) led to a gradual recovery in the global economy. He established the Strong Cities, Strong Communities programme in 2012, which provided technical assistance to economically depressed communities, with a particular focus upon urban areas; supported international commitments to increase development aid to poorer countries in the global south; and funded renewable energy and climate change adaptation and mitigation programmes building upon the powerful campaign to educate people about global warming by former Vice President, Al Gore.

The year before, hopes rose across the Middle East and North Africa (MENA) region with the Arab Spring democracy movement led by middle-class professionals and students alongside trades unionists and activists from poorer areas. This region had long been run by military and monarchical authoritarian dictatorships installed and supported by the West. Throughout the period since the 1950s these regimes had adopted top-down approaches to development. Notions of citizen participation in local decision-making, for example over the building of new urban communities and redevelopment of old, had been negligible. The unplanned growth of mega-cities like Cairo had created huge urban development problems. Poverty levels had increased and the tackling of the needs of disadvantaged and vulnerable communities across the region had been neglected, other than by Islamic and Islamist charities and international NGOs. Across most of the region, authoritarian governments stamped down violently upon calls for democracy, notably in Syria, leading to civil war and the displacement of ten million refugees. For development agencies this humanitarian crisis, called for the urgent creation of camps for refugees, for health care, warm clothing, clean water and food and the protection of vulnerable children, girls and women, the disabled and the elderly.

The Latin American region had since the 1980s and 90s witnessed the emergence of democratically elected governments replacing longstanding authoritarian military dictatorships in many countries, most notably Argentina and Brazil. As with MENA, this was a region with huge disparities in income and wealth and in particular land ownership and with considerable discrimination towards indigenous communities. Unlike the Middle East, democracy was able to take roots. Community development programmes as we have seen were not new to the region, but democratization brought a strong interest in decentralization initiatives and an increased focus upon poverty reduction measures. We saw the municipality of Porto Alegre pioneering handing over eventually a quarter of its budget annually to local communities to participate in determining their development priorities.[64] Called participatory budgeting, this model took off across many countries outside Latin America to become a regular source of funding for community-led development initiatives.[65]

Without Community Development There is No Sustainable Development

"Thinking globally: Acting locally" had begun to appear as a mantra in community development practice as far back as the 1970s influenced by writers such as Ernst Schumacher and his book "Small is Beautiful".[66] This highlighted the links between underlined global social, economic and environmental trends, and their impact upon underlined local communities. Although there had long been silos in the development world between those working on poverty and social justice concerns, and those working around ecological and biodiversity concerns, sustainable development ideas had gained traction amongst both by the new millennium, recognizing the inter-connections between the economy, society and the environment and once again calling for joined-up programmes bridging disciplinary silos. New thinking and programmes emerged in community development practice at this time, informed by ecology, green economics, ecocide and eco-systems thinking.[67] These focused upon transitioning towards a low carbon future, including recycling projects, local renewable energy, reforesting, community agriculture, the rights of animals and nature and local food production. It also began to highlight the interdependencies between urban and rural community development practice. The residents of cities and now mega-cities were connecting more with the importance of the countryside. Questions were being increasingly asked by civil society activists about damaging monocultural farming methods, loss of biodiversity, poor animal welfare, the sourcing of food, its quality and its carbon footprint, rights of access to the countryside, land ownership and rural depopulation, sometimes forced.[68]

This concern for the environment reflected the growing scientific understanding about the effects of the catastrophic loss of global biodiversity, ever increasing industrial and agricultural pollution and criticism about approaches to development measured only in terms of GDP (Gross Domestic Product) – the "stuff" countries produced as economies.[69] We saw a new generation of community development practitioners more passionate about climate change and biodiversity loss than before, not least in Latin America inspired by the UN Earth Summit held in Rio and quickly spreading around the world.[70] The Brundtland World Commission on Environment and Development report[71] chaired by the former Prime Minister of Norway, had called for a paradigm of development that met the needs of the present without compromising the ability of future generations to meet their own needs, calling this sustainable development. They urged the UN to establish a Programme of Action on Sustainable Development, which it did. Increasingly the worlds of community development practice, social action and environmentalism were working together, with development practitioners applying their expertise in community mobilization to support resilience, adaptation and mitigation projects.

In 2015 the UN announced its most ambitious programme yet – the "Transforming our World: 2030 Agenda for Sustainable Development". Significantly the SDG (Sustainable Development Goals) was the first global development programme applicable to every country, north and south. The SDGs were of course a political compromise agreed between governments of many complexions. Other than the reference in Goal 10 to reducing inequality, there was no mention of the need for a redistribution

Figure 1.1 The seventeen Sustainable Development Goals. Image credit: United Nations Development Programme.

of wealth. Civil society led the calls for increased taxes upon the rich to help pay to realize the SDGs, but this was a challenge that only governments and inter-governmental bodies committed to redistribution stood any chance of changing. At the time it was estimated that the twenty-two richest men in the world had more wealth than all the women in Africa.[72] The words "promoting human rights" do not appear in the SDG Agenda, nor "promoting democracy". Although providing capacity building support for disadvantaged and vulnerable communities does appear in the wider text, as does recognition of the need to "empower and promote the social, economic and political inclusion of all, irrespective of age, sex, disability, race, ethnicity, origin, religion or economic or other status". It was clear however that the wide range of agencies and disciplines now adopting community development approaches could play a significant role in realizing most of the SDGs and were keen to do so.

IACD participated in the UN consultations that led to the SDGs and at an IACD event linked to the UN's SDG High Level Political Forum, launched its *Without Community Development There Is No Sustainable Development* three-year roadshow. This was subsequently to embrace several conferences and study trips around the world, publications, and an on-line resource bank to support practitioners to understand the SDG 2030 Agenda and to share their practice. The IACD Board believed that the SDG 2030 Agenda presented a huge opportunity to raise the profile of community development practice once again at national and international level, and to convince governments and other development partners that without professional and technical assistance, disadvantaged and vulnerable communities would be far less resilient, prepared or able to deal with the huge challenges they already faced and would face over the coming fifteen years.

This did not, of course, mean that the SDGs were the only issues community development practitioners should focus attention upon. Local issues rather than the concerns of inter-governmental agreements will almost always be the trigger points for local community action. But these local issues were not as unique as perhaps thought in the past. What all this should be telling community development practitioners was that localism was not enough. Community development practitioners were increasingly thinking and acting both globally and locally. But how to scale up the education and organization of disadvantaged and vulnerable communities in the face of such challenges? How to build collaboration and learning between communities in different countries, working on similar issues?

With laptops and smart mobile phones becoming more widely used worldwide, and some governments and the new philanthropic foundations set up by the tech giants providing funding and equipment to community groups in disadvantaged areas, the requirement to use digital skills and of helping overcome the digital divide became a core competency for community development practitioners.[73] Community development projects began to join up their efforts using the global networking and learning exchange opportunities that the revolution in information and communications technology, and the creation of on-line communities offered. Cross-national and cross-community collaboration and partnership was not new, but the opportunities to realize it multiplied year on year. The use of these digital technologies and social media for community education and organizing grew. It was also proving transformational in the blended learning delivery of community development professional training.[74]

Charlie McConnell

Part Three: Towards International Standards for Practice

It was in light of the opportunities presented by what appeared to be a more optimistic geo-political landscape, that the IACD Board issued a statement in 2016 on community development intended to raise its visibility internationally, but also to promote consistency of meaning worldwide. In reviewing publicized graduate community development education programmes around the world, it was clear that what was being understood as community development practice was not being used in a common way across all countries. In other words, perhaps unsurprisingly, the term community development (and in translation) was meaning different things to different people. Although the literature made regular reference to the U. N's statement in the 1950s about community development being a way of reaching out with technical assistance on the ground locally, there was no globally agreed statement about what community development practice actually entailed, and thus the approaches or competencies expected of practitioners.

The Board consulted association members and the wider field on a draft global statement which, building upon community development practice and scholarship over six decades, sought to highlight the purpose of community development no matter where it was being practiced. The IACD statement saw this as being to promote *participative democracy, sustainable development, rights, economic opportunity, equality and social justice*; and the role of the professional community development practitioner, irrespective of their occupational discipline, as being to help realize these through the *organization, education and empowerment of people within their communities*. The new statement was adopted unanimously at the international community development conference in Minnesota, USA and subsequently endorsed by national associations around the world. The statement sought to promote an internationally agreed understanding of professional community development practice and to highlight the contribution such approaches made and can contribute to public policy and programmes for tackling some of the world's major problems – the crisis in democracy, climate change, biodiversity loss, conflict and human rights abuses, xenophobia and inequality. This is the statement:

> Community Development is a practice-based profession and an academic discipline that promotes participative democracy, sustainable development, rights, economic opportunity, equality and social justice, through the organization, education and empowerment of people within their communities, whether these be of locality, identity or interest, in urban and rural settings.[75]

This international statement was also the clearest yet that the international association saw community development practice as a professional field, embracing a wide range of disciplines adopting shared approaches, methods, values and goals. And as a professional field it needed to ensure that its practice was of the highest standards in the service of disadvantaged and vulnerable communities across the world. This was why following adoption of the new statement, the IACD Board set up a working group to look at whether nationally agreed professional standards adopted in some countries for over a decade, had played a significant role in improving the quality of community development practice.[76] This initiative also built upon earlier work presented at the IACD conference in New Zealand in 2001.

A disconnect between what was taught in HEIs and the labour market was the main cause of what was called the "competency" movement. Employers (governmental and non-governmental) had become increasingly critical that graduates were applying for jobs knowledgeable about social and environmental issues, but not competent to do the job. While it was true that new applicants could learn some skills on the job, letting an unskilled and ill-informed practitioner work with a community could be damaging. So, community development employers began to introduce competency requirements with which job applicants had to comply to get a job as a practitioner. The first National Occupational Standards for community development practice were produced in the UK. These described what the practitioner needed to do, know and understand in their job in order to carry out their role in a consistent and competent way.[77]

For a minority of teachers of community development in the HEIs there was strong resistance to this move as a supposed attack on academic freedom. Most however welcomed a partnership with employers and practitioners in agreeing the competencies, designing course curricula, and adopting a peer review process where employers, practitioners and community development teachers from another HEI comprised an independent endorsement panel to look at the community development course being offered. HEIs in those countries influenced by the "competencies" movement redesigned their courses to adjust them to what was also expressed as being important by the field. This was then linked to nationally agreed standards adopted after extensive consultation across the field involving national community development associations, trades unions, HEIs and employers.[78] There was no evidence that as a result the content of these courses was academically compromised. And in an increasingly competitive and global higher education marketplace, having a course independently endorsed and recognized by a wide range of employers was a marketing advantage, and increasingly attractive to fee paying student applicants.

It was in light of these developments, that the IACD working group then undertook a consultation with IACD members and others in the field and academia on the proposal to publish a set of international standards for community development practice, building upon the national standards introduced in some countries. The large majority of responses were strongly in favour of this initiative. However, a handful of submissions, primarily from academics, argued that IACD's preoccupation with professionals had sidelined the role of the unpaid community activist in community development and that professionals were creating distance between their expertise and the people they support. Community development practice is no different in that regard from any other field. And such risks must be taken seriously, although it has been the academics in our field and not practitioners who have too often written in an inaccessible language rarely read by practitioners, let alone local communities. Ironic to say the least in a field where the ability to communicate in plain language is so important.

These critics were also concerned that the emphasis upon professional competence and standards would lead to managerial approaches to service delivery, with an increased emphasis upon accountability of the practitioners to their employers. There was some truth in this. It was hardly surprising that employers and funders of community development programmes would expect accountability over the use of resources – time and funds. Nor had they appreciated that practitioners in all countries valued relevant professional training and continuing professional development and public recognition of their professionalism. And nor did they appear to understand that by organizing themselves and seeking sectoral recognition by governments and employers, among others, community development practitioners were simply practising what they preach – that to get recognized in terms of public policy and investment you don't agonise, you organize.

The failure of community development practitioners and academics in some countries to create and sustain national associations, national institutes, professional courses or to advocate for professional recognition, contributed to the ease with which the neo-cons could argue that community development was little more than about promoting self-help and volunteering and did not require professionally trained development practitioners. In other countries the field remained better organized and recognized by governments and other supporters. IACD was keen for practitioners and community development educators in all countries to learn from that and thus the launch of the world's first international standards for community development practice at the 2018 World Community Development Conference (WCDC), the annual gathering where so many disciplines involved in community development, from so many countries meet together to exchange their experience and scholarship.

The final report was called Towards International Standards for Community Development Practice. It was approved unanimously by the IACD Board and launched at the WCDC in Ireland in 2018.[79] The International Standards have since been translated into a dozen languages and become IACD's most disseminated publication. They recommend eight core areas of competence necessary for effective practice and which needed to be demonstrated in order to be a community development practitioner. Distilled from decades of experience, these competencies were seen as essential for all community development practice, whether you are a community worker, health worker, environmental worker, social worker, economic development worker, cultural worker et al, and which applied equally to work in urban or rural communities or with communities of identity or interest anywhere in the world.

Each of these is examined and illustrated in more detail in the following chapters.

Table 1.1 The eight core competencies required of all community development practitioners.

The ability to apply professional ethics and values in practice
The ability to engage with communities
The ability to ensure participatory planning
The ability to organize for change
The ability to support learning for change
The ability to promote diversity and inclusion
The ability to build leadership and infrastructure
The ability to evaluate and improve policy and practice

To do this often complicated, challenging, sometimes dangerous work, the International Standards report recommended that:

> Practitioners also needed an understanding of political, social and ecological sciences to give them wider insights into the interconnected realities of people's lives, of the social, political, cultural, economic and environmental contexts within which people live and of how to achieve change that empowers people.

The report concluded that:

> In developing these standards, our intention is to offer them as a guide for practitioners, education and training providers, employers, regional and national CD associations and national governments, to be used to enhance the quality of community development practice and the quality of professional development programmes ...

In other words, these competencies, informed by the political, social and ecological sciences, should be included in the pre-service training and through the continuing professional development of all community development practitioners, irrespective of their specialist discipline in all countries in the years ahead. The report did not make specific recommendations regarding course design, although the inference was that they would inform modules and practice elements within the professional training programmes. For professional education courses specifically called community work or community development, content relating to these required core competencies should form a central part of professional training. For other disciplines, modules should be included alongside discipline-related modules required for example to be a health worker, arts worker, environmental worker or social worker.

The adoption and dissemination of IACD's statement on community development and the International Standards, was a central part of the association's strategy to raise greater awareness about the contribution a community development approach had made for six decades; and why governments, NGOs, professional bodies and international donors should be investing in such strategies, programmes and skilled practitioners. The following chapters look at the contribution community development programmes and practitioners have already been making in relation to the global SDG Agenda 2030, as well as the many local agendas of concern facing disadvantaged and vulnerable communities. Since the UN adopted the SDG Agenda 2030, the world has been affected by growing far right anti-state, nationalist and racist ideologies, by the Covid-19 pandemic and global recession, and by further scientific evidence of the disastrous consequences of global warming. The following chapters make reference to these challenges. Chapter Ten builds upon this to outline what this means for community development policy, practice and professional development over the coming challenging decade in all countries.

Notes

1 For example, W. Biddle (1966). The "Fuzziness" of Definition of Community Development. *Community Development Journal*, Vol. 1, No. 2, April 1966.
2 A fourth use of the word community has emerged in recent years due to wider access to the internet, with communities on-line. This is not a discrete form of development practice yet, but it might become one, and is being increasingly used as a virtual platform by community development practitioners to network members of the previous three nationally and internationally and through both the web and social media, as an educational and organizational tool.
3 G. Wallace (2014). *Beethoven's Letters*. Cambridge University Press. DOI: https://doi.org/10.1017/CBO9781139940535
4 R. Putnam (2000). *Bowling Alone: The Collapse and Revival of American Community*. Simon & Schuster. New York.
5 K. Popper (1999). *All Life is Problem Solving*. Psychology Press.

6 I am taking as a common starting point for a book on international community development practice, the adoption and promotion of the term by the United Nations in the 1950s. There were of course earlier origins in different countries, but it was only after the 1950s that community development as a recognized and named area of professional practice began to take off internationally.

7 IACD (2018). *Practice Insights* magazine. Special 65th IACD anniversary issue.

8 In 1978, the World Health Organization convened an International Conference on Primary Health Care in Alma-Ata, capital of the Soviet republic of Kazakhstan. This conference was seen as a global landmark in advocating a community-based, social justice-oriented approach to health.

9 I. Illich (1973). *Deschooling Society*. Penguin

10 S. Arnstein (1969). A Ladder of Citizen Participation. *Journal of the American Planning Association*, Vol. 35, No. 4: 216–224.

11 S. Alinsky (1971). *Rules for Radicals*. Random House.

12 P. Freire (2003). *Pedagogy of the Oppressed*. New York, Continuum.

13 M. Loney (1981). The British Community Development Projects: Questioning the State. *Community Development Journal*. Vol. 16. No 1.

14 D. N. Thomas (1983). *The Making of Community Work.*, London: Allen and Unwin.

15 P. Henderson and D.N. Thomas (2016). *Skills in Neighbourhood Work*. 4th edition. Routledge; C. Forde, C. and D. Lynch (2015). *Social Work and Community Development*. Palgrave, London.

16 J. Hubley (1980). Community Development and Health Education. *Journal of the Institute of Health Education*, Vol. 18, No. 4.

17 L. Bidwell and C. McConnell (1982). *Community Education and Community Development*. Dundee; T. Lovett Adult Education (1975). *Community Development and the Working Class*. Ward Lock Educational.

18 HMSO (1969). *Youth and Community Work in the 70s*. London.

19 A. Kruger and C. Poster eds (1990). *Community Education and the Western World*. Routledge. London.

20 J. Jacobs (1961). *The Death and Life of Great American Cities.*, New York: Random House and Vintage Books; W. Roling and R. Hackney (1969). Community Architecture and its Role in Inner City Regeneration. *RSA Journal*, Vol. 137, No. 5391: 149–162.

21 Calouste Gulbenkian Foundation (1968). *Community Work and Social Change*. Calouste Gulbenkian Foundation.

22 There were very limited opportunities to study community development at undergraduate or graduate level before the 1970s.

23 The founding Commonwealth members were Australia, Canada, India, New Zealand, Pakistan, South Africa, Sri Lanka and the United Kingdom. From the 1950s to the 1970s over forty further countries joined as they secured independence. All Commonwealth countries have supported community development programs.

24 G. Craig (ed.) (2017). *Community Organising against Racism: "Race", Ethnicity and Community Development*. Policy Press.
   M. Mayo (ed.) (1977). *Women in the Community*. Routledge and Kegan Paul.

25 P. Townsend (1993). *The International Analysis of Poverty*. Routledge.

26 G. Craig (2020). *Handbook on Global Social Justice*. Edward Elgar Publishing. London.

27 A. Barr (1991). *Practicing Community Development: Experience in Strathclyde*. CDF. London.

28 E. Hahn, E. and U. Simonis (1991). Ecological Urban Restructuring: Method and Action. *Environmental Management and Health*, Vol. 2, No. 2: 12–19.

29 K. Kraft and O. Wilkinson (eds) (2020). *International Development and Local Faith Actors, Ideological and Cultural Encounters*. Routledge.

30 C. McConnell (1977). *The Community Worker as Politiciser of the Deprived*. Paisley.

31 C. Dorn and K. Ghodsee (2003). *The Cold War Politicization of Literacy: Communism, UNESCO, and the World Bank*. The Journal for Historians of American Foreign Relations.

32 M. Albert, M. Richon, M. Viñals and A. Witcomb (eds) (2012). Community Development through World Heritage. World Heritage Paper 31. UNESCO.

33 A number of community development writers prefer to use the term neo-liberal. The term neo-con embraces the neo-liberal's belief in laissez faire economics but adds to that the rolling back of liberal/social democratic social reforms and environmental protection regulations.

34 D. Tsikata (1995). *Effects of Structural Adjustment on Africa*. Global Policy Forum.

35 J. Pearce (2003). *Social Enterprise In Anytown*. Calouste Gulbenkian Foundation.

36 European and American foundations interested in social justice and environmental philanthropy periodically gather together to share their work and explore opportunities for partnerships.

37 A. Kilmurray (2019). *Then, Now, The Future 1979–2019. The Role of Community Philanthropy in Progressive Social Change*. Community Foundation of Northern Ireland.

38 J. Kretzmann and J. McKnight (1993). *Building Communities from the Inside Out: A Path Toward Finding and Mobilizing a Community''s Assets* (3rd ed.). Chicago, ACTA Publications.

39 J. Bamburg (2017). *Mondragon through a Critical Lens: Ten Lessons from a visit to the Basque Cooperative Confederation*. Fifty by Fifty: Employee Ownership News.

40 M. Yunus and A. Jolis (1999). *Banker to the Poor*. Public Affairs.

41 M. Westgate (2011). *Gale Force: Gale Cincotta: The Battles for Disclosure and Community Reinvestment*. Harvard Bookstore.

42 Community Development Corporations (CDCs) are non-profit, community-based organizations, often set up with private sector financial support and that engage for example in building low income housing or community economic development projects.

43 A. Van Hoffman (2013). *The Past, Present, and Future of Community Development*. Shelterforce.

44 B. Dinham and Satinath Sarangi (2002). The Bhopal gas tragedy 1984. The evasion of corporate responsibility. *Journal of Environment and Urbanization*, Vol. 14, No. 1 (April): 89–99.

45 G. Mombiot (2002). Business of betrayal. *The Guardian*. Tue 15 Jan. 2002

46 It was at this time that ideas from the business world such as the SWOT analysis were adopted across the community development sector, offering a simple yet systematic approach for analyzing options, prioritizing actions, making decisions, and focusing efforts for the greatest impact.

47 H. Binswanger-Mkhize, J de Regt, S. Spector (eds) (2010). *Local and Community-Driven Development. The International Bank for Reconstruction and Development*. The World Bank

48 A. Barr and S. Hashagen (2000). *Achieving Better Community Development*. Community Development Foundation London; N. Walzer, J. Leonard, M. Emery (eds) (2017). *Innovative Measurement and Evaluation of Community Development Practices*. Routledge.

49 IACD (2005). The Budapest Declaration: Building European civil society through community development. Published in association with the Combined European Bureau for Social Development. Readers will find this on the IACD website.

50 For the example the Council of Europe's 1989 report on community development which encouraged all municipalities and regions to support such initiatives. Council of Europe membership embraces the whole of the continent of Europe, not just E.U. member states

51 E. Shomina (2018). Supporting Community Development in Russia. Article on IACD News website.

52 W. Lang and B.F. Li (2004). *Public Participation in Old Town Reconstruction —— A Case Study on Tongfeng Community in Wuhan. Planners* (in Chinese), 8, pp. 26; N. Kenton (ed.) (2011). Wagging the dragon's tail: emerging practices in participatory poverty reduction in China. *Participatory Learning and Action*, Issue 62. IIED, London.

53 C. O'Brien (2007). Integrated community development/conflict resolution strategies as "peace building potential" in South Africa and Northern Ireland. *Community Development Journal*, Vol. 42, No. 1.

54 A. Donahoe (2017). *Peacebuilding through Women's Community Development*. Palgrave Macmillan.

55 A. Kilmurray (1995). Community action in Northern Ireland: post cease-fire. *Community Development Journal*, Vol. 30, No. 2: 205–208.

56 J. Ife (2009). *Human Rights from Below. Achieving Rights through Community Development*. Cambridge University Press.

57 https://www.unicef.org/child-rights-convention/what-is-the-convention

58 https://www.un.org/development/desa/disabilities/convention-on-the-rights-of-persons-with-disabilities.html

59 A. McIntosh (2004). *Soil and Soul*. Aurum Press.

60 I was the IACD Board member who proposed the move to transfer IACD to Scotland, to be housed at the Scottish Community Education Council where I was CEO. Following negotiations, we were able to transfer the name, but not the assets. In other words, we had to re-create and relaunch the organization. Over the following years the volunteer board and staff created the vibrant association we see today.

61 I chaired this working group and led the presentation at the 2001 IACD conference. At that time, we felt it premature for IACD to be proposing international standards for two reasons. The initiatives being taken in some countries to agree national standards needed to be evaluated. And secondly, we needed to focus upon re-creating IACD, building up its membership, financial sustainability and legitimacy as the international voice for community development.

62 The World Bank (2017). *Piloting Community-Driven Development and Financing with Chinese Farmers. Results brief*.

63 D. Bräutigam (1998). *Chinese Aid and African Development*. Palgrave Macmillan.

64 Y. Cabanes (ed.) (2017). *Another City is Possible with Participatory Budgeting*. Black Rose Books.

65 G. Baiocchi and E. Ganuza (2016). *Popular Democracy: The Paradox of Participation*. Stanford University Press.

66 E.F. Schumacher (1973). *Small is Beautiful*. Blond & Briggs.

67 F. Capra and P. Luisi (2014). *The Systems View of Life: A Unifying Vision*. Cambridge University Press.

68 K. Cahill (2014). *Who Owns the World: The Hidden Facts Behind Landownership*. Random House.

69 A. Leonard (2007). *The Story of Stuff*. This excellent animated film has been viewed by more than 50 million people online around the world and used extensively in schools and community education. Readers can find this film at https://www.storyofstuff.org/movies/story-of-stuff/

70 P. Lachapelle, I. Gutierrez-Montes, C. Butler Flora (eds) (2020). *Community Capacity and Resilience in Latin America*. Routledge

71 Our Common Future: U.N. World Commission on Environment and Development (1987). Oxford University Press. New York. This commission was chaired by the former Norwegian Prime Minister Gro Harlem Brundtland and is often referred to as the Brundtland Commission.

72 M. Lawson (2020). *Time to Care*. Oxfam

73 See D. Schoech (2013). Community Practice in the Digital Age, in M. Weil, M. Reisch and M. Ohmer (2013). *The Handbook of Community Practice*. Sage Publications.

74 IACD undertook a website review of undergraduate courses around the world in 2015. This study identified several hundred undergraduate degrees.

75 IACD (2016). International Statement on Community Development.

76 IACD (2017). Draft Guidance: Towards Common International Standards for Community Development Practice.

77 A. Clarke (2009). *A Guide to Using Community Development National Occupational Standards.* Federation for Community Development Learning.

78 The first national standards setting body was set up and approved by the UK government in 1999. I was its first chair. The new agency was given sectoral recognition by the government, together with funds a. to undertake labour market forecasting in order to estimate how many practitioners might be needed by employers and thus would need to be trained, and b. to undertake the process of agreeing, producing and reviewing national occupational standards for the next generation of practitioners.

79 IACD (2018). Towards Shared International Standards for Community Development Practice. Final Report.

Chapter 2

Putting Ethics and Values into Community Development Practice

Anna Clarke and Anastasia Crickley

Introduction

"Different people have different definitions of fairness, some of which may be fairer than others."[1] This quote by Danny Dorling highlights a key challenge for community development practitioners. When we talk of values and ethics, do we have a shared understanding of what we mean? Often the answer is no. This chapter will explore some of the key texts that have influenced thinking around values, ethics and community development practice, and by way of case studies from around the world, look at how practitioners, working in different areas, have handled values and ethical issues and the dilemmas related to these in their community development practice. While not extensive (yet) the discourse around ethics and community development is growing.[2,3] Community development is and ought to be an ethical and values-based field of practice because it is about social change.

Values and Ethics-Based Practice

While they are sometimes used synonymously, ethics and values are different, but should be complementary.

      Ethics. Ethics are a set of rules that govern the professional practitioner's behavior. These are usually agreed by the practitioner's profession or employer and are expected to be adhered to by the practitioner. In many countries this has led to professional codes of

DOI: 10.4324/9781003140498-2

conduct, setting out expected standards not in relation to the field of practice per se, but equally as ethical standards in public life. These will often include:

- **Selflessness** – acting in the public interest
- **Treating people equally** – while recognizing diversities including those of ethnicity, gender and disability
- **Integrity** – acting for the public benefit and not for financial or material gain. Declaring and addressing any conflicts of interest
- **Objectivity** – acting impartially and making decisions based on fair assessment and best evidence
- **Accountability** – acting with responsibility for decisions and actions taken based on clear and appropriate practice and procedures
- **Honesty** – acting in a truthful manner and building trust
- **Transparency** – acting in a transparent manner and be open to scrutiny
- **Duty of care** – acting in a protective way when working with children and other vulnerable people who may be at risk of exploitation
- **Respect** – acting in a way that is respectful of staff and volunteers working with the agency and with community members
- **Trust** – acting in ways to build relationships that embody trust, demonstrating through their actions that they value and respect the importance of trust within the relationship
- **Compliance** – acting in ways that acknowledge any regulatory frameworks that promote and encourage good practice. Part of the role of the practitioner is about critically engaging with discourses around what is collectively considered to be good practice and to contribute toward codifying that
- **Autonomy** – acting in ways that recognize the independence and the right to self-determination of people and communities

Such ethical standards and expected conducts of behavior are common across many 'people professions' such as social work, teaching and healthcare. They are generally seen as good practice in organizational governance across governmental and non-governmental employers and should be agreed by all stakeholders including practitioners and the communities they work with.

Values. Values are guiding beliefs and the lens through which the practitioner sees the world. The values we hold shape how we think, what we say and what we do. Since its early days as an area of professional intervention, community development work has not taken a value-neutral stance but has made a commitment toward social and economic development. Community development practice was born out of ethically oriented development charities, liberation movements, commitment to the social and economic advancement of poorer countries, and the introduction of welfare states committed to more effective planning and socio-economic opportunity. The values underpinning community development practice emerged over decades and build upon international mores promoted by the UN committing to greater equality of opportunity, freedom of thought, democracy, human rights, social justice and more recently environmental justice. As we have seen in Chapter One, these have been reflected in international agreements about the rights of discriminated communities and most recently within the Sustainable Development Goals. From the 1970s feminist and civil/human rights practitioners and writers concerned with inequalities around gender, race, ethnicity, disability and sexual orientation brought a greater focus upon cultural empathy and relativism and focused again on the idea that "the personal is the political".[4]

Values are central to, and the fundamental foundation of what community development practice is about. Community development practitioners should be working with communities to achieve solidarity and agency, by facilitating, modeling, practicing and advocating **for** solidarity and agency. This is what Bhattacharyya refers to as "teleological" in nature – charting action toward a goal, elaborating a vision of a desired future – and articulating a methodology to get there. Community development methods of organization and education have long focused on how participants can self-organize as well as being supported to organize more effectively to address some identified problem or challenge, to understand its causes more clearly and by linking together action and learning. This process is based upon building dialogue, mutual trust and respect between community members and the community development practitioner and agency.

Most definitions and descriptions of community development refer to values[5] Let us look again at the International Association for Community Development (IACD) definition published in 2016:[6]

> Community Development is a practice-based profession and an academic discipline that promotes participative democracy, sustainable development, rights, economic opportunity, equality and social justice, through the organization, education and empowerment of people within their communities, whether these be of locality, identity or interest, in urban and rural settings.

This definition embodies a set of underpinning values, a purpose and a set of methods for work. The purpose of community development is seen as… *"To work with communities to achieve participative democracy, sustainable development, rights, economic opportunity, equality and social justice."* This high-level purpose statement can be used as a template against which to measure both the journey and the destination of community development practice. In other words, there are both explicit and implicit statements here about the values that should underpin practice; these being the *"commitment to rights, solidarity, democracy, equality, environmental and social justice."* This statement positions community development practice as both promoting certain values-based goals such as greater equality or environmental justice, and for the practitioner to practice what they preach, in the ways in which they work, i.e., through the organization, education and empowerment of people within their communities.

Different cultures may emphasize different values. However, the values of a profession/field of practice such as community development, should be consistent in all contexts and as such universal. Amartya Sen[7] talks of *"social values and prevailing mores, which people enjoy and have reason to treasure."* Values shape and mediate ideas about shared norms, ethical standards, and are influenced by public discussion about the same.

While there is no single definitive set of values for community development, these appear to be generally common.[8,9] A commitment to:

• **Participation** – working to ensure the active and democratic participation of people and communities in planning and decision-making processes on all matters that effect their lives.

- **Sustainable development and environmental justice** – working to ensure that social, economic and environmental development are based upon climate justice, respect for biodiversity, the rights and protection of the natural environment and all life on earth.
- **Equality and human rights** – working to ensure that fundamental and internationally recognized human rights are respected, promoted, protected and realized. Promoting and respecting the equal worth, dignity and diversity of all people and communities and working to ensure their equitable access to resources, services, opportunities and outcomes.
- **Social and economic justice** – working to ensure a just society through collective action that challenges injustice, poverty, inequality, discrimination and social exclusion through policies and procedures that lead to the fair and equitable distribution of resources, sustainable production and democratically controlled decision-making.
- **People empowerment** – working to build people's power and capacity to shape change through collective action, in ways that values their lived experience, builds on their strengths and enhances their critical awareness, knowledge and skills.
- **Collectivity** – working for collective outcomes and benefits for the whole group or community, which builds from individual need to collective concerns.

While values are often presented in the form of a list, as here, it is important to note they are neither disconnected and separate from each other, nor in any order of priority or importance. Each is connected and there is a complex relationship between them that is also evolving. These values need to be reflected in the practice of all disciplines using a community development approach.

Why Values are Important in Practice

Mayo notes that community development practice is talked of as a contested arena.[10],[11] Not least because it often challenges policy, systems and practices which create and reinforce inequality and social injustice. Because of that, and without a strong focus on agreed values to underpin and inform community development practice, Ledwith believes that the field is *"open to manipulation and dilution"* from external influences such as state agencies, funders, politicians and others with their own interests.[12] A clear and collectively agreed set of values provides unity for any professional field.

National and international professional associations, governmental and non-governmental employers, as well as practitioners and academics, philosophers, political movements, secular and religious players from different countries around the world have contributed toward informing the key values that underpin community development practice. Ledwith likens these as the framework that practitioners can use to ensure the integrity and authenticity of practice, whether this is in the context of individual encounters with others or engagement collectively with others toward local as well as global action. This is about working with people through an ideology of treating them with equality, a lens through which to frame, explore and check everything community development practitioners do.

Within the field there have been debates regarding whether the practitioner should be directive or non-directive, whether they should be focusing on alleviating symptoms or working with the community to address the root causes of people's disadvantage.[13] Community development practitioners, as organizers and educators facilitate what Freire called critical consciousness.[14] In doing so, they are basing this upon a belief that it will support people experiencing disadvantage and marginalization to better understand the situation they are in and how to change things in their interest.

Popper[15] is a strong advocate for "open societies", where being open to ideas is given high value in helping people deal with change and problem solving. Popper believed that science provides a model for life about how best to solve problems. This requires an open mind to test out our actions, and to reflect upon these and change direction if they are not working. A key part of the community development practitioner's role is to encourage and enable new thinking through exploration of new ideas, practices and ways of working, as well as encouraging people to be open to re-examining the effectiveness of traditional ways of knowing and doing that may have been long and standard practice.

Challenges

Practitioners are constantly dealing with how to grapple with ethical dilemmas and tensions as they work with complex issues and circumstances, varied contexts and not least diverse groups and communities. Some of these challenges include:

- gaining consent in divided communities;
- maintaining boundaries appropriate to the discipline and its values;
- respecting and learning from indigenous values and philosophies as well as from the diversity of cultures within which the practitioner may work;
- developing new paradigms for transformative community organizing, sustainable development and ethically sensitive practice;
- practicing within an employing organization that might be somewhat tokenistic toward community development values;
- working with inadequate resources to address issues experienced locally but rooted nationally or globally;
- working within a country that is not democratic and abusive of human rights.

Within the realm of contestation and ethical dilemmas lie also debates about the "professionalization" of community development work itself. These debates often hinge around interpretation of terms such as "professional" and "professionalization." Do they mean simply someone who is in a paid role? Or someone who has a "relevant" qualification? Or both? And then, what is considered a "relevant" qualification for a community development practitioner? Who makes those determinations? And so on. If these are the only criteria for determining who is considered professional, where does that leave those who are skilled, experienced and passionate community activists who give their time and energy freely to work with others to bring about positive change in and for their communities? For other commentators, the term "professional" is linked more to matters of approach, behavior and conduct – ethical standards.

This is why community development practitioners and professional associations in several countries, (including Ireland, the United Kingdom, South Africa) have created national standards for community development practice, which reference codes of expected ethical behavior and conduct as well as the values specifically relating to the field of practice. Such standards for community development have helped to bring clarity and collective agreement about community development as a recognized field of practice, with a clear purpose, underpinning ethos and values and processes. Such national standards are also now reflected in new qualifications frameworks and supporting bodies. It was by building upon these national standards that IACD developed the International Standards for Community Development Practice to help practitioners around the world explore:

- how to understand and express the ethics/values within the processes and outcomes of community development and the practitioner's role
- how to handle areas of potential conflict between the practitioner's professional ethics/values, the ethics/values of their own and other agencies they may be working with, and the ethics/values of the individuals and groups they may be working with
- how to support and promote community development ethics/values within their own agency and other organizations with which they may be working
- how as a practitioner they should commit to their own continuing professional development

There are, as mentioned here, ongoing and emerging challenges for community development standards, practice, learning and qualifications in the decades ahead. Community development practice based on the values set out in this chapter, needs now, more than ever to explicitly acknowledge, articulate and address the ongoing legacies of slavery and colonialization as well as all forms of racism, some of which may even be hidden in the discipline's own roots. Finally, based on these values, the key roles of women, everywhere and in all our diversity, as participants and practitioners need to be reflected at all levels and in all arenas.

Case Studies

The following five case studies explore some of these issues working in communities. The first from India describes work with garment workers in India and at ways in which the practitioners challenged the caste system and discrimination within the village toward Dalit people and how far the practitioner should confront entrenched institutionalized discrimination. The Irish/Scottish case study highlights how community development practitioners have collaborated to use a human rights approach to build agency, develop alliances, challenge inequalities of power and lever economic and social change. The third case study looks at how discrimination toward women and girls sex workers in Kenya led to the creation of a new community development organization that challenged the attitudes and values of the traditional "male" community leaders and others at government policy level. The fourth case study, from Australia is about a values-led project with Indigenous communities which harnessed both traditional values ways of working with new ideas based on the empowerment of young men. The final case study from looks at how at how the agency responsible for setting national community development standards in Scotland developed a code for practitioners on ethics.

Figure 2.1 Promoting social justice in garment work districts in Tamil Nadu, India. Photo credit: Pradeep Narayan.

Case Study 1 – India

Promoting Social Justice in Garment Work Districts in Tamil Nadu

By Pradeep Narayanan and Sarah Banks

Background: Garment Work and the Caste System

This case focuses on community development work with garment workers in Tamil Nadu, India, where millions work in ginning and spinning mills and stitching units. The industry employs many adolescent girls, bonded labor is prevalent, and many workers receive neither minimum wages, nor social security. NGOs (Non-Governmental Organizations) therefore have programs to sensitize garment workers to their entitlements. Often it is difficult to reach workers in factory premises, so programs work in villages using a prevention framework based on education and awareness-raising.

The case is located in a village in a district with a number of spinning mills, which recruit workers from adjacent villages. Many villages comprise smaller hamlets, which segregate inhabitants according to caste status. Although untouchability is illegal in India, the hierarchical caste system still operates in many areas, meaning that people born into different castes observe various customs linked to purity and pollution, which govern interactions among people. Dalit communities at the so-called "bottom" of the caste hierarchy, face the worst forms of discrimination and are denied dignity even in public places.

Establishing a Tuition Center

An NGO, working on empowering women workers, has been working in twenty villages implementing an awareness-raising program among garment workers and organizing them to stand up for their rights. The program officer (PO) has to evolve, in each village, a community support group (CSG), to advise the program how to reach existing and potential garment workers. The CSG meets monthly, comprising villagers from a range of identities and backgrounds (gender and caste). The PO is responsible for recruiting a villager to run a tuition center to teach children. The center builds the NGO's credibility in the village, and helps children continue their education, instead of considering garment work at an early age.

The case is based on work in one particular village, with ninety garment workers, across three hamlets. These hamlets are largely homogenous in terms of caste composition. Hamlet A has about eighty families from the so-called "highest" caste, with twenty-seven garment workers. Hamlet B has about a hundred families from "middle" castes, with thirty-five garment workers. Hamlet C is a Dalit colony with ninety-five families and eighteen garment workers. In 2018, the PO decided to start the center in Hamlet B. It was a "natural" choice since Hamlet B had the most garment workers, and siting the center there would make the greatest impact on the programmer's target criteria. The center started and children from all three castes attended, many of whom were family members of garment workers. The program accessed more than sixty garment workers across three hamlets, enabling them to participate in various sensitization programs.

Reflection Visit

In October 2019, a new leadership team under a different NGO, Partners in Change (PiC), took on management of the program. The team members involved in implementation, including the PO, remained largely the same, continuing the work, but now under the leadership of PiC, an NGO committed to promoting equity and anti-stigmatization through participatory community development. After six months, a program reflection team (comprising a community member, the PO, the program manager and two PiC staff from outside the area) visited the village. During the visit, the reflection team became aware that only children from Dalit castes had to remove their slippers before entering Hamlet B to attend the center. Although no children from any caste, nor the teachers, had complained, the team felt it was important to discuss this issue, as the location of the center seemed to be causing caste-based discrimination against some children.

The PO facilitated the reflection team's discussion with several CSG members. It became clear that caste segregation was very high. When residents from the Dalit colony entered the other hamlets, they had to remove their slippers and shoes. While most schools, shops and essential services were in a common area, the program did not have resources to start a center in the common area. It was agreed that Dalit children removing slippers outside the hamlet to participate in the center was not acceptable. The PO stated that the decision to have a center at Hamlet B was taken in consultation with the village-level CSG. The PO explained: firstly, opening a center in either of the other hamlets did not make sense as they had less garment workers; and secondly, if a center was placed in a Dalit hamlet, families from other hamlets would not send their children there, as they would be afraid of a social boycott from their own community. When asked whether the CSG discussed all these issues, the reply was "no". However, a couple of CSG members present in the meeting stated that these challenges were in the back of their minds at the time. Often such sensitive points are not openly discussed in mixed caste groups. It is assumed that everyone understands them.

A week after the visit, the PO and program manager further deliberated on potential solutions with a few CSG members from all hamlets. One proposal was to start another center in the Dalit hamlet, for Dalit children, so they did not have to suffer discrimination. While a few participants accepted this proposition, others heavily criticized it, for reasons of both resource availability and perpetuation of caste discrimination. A further complicating factor was raised: access to garment work itself is contaminated by caste rules, which discriminate against Dalit residents. Caste determines access to mill work, for example, since mill workers are often recruited through existing permanent workers or contractors, who are generally from dominant castes.

The program team and CSG members concluded it was important to confront the caste system, rather than find solutions within it. They also knew that this decision would not sit well with local elites, nor with many Dalit leaders who had developed a coping system that involved choosing their own time to challenge caste rules.

Bearing in mind all these factors, it was decided to shift the center to the Dalit hamlet for a year, monitor how it worked and then take a final decision accordingly. In March 2020 the center moved. It is functioning, but with a limited number of children due to Covid-19 restrictions. Hence the impact of the move is not yet known.

Uncovering Hidden Assumptions and Unsettling the Status Quo: Whose Values Count?

The initial location of the center aimed to achieve the program target: to reach the most garment workers at the earliest opportunity. While caste issues were not overtly considered, CSG members were aware of them. The caste system is so normalized that it was never a point of contestation.

However, with the change in program leadership, also came a change in the ideological and ethical lens of the organization. PiC was actively looking for caste discrimination in its field operation, which is why the program team could actually bring "caste discrimination" into the zone for consideration. In discussions following the field visit, it was realized that allowing caste-based discrimination to occur in an institutionalized way violates human rights. Subsequent discussions revealed further ethical complexities about the conflicting rights and interests of different parties in the decision about center's location. For example, how should the program team weigh protection of Dalit children from discrimination against protection of upper caste families from social boycotting?

Reflections on Ethical Decision-Making: The Hard Work of Putting Values into Practice

The decision to move the center was based on values of equality and human rights in relation to Dalit people: they should not be subject to discrimination in accessing education. It drew on PiC's commitment to work toward social justice in Indian society through challenging the caste system. While the decision to relocate appears to have been made democratically with CSG members, it was recognized that some Dalit leaders might not have chosen to fight this battle. This case raises questions about whether, how and when community development organizations should facilitate the empowerment of oppressed people to confront entrenched institutionalized discrimination. Confrontation may result in negative consequences not only for those currently benefiting from the discriminatory practices, but also (at least in the short term) for the oppressed group, as the status quo is unsettled, and they are put under the spotlight.

The unfolding complexity of the ethical decision-making in this case highlights the challenging roles of community development workers as consciousness-raisers, mediators between different groups, and advocates for socially just change. It highlights the importance of careful ethical deliberation to uncover hidden assumptions, weigh the rights and interests of different groups and build collective courage to tackle entrenched social injustices.

Many decisions in community development work are based on invisible assumptions, aligned with discriminatory practices. Community development projects often ignore them because they are the "normal" lens through which everybody looks, decides and acts in everyday life, and they are difficult to challenge. However, if we consciously switch to an ethical lens, based on the values of community development, and ask ourselves how these values play out in practice, it encourages us to stop, reconsider, and perhaps change our practices.

Figure 2.2 Leith, Scotland. Photo credit: Michael Rea Media.

Case Study 2 – Ireland and Scotland

Small Places Close to Home: Housing Rights in Practice

By Dessie Donnelly and Clare MacGillivray

> Where, after all, do universal human rights begin? In small places, close to home – so close and so small that they cannot be seen on any maps of the world.
>
> *Eleanor Roosevelt on signing the Universal Declaration of Human Rights 10th December 1948.*

The promotion and protection of human rights are often viewed as being the responsibility of distant international and domestic mechanisms, bound in legal specialisms and out of reach of the very people they are designed to protect. While marginalized communities experience human rights violations everyday: food insecurity, extreme poverty, homelessness, inaccessible health services, insufficient welfare, lack of access to education and so on, few would be aware of the content, never mind the application, of the United Nations Declaration of Human Rights (UDHR) or the raft of general comments which are meant to give substantive content to rights.

Despite this disconnect, IACD places rights at the center of community development practice: *"To work with communities to achieve participative democracy, sustainable development, rights, economic opportunity, equality and social justice."* But what does it mean for a community development practitioner to employ a human rights-based approach (HRBA)? This article highlights how community development practitioners in Scotland and Ireland have collaborated to use a HRBA to build agency, develop alliances, challenge inequalities of power and lever economic and social change. It explores the challenges and ethical dilemmas for practitioners working in spaces where entrenched inequality, power imbalances and tensions define communities' interaction with the states. Most importantly it demonstrates how a synergy in values-based work, a shared understanding of methodology, the commitment to learning and collaboration across different contexts, mixed with strong and enduring inter-personal relationships, can build solidarity, create formidable partnerships, and strengthen grassroots community development and human rights work in practice.

Housing Rights in Practice

As part of Scotland's National Action Plan for Human Rights (SNAP), the Housing Rights in Practice (HRiP) project was set up as a partnership between the Scottish Human Rights Commission ("the Commission"), Belfast based Participation and the Practice of Rights (PPR) and Edinburgh Tenants Federation (ETF) to support residents in Leith, Scotland address poor housing conditions. The right to adequate housing is a human right under international law containing standards which governments and public authorities are obligated to meet.

ETF staff supported participative democracy in the HRiP, while the Commission staff brought human rights training, with PPR sharing expertise of employing a HRBA in practice. Practitioners from the three organizations worked with people experiencing chronic problems with damp, mold, ineffective or broken heating, pigeon, rodent and insect infestations, and maintenance issues. From 2015–2019, residents were supported to use a HRBA to assert their right to housing by monitoring progress in their housing conditions and developing strategies to hold City of Edinburgh Council (the local authority and landlord for some of the residents) to account and realize £2.3m of investment in their homes.

Developing a Shared Understanding and Building Relationships

PPR have been using a HRBA in Belfast since 2006, putting the collective resource and expertise of traditional human rights advocates (NGOs, academics, community development organizations, lawyers) at the service of marginalized communities. In 2014, the project team from Scotland spent time with activists in Belfast learning about the values underpinning human rights work, the methodologies employed, the challenges faced and the practical application of rights in a summer school run by PPR. Learning and exploring theory and practice in the summer school, and sharing cultural and social activities amplified the project team's shared values and created a culture of mutual respect, trust, and authenticity in personal relationships of practitioners and activists who would be working together.

A Human Rights-Based Approach

The HRBA provides a set of principles for understanding the exercise of power. The HRBA "PANEL" principles of Participation, Accountability, Non-discrimination, Empowerment and Legality provide a framework for understanding whose voices are elevated, whose experiences are valued and what interests are promoted in official decision-making processes. A focus on power relationships enabled partners to explore the relationship residents (as rights-holders) had with public authorities (as duty bearers) and understand that inequalities and human rights abuses are not accidental outcomes of a decision-making process; they are intended outcomes of processes which serve particular interests in society.

How the Project Worked in Practice

In 2015, practitioners from ETF and the Commission supported a small group of residents to plan and run an open meeting inviting neighbors to discuss new ways of addressing old problems. This resulted in a core team of residents being established to learn about and carry out participatory action research on housing problems. This team of community researchers carried out a monitoring exercise with just over half of the 182 homes participating.

After analyzing the results, a series of public meetings were organized to prioritize residents' concerns and learn about specific housing rights related to their priorities; international human rights standards, as well as domestic Scottish law governing habitability standards which public authorities were obligated to meet. Practitioners then supported residents to develop human rights indicators and benchmarks capable of measuring state compliance with human rights commitments. The indicators were published widely and presented by residents directly to the Council as primary duty bearer in a public meeting.

Residents monitored the indicators at intervals doing door-to-door surveys, collecting photo evidence, holding soup day drop-ins as well as providing neighbors with thermometers to record temperatures in homes. Traditional media and social media were used to shine a spotlight on their issues and secure strong engagement with politicians at local and national levels. A film on the project made by the Commission was screened at the Scottish Parliament on International Human Rights Day in 2016 to 90 participants including the Minister responsible for Human Rights in Scotland.[16]

Activating international human rights mechanisms was a key strategic plank in gaining traction for residents' issues and validating their approach: Chair of the UN Committee for Economic, Social and Cultural Rights Virginia Bras Gomes visited the project and praised the efforts as a model for other communities to emulate. Such interventions helped build momentum for a human rights compliant method of engaging with the duty bearer. Six months after the report's launch, a participatory process was established with residents and the Council engaged with a singular focus on progressing the human rights indicators and benchmarks.

Over a four year process the Council invested £2.3m into the flats, including a heating and window replacement program, new kitchens and bathrooms and a raft of external works. By the end of 2019, residents reported improved physical and mental health, improved feelings of self-worth, confidence and pride, reduced fuel poverty and a better sense of community. Throughout this time, practitioners continued to support residents to learn about human rights, participatory action research, analyze power, and to strategize campaigning methods to effect change. A powerful example of using human rights in practice, the Commission published Housing Rights in Practice: Lessons Learned from Leith, capturing reflections of the process from rights-holders, duty-bearers, support staff and the Commission.[17]

Challenges and Ethical Considerations

Using a HRBA to challenge systems that disenfranchise the most marginalized disrupts existing models of decision-making and the relationships between the public, private and voluntary sectors which underpin them: consultative processes, partnerships and service-level agreements.

Although the Commission provided human rights training to some Council staff, the Local Authority at a senior level never acknowledged that the housing conditions experienced were a breach of human rights standards. This caused tensions particularly for community development practitioners based at ETF, since their employment was almost exclusively funded by the Council. Balancing this, and the practice of a more participative approach with traditional models of representative democracy also challenged dominant community-based power structures.

The Council's response to the project created a hostile environment for practitioners and activists. For practitioners, this response was challenging; juggling the pressure of funders, with that of employers and freely supporting residents became an ongoing tension. While attempts were made by partners to work directly with Council officials on the HRBA, the Council's responses escalated from defensiveness to disengagement to tactics aimed at discrediting the residents' case.

Practitioners and activists used the values of community development to build consciousness; to name and understand the agendas behind Council's actions and develop strategic and creative ways of responding which kept the issues in the public spotlight. Practitioners built an active support network as a reservoir of solidarity to tease out tensions in the methodology and underpinning values for this praxis work.

Nevertheless, these tensions raise important questions about the need for non-state funding for communities and organizations using a HRBA. Importantly, the necessity of creating a resilience framework to protect the health and well-being of community activists and community development practitioners as human rights defenders was essential for future initiatives.

Making Rights Real

Following the completion of the project practitioners from the HRiP have used the experiences and learning to found a national independently funded organization, Making Rights Real to enable and empower communities in Scotland to use the power of human rights to achieve participative democracy, economic, social and cultural change and social justice.

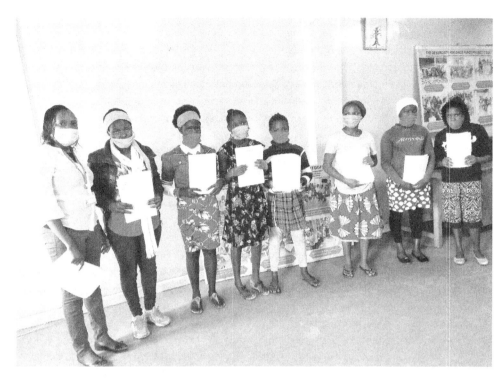

Figure 2.3 Students receiving study materials for use during Covid-19 school closure – Kenya. Photo credit: Lifebloom Services International.

Case Study 3 – Kenya
Case Study Life Bloom Services International
By Catherine Wanjohi and Meriba Mwende

This case study examines the work of Life Bloom Services International in Naivasha, Kenya, which helps survivors of sexual exploitation to build a strong survivor network and transform their households (and communities) using peer to peer support as the main pillar. Naivasha has a flourishing tourism and hospitality industry as well as flower farming, mining and horticultural industries resulting in high movement of tourists, businesspeople and workers into the area. Despite this, poverty is widespread within the region which includes a number of low-income urban settlements. Poverty impacts in many ways for women and girls. Many are forced to leave school early in search of some kind of income as households are desperate for money. Many families cannot afford to provide sanitary pads; thus, girls are often left to fend for themselves. Leaving school at an early age results in educational underachievement and limited access to develop knowledge and vocational skills for decent employment opportunities.

Within this environment women and girls are particularly vulnerable to Sexual Gender-Based Violence (SGBV), local and global trafficking in persons (TiP) and sexual labor. These and other forms of exploitation are widespread within Naivasha and the surrounding area. Women and girls experience further marginalization at the hands of judgmental moralists within their communities. Teenage pregnancy rates are high.

Disregard and exclusion of this population from programming/planning for service delivery by government and other development key players has been common. Because of the moralist approach and the voices (needs) of those in sex work (or those trafficked and sexually exploited) not being represented at policy development round tables (board rooms), then programs and budgets to mitigate are not included in our annual government development plans. Often, it is assumed that women and girls in sex work or sexual exploitation will have the capacity to form and register Self Help Groups, and so can access government affirmative funds like any other women/girls. However, the need for acceptance in the community and confidence building so that they can even see themselves as worthy and deserving (and very importantly that it's their right!) to access the funds.

Life Bloom is unique way of addressing this gap in that we begin with the women and girls from the point of addressing stigma and discrimination, building self-acceptance and confidence skills, so that they can reach the same bargaining level to marshal especially for competitive services like the group funds loaned by the government. Recognizing the need to address these issues and support girls and women, the community development worker initiated conversations with other community members concerned about the exploitation they experienced and the challenges of how to address the growing issues they faced. Following successful lobbying they engaged key strategic stakeholders including village chiefs and relevant government departments with remits for women and children,

Life Bloom Services International (LBSI) was founded in 2004 in Naivasha Sub County of Nakuru County, Kenya. Community development practitioners within the organization began by supporting community leadership capacity development, skills for enhancing employment opportunities, offering counseling services, and offering practical support such as providing menstrual hygiene packs accessible to women and girls. Quickly, the initial women and girls who joined the project brought with them others in need of the services.

From its inception, the founders adopted a values-based community development approach and sought to engage the community to create community-based and owned models of transforming communities. Social and economic justice for girls and women is an underpinning value of the project, shaping work in addressing gender-based exploitation. This has included guided community dialogue, exploring values and the dynamics of change processes within communities as well as working with other stakeholders such as NGOs, churches, government departments. Stakeholders are engaged in ways that uphold professional integrity, accountability and confidentiality.

Empowerment is also a core value of the project, both as a process and an outcome. There has been a strong emphasis on building community members as champions, leaders and transforming agents in their own communities. Since 2004, each new recruited group has identified their emerging leaders who have been trained to support them in leadership roles. Practitioners within LBSI also recognize the importance of working in inclusive and participatory ways with the communities they work with. The communities know best what their issues are, and if offered a safe environment and their capacity is supported, they also know how best to navigate around their circumstances and find the solutions they will own and be proud of and defend moving forward. This includes recognizing, respecting and building on community ways of life like communal approaches to challenging situations through Self Help Groups, and the government developed a model of "Nyumba Kumi" literally meaning "ten houses in the neighborhood" who watch over each other, support each other, etc.

To further promote the values upon which community development is based, community mentors are recruited through an open and inclusive process to ensure that mentors work to appropriate values in their support of mentees. This mentoring work runs on a rolling process, mobilizing new beneficiaries and using the existing beneficiaries to support the new ones. In this way, the beneficiaries are the key drivers of the project. In this way a new movement of champions of 1661 mentors have been raised to raise and amplify the voices. It is this strong volunteer mentor tradition that self-propels the project and makes it highly sustainable as the most investment is focused on beneficiaries in the community.

The project operates on a revolving cycle of processes. There is continued assessment of needs, recruitment of new potential beneficiaries, service provision and building of the beneficiaries' capacities with most beneficiaries making milestones in their transitioning to the lives they desire even while they continue to mentor and coach their peers. As some may move on, more potential beneficiaries join the project. Practitioners have worked with beneficiaries to create support networks that all can remain engaged with and part of. Through this way, the project has built a solid foundation that is strengthened along the way. Community engagement is also an ongoing process, as is training and capacity building. The most significant aspect of the project is the participation of the beneficiaries as the key drivers of their processes.

Several beneficial outcomes have been achieved through the values-based approach that has been implemented by practitioners within the project.

- Currently about 420 active Community Volunteer Mentors are leading different projects including with teen mothers and teen survivors of sexual exploitation and domestic human trafficking. These are supported by the practitioners from LBSI.
- More than 10,600 households now have different income streams, reducing the impacts of poverty and vulnerability to exploitation.
- A Women's One Stop Center has been developed as a central safe space for women and girls. Other safe spaces in the neighborhood are continuously expanding and offering opportunities for women and girls to realize better life outcomes.
- Two emergent movements, Women Champions for Change (WC4C) and Girl Champions for Change (GC4C) are growing in strength and helping to transform the circumstances in their lives and their communities.

Formal or informal education is a prerequisite to shape the future lives of the girls in the project. Education helps to break/prevent the cycle of abuse and poverty for those engaged with the project. The women and girls are all members of their own communities, and they may still be exploited by others at the community level. Consequently, the LBSI practitioners have learned to involve the community in major parts of the project and decision-making such as during stakeholders' meeting, sanitary towels distribution and during observation of international days intended to raise awareness among the community of different issues affecting girls. This has been possible by maintaining and creating partnerships with likeminded civil society organizations and government departments. The COVID-19 19 pandemic has threatened the economic security of women and families, in turn making women and girls vulnerable again to exploitation and sexual trafficking. By working with others collaboratively the capacity to develop and implement responsive strategies to address the local and global socio-economic dynamics that result in marginalization or exclusion of people and communities has been strengthened.

Figure 2.4 End product – furniture from felled trees and recycled industrial material – Australia. Photo credit: Andy Grieg.

Case Study 4 – Australia

The Agunya Project

By Anne Jennings and Andy Grieg, Australia

In the remote Kimberley region of Western Australia Indigenous people, and more specifically young Indigenous men, have been severely disadvantaged in their efforts to attain positive training and employment opportunities. The Agunya project was established to upskill young Indigenous men in a wide range of areas including building construction, carpentry, creative arts, machinery usage, and communication/self-development, as well as expanding participant's competences into mentor roles. As a social enterprise it generates 60% of its own income, with over 90% of products being fashioned from recycled materials. Consequently, the benefit to the community is extensive.

The core values within this project included using indigenous knowledges, beliefs, and expectations from within their communities. While at the same time recognizing that the values of Western "colonization" were still impacting upon Indigenous people and that some of these values could be included. So, the project included bringing the Elders together with non-Indigenous people to assess current activities and provide knowledge and direction to direct future pathways. Thus, a commitment to equity and human rights, along with other values including social and economic rights and individual and community empowerment were adopted for transformational change,

For years Andy Greig, an experienced building/construction professional living and working in remote Indigenous communities in Australia, grappled with culturally and environmentally inappropriate (design and materials) housing - as well as lack of employment and skills development for young people given many Indigenous communities may have one shop, others none and most services fly in-fly out by external agencies. Andy had also taken a diploma in community development work and became the practitioner supporting the Elders to devise a collective response, this led to Agunya, a not-for-profit social enterprise, being formed to engage in ecological community and economic development projects.

Agunya commenced working with small, remote Indigenous Community Governing Councils on housing projects, training local people through practical skills application. Those trained then undertaking ongoing repair works within their own communities. Agunya also established a central training venue, creating opportunities for more trainees and for collaboration with more organizations.

The project participants undertook detailed carpentry out of recycled timber as well as old cast iron machinery parts. Overall recycled products account for over 90% of production materials, with some timber coming from trees uprooted during cyclones, to make stunning one-off creative works of furniture and original art.

Agunya is also establishing a sustainable food garden to assist programs aimed at alleviating anti-social behavior, with support being offered to new participants by a group of current trainees. It is currently setting up a new project supporting young men returning home from Juvenile Detention thousands of kms away. Agunya's previously trained participants are being trained as peer mentors for the new project to bring about maximum benefit to all involved.

What Works/Worked Well

- Linking values and practices through to outcomes - participants were encouraged to continually discuss their values and reviewing their work on completion within those values. This has been a totally new approach for most of them, which they have reported back as having high personal value.
- Engaging communities by building and maintaining relationships – for many young people this was the first time they had engaged with the broader Indigenous and non-Indigenous community as many come from small Indigenous-only communities (most under 100 people). From an often-frightened start they moved forward building and maintaining relationships that have the potential to both assist Agunya's professional approach and to personally build confidence and skills.
- Organizing for change, while delivering practices that recognize and respect diversity, and then

evaluating activity to inform future practice. As participants moved through the program, at their individual pace, they realized their own worth and skills (which many articulated came as a surprise to them) as well as respecting both cultural and skill-based diversity. They then contributed significantly to the project's strategic direction, thus informing Agunya's future practice.

Challenges included:

- Establishing a new, innovative project that does not "fit" existing values systems takes time, as a strategy of community education was required and enacted. Then it takes time to develop value-based relationships with other likeminded community organizations who will contribute to, as well as benefit from, this program.

- In addition, developing new funding/income stream arrangements for innovative activities created "outside-the-box" was quite demanding and took the community development away from their other roles.
- A challenge for the project instigator related to working within trauma informed and culturally sensitive spaces, which meant he had to "carry on regardless" without showing his emotions when participants had disturbances in their lives. This he found exhausting and it pointed to the importance of setting up personal support/debriefing systems early in a project – which is now being addressed.
- And, of course, COVID-19 after seven months of project shut down Agunya arrived at the point where it was about to close – however thanks to a philanthropic contribution the rent was covered. Agunya is now back on track, slowly but surely.

Learning and Future Plans

This whole project has been continual development and learning (often on the run), however after six active, roller coaster years it is now at the point where it can consolidate, reflect on experiences and learnings, and move forward. This has been supported by co-author Anne Jennings, (a community development university researcher) who regularly reflects on and documents the program. She has reported how this project's values encompass (a) Participative democracy – as the young people involved develop active participation in planning and decision-making; (b) Sustainable development and climate justice – with the demonstrated 90%+ use of recycled, within a social and climate justice framework; (c) Equity and human rights – respecting participants dignity and ensuring positive opportunities; (d) Social and economic justice – combining the points above, undertaking collective action that challenges injustice, poverty, inequality, discrimination and social exclusion; and (e) Empowerment – with Agunya working collectively with participants in ways that values lived experience, builds on existing strengths and supports the development of understanding, knowledge and skills, contributing to greater participation and collective action.

This empowerment process is key to the establishment and continual expansion of activities and diversity of actions within the project – without which Agunya would have become another project that tried, but could not produce, the creative outcomes required to bring about distinctive social change in the lives of participants. To keep this on track Andy has devised a three-year strategy, continuing to mentor a group of young men to the point where they will take on full responsibility for the project, supported by their Elders and other community organizations and collaborations they continue to nurture and develop.

Figure 2.5 Open space practice discussion – Scotland. Photo credit: Community Learning and Development Standards Council Scotland.

Case Study 5 – Scotland. UK

Developing a Code of Ethics
By Maggie Paterson and Kirsty Gemmell

> Can you do your job just by doing what you're told? Is your practice just a set of techniques?
>
> *("Ethical Practice – Competent Practitioners", Community Learning and Development Standards Council)*

Context

The Community Learning and Development Standards Council was established by the Scottish Government in 2008 to:

> Work with the sector to establish and maintain high standards of practice in Community Learning and Development (CLD) across Scotland.[18]

It is the body responsible for the registration of CLD practitioners, the approval of training courses, and the continuing professional development of the sector workforce, including volunteers. Its vision is "that the communities and people of Scotland are served effectively by

CLD practitioners who are recognized as competent, confident and committed to equality, empowerment and life-wide learning for all". While continuing to be a Scottish Government agency, the Standards Council now has a membership of around 2,500 CLD practitioners, who lead its work through its committees. These include both field practitioners and CLD educators.

The Standards Council sees community learning and development primarily as a profession, identified through shared values and methods of practice. Conscious that its vision and functions only make sense within the context of a shared understanding of the purpose of CLD and the values of CLD practitioners, the Standards Council began to develop a Code of Ethics for CLD.

Why a Code of Ethics?

For CLD practitioners, the Code of Ethics provides a point of reference connecting CLD values to the CLD Competences. It does not provide a set of rules for conduct. Not only are the circumstances and issues that CLD practitioners encounter too varied and complex for this to be feasible; it is also essential to ethical decision-making that the individual practitioner takes responsibility for applying a set of principles to their own situation.

In order to carry out any and all of its responsibilities, the Standards Council needs to have a rigorous basis for its work and its decisions. To secure credibility and command respect, it needs to be able to demonstrate this rigor. The Code is also a point of reference for participants and communities, enabling them to hold CLD practitioners accountable. Underpinning all of this, the Code is designed to encourage practitioners to consider their own position and interventions in daily and ongoing practice contexts.

Process of Developing the Code

The Code was developed using an inclusive, participatory process, designed to reflect the reality and diversity of CLD contexts and practice. An initial series of discussions involved members of the Standards Council's committees and were informed by input from experts in the field of professional ethics. In particular, ideas of professionalism that emphasize inclusion and accountability as well as knowledge, skills and understanding, were highlighted.

Building on these discussions, a draft Code was formally presented to the Standards Council's Committees in 2010. A wider consultation then took place which included five events spread geographically across Scotland and three events for practitioners with a specific focus on youth work, adult learning or community development to discuss the Code as it relates to that context. In addition, there was an online discussion. The Code was amended to take account of comments received through the consultation and the final version was approved by the Standards Council's Committees in 2011. The discussions on ethics and professionalism, and the engagement of members in the process of developing the Code, helped the Standards Council to grow its understanding of how to be a professional body while continuing to base its work on the values of CLD.

Following experience of applying the principles in practice, a member-led working group was established to review and refresh the Code of Ethics. This was published in Autumn 2017.

The Code

The Code (https://cldstandardscouncil.org.uk/resources/code-of-ethics/) currently has 12 clauses, each with a heading and an explanatory text; all of these were subject to rigorous debate. For example, the first clause is "Primary Client", for which the text reads:

> Our primary client (our "constituent") is the individual, group or community with whom we engage. We will ensure that the interests of the constituents we work with are at the center of everything we do in our work. We will not seek to advance ourselves, our organizations or others, personally, politically or professionally, at the expense of our constituents.

There was disagreement about this terminology; the conclusion was that it was the best available way of articulating practitioners' primary responsibility to the communities, groups and individuals they work with.

The other clauses focus on:

- Social context
- Equity
- Empowerment
- Duty of Care
- Transparency
- Confidentiality
- Co-operation
- Professional Learning
- Self-awareness
- Boundaries
- Self-Care

Supporting Practitioners in Applying the Code

To encourage and support the application of the Code, the Standards Council published the "Ethical Practice – Competent Practitioners" resource.

https://cldstandardscouncil.org.uk/resources/ethical-practice-competent-practitioners/

The purpose of this resource is to assist CLD practitioners, and everyone with an interest in CLD practice, to use the Code of Ethics to inform, develop and challenge practice; and to promote the use of the Code in their organization and with partners.

The resource looks at:

- What do we mean by "ethics"? Theories, frameworks and professionalism;
- Ethics in CLD – boundaries, accountability and professional identity;
- Using the Code of Ethics in developing competent CLD practice; and
- Embedding the Code of Ethics in practice.

In addition to this resource, a short Professional Learning program highlighting the importance of the code and supporting its application was designed and has been delivered to local groups of practitioners as well as at national events. This has resulted in additional material illustrating application of the ethics being generated by practitioners themselves and shared on our website.

An example of these materials is a session on Professionalism & Ethical Standards which supports practitioners to consider practice and actions within a range of dilemmas (fictional but based on community development practice experience). The objectives of the session are:

1. Assist participants to understand the relationship between professionalism and ethics.
2. Assist participants to manage ethical dilemmas in practice.

Examples of the dilemmas include:

If a group you are working with is starting a campaign against something your employer is doing, how do you decide what to do?

Douglas attends a group you support. He's reputed to be a good plumber. Your bathroom drains are blocked, and you know he'd be cheap. Do you ask him to come and have a look at the job?

When did you last ask, "Can this group do without me?"

Pawel and his wife, Helena, who are participants at your community center, are struggling for money. Your co-worker, Angela, tells you that she felt sorry for them and has bought them some food shopping. Is this okay?

Through group discussion, participants are asked to consider which of the ethics is relevant to their considerations and how these can help them form actions and responses to the situation.

How the Code is Being Used by the Standards Council and by Practitioners

To Help Deal with Tensions with Other Partners and Define Our Limits in Partnership Work

Partnership working is a vital component of CLD, but in practice can be very challenging and it can take time for mutual trust and respect to be established between partners from different backgrounds. Having a clear set of values and the code of ethics in place, sets a foundation for identifying and agreeing common ground and purpose.

To Support and Inform Accountability

The Standards Council's Guidelines for Approval of CLD courses and qualifications have a clear focus on CLD Values and Code of Ethics, alongside the practice Competences for CLD. The Approvals process is peer-led by Standards Council Committee members.

Where issues arise over whether the conduct of individual students on CLD programs is in conflict with CLD values, and how this is managed by academic institutions, having the Code of Ethics enables discussions and decision-making to be both rigorous and values led.

To Offer Reassurance and Protection and Secure Standards of Practice

The Code of Ethics is a vital component of the registration process. To register with the Standards Council, practitioners must make a formal commitment to:

- The values underpinning CLD;
- The Code of Ethics for CLD;
- Practice using the CLD Competences;
- Continuing professional learning;
- Challenge discrimination; and
- Maintain standards of professional behavior.

They must also provide a referee who can confirm that they have evidenced these commitments.

Alongside this a process for de-registration has been put in place to address situations where serious issues of conduct, breach of the Code or poor practice arise, providing an important safeguard for communities.

To Promote Professional Dialogue and Understanding

Standards Council members can find themselves working within an organization that does not fully subscribe to their values and code of ethics. The "clauses" within the code provide sufficient context and detail to support practitioners to reflect on their own practice within their employing organization and to explain to their employers why certain courses of action create an ethical issue for them.

To Challenge, Examine and Reflect on our Practice

The Code of Ethics sits alongside the CLD Competences as a key part of the Standards Council's Competent Practitioner Framework, both defining a professional identity and guiding practice. It enables the Standards Council to put a focus on values at the heart of its remit for standards. Experience has shown that that often it is the Code that provides the most fruitful route into the challenging discussions through which practice is developed and sharpened.

The Code of Ethics is a living document that is maintained by the Standards Council and owned by practitioners.

Anna Clarke, Anastasia Crickley

Notes

1   D. Dorling (2013) Fairness and the changing fortunes of people in Britain, *Journal of the Royal Statistical Society. Series A (Statistics in Society)* Vol. 176, No. 1 (JANUARY), 97–128.
2   S. Banks and P. Westoby (eds) (2019) *Ethics, Equity and Community Development.* Policy Press.
3   S. Banks and P. Westoby (eds) (2019) *Ethics, Equity and Community Development.* Policy Press.
4   "The personal is political" was a frequently heard feminist rallying cry, especially during the late 1960s and 1970s. The exact origin of the phrase is unknown and sometimes debated.
5   S. Banks (2019) The Ethico-political context, in S. Banks and P. Westoby (2019) *Ethics, Equity and Community Development.* Policy Press.
6   IACD (2018) *Towards Shared International Standards for Community Development Practice.*
7   A. Sen (1999) *Development as Freedom.* Oxford University Press.
8   G. Craig, K. Popple and M. Shaw (eds) (2008) *Community Development in Theory and Practice; An International Reader,* Spokesman, Nottingham; European Community Development Network (2008) *Community Development in Europe — Towards a Common Framework and Understanding.*
9   G. Craig, K. Popple and M. Shaw (eds) (2008) *Community Development in Theory and Practice; An International Reader,* Spokesman, Nottingham; European Community Development Network (2008) *Community Development in Europe – Towards a Common Framework and Understanding.*
10 M. Mayo (2008) Community Development, Contestations, Continuities and Change, in G. Craig, K. Popple and M. Shaw (eds) (2008) *Community Development in Theory and Practice; An International Reader.* Spokesman, Nottingham.
11 M. Mayo (2008) Community Development, Contestations, Continuities and Change, in G. Craig, K. Popple and M. Shaw (eds) (2008) *Community Development in Theory and Practice; An International Reader.* Spokesman, Nottingham.
12 M. Ledwith (2011) *Community Development a Critical Approach.* Policy Press.
13 R. Batten and M. Batten (1967) *The Non-Directive Approach in Group and Community Work.* Oxford University Press.
14 P. Freire (1972) *Pedagogy of the Oppressed.* Penguin, London.
15 K. Popper (2011) *The Open Society and Its Enemies.* Routledge.
16 'Housing Rights in Practice' film on YouTube https://youtu.be/_dU44dIGsaA
17 Housing Rights in Practice (2020) *Lessons Learned from Leith.* Scottish Human Rights Commission.
18 In Scotland the term community learning and development has been adopted for the profession.

Chapter 3

Engaging with Communities

Charlie McConnell, Anita Paul and Kalyan Paul

Introduction

Engagement with the community is the starting point of any community development process. The initial engagement sets the tone for the subsequent programme.[1,2] Some community development activity is characterized by a focus on just getting on and "doing", perhaps because of time and resourcing constraints or the urgency of the problems to be addressed, for example in an area affected by an earthquake or a pandemic. So, there will always be times when development agencies intervene quickly with technical expertise to help solve an urgent problem. And at such times this intervention may need to be more directive and at a reduced level of community consultation. This is not necessarily the wrong approach to take. However, where this is the case, it is essential that the community development agency and practitioners communicate quickly, clearly and regularly with community leaders and the wider community, throughout the process and afterwards. But rapid interventions can be like "a bull in a china shop" and lead to mistakes and sometimes cause harm. In most cases time needs to be taken to meet and consult with community leaders and members to find out about the nature of the problems/issues they are trying to deal with and agreeing with them the ways of resolving these. Community development practice is therefore more often typified by taking time to do background research, to meet with members of the community, listening to their ideas and building a trusted relationship with them.

This chapter will explore the knowledge and skills associated with how to engage with communities (whether of locality, identity, or interest) and how the processes of engagement inform outcomes. It examines how to get to know a community, to

DOI: 10.4324/9781003140498-3

understand its demographics, its history and culture, its ways of communicating, its assets, needs, interests, motivations, hopes and the barriers that may exist for more vulnerable members to have their say. It explores what community development practitioners, whatever their discipline, need to do when engaging with a community for the first time, recognizing that within any group of people there will be a diversity of views, concerns, and interests, depending on such factors as age, gender, ethnicity, political views, faith, cultural values, economic circumstances.

What Do We Mean by the Term "Community Engagement"?

Community engagement is an intentional act by development agencies and practitioners to intervene within a community in order to gather knowledge and understanding of that community and the problems and challenges it faces; to develop relationships and trust in order to agree how best to organize collaborative action and sustainable change. The basic skills employed in engagement are clear communication, relationship building, listening, observation and research. By engaging with people practitioners are then more able to engage them in community development activities and projects.

If you are a community development practitioner employed by a governmental agency or a national or international non-governmental organization (NGO) or community-based organization (CBO) that is already known by the community, it is highly likely that the reputation of the past performance of that organization (good and bad) will impact upon how you are at first seen, perhaps as yet another official at the end of a long line of people who have promised much and delivered little. Or conversely as a highly supportive agency that employs staff who have done a good job. Many disadvantaged and vulnerable urban and rural communities will be less familiar with development agencies that want to work with them in both the identification of problems and in finding solutions, rather than imposing those solutions. It is therefore vital from the outset that practitioners are clear as to how to introduce themselves, how you explain what the agency does, what they are able to offer as a community development practitioner and how they wish to work collaboratively with the community.

In most instances, the agency community development practitioners work for will have its "development" agenda – this may be to promote healthcare, to create jobs, to improve a denuded environment, to help with conflict resolution. And it may have been invited by a government or other body to go into an area or to work with a community of identity/interest. As we have seen in chapter one, community development can take many forms and can be instigated by different types of agencies from the state to international donors, from NGOs to Community Development Corporations. Sometimes community development agencies may have not been invited into the community by its leaders, activists and members. Rather it may have been that the area or group has been seen by officials as being in need. In other instances, it is the communities themselves who have sought out technical experts to assist them deal with an issue of concern.

Whether working for an agency that is proactively engaging with a community, or reactively responding to a request for support, a central principle of good community development practice is negotiation, seeking a transactional relationship that has confidence in the expertise the team can bring, together with respect for the knowledge and insight the community members have. Community development practitioners are not the only experts in such a relationship.[3,4] Development agencies bring to the community additional expertise and resources. Community members have local knowledge and a wide range of skills and any subsequent activity will be dependent upon the active involvement of them. Underpinning any community development project must be a commitment to the community having a strong voice in co-designing and agreeing the direction of travel of any programme or activity.

The diagram below highlights six requirements for good engagement:[5,6]

1. Clarity of purpose, based upon shared understanding of the issues to be addressed
2. Commitment to working collaboratively
3. Using a range of engagement methods that are fit for purpose
4. Clear and regular communication with the people affected
5. Identifying and including all the people and organizations affected
6. Overcoming barriers to participation

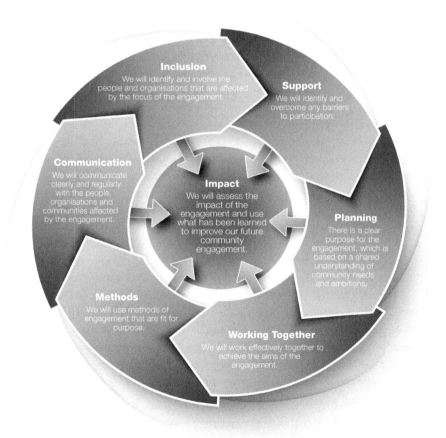

Figure 3.1 The National Standards for Community Engagement. Image credit: What Works Scotland and the Scottish Community Development Centre. Updated 2016.

Whether the agency has decided to proactively engage with a community, or whether invited into the community by local leaders and activists, first impressions count. Before meeting the community, these are some basic questions that are useful to consider:

- Have I done background research to prepare for meeting with community leaders and members?
- Are you from the community and if so what advantages and disadvantages might this give you?
- If you are not from the community, how might you be perceived by the community?
- Has your employing agency already worked with this community and if so, how has it been thought of?
- How will you explain what expertise and resources you can bring to the community?

Stage One: Undertake Some Basic Background Research.[7]

Before meeting with community leaders and activists and other members of the community, it is important to do some preliminary research about the community and its possible needs and problems.[8] Most governments and local authorities and international bodies such as the World Bank, will have census and demographic data and poverty statistics that will help inform you about the nature of the community, the number of people living and working there, gender and age spread, ethnic makeup, number of unemployed, number of men and women in the labour market, whether people travel far to find work, the main areas of employment locally such as farming, coal mining or seasonal tourism work. It will be useful to do some research about the nature of the environment. For example, is the community vulnerable to flooding or deforestation? Is there industrial or other pollution? Who owns the land? Find out about which governmental agencies, NGOs and CBOs are working in the area and what they do. Such information will help appreciate some of the problems the community may be faced with and inform initial discussions with them. Such information will have been gathered by local government or other agencies already working with the community. And there may already be reports and surveys undertaken about the community. It will be useful to obtain a map of the area and use coloured markers to draw upon it housing, shops, community facilities, industrial or agricultural areas, green spaces. If reports about the community are not available, the information above will help inform yours.

But don't just rely on official reports and quantitative data. Check out how the community or the media discuss issues of concern affecting the community. Local newspapers, TV, radio and social media can be invaluable in getting a take on the views of community leaders and activists around particular issues (past and present), and what kind of tensions and conflicts might exist within the community and between it and outside agencies. And then go and talk with people.

Stage Two: Meeting the Community Leaders/Activists and Wider Members

Community development practitioners can be either generalist community workers or they may have areas of expertise for example as community architects, community health workers or in community economic development or environmental protection. Whichever it is important that you are prepared to explain clearly what you can and cannot offer, to explain what your expertise is and how you might be able to help the community to work together to deal with particular issues of concern or aspirations for change. So, after preliminary research, go and introduce yourself to community leaders and activists. Agency colleagues or other people working with the community should be able to open doors for you and help you identify these people. It is likely that you will need to meet with a range of community organizations, faith groups, social and environmental groups within the community and not just the leaders/activists of one organization.

Community leaders and activists are not necessarily the gatekeepers who know everything there is to know about the community, but they will know a lot and might become active players in any subsequent development programmes. Some may be indigenous members and longstanding residents; others can be more recent incomers especially within more fluid urban areas. What they share is that they are the more active members of any community. This is not only a courtesy, but about gaining trust from and giving respect to people who may prove invaluable in the future. Remember that community leaders and activists may have reason to be suspicious of your intentions. They may have been trying for years to deal with problems and issues facing their community. And they may have endured previous well-meaning experts from "outside" parachuting in. When contacting them requesting a meeting ask if they might make some time available for you to explain what your agency does, and that you want to find out their views on what they see as the issues facing their community.

This is a checklist to think about before meeting with community leaders and activists, and subsequently with other members of the community:

- Take an interpreter if required.
- Ask someone known to the community to introduce you.
- Dress code needs to be respectful.
- Go to them, do not expect them to come to you.
- Ensure the meeting place and time is convenient, accessible and appropriate.
- Make your presentation short, in plain language and visually engaging.
- Build in time for listening and story sharing.
- Be prepared for questions and to ask questions.

Begin by explaining what the agency does in clear language familiar to those you are meeting with, sharing examples of work the agency has done in the past with which they can identify. Avoid technical jargon. Present a short video or illustrated posters explaining what you have to offer. Photos are often better than text. Don't use power point. Keep it brief and invite questions. In many cases people may have a pretty good idea what a community health worker does, but they may have never heard of a community architect. It is important when preparing presentations to try to get into the role of the people listening. Good advice is the KISS approach (keep it simple stupid). Never talk down to people. But as the same time, you are being paid to offer expertise, so explain what that is and how it might help. Most community leaders and activists are highly articulate, so above all listen carefully to their stories and experiences and do not judge, discount or dismiss the importance of what you are hearing. At the same time, ask questions as to what they deem the problems in the community to be and what they think the causes and solutions might be. A key skillset required of any community development practitioner is that of an educator, so use creative ways of capturing their ideas using, if appropriate, flip charts and post-its. What is for sure, it will take more than one introductory meeting.

Do not assume that community leaders and activists represent the whole communities' feelings and experiences. After meeting community leaders and activists explain that you want to go out into the community to meet and talk with other people, especially those who for one reason or another are not usually involved in community action but may nevertheless be affected by the issue. Communities, especially those that are quite large geographically or in population, are rarely homogenous. Community development practice is concerned with reaching out and engaging those whose voices are rarely heard, who may feel marginalized. You are likely to find gender and age inequality, especially in leadership roles, with community leaders very often being men. Meet different members of the community, listening sensitively without imposing your views, but again clearly explaining the expertise and resources your agency has to offer. Explain that you want to build a consensus of views as to what together with your agency's assistance may be addressed.

When meeting with members of the community, you may find some deference and that some people don't at first ask questions especially in more traditional societies. Ensure such meetings are unintimidating and informal yet structured in a way that people feel comfortable with. Ideally hold such meetings in small groups, to give people more confidence to speak. Give people space to share their stories and experiences. Never assume that you know what the experience of being poor, disabled or discriminated against means.

You may come across people with views that differ with your own. You may find people who are racist and sexist and who blame other people within their community for its ills. Some traditional communities may adopt practices that deny basic human rights, such a female genital circumcision. In initial meetings it generally best to listen and take stock. Don't rush in. Take time to reflect and to consider how to best to respond. Community development practitioners and projects should not be assisting people who deny human rights or are violent towards others, but as educators enter into a dialogue with people with discriminatory ideas and explore how best be able to change such views. Again, this will take time and may be impossible. Hopefully, as the community projects your agency is assisting and initiating are seen to be helping the communities' social, economic and environmental development in a fair and equitable way, you will find more and more people supporting them.

Engaging with Other Agencies

There are tens of thousands of isolated communities around the world with which external agencies rarely engage. But increasingly communities of all types come face to face with the state, with corporations and NGOs. In most countries and in such agencies, you will find people wanting to help disadvantaged and vulnerable communities to improve their situation. There will always be officials and systems that are less open to working with your agency, or who are part of the problem. Do not jump to immediate or prejudiced first impressions. A skill you will need in community development practice is to work appropriately with state and corporate bureaucrats. At an early stage introduce yourself to the staff of other agencies working within the community, to headteachers of schools, faith leaders, the police, doctors, business leaders, local authority officials etc. If you are lucky the agency you are working for will already be part of a collaborative of agencies and professionals supporting that community. Relationship building with these players will prove invaluable, not just as a source of information, but for the sharing and pooling resources and as a support group, where you can share any apprehensions or difficulties you may be faced with. Again, it is all about building trusted and respectful relationships within these agencies.

Getting to know a community may take weeks or months dependent upon how big and diverse it is and is indeed an ongoing process. Authentic engagement is about listening and evidencing that your agency is keen to learn from the community and from colleagues about the ideas they may have about problems and issues the community is facing and about ways of improving the situation. This highlights another reason for taking a measured and sensitive approach to the engagement process. By ensuring that the process of engagement is seen to be inclusive there will be greater buy-in and a greater sense of "whole community" ownership of any programme/action.

Another important reason for investing this time in this engagement process is to use it to map what assets and resources the community already has. The community capitals framework can be a useful tool for identifying these. This framework was created as a simple tool to map the assets all communities, including those that are disadvantaged and vulnerable, may have and that might or already are being harnessed to help tackle issues of concern. Stronger communities are generally ones that leverage their community capitals.[9] These are:

1. Financial – money that might be available for projects
2. Built – buildings for community use or potential use
3. Social – the strength of social organization, self-help and neighbourliness
4. Cultural – the traditional wisdom, beliefs, creativity, diversity
5. Natural – the land, forests, rivers etc
6. Political – the understanding, experience, and effectiveness of dealing with power
7. Human – people's existing knowledge and skills

Don't undertake this exercise yourself but do it at meeting/s with community members, leaders and activists. There are a range of participatory approaches that can be adopted and this is looked at in more detail in the chapter on participatory planning.

At the same time, by talking with the other agency players try to assess the capital assets they might have and are either already bringing or might be willing to bring towards new community development projects, for example workspace or equipment. This mapping exercise should also explore the gaps as to what additional capital, expertise and resources may be required to help the community to realize its development goals, that may need to be brought in as new community development projects take off, or to strengthen existing ones.

By gathering information about the community and hearing people's experiences of dealing with issues and problems in the past, you will be identifying people keen to get involved, both existing community leaders and activists, other community members, as well as other agencies. In many cases it will make sense to work through existing community organizations, in others, to work with people to establish new ones more fit for purpose. For example, if your agency wants to promote a health or environmental programme you are beginning to identify local people to help with this work and who may require some basic training or who are interested in creating some sort of local enterprise.

The general lesson is not to tackle the hardest problems first. Go for those where there is a good chance of success, where a number of community members are keen to get involved, where you and your agency have the technical expertise or know where to get it, and where funds already exist or are easy to obtain. By achieving a quick success with local people and their organizations, your reputation for being useful will spread. And you will find ongoing community engagement as a result much easier. Action speaks louder than words. We discuss how to co-design activities and projects in participatory ways in the next chapter. And how organize communities and to enhance community learning in chapters five and six.

Case Studies

The five case studies that follow, from India, Nicaragua, Mongolia, Peru and Kenya, illustrate the engagement process in a variety of settings and how by getting the engagement process right it is possible to mobilize communities quite quickly around a variety of issues. The challenges and opportunities of engagement are illustrated as well as how to use research and communications skills in doing this. Practitioners are observed seeking out and engaging with all sections of the community, listening and always having regard for the unspoken or least powerful voices.

The case studies explore:

- the social, political, economic, cultural and environmental factors impacting upon these communities
- how the community development agency and practitioners got to know the community
- how they sought out and engaged with all sections of the community and other agencies
- how they built relationships
- how they identified assets and resources
- how they worked towards identifying the projects/actions to be taken

Figure 3.2 Typical monthly meeting of SHGs – bedrock of sustainable change at the grassroots – India. Photo credit: Pan Himalayan Grassroots Development Foundation.

Case Study 1: India
The Grassroots Story
Anita Paul and Kalyan Paul

> Where do correct ideas come from?
> They do not drop from the sky
> They come through social action.

The Pan Himalayan Grassroots Development Foundation (Grassroots) is a voluntary organization engaged in spearheading holistic interventions in the mountain ecosystems of the Indian Himalayan Region. The co-founders of this organization are trained community development professionals who believe that community members have the desire, the right and capability to promote their own welfare and prosperity and to participate in decisions that affect their lives. Our work is about channelling resources – managerial, technical and financial – directly to people and associations of the communities, working at the village/watershed level. The emphasis is on self-help participation and the belief that improvement in quality of living here and now will also encourage communities to participate in long-term engagement for effecting sustainable change and development. Grassroot's approach and methodology are the promotion of the entrepreneurial spirit – the belief that people can determine their own destiny, establish goals, take risks and invest their time and energy to achieve their aspirations for a better life.

The effects of global warming, globalization of trade, degradation and desertification of land, diversion of land to non-agriculture uses, rural urban divide and marginalization of small land holding farming families and indigenous communities are issues that we as community development practitioners have had to engage with more intensely over the last decade. Collective action through active engagement with different advocacy groups and networks is an emerging methodology for putting the last first. Digital empowerment has facilitated this process of enabling the voices of all to be heard through local testimonies, video clippings and media engagements. Socially aware consumer base and people's movements demanding Fair trade not Aid, ethically produced food, clothes and awareness regarding ecological footprints are opportunities for giving voice for local with a global reach.

As community development practitioners the values of listening and appreciating traditional knowledge systems was the first step that assisted us in understanding the underpinnings of mountain communities. Folklores, festivals, songs, local deities all pointed to the significance of natural resources in their lives. Poor infrastructure and rough terrain were other challenges that we had to address in formulating our strategies. Dependence on urban human resources as members of a spearhead team did not seem to be the model that would give the desired results. Concepts of small is beautiful, that build on local human resources, decentralized planning, implementation and monitoring of change and impacts has assisted us in developing trust and transparency among the communities and our colleagues.

Recognizing our roles as catalysts for effecting change, as the community development practitioners, we realized the need to respect and understand the rhythm and life forces that guide these mountain communities as the first steppingstone for our engagement. The first message that came out loud and clear was the interface between people and nature as a necessary condition for life itself. The loss or lack of title to environmental assets was therefore viewed by Grassroots, as an additional component of poverty, leading to the conclusion that environmental conservation is a necessary fundamental to poverty alleviation.

The form of organization at the grassroots that would enable active engagement of communities was the first question that needed to be addressed. We decided to adopt the approach of empowering communities through participatory approaches to engage and strengthen grassroots democracy by contributing in the following ways:

- Empower community members to question and challenge local governance systems
- Build upon the administrative and legislative capacities of CBOs
- Build community leaders with strong connect to local realities
- Enable informal local decision-making as a key component for sustainable development
- Encourage small holder women farmers to form self-help groups and create "social capital" and thereby
- Enhance confidence and self-worth as a tool and asset for addressing challenges

Since we entered a community as stark outsiders we had to spend considerable time to introduce ourselves, as well as the very concept of civil society organizations, an alien concept in 80s.

We took the following initial steps to engage with communities:

- Introducing ourselves, goals of our organization and frankly letting communities know that there were no fixed programmes that we had come to "sell"
- That the programmes would be worked out in consultation with them based on their felt needs and our own capacities to intervene
- That their engagement and ownership of assets created was an *a priori* condition, to be demonstrated through sharing of programme costs, in kind or cash
- Participatory rapid appraisals to understand natural and human capital of the region
- Meetings with communities as prime stakeholder for programme planning with focus on attendance by all segments of the society and gender inclusiveness
- Building on the capacities of local youth and women as changemakers
- And, finally, an agreement at the community level to adopt measures outlined in their plans in a participative manner and take responsibility of implementation, operation and maintenance
- For which a Village Development Committee had to be formed along with minutes book, set of records books and a bank account
- So as to enable communities to reach a stage when they could reflect and say that "we did this ourselves"

Based on our understanding through interactions, we developed a holistic intervention strategy based on our own strengths as changemakers. Conducting successful pilots with some selected communities with visible leadership and some lead farmers was the methodology adopted. Actions speak louder than words have been our guiding principle, as stories of positive interventions soon spread from one community to another through word of mouth. Experiential learning as a methodology has a lot of positives, organizing inter and intra basin dialogues for communities and farmer to farmer exchanges has worked as a tool for community extension work.

In a situation where demand outstrips the annual incremental growth/recharge of natural resources, the need to introduce some appropriate technology options was soon apparent. We realized that recruiting a cadre of local people with necessary skills and knowledge will be best suited for providing the services and hence we met with and carefully selected school dropouts and trained them as barefoot engineers. This helped them in earning sustainable livelihoods and prevented them from migrating to look for work hundreds of miles away in urban areas of India. They continue to live and work in their communities and market forces have also recognized their importance and they are able to generate work for themselves and mobilize resources too.

We sought to promote self-help groups (SHGs) of women engaged in micro finance for creating social capital, village water and sanitation committees, village development committees, farmers' collectives practicing climate resilient agriculture based on agro-ecological practices. We also introduced to local communities the idea of the Participatory Guarantee System (PGS) as a mechanism for farmers to engage with distant markets by strengthening their dignity and voice for the quality of their farm produce versus third party certification, together with the guilds of local youth trained as barefoot engineers promoting appropriate technologies and skill-based collectives are some examples of community-based organizations that we have supported.

Grassroots works like a spearhead team and believes in having a clear exit policy after a stipulated period of time. The programmes mentioned above are institutional structures and social and human capital created are the tools for engaging and continuing to strengthen the voices of communities. Adapting to climate change challenges in order to build resilient communities are new and emerging issues wherein for the first time, macro issues and policies also have bearing to everyday existence. Breaking stereotypes, energizing and resurgence as a continuous process of effective leadership and intergenerational justice was a challenge that we had to address as an ongoing process. This included navigating power structures and engaging with policy makers through the formation of multi-stakeholder platforms and actively engaging in issue-based networks with common agendas for advocacy.

Engendering government policies and voicing for gender equality in all spheres of life, from representation in policy forums to active engagement in implementation and monitoring of programmes as a key stakeholder has been a major area of our engagement. Currently the focus is on Water and Gender and Women in Agriculture and their role as collectives and entrepreneurs accessing markets based on value chain approaches. Post Covid19 Farmer Producer Organizations and other community-based organizations as a forum for building resilience, and community responses to livelihood, food and health crisis in rural eco systems has gained significance.

Our focus is on skill assessments and entrepreneurial development, but the challenge is not to lose the inherent strengths of such collectives of indigenous communities and their food systems based on agro-biodiversity versus market-oriented push on single crop contract farming models. As community development practitioners we continuously strive to focus upon a methodology of appreciating the web of life with all its intricacies and challenges and assist in providing the required space for co-existence instead of one fix for all. Enabling the voices of invisible yet invincible communities to get amplified especially for women farmers who are still not recognized as farmers in their own right remains a challenge that needs to be addressed.

We feel that community development practice has to have a resurgence in order to address the sustainable development challenges globally in a manner that centre stages the ethos of "communities are the answer" and "without community development there is no sustainable development". We believe that the current push of the social entrepreneurship model with a focus on "Everyone a Changemaker" providing scalable market oriented quick fixes promoted through digital platforms, has compromised their value to some extent. Community engagement as an essential condition for successful implementation of programmes is being recognized but in practice this engagement more often than not is of a superficial nature in order to tick the boxes and very rarely gets assimilated as a behavioural change and used as a tool for decentralized governance mechanism.

To conclude, our story which started as a dream to live in mountain ecosystems and contribute to the wellbeing of neighbourhood communities, has enriched our lives in more than one way. It started for us with addressing the water shortage crisis resulting due to environmental degradation and culminated with setting up pro poor community owned social enterprises, guided by the concerns of ecology and fair trade. This anchor is currently being nurtured as the vehicle of change and development owned and managed by community members themselves. Due to the high out-migration of male members, women have been playing a critical role in taking leadership roles in order to build an iota of dignity and happiness in their lives. Assisted by the youth of the region whose skill and knowledge have been upgraded as barefoot engineers and service providers in water, renewable energy and environmental sanitation sectors, the quality of life for these communities has certainly improved, through the enhanced availability of critical resources such as water and cooking energy.

All of these communities participated in the process of change, firstly, through sharing the cost of all social development investment and secondly by building upon their own social capital for the future, through thrift and credit mechanisms. The challenge for the future is to recognize and accept the way these human resources, developed over the years, will lead the way forward in the coming times and also address issues of rotation of leadership in order to maintain continuity. Community development practitioners ought to understand the nuances of aspirational changes over a generation and create mechanisms to address this critical issue adequately.

Figure 3.3 Community member and community development practitioner open water nozzle at inauguration event for the water system – Nicaragua. Photo credit and copyright: AVODEC.

Case Study 2: Nicaragua

Hope and Clean Water

By Anna C. Ortiz and Victorino Centeno

With limited access to solely dirty water, rural communities in Nicaragua often are left to organize and find their own solutions. The Association of Volunteers for Community Development, or AVODEC by its Spanish acronym, is a Nicaraguan non-profit organization that leverages community leaders in rural communities to provide training and equipment to improve food security, health education, access to clean water and safe housing. AVODEC partners with communities to develop grassroots solutions to their most pressing priorities. Their comprehensive network of volunteer community leaders has promoted local accountability and the long-term sustainability of projects.

This project was initiated when residents of San Isidro identified potable water as their number one priority. San Isidro is a small, remote community of about 120 residents located 40 km from the regional capital. Most families in San Isidro make a living working at local coffee plantations or working their own small coffee plots. Through their partnership with AVODEC, the community of San Isidro successfully built and continues to manage a solar-powered water system that pumps clean water to twenty-three homes, twenty-four hours a day.

Extremely rural communities in Northern Nicaragua lack infrastructure for potable drinking water, electricity, sewage, and trash disposal. The Nicaraguan government offers little support to provide the necessary infrastructure, therefore communities are left to find their own solutions. Forced to advocate for their health, communities have organized and partnered with non-profits to meet their basic needs. In San Isidro, a small group of community members came together to voice their mutual concerns and organize to find a solution. A community member, who also happens to be a volunteer community leader for AVODEC, decided to formalize this process by inviting AVODEC to the conversation. AVODEC requires that community leaders present a formal proposal including a list of available community assets, resources, and needs to get involved with a community project.

AVODEC's community development practitioners engaged with San Isidro residents through several community meetings during which top concerns, commitment, and community assets were discussed. They identified access to potable drinking water as the top priority. Considering the community is spread out and cell phone service is spotty at best, face-to-face meetings were the best way to communicate information to the entire community. Meetings were planned well in advance and all community members were notified to involve as many residents as possible. The first couple of meetings were used to confirm the information put forth in the formal proposal. Residents vocalized their concerns and challenges and shared about their technical skills and resources. AVODEC then helped identify and establish a Potable Water and Sanitation Committee (CAPS by its Spanish acronym) comprised of community members who were democratically elected to administer and safeguard the water system and sanitation in the community. Residents could nominate each other or themselves for the CAPS. AVODEC's community development practitioners ensured the election was fair and private. From this point forward, all community meetings and issues regarding the water project were managed by the CAPS, thereby creating ownership over the process and outcome. San

Isidro already had a history of vocal and engaged residents, therefore, it was not difficult to find enough people to step into leadership roles.

AVODEC sees community development as a true partnership. While AVODEC provides technical oversight and most of the funding, community members provide labour, partial funding, and commitment to see the project through. CAPS members carry a lot of responsibility of oversight and management; however, all community members must do their part to contribute to the project. A major part of their contribution is in physical labour. Each household is assigned the amount of labour hours they are responsible for and will result in the construction of the water pump, well, storage tank, and distribution network. This collective action leads to the physical and administrative infrastructure for a water system that will deliver potable drinking water to each home, while maintaining community consensus throughout the process. AVODEC's community development practitioners work with community members to resolve technical construction challenges as well as disputes or other logistical issues that may arise. This project required the involvement of up to three community development practitioners throughout the process. Practitioners are well versed in rural development and community engagement strategies.

This project took place between March and August 2007. At its completion, this project established a well with a solar-powered pump, storage tank, distribution network, and usage meters at twenty-three homes, bringing potable water to 115 residents. Eight community members, half of which are women, received training to administer and maintain the financial and physical responsibilities of the water system. They are viewed as leaders in the eyes of their neighbours and are often approached to help resolve other community challenges. Community members at large also participated in training about proper water storage, prevention of water-borne illnesses and hygiene.

The strength of this project lies in its participatory nature. The non-profit AVODEC cannot sign-on to a project without the community's full commitment. These projects can often carry on for months or years, so a community's commitment is essential to a project's success. Community commitment was achieved by formalizing roles with the CAPS committee and formalizing resident's commitment to the project. Each household had an equal amount of labour hours to contribute to the project and the head of household had to sign a document, binding them to the completion of those hours. The contribution of labour hours was assessed throughout the project. CAPS members would reach out to residents who had not completed their hours and ensured they honoured their part of the agreement.

Every step of this project builds towards community ownership of the process, structure, and outcomes. Once the project is completed, communities can reach out to AVODEC for technical assistance or guidance, but the community themselves owns and maintains their system, so community ownership becomes essential to the project's survival. The formalization of the CAPS through implementation of elections, extensive training, and legalization through local government, provides sufficient structure to ensure the project's sustainability.

The initial stages of the project were challenging because not all community members trusted AVODEC or the process. This resulted in searching for an alternative water source because the one the community had been using for years was on privately owned land, and the owner was no longer willing to allow free access to it. Though an alternative source was identified, it was further and lower than the original, therefore, the design and budget had to be revised. When the untrusting community members saw that AVODEC followed through with this unforeseen challenge, they understood that AVODEC is dedicated to their work and the communities they support for the long term. Community development practitioners built rapport with residents during capacity building opportunities where each were seen as experts in their own domain – practitioners as experts in the technical aspects of the project and residents as experts of their community and its needs.

The key to this project was identifying committed local leaders who already have the attention and respect of the greater community. Some of the leaders had worked with AVODEC previously through their different health initiatives, however, the magnitude of infrastructure for this project required greater involvement. The process of democratic elections to fill the CAPS proved to be extremely successful as we had more than enough candidates to fill the required positions. By understanding and respecting the local informal hierarchy and leadership, AVODEC was able to gain the community's trust and respect. Collective engagement was key to ensuring the long-term success of such transformative projects. The community is already working on adapting the water system to include new homes in the distribution network and potentially expand it by adding another water source.

Figure 3.4 Promoting diverse local food baskets – Mongolia. Photo credit: ADRA, Mongolia.

Case Study 3: Mongolia
Partnership for Organic Farming
By Tsetsgee Gavaa

Mongolia is a land of blue skies and beautiful nature with three million population. It borders with Russia and China. Mongolia won its independence from China in 1921, when the Mongolian People's Republic was then established with USSR influence. Following the dissolution of the USSR, Mongolia had its own relatively peaceful democratic revolution in the early 1990s which led to a multi-party system, a new constitution and a transition to a market economy.

This transition resulted in an upheaval of structures that had been in place for seventy years and saw Mongolia's trade with Russia decline by 80 per cent, which had a strong impact on peoples' lives. After the collapse of the communist system people did not know how to live in the market economy and earn enough money to live a decent life, even though they welcomed many freedoms such as freedom of speech and having a passport to travel abroad. Unemployment, school dropouts, poverty and malnutrition became the reality of life for most people who lost jobs after the communist system collapsed.

In that difficult time, community development projects and programmes started in various parts of Mongolia. The Adventist Development & Relief Agency (ADRA) was one of the development agencies that began its activities in Mongolia during 1994. In the early years, ADRA Mongolia implemented mainly relief projects and provided food and clothes aid to Mongolians. Then programmes on education, health, agriculture, micro-economic development programmes were launched and implemented successfully. Since that time, ADRA Mongolia has reached one third of the Mongolian population through its community development work and other projects and programmes.

To engage with local communities, ADRA needed to understand them. First, we did desk review reports and records and gathered economic and social data related with each local community. Then we analyzed and prepared questions for interviews and focus group discussions, ensuring participation by ordinary citizens, poor and marginalized groups, representatives of civil society, businesses and local government. We organized meetings with communities to understand the local situation. After conducting needs assessment, we helped each community to set up a working group or steering committee which would plan next steps in order to address the priority issues or concerns of the community. The steering committees planned and developed project proposal and did fundraising, with the community development practitioner's support.

We mainly used the following tools and approaches to gain knowledge about the social, economic, cultural and environmental factors impacting local communities:

- Community Meeting
- Observation & Mapping tools (resource mapping, community mapping)
- Interview/Informal discussions
- Participatory learning approach (bottom-up)
- Appreciative inquiry approach (sharing best experiences and telling stories)

As community development practitioners our main task was to enable communities to gather sufficient confidence as change makers and add dignity to their lives. Alongside, we played the role of an expert, a guide, an enabler, advocate and a mediator. Community engagement was essential for agreeing pressing issues and needs. Communities identified their priority needs and discussed ways to resolve issues in a participative manner. From this early engagement, ADRA's community development practitioners worked with local communities to develop simple project proposals to raise funds.

ADRA proposed cooperatives as the primary format for local participatory engagement and organizing and we worked with the communities to achieve a shared vision. Cooperatives required joint investment, joint decision-making, total family-level involvement and a genuine leadership selection process. Step by step, beneficiary communities were learning from their experiences with the clarity that only the community itself could decide about how to use local resources in ways that would avoid conflict.

Over the past two decades and half, ADRA Mongolia has implemented over 200 projects and contributed significantly to community development in terms of reduction in childhood malnutrition and improving food security. To give one example, Mongolians did not have much experience in growing and eating different vegetables for many years due to their nomadic way of life. ADRA Mongolia's Food Security Programme improved access to food for many rural and urban households through the establishment of agricultural self-help groups and cooperatives in Zavkhan, Bayankhongor, Bayan-Ulgii and Selenge provinces and Ulaanbaatar, our capital. It has helped hundreds of households and cooperative members to learn the basics of vegetable gardening to provide sustainable access to diverse food baskets. Besides this, communities jointly established small workshops using local community resources, such as bakery, wool felt, vegetable preserving, sewing and carpentry and established a supply chain for serving communities with bread, noodles, and agricultural products.

ADRA Mongolia pioneered an organic agriculture programme in 2018. Concern for food safety has also increased among the urban middle class and thus there is growing interest and demand for organic products in Mongolia, particularly in the capital city of Ulaanbaatar, where one third of the country's population lives. A comprehensive programme for the period 2018 to 2021 called – Partnership for Organic Agriculture (POA) – was launched with the primary aim to promote organization of organic producers in Mongolia. In order to produce qualitative organic vegetables and natural honey, small-scale farmers and beekeeper cooperatives of Selenge province participated in organic agriculture training.

Most of ADRA staff have worked with the community for many years and gained experience of community engagement and advocacy. Since its programme start, ADRA has focused on food security and food diversity through growing vegetables. Agronomists organized organic agriculture training for small-scale holding farmers as well as some other experts and consultants who conducted training such as "Cooperative governance and management" and some specialized training on organic practice related to preventing weed and insects.

These training programmes led to the development of a basic organic agriculture traceability book for farmers and beekeepers and a code of conduct defined by an oath for organic farmers and beekeepers. The farmers and beekeepers of each village had a meeting and finalized internal bylaws for a Participatory Guarantee System for Local Groups (producer groups) and documents for peer review and management information systems. This led to them establishing "Selenge Organic" Participatory Guarantee Organization, including consumers representatives in June 2019. In 2019, 112 organic producers grew vegetables over 80 hectares of land. Within a year about 250 farmers were growing twenty-two kinds of vegetables over 204 hectares. This project has been extremely successful with growers being certified organic and selling 2,500 tonnes of twenty-two types of products through their PGS Local Groups and the Selenge Tavan Khairkhan Cooperative Union, a key partner in the project.

The POA programme has been crucial for building local and national level capacity, promoting organic agriculture through institutional, technical, and human resources developments. In the process, Mongolia has joined other nations on the path towards promoting sustainable and commercially successful organic agriculture development.

Our lessons from our community engagement activities have been:

- Community leaders must obtain skills of identifying priority needs of the community and thereby ensure equal participation of all generations of women and men.
- Community leaders need skills for planning, fundraising, capacity building and implementation of programmes.
- Community leaders need to be trained on techniques for mobilization of the community and the management of natural resources.
- Community leaders need to initiate dialogues with citizens, farmers, local government and businesses in order to resolve issues and reach sustainable solutions.
- Local government engagement is essential for long-term change.

To initiate the first organic agriculture programme in Mongolia was quite challenging. We were treading into uncharted territory and had to find bio-fertilizer, good quality seeds, introduce participatory guarantee systems and establish market linkages with potential con-sumers. The project action team conducted needs assessment and identified priority needs of small-scale farmers of cooperatives involving local government and other stakeholders. Side by side small-scale farmers and beekeepers had to participate in several orientation and training programmes to understand the nuances of organic farming systems.

Through these interactions it was also essential to introduce appropriate technological solutions in terms of post-harvest tools, storage, packaging and branding. Finally, communities were enabled to form participatory guarantee systems and local groups with the understanding of peer group reviews to sustain the movement. Currently, such local groups of small-scale farmers and beekeepers of Selenge Province are sufficiently empowered to enjoy enhanced incomes through sustainable production and marketing systems and commitment to create a sustainable value chain for organic agriculture in Mongolia.

Figure 3.5 Tree-planting drive in Cerro Verde del Milagro, Peru. Photo credit: Periferia.

Case Study 4: Peru
Constructing a Metropolitan Green Belt
By Anna Zucchetti, Taícia Marques and Yamile Sánchez

The metropolis of Lima, the capital of Peru, contains almost 10 million inhabitants, 30 per cent of the country's population and 30 per cent of the national GDP. The city, located on the coastal desert with very limited water resources, grew demographically and spatially, squeezed between the Pacific Ocean and the lower Andean hills, expanding horizontally to accommodate the high influx of people from the 1970s onwards. Its spatial organization shows a very fragmented urban space, with clearly segregated socio-economic areas, expressing the weaknesses of land use and urban planning policies and urban public service provision.

While middle and high income districts occupy mainly central Lima and are usually placed on flat lands, low-income informal settlements stand mainly in the peripheral desert hills and steep slopes around and in the city (*laderas*), forming a peri-urban belt of poverty that exposes people to natural hazards and threatens the fragile seasonal ecosystem of *Lomas* (an ephemeral green landscape that appears annually with the winter fogs occupying between twenty and a hundred thousand hectares of the cityscape). This socio-economic segregation and the fragmented governance of the city into forty-three autonomously administered districts, increases the challenges to provide even access to public services, including the maintenance of publicly accessible green and natural spaces throughout the city.

The social mobilization to protect and conserve the natural *Lomas* ecosystems started almost 15 years ago, with the implementation of a demonstrative project in approximately 200 hectares of the peri-urban community of Quebrada Verde. Thanks to strong local leadership, Quebrada Verde implemented the first community ecotourist circuit and experimented with small-scale enterprises for snails production, *tara* cultivation, orchards, gastronomical services. Almost twenty years afterwards, the project has consolidated itself as a Community Conservation Area that provides recreational services to the local and metropolitan population and, especially, as a model for the defence and communal management of *Lomas* ecosystems in an urban context.

The Quebrada Verde experience inspired a social movement for *Lomas* protection on a metropolitan and national scale (*Red Lomas del Perú*): today, more than ten thousand hectares of *Lomas* have been declared a Regional Conservation Area by the Lima government and a Management Plan is currently being designed with the participation of local communities. This experience also sparked the discussion on the need to mobilize urban and peri-urban communities around the consolidation of natural or green urban borders ("metropolitan green belts"), in order to limit urban expansion on high-risk areas while, at the same time, creating opportunities for habitat improvement, new public spaces and small-scale enterprises in the interphase where the city meets the slopes (*laderas*) and the slopes meet the *Lomas*.

This discussion is currently being converted into a new concrete initiative in the northern district of Independencia (211,360 inhabitants, 18.6 per cent of which live in high-risk conditions on this interphase). An initial plantation of 3,000 trees on *laderas* implemented with international funding, is now being complemented with 1,500 more trees as well as a diverse array of small-scale Nature-based Solutions (NbS), such as orchards, productive *andenes* and fruit trees, financed by the local Municipality, the community and a private construction company which needed to compensate its carbon footprint. Periferia, a small public benefit company, is playing a pivotal role in linking local needs of the Municipality and the community to the carbon compensation demand of the private constructor. This synergy creates an opportunity for mutual solution where the carbon footprint of a residential building in Lima is being partially compensated by expanding the urban forest of Independencia district. The Green Belt hopes to become a collective solution to a common problem, using a holistic approach that integrates different stakeholders: the municipality, the community, the private sector, as well as the academy and NGOs, in a reciprocity cycle.

The methodology used to conduct the social process is based on four general stages, which decant from many years of community development work in urban settings:

1. Get to know the community and other stakeholders, create trust and companionship;
2. Co-design and co-create the initiative;
3. Co-implement, organizing the work and mobilizing different resources;
4. Co-maintain and co-monitor, to ensure sustainability of results and measurement of impacts.

Each stage contains a specific set of activities designed for and with the local community and, as such, can be considered as an open-ended method that guarantees a certain degree of flexibility to attend the specificities – in this case – of the Independencia context and needs (See Figure. Reciprocity cycle related to methodological stages.)

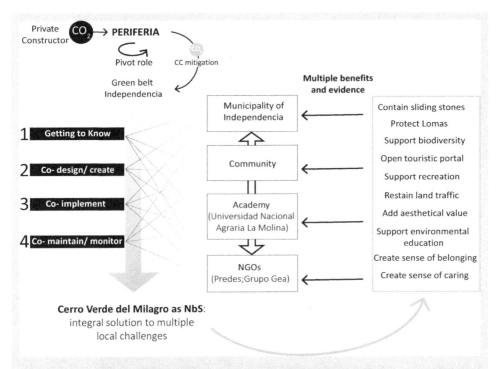

Figure 3.6 Reciprocity cycle related to methodological stages.

Independencia was selected based on a clear local commitment from both the Municipal government and the community and strong social leadership. This created a fertile ground for a process of further social empowerment and engagement. Restrictions imposed by central government due to the Covid-19 pandemic added additional challenges for the application of the methodology. Virtual meetings and non-contact training sessions became part of the process.

Activities such as presentations and virtual meetings with local community leaders, workshops with leaders and community members, including women, youth, children and elderly, were conducted in a gradual process that enabled the Periferia team to inspire, create trust and motivate everybody to voice their wishes for the future of Independencia. This was accompanied by site visits, or "walk-and-talk" tours of the area, that enabled us to identify together the challenges and opportunities. It was thus possible to map areas of conflict, geophysical restrictions, shades, and variations of ecosystem vegetation according to local climatic conditions, desires, and expectations of different sectors of the community.

The visits were complemented by "imaginative workshops" where people started to design their green dream for Independencia, answering the questions: *How I wish Independencia to be? How do I imagine the laderas?* Workshops included interactive games to further build trust, as well as specific training on planting, tree species selection, tree care by an urban forestry engineer. As a strategy to build a sense of belonging, the community was asked to propose a name for the project, now baptized as "Cerro Verde del Milagro", and celebrated the first planting of a tree. To convert all the information collected during this co-creation stage into a forestation plan, virtual meetings were conducted with municipality representatives and the neighbouring committee currently responsible for the maintenance of 3,000 trees, who provided a rich expertise regarding the definition of planting and irrigation sectors, based on site experience.

The next stage, co-implementation, will be focused on further training sessions that include compost production, tree growth measurement and monitoring, plague control and fertilization. The final plantation will be held in November 2020 when volunteers from the academy, NGOs, the supporting private company, and other civil associations will be invited to join the community, every Sunday of the month.

Finally, for the co-maintenance and co-monitoring stage, members of the community will be trained, a monitoring calendar developed, and tree monitoring information will be published systematically on a website, making it publicly available. Complementary research will also be carried out by university students and researchers on topics such as CO_2 sequestration, urban biodiversity, urban greenbelts by social urban forestry and social processes and impacts.

Charlie McConnell, Anita Paul, Kalyan Paul

Figure 3.7 HURIA Executive Director addressing community members in a community sensitization forum – Kenya. Photo credit: HURIA.

Case Study 5: Kenya
A Community-Based Approach to Tackling Violent Extremism
By Halimu Suleiman Shauri and Yusuf Lule Mwatsefu

Human Rights Agenda (HURIA) is a human-rights-based, non-governmental organization in the coastal region of Kenya. The organization was founded in 2012 against a background of poor leadership, injustices, violation of human rights and fundamental freedoms and bad governance in Kenya. HURIA, has a theory of change, which hinges on the believe that:

> if HURIA strengthens capabilities of state and non-state actors to exercise their rights and fulfil their responsibilities as provided for in the Constitution of Kenya, 2010, other laws and the international human rights instruments, then citizens can increasingly use their improved abilities and knowledge to claim their rights, enhance their participation, demand accountability, resolve their grievances, respect others' rights and fulfil their responsibilities.

This is a commitment, HURIA as a human rights defender has been building in its team and through lobbying and advocacy tried to engender this virtue to fellow Kenyans and human rights institutions in the country and the region through partnerships and collaborations, evidence-based advocacy, human rights education, training and mentorship, partnership and networking.

One of HURIA's success stories has been influencing state and non-state actors in the prevention and countering of violent extremism (P/CVE), an area marked by many human rights violations. The most common human rights violations include alleged disappearances, abductions and extra-judicial killings. While the Kenyan government is using both hard and soft power in mitigating violent extremism through the Anti-Terror Police Unit (ATPU) and the National Counter Terror Centre (NCTC), HURIA has been in the forefront influencing the respect for human rights in dealing with the challenge of violent extremism.

The approach by HURIA staff was to first conduct research to assess the impact of Violent Extremism in Kwale County in the coast of Kenya. The research exercise entailed among other data mapping of P/CVE actors in the county and the various interventions they were undertaking with a view of avoiding duplication of what was already being done at the grassroots. The research established key gaps that needed redress, which included lack of a clear guideline in the implementation of P/CVE programmes in the county. Accordingly, the study findings were used by HURIA as a foundation in the designing and implementing its P/CVE projects.

HURIAs implementation of P/CVE programmes in Kwale County came at a time when cases of alleged abductions, extra-judicial killings and disappearances were rampant. As a result, most of the stakeholders, specifically community organizations, were not willing to be engaged in violent extremism discussions. As a matter of strategy therefore, HURIA decided to partner with the national and local governments in the development and implementation of its P/CVE interventions and the development of the Kwale County P/CVE Action Plan.

However, this was not taken well by community leaders who identified themselves as "gatekeepers". These included community champions and village elders who were already involved in peace and security matters in their villages. Family members of victims of terrorism incidences, enforced disappearances and extra-judicial killings saw the partnership with the state apparatus as an endorsement of their alleged atrocities to the community. This therefore bolstered mistrust and resistance for meaningful engagements.

In order to reach out to community "gatekeepers", HURIA ensured their inclusion in the validation processes and in implementation of the project. The idea was to ensure ownership by all stakeholders and accountability for their actions. As part of this strategy, HURIA also started engaging and building community capacity, especially of upcoming community-based organizations in the implementation of P/CVE programmes through mentorship and provision of seed grants. The organization mapped out existing CBOs interested in P/CVE work and helped members of the communities in setting up formal structures for engagement. This was critical in expanding the network of influencers in the affected communities.

To ensure the P/CVE programming had an impact, HURIA community-based development staff conducted community sensitization meetings in all the four sub-counties of Kwale. During these meetings HURIA staff were able to flag up and take note of the community needs, which informed other interventions connected to mitigation of violent extremism. One of the identified gaps identified in these meetings was the lack of community coordination structures with regard to matters of peace and security. Accordingly, HURIA staff also supported the reconfiguration of various community led structures that coordinate peace and security activities in Kwale County. These included district peace and community policing committees as well as *nyumba kumi* (household neighbourhood watch) which had either collapsed or been infiltrated by members of criminal gangs. HURIA staff supported their reconstitution using newly launched guidelines by the state. This boosted the trust, morale and efficiency of the structures in supporting P/CVE conversations at the village level.

To ensure that the community was included and in securing their buy-in, especially with a view towards ensuring community ownership, the following steps were taken by HURIA's community development staff working directly with the targeted communities:

- Engaged communities within target implementation areas in a baseline research and included the community recommendations by ensuring community suggestions were given priority in HURIA's design and implementation of its various P/CVE projects.
- Strengthened community capacity including their Peace and Community Policing structures as an approach to Countering Violent Extremism.
- Sought external support from community champions to provide psycho-social support and created safe social spaces for vulnerable and at-risk community members in order to discuss and demystify P/CVE issues. This made significant impact in opening up community social spaces where P/CVE issues hitherto discussed in secret and with fear, to now being discussed in several open social spaces such as community meetings, schools and religious spaces.
- Invested in ensuring feedback to the community on the progress of various projects was done promptly and effectively, especially during reflection meetings with the community. Feedback is key in registering success, building community confidence and staying in focus with the community as programme implementation continues.

Owing to the disappearances, abductions and alleged extra-judicial killings that were happening in the county predating HURIA's entry, there was tension and fear in the community engineered by these human rights violations. More precisely, fear and anxiety manifested itself in many of our engagements with the community whenever issues of violent extremism were mentioned. The silence whenever such issues were mentioned and the discomfort of participants speaking freely were not difficult for one to note as it showed the pain and difficulty the community was experiencing.

However, through our community engagement approach, HURIA won the hearts and minds of the community members, albeit gradually, and transformed them into solid partners in P/CVE work. Evidently, the community's embracing of HURIA interventions in the county is proven by the milestones achieved. The KCAP-P/CVE is in place and now under review with HURIA's guidance, robust community structures on peace and security are now visible, safe social spaces to engage in P/CVE work are in place and above all the community now speaks freely of human rights violations with regard to disappearances, abductions and extra-judicial killings related to violent extremism in the county and beyond.

Human rights work must be guided by ethical considerations. It is highly sensitive and more so where there were allegations by the community of forced disappearances, abductions and extra-judicial killings as in this project. This meant that HURIA development staff needed tact and experience to make an entry into the county and help in mitigating violent extremism within the framework of protecting human rights. To achieve this HURIA's approach placed ethics and human rights principles at the fore of its interventions. From respectful entry into the community to adherence to research and programme implementation ethical standards, HURIA ensured support. This was manifested in the good working relations with the community, informed consent from the community through information sharing and excellent communication and feedback mechanisms, and a Do No Harm approach in all its P/CVE projects. HURIA also ensured confidentiality of sensitive information shared by the community.

HURIA staff learned that for successful implementation of P/CVE interventions, there is need for frequent research on the changing international, national and local context on P/CVE and dissemination of the findings with the local community. This way, P/CVE interventions can then remain focused and relevant within such dynamics. In the process of implementing the P/CVE intervention, HURIA also learned the need to have a clear *community entry strategy*. The importance of *establishing trust and mobilizing support* from local networks and influencers in project planning, designing, implementation, monitoring and evaluation was key for our success. The idea is to be as inclusive as possible and be able to secure buy-in that ensures project ownership by the local community.

During the implementation phase of the HURIA P/CVE intervention, it was clear that success could not be achieved without partnerships. There is therefore a need to expand partnerships with community champions and village elders beyond state and non-state actors with a view to minimize risks at all levels. Successful P/CVE intervention needs careful stakeholder analysis and understanding of the partners' roles in the project. The importance of partnerships in the successful implementation of the HURIA P/CVE intervention cannot be gainsaid. Finally, HURIA learned that the success in any P/CVE intervention requires the transfer of capacity from the implementing agency to the local community, which is critical as an exit strategy.

Notes

1 P. Wilson. (2019) *The Heart of Community Engagement: Practitioner Stories from Across the Globe*. Routledge.
2 P. Wilson. (2019) *The Heart of Community Engagement: Practitioner Stories from Across the Globe*. Routledge.
3 G. Blake, J. Diamond, J. Foot et al. (2008) *Community Engagement and Community Cohesion*. Joseph Rowntree Foundation.
4 G. Blake, J. Diamond, J. Foot et al. (2008) *Community Engagement and Community Cohesion*. Joseph Rowntree Foundation.
5 The National Standards for Community Engagement. (2016) What Works Scotland *and the Scottish Community Development Centre*.
6 The National Standards for Community Engagement. (2016) *What Works Scotland and the Scottish Community Development Centre*.
7 P. Henderson and D.N. Thomas. (2016) *Skills in Neighbourhood Work*. 4th edition. Routledge.
8 M. Hawtin and J. Percy-Smith. (2007) *Community profiling: a practical guide: Auditing social needs*. McGraw-Hill Education.
9 R. Putnam. (2001) *Bowling Alone: The Collapse and Revival of American Community.*, New York, Simon and Shuster; M. Emery and C.B. Flora (2006). Spiralling-Up: Mapping Community Transformation with Community Capitals Framework. *Community Development: Journal of the Community Development Society* 37: 19–35.

Chapter 4

Ensuring Participatory Planning

Dee Brooks, Huston Gibson, and
Asnarulkhadi Abu Samah

Introduction

This chapter provides cases of exemplary participatory planning practices in community development from various geographies and contexts; "empowering partnerships and supporting communities".[1],[2] Community development planning processes may take on many forms, involving a multitude of stakeholders and methods, or practices, of inclusion. Participatory planning is a process of involving, or empowering, communities in strategic processes and decisions about their future. Those empowered have the means to influence the actions and outcomes of the decision-making process. How and which stakeholders are involved, and the sincerity of such involvement, may vary depending on how the participatory framework is structured. Participatory planning can and has faced differing levels of barriers and challenges due to, among others, politically dominant power structures.

Sharing international examples through the lens of various frameworks of participatory planning practices enables community development practitioners to examine (i) the process of participation, (ii) the types of stakeholders involved, (iii) methods and strategies of participatory planning, and (iv) barriers and challenges faced. Participatory planning is generally recognized as a dynamic process. Embedded in that process is human behavior which is influenced by culture and power. Different cultures practice different levels of socio-political presentation, and these may shape the dynamic of people's participation in planning. Through examples, practitioners will learn how people maneuver their participation space, meeting their needs and achieve common goals in the community's interest.

The extent of public participation in planning may also be influenced by the type of community, location, and/or specific groups within the community. Whether an urban,

DOI: 10.4324/9781003140498-4

urban-fringe, or rural community, minorities, or indeed whole communities are often marginalized. These disadvantaged groups become the social context where community development is most vital. Community development work primarily focuses on the local level for meeting the local needs, and demands, and addressing local and sometimes wider problems, it is also about work with communities of identity and interest. Community development most often takes place from the bottom up, with grassroots groups, villages, sub-districts, on up to districts and/or municipalities of different geographies and population.

Process of Participation

The International Standards for Community Development report calls for community development practitioners working in a range of disciplines to demonstrate that they know how to:

- Assist communities to understand local, national, and global political processes and where power and influence lie.
- Enable communities to understand and utilize both existing research information and the application of research methods in their own setting.
- Initiate and participate in partnership and collaborative working for the empowerment of communities, acknowledging and addressing conflicts of interest.
- Promote relationships between communities, public bodies, non-governmental organizations, and other agencies for the empowerment of communities and in pursuit of their interests.
- Influence public bodies and other decision-makers and service providers to build effective and empowering relationships with communities.
- Work with communities and agencies to identify needs, opportunities, rights, and responsibilities, acknowledging and addressing conflicts of interest.
- Break down barriers to community participation and enable community representatives to play active roles in strategic planning, decision-making and action.

Participation practices can range from offering "a seat at the table" from the beginning to supporting opportunities such as stakeholder group meetings, focus groups, key-person interviews, surveys, simulations and scenario development, charrettes, public hearings, and other public meetings.[3,4] Providing access is only the first step on the ladder for meaningful community engagement, the second is framing the power dynamic, which may range from manipulation, which clearly embodies little community power, to informative/tokenism (i.e. a one-way, top-down flow of information disguised as participatory planning), to real community partnerships and grassroots, bottom-up control through communal decision-making.[5,6]

Sherry Arnstein was one of the pioneers of participatory planning in community development. For Arnstein "*the idea of citizen participation is a little like eating spinach: no one is against it in principle because it is good for you.*" Her "ladder of participation" will be well known to students and teachers of community development, and community practitioners across a wide range of disciplines.

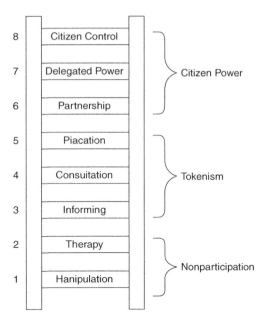

Figure 4.1 Sherry Arnstein's ladder of participation.

- The two bottom rungs are in effect little more than a public relations exercise by planners and developers whether corporate, governmental, or non-governmental about a top-down plan they are proposing that will impact upon a community.

- The third rung aims to be more informative but tends to remain a one-way flow with little or no opportunity for community feedback. The fourth and fifth rungs are more consultative, using attitude surveys, neighborhood meetings and public enquiries. But again, this tends to be about consulting on an already prepared proposal or range of options, where citizens can give their feedback, but the developer retains the right to decide whether to accept that the advice.

- Rungs six and seven move toward more genuine partnership and co-production and is generally advocated as better community development practice. Here there is real negotiation with communities, co-planning and co-decision-making responsibilities are shared, and power over the decision-making process can even be delegated to the community, with their representatives having powers to make decisions.

- The top rung is where the planning, policy making and managing of the program, including control over the resources to realize it lies within community control.

The skill required of community development practitioners is to be able to judge how far the community might want to go. It may for example be disempowering to hand over full responsibility and resources to a community group over a major economic, social or environmental development when they may at first not have the capacity or may not want to take on such responsibilities. On the other hand, control over planning and decision-making may be exactly what a community wants, and their organizations indeed have the capacity to take this on. Most community development projects and practitioners will move across the rungs at different times working with community members and the other stakeholders to secure outcomes that benefit all. Important to our discussion in this chapter is the notion that the processes and the outcomes, means and ends are not mutually exclusive.

No matter how good an agreement is by some standards, if it was reached by a process that was not regarded as fair, open, inclusive, accountable, or otherwise legitimate, it is unlikely to receive support.[7]

Stakeholders in Participatory Planning

Any urban or rural development proposal involves various types of stakeholders, namely government (and their agencies), private sector, non-governmental organizations, local activists, and beneficiaries. Stakeholders may be defined as those who can affect or are affected by a decision or anyone that gains advantage and disadvantage from a project process and outcome.[8] They range from the promoters of a proposal, for example a local authority may wish to redevelop an urban neighborhood, to participation in projects and initiatives led by a community itself. The various players or stakeholders can range from governmental, private sector to NGOs (Non-Governmental Organizations) and CBOs (Community-Based Organizations), from the implementers of the proposal and on to community members upon whom any decision may impact, positively or negatively. Stakeholders are the important parties at the core of the planning process.[9] Early identification of the parties involved in the proposed plan is important to clarify each expectation and view as this will influence participation levels during the planning process.[10]

Stakeholders in planning depend on the type and or form of proposal being planned. Some public participation planning processes may have been designed by the state authority, and locally implemented in the realm of urban redevelopment, coastal protection construction, windfarms, social amenities provision, socio-economic income-generating activities, extension and social services, and health delivery. In addition, there are community-initiated projects mooted by members of the community to meet their local needs or for solving their shared problems. In all these cases, participatory planning becomes essential so that the people concerned are part of the process from the ground up, and they do not end up getting hurt in the process.[11]

A community development approach to participatory planning should aim to:

1. Engage all appropriate parties in a meaningful manner.
2. Be purpose-driven toward an agreed upon goal or set of goals.
3. Operate within an agreed upon framework.
4. Integrate facts and nurtures ideas.
5. Reach an outcome only after all issues have been fully exhausted.

However, this assumes that all the players with a stake in the planning process can work collaboratively and have a high degree of consensus over the outcome. In some cases, there may be conflicts of interest within any community and between the community and outside players. The extent of stakeholder consensus will be influenced by the participatory methods and strategies applied.

Methods and Strategies of Participatory Planning

The choice of methods and strategies adopted for ensuring effective participatory planning takes place will be dependent upon the issues being addressed; matters of location, space, and timing just as much as the practical application of tools and techniques that are adaptive and responsive. The methods and strategies to adopt will also be dependent upon the extent to which other stakeholders in the planning process, for example a local authority or building developer recognizes the value of engaging the community against other arguments, e.g. it will cost money. In some countries, communities will have legal rights to participate in planning processes around developments that impact upon them. In other countries such legal rights may not exist. So, community development practitioners will need to be appraised of the legal rights for community participation and to be prepared to use those rights to best effect. In situations where there are no legal rights, the community development agency and practitioner will need to consider other options with community leaders and activists, as well as gauging the views of the wider community concerned.

When approaching any systems change, a community development practitioner's lens tends to focus upon the problems, challenges, concerns the community they are working with may have. This is known known as a needs or problem-based approach. Or they can focus on the opportunities and strengths, any community will have. This is known as an asset or strengths-based approach. [12] From an asset-based approach, it is necessary to identify the assets and strengths that the community has before addressing challenges and to ensure that the community are best prepared to engage in any participatory planning process with other stakeholders.

Whereas a needs assessment focused on what was not in a community and developed a wish list of project and programs, as asset-based approach links the various capitals existing in a community to see how they can be recombined to achieve a desired future condition. [13]

Community development practitioners will often find that the asset or strength-based approach is seen as a less risky "entry point". [14] Here community development practitioners work with communities to first discover what is strong in the community, instead of what is wrong, in order to then address the identified issues. Communities and their representatives are likely to be stronger players in any participatory planning process if they are confident of their strengths. This approach focuses on the glass half full. In comparison, the half-empty glass views communities as having weaknesses when it comes to tackling problems whereas the half-full glass views communities as having strengths, capabilities, and assets. It is the half-full glass that gives us something to work with. [15] McKnight and Russell, proponents of this approach offer three questions which can help communities during participatory planning to identify what they have, to get what they need and how to make collective decisions about engaging internal and external support:

1. Start with what the community can do themselves as an association of citizens, without any outside help.
2. Then looking at what they can do with outside help.
3. Finally, once these local assets have been fully connected and mobilized, citizens decide collectively on what they want outside agents to do for them.

"The order is critical. When we start with the third, as often is the case in traditional helping endeavors, we preclude citizen power."[16]

So, when supporting community participation, practitioners should:

- Apply strengths focused practices where possible.
- Identify local assets (people, resources, organizations etc).
- Agree on principles for working together.
- Agree on what the community wants to achieve, both in the short and long run.
- Use information with transparency and accountability.
- Offer flexible options to participate.
- Use inclusive language.
- Focus on capacity and skill building.
- Strengthen, nurture, and maintain relationships.
- Notice and address power imbalances.
- Create and invite diversity of people and views.

There are a wide variety of methods and strategies for strengthening community participation in planning and decision-making. These include:

- Recognizing community members as experts who can provide knowledge and stories.
- Ensuring meaningful engagement and collaboration by all parts of the community concerned, not just community leaders and activists.
- Identifying the community's capacity for taking on an issue or project.
- Co-creating maps and charts that can visually help people understand the planning process.
- Helping people to understand trends and the implication of doing or not doing anything.
- Scaling and ranking the challenges to be addressed and timelines.
- Identifying what outside technical assistance or resources may be required that are not available within the community.
- Ensuring transparency especially where this involves money and budgeting, monitoring and evaluation.
- Organizing public consultation through hearings, panels, and debates.
- Facilitating community conversations, forums, and focus groups.
- Appraising and reviewing progress.
- Introducing different approaches to community led governance if that is the desired outcome.

Using Online Tools to Widen Participation

These days it is also important to consider online engagement methods particularly when considering access for individuals who may be differently abled or may be unable to attend community meetings. Local authorities and other public bodies are increasingly using online ways of consulting the public. Similarly, they can be used by community development practitioners to ensure that everyone's voice is heard. "Online communities are new social structures dependent on modern information technology, and they face equally modern challenges.".[17] However, people will only use online platforms if they feel valued, heard, needed, and satisfied. And it is important to recognize the digital divide, with poorer communities, especially in developing countries often unable to access such technologies.

Barriers and Challenges in Participatory Planning

Community development does not come without barriers and challenges. For example, in participatory planning, we must ask ourselves questions such as: How do we be mindful in terms of appropriate language and process in different cultural and indigenous contexts? How do we speak in a common language which is understood by all parties, regardless of educational background? How do we reach out to engage those within any community who may not traditionally have a voice? Not every culture or community lends itself to similar levels of participation and by approaching each community with the purpose of listening and asking, without making assumptions, we can discover different levels of local knowledge, preferred times for meeting, issues of accessibility for people who may be differently abled or regarding ability to use tools such as the internet.

As we have discussed in chapter three on engaging with the community, the community development practitioner needs to prepare before meeting with community leaders and activists, and then to listen to their views before jumping in with suggested ways of participating in planning processes determined by external bodies, or in planning projects determined by the community itself. This is not to say that practitioners should be non-directive. Professional community development practitioners can include health workers, social workers and community architects who have expertise and are paid to share that. Indeed, in many cases it will be the community development agency that is proactively seeking to engage participants in its programs, e.g. for health education. But good practice would be to strive to know the views of the wider community and to be cautious not to accidentally, or intentionally, leave anyone behind or exclude them just because, at first, they seem less active or concerned. Practitioners, of whatever discipline, must authentically involve people as opposed to simply creating the illusion of doing so.

Grassroots development is a term used when advocating for engaging community members in participatory planning. Another term used is "'grass tops' democracy," which refers to when "local elites have considerable leeway in making critical decisions" and influence in their communities.[18] Thus, what may appear to be grassroots development, may be grass tops democracy at the community level, driven by local elites and thereby perhaps marginalizing those with less community status and influence. The challenge for community development practitioners is to be able to involve the grassroots and not just the grass tops in any project's participatory planning processes.

Community development practitioners should therefore be aware of and sensitive to such barriers and challenges to non-participants, and be willing to listen and learn from a broader range of community members to ensure more inclusive and diverse participation, helping people to work collectively together to achieve better outcomes in everyone's interest.

Case Studies

The following five case studies, drawn from around the world, illustrate in more detail what we have been discussing here, demonstrating how participatory planning contributes to more sustainable community development outcomes over which communities feel a sense of ownership. From Croatia we see how after the civil war in former Yugoslavia, communities renewed and recovered after devastating physical and economic destruction and how initiatives in local rural communities, at the border with Bosnia and Herzegovina, helped facilitate post-traumatic recovery and regain mutual trust. In the Hong Kong story, it is highlighted how city planners can work effectively with a wide range of stakeholders, including community residents, to address community challenges such as street market hygiene, by adopting a bottom-up approach and a commitment to use participatory planning to discover a mutually beneficial outcome for all. The Australian story shares how participatory planning played a major role, during the global coronavirus pandemic, to bring like-minded practitioners and communities together, from around the world, and achieved a forty-eight-hour rolling event, across twenty countries. From New Zealand/UK, the story is about a group of nursing students who undertook a community development project for their Primary Health Clinical Practice to discover how to work collaboratively with community members and stakeholders and identify specific health needs of rural communities. Finally, from South Africa, the story shares how corporations can effectively collaborate with local communities, who have suffered from vandalism and unrest, in order to both design a new highway through these communities and support them to develop and thrive through small- and large-scale local initiatives.

Figure 4.2 City of Hrvatska Kostajnica and Una region, Croatia. Photo credit: Marina Pavlić.

Case Study 1 – Croatia

Putting the Pieces Back Together

By Dragana Knezić, Ana Opačić, and Dijana Vuković

This article presents the work in post-war communities in Croatia over the last 25 years and can be divided into three phases: the renewal phase, phase of recovery and empowering the population, and the phase of community development. Here we describe experiences and initiatives in local rural communities placed at the border with Bosnia and Herzegovina.

Immediately after 1995, when the war officially ended in Croatia, numerous consequences affecting communities had to be faced. Besides the loss of human life, the war also caused physical and economic devastation, deep demographic changes (the exiling and forced relocation of the population, and the migration of exiled habitants from Bosnia and Herzegovina), as well as long-term social and psychological consequences. Many people became seriously traumatized developing acute and chronic traumatic disorders, while social relationships in communities, which prior to the war were ethnically and religiously mixed, broke apart and deteriorated due to long-term animosities and distrust. Moreover, people and communities became impoverished, thus it was increasingly difficult to ensure existential conditions and basic services.

The aim of the initiatives in the community was primarily to facilitate the post-traumatic recovery of individuals, reconcile and build again mutual trust while supporting social and economic empowerment of people, and develop social services which were lacking. As the community become more empowered, the preconditions for greater inclusion in managing their own development were created.

Continuous Projects in Post-War Communities

The initiatives within the community, which are presented in this case study, began immediately after the war, and included projects for assisting people and renewal. In this particular phase, social workers, working also as community development practitioners, were engaged in building a civil society, establishing voluntarism and involved in home visits to the most vulnerable users of social services (about 1,500 visits a month). A total of 250 actions were organized to renew the social fabric of disorganized communities. This part of the work was strategically led by UNHCR (United Nations High Commissioner for Refugees) and the American organization USAID (US Agency for International Development) who encouraged systematic cooperation between local committees, associations, as well as the public and private sector.

After this first phase, at the end of the 1990s and into the 2000s, initiatives were primarily directed upon post-traumatic recovery and social reconstruction of communities were implemented, with the aim of encouraging reconciliation and renewal of trust and life together. What is typical for these phases of post-war renewal and rehabilitation is that the initiatives were mainly established and led by stakeholders outside of the community, i.e. international organizations and donors, in partnership with non-government organizations from Croatia, which were at that time specialized in providing psychological and social support for trauma recovery, as well as overcoming conflicts and transitional justice. In the latter phases of community renewal, most of the projects were directed toward social and economic empowerment and inclusion and the development of social services which communities were not able to ensure for their most vulnerable members. What is typical for this final phase is that initiatives and the identification of needs came from the community, who merged their efforts with partners from outside of the community, and with whom they developed a relationship of trust and acceptance.

In the final phase, from 2010 to this day, a community development model has become increasingly prevalent. After years of systematic work with local stakeholders, an empowered community has clearly gained capacity and motivated local actors who began to autonomously manage development projects and, even more so, community development is now viewed strategically, and a culture of evaluating development activities is nurtured including cooperation with a wide scope of stakeholders, including development-service-learning programs.

In the initial phases, the primary step was to ensure basic existential conditions for life and a return of the population, material renewal and ensuring basic infrastructure for functioning of the community. Moreover, significant efforts were invested into building a civil society which practically before the 1990s had not existed in socialist Yugoslavia. Projects directed to post-trauma recovery and encouraging reconciliation and social reconstruction of the community were primarily initiated and run by stakeholders and experts outside of the community, whereas stakeholders from within the community were mostly end users of such projects. In the initial phases, this approach was justified to some extent. Namely, the goal was to ensure rehabilitation of individuals who had survived serious traumatic experiences, for which the community in post-war circumstances did not have its own resources and capacities. Moreover, while the wartime conflicts were still fresh and the process of returning the population that had once fled remained unfinished, importance was placed on reconciliation and building trust, even if it had to be done by stakeholders outside of the community.

In subsequent phases, the role of stakeholders from local communities became stronger, and who identified needs for support and development of specific services and programs and required outside partners. These initiatives came from representatives of local authorities, local providers of social services and schools. The aim of these initiatives was to empower vulnerable groups of the population socially and economically – women, the long-term unemployed and poorly educated people. The aim was to ensure psychological and social support as well as social services in order to prevent social exclusion of the most vulnerable members of the community – children and families at risk, the elderly who live alone and disabled people. These initiatives were the result of participatory development and the implementation of ideas initiated by people from the community and implemented in partnership with civil society organizations that possessed many years of experience and recognition among members of the community.

The final series of projects in the third phase was specifically directed to strengthening the leadership and capacities of local actors so that they become the bearers of community development. These activities meant that significant efforts were invested in strategic planning, program evaluation, education of local experts and socially useful learning programs. Continual work over the last twenty-five years has clearly shown that maximum endeavors have been made to implement empowering practices while moving focus on action from external actors to a wide circle of internal actors. Moreover, throughout the entire period of work undertaken in the post-conflict community, the imperative has been the protection of human rights. The continuity of work which has always been more of a partnership than anything else, but has also been compliant and coordinated, testifies to the fact that the work in a community is based on partnership values, building trust and, finally encompassing a wide spectrum of activities which stem directly from identifying needs out in the field has led to nurturing the idea of progressive social change and the value of social justice.

In the last phase, the community development model is evident primarily in the well-developed network of local stakeholders who come from local leaders with authentic legitimacy. Furthermore, the community is very responsive to identified needs of the population, indicating the presence of very live communication between local stakeholders and the population. Capacities of local organizations are constantly changing, and efforts are made to provide continual assistance in acquiring new knowledge as well as through supervision of work. Community development is best evident in practical terms when internal actors initiate various project activities, and their outcome becomes clearly synergetic. Their consistent cooperation resulting in exceptionally diverse content for citizens is not an unusual outcome.

In the first phase, an important factor in success was the legitimacy and influence of international organizations that strongly promoted the participation, inclusion, and networking of local actors from the start. Subsequent initiatives were especially successful and relevant in contributing to the creation of new structures in the community around which local resources were organized and mobilized, as is the case with social services for persons with disabilities or home assistance services for the elderly and infirm persons. In the case of services for people with disabilities, local authorities from five communities decided, in solidarity, to ensure conditions for maintaining them in partnership with a civil society organization which, thanks to its capacities and resources, initiated and implemented the initiative. Local stakeholders such as schools, local organizations, sporting associations and businesses, supported and got involved in implementing the program which has the goal of including people with disabilities in the community. The project for assisting the elderly and infirm led to the mobilization of women's groups who, with the help of external stakeholders and thanks to self-organization, developed capacities for providing quality services to this very vulnerable group, while respecting their dignity and autonomy.

The many years of cooperation and working together on the described initiatives has led to a partnership between stakeholders who are also key members of the community – local public providers of social services, local authorities, schools and organizations rooted in the community, and possessing the relevant competencies and network of allocated resources outside of the community which, if needed, can be mobilized. Finally, the most successful projects were those initiated, planned, and fully run by internal actors possessing partnership legitimacy and who have proven themselves as leaders in the community.

Post-war circumstances have long-term consequences in these communities. All the initiatives undertaken in them had to take these consequences into consideration and bear them. This is especially apparent in phases of economic crises, which more strongly affects communities still experiencing post-war recovery. Poverty and insufficient resources in a community leads to frustration which then more easily revives animosity. A constant lagging in development and internal inequalities further weakens the motivation of citizens to participate and their belief that they really can have an impact on the development of their community.

In the past decade, depopulation of these communities has been increasing as a consequence of deindustrialization and insufficient number of good quality jobs. Accordingly, the community has become poorer, older, and at the same time has an increasing need for social and healthcare services. These challenges are currently overcome by attracting and utilizing money from EU funds, and which supplement needs the community cannot autonomously meet. A multi-sector approach has been credited as the underlying reason for succeeding in drawing these additional funds, an approach established in the development and implementation of the described initiatives.

The post-conflict renewal and development of local communities is a complex, long-term and uncertain process. In that process, post-traumatic recovery, in terms of the individuals and the community, requires integration with economic and social strengthening and inclusion. One without the other two components of renewal and development of post-conflict communities has little chance of success. The experience described here shows that initiatives stemming from the community and which the community views are its own, have a greater chance of contributing to its renewal and development than initiatives imposed or initiated externally. Therefore, the prospect of any future work is to provide support to key stakeholders in the community in order to achieve projects for addressing key challenges and, accordingly, to optimally utilize resources and strengths inherent in the community. A future challenge to a larger extent will be the activation of citizens and their potential in community development.

Figure 4.3 **Different stakeholders participated in "Our Kwai Fong Circuit" city-planning workshop which was facilitated by city planners to discuss their expectation on Wing Fong Street Market and their community – Hong Kong. Photo credit: Kenny Ng Kwan-lim.**

Case Study 2 – Hong Kong, China

Bottom-up Participatory Planning on Wing Fong Street Market

By Kenny Ng Kwan-lim

This project began in 2015 in Kwai Fong district, southwest of Hong Kong. The old residential area in Kwai Fong district, had been unable to resolve poor public hygiene conditions for years in the district market. The problem lay within the Wing Fong Street market which was old and crude and could not address the needs of the residents there. So, the project attempted to organize the residents together with city planners, and architects to try a bottom-up planning of the Wing Fong Street market. The project successfully organized and mobilized the residents, who with the city planners, and architects, actively participated into the whole planning and redevelopment process of the Wing Fong Street market. The Wing Fong Street market, which was built in 1982, had been unable to follow the development of the district, in terms of its population growth. It had been in a poor condition across a one-floor building for decades, it did not have any air-conditioning, nor did the market vendors improve the hygiene condition in the market. These led to a serious public hygiene problem around the market. In 2015, the Hong

Kong government launched a plan to modernize six old markets in different districts. Wing Fong Street market being one of them.

In the initial stage, the community development practitioner assisted the residents' association the "Association of the Residents of Private Buildings of Kwai Fong District" to work with Professor Ng Mee-kam from the Department of Geography and Resource Management, Chinese University of Hong Kong, and a number of city planners to come up with a bottom-up city-planning solution in the community for the redevelopment of the Wing Fong Street market. The project sought to adopt a participatory planning approach with the community because it strived to encourage the residents to actively work with the stakeholders throughout the planning process.

To realize participatory planning, this project addressed the issue of poor public hygiene in the market to the residents by setting up regular street station presentations. The project then publicized and organized "Our Kwai Fong Circuit" city-planning workshops inviting residents and market vendors. In these Professor Ng Mee-kam, city planner Ms Kate Kwok, and other city planners sought to educate the public on the importance of public participation in city-planning. In addition, the workshop successfully opened the dialogue between the residents and the vendors in the market to discuss different perspectives and considerations in the city-planning solution. The city planners made use of their professional modelling software to visually illustrate the possible solutions in the discussion. The workshop also created opportunities to exchange viewpoints and thoughts with members of Hong Kong Legislative Council, members of the District Council, and departments in the Hong Kong government. After each workshop session, the project team and the residents' association reported back to the residents through the regular street station presentations, updating on each stage of the planning process. When we encountered any query from the residents, we brought them back to the next workshop session and adjusted the planning solution to meet the needs of the residents. As a result, the planning solution became more practical, relevant, and accurate. This gradually created community consensus to the planning solution.

Combining the practical and professional solutions, different stakeholders increased mutual understanding while planning through this two-way communication manner. This process went beyond the situation that only has "support" and "oppose" dichotomous positions. Working together the stakeholders finally started exploring different possible solutions. With community consensus for the planning solution, the project team members invited Professor Chu Hoi-shan, Paul, Department of Architecture from the Chu Hai College of High Education and his team, to help participants to visualize the short, middle and long-term solutions, with the use of professional planning software. "Seeing is believing" – the visual model was effectively presented to the community and facilitated the lobbying for that solution in the District Council.

The core community development value of this project was to nurture a bottom-up participatory planning process, through the establishment of communication platforms between residents and other stakeholders in the community. We deeply believe that this community planning solution avoided the "support" and "oppose" dichotomous positions, but we also believe enhanced the residents' capacity to work out a planning solution for their community they wanted to see. They have voice to be heard and ideas to be considered in the actual physical planning. We attempted to bridge the residents with the planning professionals to work out the thoughts and ideas with the use of professional software. Capitalizing the local human capital and subsequently creating social capital were the primary assets involved in this project.

In terms of community development, we successfully worked out the community planning solution of the Wing Fong market, with the joint effort between the residents, the resident's association, the professionals, and the project team members. Importantly, this project maintained a high level of residents' participation into the planning process.

The relationship between residents, the resident's association, professionals, and the project team was collaborative and well developed in the making of community planning solution. The factors that made the relationship a success were:

- the stakeholders could work toward the same goal throughout the process.
- the project team facilitated the communication between the stakeholders and the community with quick, transparent, and reciprocal communication.
- the resident's association learnt how to participate into the work of community planning solution in the workshop.
- the project team also ensured that the communication platform was inclusive throughout the process.

The strength of this project is that the team networked to bridge up different professionals, the councils, and the Hong Kong government. It facilitated the synchronization between different stakeholders. It also had expertise to nurture the relationship and capacity among the residents. All in all, we collaborated and worked as one team to meet one mission.

The community planning solution involves lots of technical knowledge. The residents at first felt difficulties in participating in the discussions. Therefore, we addressed this problem step by step through the workshop, which gradually found the focus and examined particular possible solutions. Also, the project team strived to simplify the community planning solution, using visualization software to facilitate the discussion toward the consensus of the solution, while at the same time increasing the resident's understanding and realization. This project was a successful community development experiment about how to bridge up different stakeholders in the community, how to build up a common imagination in the process, how to raise the awareness in the community, and how to encourage the community actively to participate in the change. Indeed, participatory planning with the community was the core to the community development process.

Figure 4.4 Graphic harvest of the ABCD (un)Conference. Photo credit: Fiona Miller, Jeder Institute.

Case Study 3 – Global

A "Glocal" Assets- and Strengths-Based (un)Conference: Co-Creating Our Stories of Hope and Action

By Dee Brooks

This case study reflects upon ways in which community development practitioners committed to an asset-based approach worked together to plan an online community of practice support event during the global pandemic. The (un)Conference was responding to asset-based community development and strengths focused practitioners, during the time of a global pandemic, to offer them a space to continue to connect, share and learn from each other. Inspired by a discussion during a meeting of international Asset-Based Community Development (ABCD) Institute faculty members, the (un)Conference aimed to build on the skills, abilities, talents, and passions of everyone involved. What the ABCD community ended up achieving was a forty-eight-hour rolling event, across twenty-two countries and thirty-nine sessions, where over 2,575 individual registrations were taken and 1,259 practitioners were able to attend as many sessions as they wanted to, for free.

In January 2020, Dee Brooks made a note on her phone to talk to her colleague, Michelle Dunscombe about the possible idea of hosting a virtual ABCD event. Together, they took this idea to the next international ABCD Institute faculty meeting where it was well received. Initially, there were eight people involved and after a call out to the international ABCD community about who would like to be part of the planning team, we ended up with fifty-two people, across ten countries and nine planning teams, who all stepped up to offer their skills and abilities.

People said they felt valued by being invited in to help with the planning. They felt "buy in". They felt they could add value to what we were already planning, and they turned up to the weekly meetings and would take away some tasks to complete, like developing a flyer or co-creating invitations.

The small teams took on a life of their own and started meeting outside of the main weekly meetings. Someone from each team, if not all of the people, would attend and feedback their updates each week to the global planning team. The (un)Conference only happened because of the commitment of dozens of people, around the world, who saw the event as something for practitioners to be part of as hosts, planners, participants, and organizers. Everyone put their community development skills forward to ensure the event ran smoothly.

The small teams that each person chose to be part of were:

- Co-design document team
- Zoom team
- Website and social media team
- G-Host team
- Mentor team
- Timezone team

The supporting organizations involved were:

- Tamarack Institute
- Jeder Institute

- The Constellation
- Om Dhungel
- The Unconference
- UIN Sunan Ampel Surabaya
- International Association for Community Development
- ABCD Asia Pacific Network
- ABCD in Action
- Embrace Communities
- SPACE 4 Impact
- Ikhala Trust
- Irwin W. Steans Center
- Coady Institute
- ABCD Institute
- SPiCE

There was also, very importantly, a backend support team who helped the registration and technical side of things run smoothly:

- Sam from Humanitix, Australia
- Chris from APACMS, Australia
- Nathan from Department of Internal Affairs, New Zealand
- Howard from Irwin W. Steans Center, DePaul University, Chicago, IL
- Kim from ABCD Institute, Chicago, IL
- Michelle from Firefoxes Australia

The timeframe from idea to commencement of the event was eleven weeks and could not have been done without all of the people involved. By being constantly guided by the principles of ABCD, we tapped into the skills, abilities, networks and resources of the whole global planning team. We used practices and processes from participatory community building to move us along the planning trajectory and included those principles in the documentation we offered to session Hosts. We offered mentor sessions a week before the event where session hosts could join and learn from those of us who had skills in delivering participatory workshops online and set up an internal support system so that Hosts would never be alone.

The expression of interest which each Host submitted asked them to only apply if they had a small team of two to three people to deliver their session and were informed once approved that someone from our global planning team (G-Host) would join their session, in case they needed advice, support or back up. The role of the practitioners in the planning team was to be available, where possible and to offer what they could and ask for what they needed.

The core values of the (un)Conference were based on ABCD principles and Participatory Leadership practices and processes:

- Focus is on community assets and strengths, rather than problems and needs
- Identifies and mobilizes community and individual's assets, skills and passions
- Builds on community leadership
- Builds, maintains and nurtures relationships

- Deepens practices and increases confidence in hosting group processes
- Generates connection and releases wisdom within groups of people

The assets which were harnessed throughout this process were:

- Individual assets; talents, skills, abilities and passions
- Associations; community groups and networks
- Institutions; government and non-government organizations and services
- Physical assets; land, buildings, infrastructure
- Economic assets; small businesses, consumer spending power
- Stories; culture, local values, local identities

The assets above were identified as we pushed forward, not as a particular exercise, and they internally focused on each task at hand, if we could find someone in our already sizable planning group to step up, that was the first step. If we needed to look outside of the planning group for anything, it was through the planning groups networks and established relationships.

What we achieved, in terms of community development, was to engage individuals, associations and organizations on an "as needed" basis by putting our own strengths, knowledge and wisdom forward. It was community development at its finest, without needing to be named. What worked well was the fact that we were all community development ABCD practitioners, even at various levels of experience, and we trusted each other and that the practices and processes would help us find a way forward. This worked because we implicitly knew that someone would offer a next step, if we were stuck, and we would continue to build on each other's strengths and abilities.

The open invitation for anyone to be part of the planning team was absolutely necessary and the smaller teams which spawned from the main one made the load lighter for everyone. The capacity building and skills sharing between individuals and the strengthened relationships across cultures and countries were a visible outcome.

The people were the strengths of the event!

The challenge now is how to achieve this again next year. It was a huge amount of volunteer hours with no remuneration for anyone and while it was a great social experiment on how to run a global, online conference for free, it might be a challenge to ask people to continue to offer this every year.

The call out for next year's planning team has already commenced and I'm sure we will be having a financial discussion as part of the many other discussions over the next few months.

We held a post-event webinar, hosted by one of the global Institutions involved and we shared the outcomes and "next steps" which came from the event and the planning team's post-(un)Conference catch up. The challenge here will be to keep the momentum going for the next steps.

There were copious amounts of learning both along the way and afterwards. Some of the broader ones were:

- Invite others into planning early
- Ask planning members to invite others in around particular skills

- Lock in weekly meetings
- Develop the team's principles of working together early
- Co-create a compassionate selection process for submissions
- Never host alone
- Meet people where they are at, with what they can offer
- Leave frustrations at the door
- Stay flexible and be guided by what is emerging
- Ask for what you need, offer what you can

As one of the planning team members said, at a post-event catch up, "The success of this (un)conference was that it was emergent and not prescribed – it was walking the talk. Let's not lose that!"

Overall, the (un)Conference was a huge success and one of the participants, from a Middle Eastern country, sent a message of thanks which said, "Thank you! I would financially never have been able to attend such a quality event face to face – this online unconference has opened my world to so many more stories, people, cultures and learning" and that message made it all worthwhile!

Oh, and the final cost (which was for a website template) was $48.00, or approximately 26 cents per person and was also paid for, as a donation, by one of our planning partners.

Figure 4.5 Food box – New Zealand and United Kingdom. Photo credit: Daphne Page.

Case Study 4 – New Zealand/UK
Engaging with the CHASE Model to Enhance Community Wellbeing
By Jean Ross, Keith Whiddon, Samuel Mann and Daphne Page

The purpose of this solution-based initiative was to improve and promote the resilience and wellbeing of rural residents. It involved the application of a research and education model, Community Health Assessment Sustainable Education (CHASE) that sought to improve wellbeing when applied in partnership with rural communities. The CHASE model is an internationally recognized research model for gathering and analyzing community data to establish an action plan through participation and communication. A research process engaging with the CHASE model helps community development practitioners understand and work collaboratively to establish a comprehensive community assessment, evidence-based resources, implementation and empowerment. It is a research method that applies community development values with the aim to empower rural communities and their local organizations to sustain and improve health care. Nurses act as community development practitioners to improve health outcomes in partnership with these community members and stakeholders.

Background

The rural population accounts for almost half of the total global population and these communities are confronted with reduced access to healthcare, which contributes to increased health disparities. Nurses play a critical role to reduce health disparities but there are limited models to guide their practice in ways that assess and improve health disparity between rural and urban communities. Models of community health care are largely based on an urban-dominant view with limited understanding of the nuances of rurality. Nurses are positioned to navigate the holistic landscapes of health that integrate the socio-political, cultural, economic and environmental aspects related to the uniqueness of rural communities. While the underpinning values of social justice are commonplace the application is varied, according to place.

The Project

Living labs are spaces where educational, research and health care institutions partner together at the macro level to enable empowerment of the identified community. Community development practitioners assist and collaborate with community members, where "living lab" activities take place. This is the level at which the local, national and global political dynamics related to policy, power and influence, are acknowledged, and taken into consideration. While at the micro level activities are undertaken to highlight the community assets, deficits and capabilities, with a view to harnessing innovation and empowerment.

A group of twelve third year Bachelor of Nursing learners at Otago Polytechnic in New Zealand, undertook a community development project for their Primary Health Clinical Practice in 2020 and engaged with an education and research team, who profiled the rural English town of Bishop's Castle, in Shropshire, United Kingdom. This project was undertaken using a virtual platform involving zoom, email and photo images to collaborate with the local community members and stakeholders. The learners applied the CHASE model as the research method.

This emerging research model is a multifaceted approach to sustainability, responsive governance, cultural diversity and education, embedded within a systems framework, influenced by international, national and local factors, government and non-government agencies. Engaging with the CHASE model provides community development practitioners, in this case nurse learners, with a method to build effective and empowering relationships and consider the unique aspects of rural communities that include the socio-political; environmental; cultural characteristics; the principles of social justice and to work with "community as client" while, adapting this model to fit the unique aspects of each community. This model guides community development practitioners to view health from a sustainable and population-based approach. The goal was to work collaboratively with the community members and stakeholders and identify specific health needs.

Core Values

Core community development values range from a commitment and dedication to partner with community members, stakeholders and organizations. At all times, the respect of different ideas and cultures; being patient and mindful of responsive communication and maintaining ethical practice is fundamental. Equally valuing knowledge from different disciplines is shared in a trusting space with a collaborative aim to improve health status through change, empowerment and education.

Assets have been harnessed and include local members of the core community team who engaged and collaborated with the nurse learners. They have built up an ongoing and lasting local response to new developments in the community through availability of producing resources, for example, local vegetable boxes to improve health care and continuing with community meetings and maintaining ongoing relationships with the nurse learners and the education institution Values have been harnessed between all active practitioners and include ongoing networking, trust, respect, admiration, kindness, caring and thoughtful attention to detail.

Collaboration between the learners and the community stakeholders progressed very well. Health needs in Bishop's Castle were identified by a process of profiling the community, applying a needs assessment and developing resources to improve sustainable health care.

What Worked in the Project?

By gathering data and developing a SWOT analysis, the nurse learners identified three health needs associated with the community population aggregates:

Transport community members rely on their own vehicles or the minimal public transport that is provided, which has an impact on work, social mobility leading to isolation access to healthcare and other services, and education.

Mental Health community members stated they were concerned that mental health and suicide is a hidden problem, and that suicide has a huge impact on the Bishop's Castle community because of their close relationships and ties.

Physical Health due to the concern expressed by community members about obesity, poor diet, food poverty, lack of exercise and drug misuse taking a toll on all aspects of physical health.

The learners focused on each of these needs and developed sustainable health promotion resources which are community focused, population specific and meaningful to the identified population groups. The project engaged in relationships between inside and external organizations for example a written submission and flyer to be placed on the windscreen of all non-permitted cars occupying disabled parking spaces, demonstrating the importance of the correct use of disabled parking spaces and aiming to promote accurate use in the future were distributed to the Shropshire Council to alert them of the transport and parking issues for the disabled and elderly reducing their access to health services.

Challenges and Opportunities

The community response to the project findings was overwhelmingly positive. However, COVID-19 lockdown occurred before the resources developed by the learners could be implemented, so much is work in progress. Saying that, the pandemic has brought new opportunities and the lessons learnt though participating in the CHASE model will help to shape our community post-COVID-19 recovery plan. The ability to improve many public services lie beyond our local control, for example funding and resources to support mental health are held centrally by National Health Service, Shropshire Clinical Commissioning Group. Identifying our own community needs through this project is the first step in lobbying for improved support.

Food poverty was identified as an issue. Bishop's Castle recently established its own Food Bank, which has proved invaluable during the pandemic. Little Woodbatch market garden is now supplying the Bank with fresh vegetables ensuring that families on low incomes are receiving high quality, locally produced food and contributing to improved diet and health outcomes. Resources created by the learners with the food distributed by the local food bank include a fridge magnet and coaster delivering consistent education on the benefits of a community garden and healthy living.

The nearest Mental Health Hub to Bishop's Castle is twenty-five miles away. However, in response to the pandemic, the service is now available via telephone and video call making it far more accessible to the community. Greater community support is also now available through improved social prescribing. In response to community pressure, Shropshire Council has agreed to review the parking for disabled users in the town center.

Learning and Future Plans

The community of Bishop's Castle was warm and inviting, extremely helpful and welcoming to the nurse learners. They learnt so much about a different culture, while having the privilege to partner with the community via a virtual platform is new ground in terms of research for Otago Polytechnic Bachelor of Nursing, it has been an important learning and insight into community health developments. This case study offers an opportunity for networking and for connecting with rural nurses across the globe. It is envisaged the uptake of the CHASE model will be adapted and will further enhance understanding of rurality and provide a medium to address rural health disparities while enhancing the continual identification of potential educational opportunities, research partnerships and practice innovations.

Figure 4.6 Bakwena champions celebrating a successful ABCD course – South Africa. Photo credit: Amelia Visagie & Working Group, Zutari.

Case Study 5 – South Africa

Bafenyi ka Bakwena Community Champions Project
By Siena Shaker

Bakwena Platinum Toll Concessionaire (Pty) operates the major freeway in South Africa, which connects some major cities with each other. They suffered from vandalism and community unrest as each community next to this freeway wanted to be employed in the running of the toll road. Bakwena realized that they should partner with communities to assist with development in areas where there was desperate need due to poverty and a history of destructive behaviors related to this desperation. Zutari and Bakwena was the appointed consultant to facilitate the project.

The Project aimed at empowering the community from within and less dependent on external entities for their survival, which would often be destructive to community cohesion. Through the Asset-Based Community Development (ABCD) method, communities have developed networks, discovered assets and used these to identify and start small- and large-scale initiatives for the benefit of the entire community with a view for sustainable long-term empowerment.

Background

The initiative is a pilot project that started in Rustenburg South Africa in selected communities around the N4 highway. Two ABCD practitioners, Zutari and Bakwena, in consultation with municipal and community structures embarked on the project. Asset-Based Community Development is a method of development that depends on participation with communities to ensure that projects are sourced mainly from community assets as well as run and fully owned by community members and the networks they have developed. This method ensures a higher chance of sustainability compared to top-down development approaches where companies decide and implement what they think communities need without consulting them. The latter has not led to any meaningful or lasting change.

The Project

The project began with various engagements with community leadership structures and representatives. This was in partnership with government bodies to ensure alignment with larger development goals in the region. The process at all times remained fully independent of any government, political or community body but is enhanced by their participation. The independence of the process ensures smooth running and that the project is not hampered down or beholden to any particular group or agenda.

After these engagements we began a fair and transparent recruitment process where "community champions" were selected on a volunteer benefit basis to be the community representatives that, together with Zutari and Bakwena, facilitate ABCD in the various areas. A total of fifteen unemployed young people were originally recruited and selected to represent a total of five different wards in the Rustenburg Area. These community champions were trained in the ABCD method through an initial five-day workshop and gained further training as well as valuable life skills training in subsequent monthly workshops. All the while champions began disseminating ABCD information in their communities through hosting workshops and engaging with community members. The project started gaining momentum and early adapters to the ABCD process as well as the champions themselves started small scale projects in their communities.

The essence of ABCD is for communities to take their development into their own hands and shift mindsets from dependence and lack to empowerment and possibility. Zutari's role was to instill valuable know-how and mentor and equip champions and community members to be able to do this. Champions had just begun a digital asset mapping process, intended to optimize project identification in communities, when a nationwide lockdown was implemented due to the Covid-19 pandemic. Although Champions were no longer able to continue with face to community engagements and projects, this did not dampen their passion. Champions immediately began engaging their communities on social media and other online platforms and a "home-based" style of ABCD started to flourish. Champions and early adapters began small scale ABCD projects in their own yards related to agriculture, maintenance and even sanitizers and masks for themselves and community members to ensure that their communities could survive the consequences of Covid-19 and the Lockdown. This was so inspiring and successful that a national T.V. station is in the process of producing a documentary about ABCD and the champions.

Core Values

The core values related to this project are primarily partnership and participation, consultation, inclusion, empowerment, sustainability, community ownership. Primary assets being harnessed are the skills of the community members themselves. This includes formal and informal skills that are related to the head, the heart and the hands, land as an asset, agricultural goods and tools, household reusable and recyclable items, farm animals, mechanical tools and construction assets and infrastructure. These are some categories of assets uncovered and used but are not exhaustive of all the various and specific projects and their unique components.

The project achieves community cohesion and development. Through uncovering assets (both internal to the individual and external to them) and using them, mindsets are shifting to become more positive and less dependent on external help for their own development. The community is less divided and more involved in the ownership of their own destinies. There is less tension in communities as selected groups are not linked to external benefits that create attitudes of exclusion and partiality.

What's Working Well?

Successful engagement and consultation with communities through our champions and social media. Learning and respecting area specific cultural norms. Holiday programs in each community only using local assets were a huge success and social cohesion took place throughout this process. Trusting community members to thrive when they are handed the right tools for their own development. Using the ABCD principle of *"Everybody has something, nobody has nothing"* and *"Build on what we know and enjoy what we have!"* to assist in the development of these communities.

Challenges

Development in communities is always under threat from negative attitudes that developed from years of destructive conditioning. Development is also always threated by political agendas that seek to hijack and manipulate any benefit coming into an area. Through sincere, fair and transparent community participation and a long process of trust development, these risks are well mitigated. Communities, for the most part, are hungry for real change. Community members can instantly differentiate between genuine and agenda-driven actors. This is not easy and takes time to develop, understandably, as there has been a history of abuse and mismanagement in communities by external parties.

Learning and Future Plans

Key learnings include uncovering high levels of potential for community cohesion and existing assets that need a catalyst for mobilization. This is encouraging as it demonstrates that the key to development already exists, it just needs to be awakened. This project is ongoing and there is great potential for ABCD to be used as a nationwide strategy for economic recovery post-Covid. Existing projects will be further enhanced and built upon, and community engagement and network forming will resume. The hope is to start local SME (Small and Medium Enterprise) development and to formalize and develop projects and networks into businesses along with developing local knowledge databases to be drawn on for future initiatives and optimizing use of local resources.

Dee Brooks, Huston Gibson, Asnarulkhadi Abu Samah

Notes

1 International Association of Community Development (IACD) (2018). *Towards Shared International Standards for Community Development Practice.*
2 International Association of Community Development (IACD) (2018). *Towards Shared International Standards for Community Development Practice.*
3 E. Kelly and B. Becker (1999). *Community Planning: An introduction to the comprehensive plan.* Washington, D.C.: Island Press.
4 E. Kelly and B. Becker (1999). *Community Planning: An introduction to the comprehensive plan.* Washington, D.C.: Island Press.
5 S. R. Arnstein (1969). A Ladder of Citizen Participation. *Journal of American Institute of Planners*, 35(4): 216–224.
6 S. R. Arnstein (1969). A Ladder of Citizen Participation. *Journal of American Institute of Planners*, 35(4): 216–224.
7 J. Innes and D. Booher (1999). Consensus Building and Complex Adaptive Systems A Framework for Evaluating Collaborative Planning. *Journal of American Planning Association*, 65(4): 412–423.
8 R. Freeman (1984). Strategic Management: A Stakeholder Approach. Boston, MA: Pitman.
9 N., Hamdi and R. Goethert (1997). *Action Planning for Cities – A Guide to Community Practice.* New York: John Wiley & Sons.
10 T. Tufte, T. and P. Mefalopulos (2009). *Participatory Communication: A Practical Guide.* Washington, DC: World Bank.
11 R. Lupton (2012). *Toxic Charity: How Churches and Charities Hurt Those They Help and How to Reverse It.* New York: HarperCollins.
12 H. Nel (2017). A Comparison Between the Asset-Oriented and Needs-Based Community Development Approaches in Terms of Systems Changes. Retrieved June 4, 2020, from https://www.tandfonline.com/doi/abs/10.1080/09503153.2017.1360474
13 C.B. Flora, L.F. Jan and S.P. Gasteyer (2016). *Rural Communities: Legacy and Change.* 5th edition. Boulder, CO: Westview Press.
14 B. Peters and J. Landry (2018). Human Rights Based Approaches and Citizen-Led, Asset-Based and Community-Driven Development (CLABCD) https://coady.stfx.ca/wp-content/uploads/2019/04/HRBA-and-CLABCD-Discussion-Paper.pdf
15 G. Stuart (2013). What is Asset-Based Community Development (ABCD)? https://sustainingcommunity.wordpress.com/2013/08/15/what-is-abcd/
16 J. McKnight and C. Russell (2018). Four Essential Elements of an Asset-Based Community Development Process https://resources.depaul.edu/abcd-institute/publications/publications-by-topic/Documents/4_Essential_Elements_of_ABCD_Process.pdf
17 R. Soumya, S.K. Sung and G.M. James (2014). The Central Role of Engagement in Online Communities. *Information Systems Research*, 25(3): 528–546.
18 D.S. Wood and R.C. Ragar (2012). Grass Tops Democracy: Institutional Discrimination in the Civil Rights Violations of Black Farmers. *The Journal of Pan African Studies*, 5(6): 16–36.

Chapter 5

How to Organize for Change

Daniel Muia and Charlie McConnell

Introduction

Change is a key concept in community development.[1,2] Communities are subject to forces of change just as communities desire change and, if they have the means, can and do cause change to take place.[3,4] As Saul Alinsky reminds us, *"If people don't think they have the power to solve their problems, they won't even think about how to solve them."*[5]

For more disadvantaged and vulnerable communities their capacity to influence the direction of change is far more limited than more affluent communities and those with power such as the state and multi-nationals. Community development practitioners should support the processes of change and development in ways that ensure the needs and rights of community members are addressed and strengthened.

Organizing for change is a core area of study and practice in professional community development. Community organizing is about generating and wielding people power and enhancing "political" awareness and skills particularly among disadvantaged communities.[6,7] Community organizing is not however simply about giving people a voice – they already have it – it is creating a channel and an opportunity for them to be heard; it is about shifting the balance of power.[8,9] Organizing for change is a process of supporting people to leverage their power and the support of others. This is more likely to be achieved by people working together with others with shared interests.[10,11] This is based upon the realization that existing power dynamics generally impact negatively upon disadvantaged communities, in terms of their social, economic and environmental wellbeing. If disadvantaged communities do not understand how to influence political processes more effectively, they will

DOI: 10.4324/9781003140498-5

remain disempowered. By political processes, we mean here understanding how national and local government works, how public policy and decisions are made, how to get elected (indeed unelected) politicians and other opinion formers, such as religious leaders, businesses and local media, on your side. Moreover, things usually only change if people want to change their situation and work together to change it.

The Role of the Community Development Practitioner

Community organizing is more than simply mobilizing people or advocating on their behalf. For community development practitioners it should be more akin to Lao-Tsu's adage, "give a man a fish and you feed him for a day; teach a man to fish and you feed him for a lifetime". This is why for community development practice community organizing and community education should be related processes. (See also Chapter Six.) The role of the community development practitioner is therefore to support community leaders and others who have become active around an issue of concern, together with ensuring that the less active and often seldom heard members of any community have a say.[12,13]

   Saul Alinsky, one of the pioneers of community organizing practice in the 1960s, argued that our role should be to facilitate people to lead and participate in controlling their own destiny. From Alinsky's perspective, it is about building people power among what he called the "Have Nots" in relation to the "Haves" in any society, of creating the conditions for the Have Nots to have the capacity to influence change. In his book Rules for Radicals, Alinsky shared his reflections as a community organizer. These include:

- Power is not only what you have but what the other side thinks you have.
- Never go outside the expertise of your people.
- Make the opposition live up to its own book of rules.
- A good tactic is one your people enjoy.
- A tactic that drags on too long becomes a drag.
- Keep the pressure on.

   In supporting a vulnerable community to organize, they will become more able to confront forces that seek to retain the status quo. Thus, seeking rebalancing of the system.[14] Ideally community organizing will lead to change on all sides, where for example a landowner, a company or a bureaucracy will see the value in listening to people and will want to work together with them to improve the situation. This is certainly the case with, for example, such challenges as climate change and its negative impact upon coastal communities, or where through co-design people such as those with physical and learning disabilities are more able to access and use services. But community organizing can at times be one of the most challenging parts of a community development practitioner's job. And if for example you are employed by local government it may bring you in confrontation with your employer, and more so when playing the advocacy role.[15] This is not to imply that this is always a zero-sum process. Effective community organizing involves flexibility, negotiation and political maturity, and takes time.

Steps in Community Organizing for the Community Development Practitioner

To get the best results from community organizing, this needs to be done in a planned and systematic way, but with the flexibility that enables you and the community groups you are working with to think carefully about the most successful way of realizing their goals. It is important to have clarity as to what the issue is the community wants to address and to ensure that those affected are on board and involved in making decisions about what to do. You must work to ensure that the community is not divided if the action involves engagement with more powerful players within as well as outside the community, who are in some way impacted negatively by it. For example, this could be an oil company whose socially and environmentally irresponsible behavior is polluting your community, or a government bureaucracy whose policies are discriminating against people or failing to involve a community affected by redevelopment in the planning and decision-making process. It could also be powerful individuals within the community whose interests are at variance with the greater good of the community.

Here Are Some Steps to Guide an Effective Practitioner

Engaging with the Issue

The first step is to establish where the community is with regard to the issues of concern.[16] Researching the problem and how it is impacting upon the community will help you understand the issue and the players. The actions people take are generally based upon their past experiences, so you need to find out about people's feelings, hopes and concerns with regards to the situation. People generally act to change something if they feel strongly about it and believe they have a chance of doing something about it. Years of disadvantage can lead to a lack of self-confidence and the day-to-day pressures of experiencing disadvantage take their toll on people's energies to take individual let alone collective action.

Engaging with Community Leaders and Other Activists

It is important to identify and introduce yourself to the leaders and activists in any community to find out what they have done around the issue already. This means explaining what you and your development program can offer by way of help and in doing so gaining their support, trust and confidence. In finding out who the community leaders/activists are, you will also invariably find that communities are rarely homogeneous and include people with different opinions about what they think should be done and where they think things are not working. You will find more ideas about how to engage with communities in Chapter Three.

Engaging Non-Participants

It is vital that you also reach out and talk to those who are not the community leaders/activists. By talking with people across the community you will meet many who are concerned but not actively engaged. It has been estimated that only a tiny percentage of people in any community are ever involved as community activists and leaders. In understanding what is preventing people from getting involved, you will also find new talents and expertise. In any case they have to be supported to understand that their interests are interwoven with those of others.[17] A key principle of community development practice is inclusion. You will find more about this in Chapter Seven.

Engaging with Community Development Values

Any change can be a challenge to people's values, beliefs and traditions. Many communities where community development practitioners work, especially in more rural isolated areas, can be quite conservative and traditional. It is important that these beliefs are first understood and respected. They may define the "soul of the community".[18] So as to avoid resistance to organizing for change, practitioners need to respect the values of the community they are working in, even if they may not share them.[19] While at the same time you should practice according to professional ethics and values. Acting in a respectful manner is appropriate behavior for all practitioners. Community development practitioners and projects should not however be supporting community action that discriminates against people. This is covered in more detail in Chapter Two.

Getting the Community Working Together

To organize effectively there needs to be agreed clarity on the matters of common interest or concern. This calls upon the community development practitioner to:

a) **Listen in order to identify the issues** about which people have a passion and a willingness to take some action.[20] In doing this you have to encourage conversations with the people concerned so that a clearer picture emerges with regard to what the problem is, where things stand and why things can be better.

b) **Undertake a community stakeholder analysis** so that it can be established what stakes exist in the community and who are the parties who have the greatest interest in those stakes.[21] A key task here is to get all community stakeholders to come together to discuss and agree the issue and decide collectively upon the direction and actions to take. Establishing and agreeing matters of common interest helps in defining what is important and possible and what can be changed.

c) **Identify common goals.** Organizing for change is about organizing to pursue attainment of well-defined targets. A good starting point is to list all that the community wants to work toward. Second, rank-order these on basis of what is of immediate importance and having greatest impact upon the community while also taking into account practical realities of what is feasible and the resources required to achieve the desired change. The community should agree on the list of goals upon which a change process will be based. Experience in community development indicates that having some "quick wins" is vital. Generally, the rule is not to take on the most difficult challenges first, go for the low hanging fruit. Success breeds success as confidence grows among the community group.

d) **Deal with disagreement**. A challenge any organizer needs to anticipate is conflict within the community. Here you may have to find and deploy conflict management and resolution approaches to try to build consensus on the direction of travel. A degree of conflict might indeed serve to strengthen solidarity within group.[22] Ideally you will be able to build agreement over the issues in contention, helping different interests within the community to find a way of working together. In organizing for change it is important to anticipate that there will be resistance. Change may be perceived as a threat. We are creatures of habit, often uncomfortable and threatened outside our comfort zones. As a change agent it is important that these forces of resistance are mapped and addressed so that you can help the community move forward.[23]

Organizing for Change

Having clear goals is one thing. Having a clear road map on how to attain the goals is vital. This requires action on several fronts.

a) **Locally owned** – for change to take place and be sustained at community level, it has to be owned by the community, however defined. There should be structures that anchor the change process, ensure accountability and a sense of collective ownership. You may therefore need to help strengthen existing community organizations and or help develop new ones to spearhead action. It is these organizations and your related work as a community educator that should be keeping everyone informed and ideally speaking from the same script – focusing on the values that most people care about – the community, connections, kindness, and caring.[24]

b) **Local leadership** – As we have said one of the roles you can play is to identify and cultivate local leadership. And that includes helping unlock the leadership potential in other members of the community. For brief periods it is possible to organize mass events involving lots of people. But you will soon find there is a need for a nucleus of leaders who are able and can commit time to take on more leadership roles. As a community development practitioner, you should offer leadership skills training.

c) **Getting the right people for the job** – It is important that you tap into and include a diverse range of skills and strengths within any community. A vital factor however is to ensure that people who are spearheading the action have the ability to do it. It is unrealistic and inappropriate to expect a community representative to talk with the spokesperson of a multi-national if they feel unable to handle this dynamic. Remember that if the community is organizing against some other organization, they will be organizing too, with more money and probably lawyers at hand. *Community development practice means building up the personal as well as the collective capacity of people*. It is about building up the personal confidence and skills of people. There may be cases where the community group needs to "employ" expert advocates to speak on their behalf. If we take again the example of a company polluting a local community, you will almost certainly need to bring in sympathetic technical support of, for example, lawyers, scientists, and health experts. In some cases, these experts will help pro bono, but in many others the role of the community development practitioner will be to help raise the finance for this.

d) **Resource identification** – All communities have strengths. Some call these "community capitals".[25] Successful communities will need to leverage all of their capitals to realize the change they wish to achieve – financial, built, social, cultural, natural, political and human. You will need to work with the community to audit these so that they can be harnessed optimally for the benefit of community improvement. For more disadvantaged communities these will need to be complimented by finding such capital from outside the community. As a community organizer it important to work with the community to establish the gaps and then work out strategies for addressing these. Community development practitioners are often employed by agencies that have resources and wider technical expertise. Here the role of the community development practitioner is to help find and harness outside resources and partners in addressing issues of concern. This may also include accessing funds, equipment, and the support of other professionals with skills that you may not have.

e) **Network and partnership building** – Networking and forming partnerships, whether real or virtual, can be vital for community organizing. Vulnerable communities facing profound challenges are rarely unique. Climate change or peace building require of people to learn lessons from others facing similar challenges. Here an important organizing role for the community development practitioner is to network, build and strengthen relationships and collaboration between communities, organize the sharing of experiences and the dos and don'ts of how their actions went. The ICT revolution has made virtual networking and collaboration far easier, and your role can be to help put people in touch, so you need to find out whether there are neighboring communities or in other countries that have or are facing similar challenges. Generally, people enjoy learning from what other people did and will be open for sharing their experiences too and more so to ensure co-production of desired outcomes.

Lastly, as the pre-Socratic Greek philosopher, Heraclitus stated: "Change is the only constant in life.".[26] The community development practitioner, just like the community they seek to organize for change should embrace change as a way of life.

The following five case studies are from Zimbabwe, Canada, the UK, Peru and Hungary. They have been selected from IACD members to illustrate in more detail the range of approaches that community development practitioners can use. The Zimbabwean example comes from a poor peri-rural community not far from the capital, Harare. It is about organizing young people and the wider community to address issues including sexual violence. The Canadian case study is from the French speaking province of Quebec and looks at how community organizers employed by the health department supported a small community living in mobile homes whose water supply from a local lagoon had been poisoned leading to ill health, leading to the community and the agency taking on the company that had caused it. This issue of environmental pollution is also covered in the British case study from a small town with high levels of socio-economic deprivation in the county of Devon. Here the practitioners, who were also residents working in a voluntary capacity, created a community forum to take on a multi-national company seeking to dump toxic incinerator bottom ash on the edge of the town, with forum members then taking over the town council. The Peruvian case study comes from a coastal town close to the capital Lima and is concerned with organizing to promote sustainable tourism and a more diverse local economy in an area with high seasonal unemployment. The final example comes from a poor, isolated rural community in Hungary, where with the support of community development practitioners, the residents were able to improve the quality of their housing and form a cooperative. In all cases the original generative issue, led on to the residents addressing other problems and opportunities to build a stronger and more resilient community.

Each case study explores the role of the community development practitioner/s in:

- how to enable people to work together, identify what they want to achieve, and develop groups and activities;
- how to support communities to organize to bring about positive change; support people to effectively manage and address conflict, within and between communities or community groups;
- how to influence decision makers to recognize the potential benefits of collective action by communities and build relationships with them;
- how to support communities to access resources, funds and technical aid to realize their activities.

Figure 5.1 Equipping community leaders in Epworth, Zimbabwe. Copyright and photo credit: Bongani Madziwa.

Case Study 1 – Zimbabwe
Young People Organizing for Community Transformation
By Tatenda Nhapi and Bongani Madziwa

Epworth is a largely unplanned, informal, peri-urban settlement 15 km southeast of Zimbabwe's capital Harare city boundary. Given the colonial legacy and current socio-economic challenges prevalent in Zimbabwe, the area faces significant challenges associated with urban overcrowding, unemployment, violence, inadequate services and youth marginalization among other vulnerable groups. This leaves young people prone to crime, alcohol and drug misuse, prostitution. The Safe and Inclusive Cities Project described in this case study, had funding from Plan Denmark, Dialogue on Shelter Trust, Junior Achievement Zimbabwe and Youth Alliance for Safer Cities. The core community development values of this project were toward overcoming vulnerability of young people, especially young girls in the community and supporting their empowerment.

Some milestones in Epworth's young people mobilization and empowerment have been attained through using robust community development approaches. A number of conditions characterize fertile ground for rights violations against young people. These include high population concentration, overcrowding, low levels of social cohesion and exposure to multiple, interacting risks such as family separation, living and working on the streets, sexual exploitation and abuse, HIV and AIDS and violence.

Plan Denmark (Plan DK) was instrumental in the project's initial stages through rolling out funding targeting grassroots Epworth youths. This was aimed at supporting and strengthening their capacities as civil society actors and focused on the rights and the protection of excluded children and young people in Epworth. This project facilitated their participation in local decision-making processes as well as involvement in Epworth Local Board's urban planning platforms. This has led to the creation of inclusive child and youth friendly local governance system. The strategy also involved the Safe Cities and Safe Public Spaces Program implementation for increased recognition of impacts of Sexual and Gender-Based Violence (SGBV) in public spaces. The program was under the umbrella of the Youth Alliance for Safer Cities (YASC). This is a consortium of youth led community-based organizations, groups and individuals whose main thrust is to advocate for the realization, advancement and equality of distribution of resources to the young people.

The project goal was for enhanced protection of children and young people living in Epworth. One of the project's aims was eradication and prevention of violence against women and girls through addressing the root causes of women's and girls' inability to have a "voice", "choice" and "control" over their lives, which the project saw as essential for the empowerment of women and girls who face multiple forms of discrimination. One of the milestones for this project has been organizing young people from different community wards through the facilitation of a series of capacity building workshops. On the 29th August 2019 a tour of Epworth's Overspill Market, was undertaken by stakeholders that included the Director for Small to Medium Enterprise Development in the Ministry of Women Affairs, Gender, Community and SME Development. The Director stated that central government is working toward mobilizing investments to increase safety and economic viability of public spaces. Furthermore, a mobilization of young people was facilitated by using the platform of Epworth Junior Council. This consists of teenagers who act as representatives of young people and form their own council which acts like the equivalent of the adults' constituted Epworth Local Board (ELB). These series of workshops led to the creation of a platform consisting of the young people, representatives of the community council, ELB and ward development committee representatives. Accordingly, the platform has advocated around several Epworth issues which led to the following developments:

- Market spaces provision for young people for them to be in a position to earn decent income
- Permission granted to conduct applied action research targeting empirical evidence regarding issues related to the safety of people in Epworth's public spaces
- Conducting road shows for campaigning on greater human rights awareness
- The reuse of one-time defunct public transport terminus in all wards
- Solar powered streetlights installation at crime hotspots
- Provision of police trained dogs for more efficient police night patrols

One of the community development processes used in the project has been the establishment of communal water collection points to overcome portable water scarcity that is pervasive in some parts of Epworth. However, at these water collection points sexual violence toward women and young girls became prevalent. Water committee members in whose remit is the management of the water collection points were trained in identifying suspected perpetrators and victims. The training was also to sensitize Marshalls manning water collection points to be proactive to minimize such violence and those responsible for managing and maintaining water points were trained on gender-based violence.

Community development practitioners from the Department of Social Services and another collaborating NGO, OASIS Zimbabwe conducted a joint assessment resulting in a series of ward level child protection committees training workshops. The joint assessment's specific focus was on reaching and including women and girls who are often isolated and most vulnerable to SGBV due to intersecting forms of discrimination. Thus, empowerment models that are inclusive of life-skills, social skills, gender transformation models and other components that focus on empowering women and girls to have and exercise their agency were explored by the joint assessment.

In accordance with the 2030 SDG Agenda principle of leaving no one behind and "reaching the furthest first", women and girls in the most impoverished communities are the prioritized beneficiaries. The program activities targeted desired outcomes of contributing to the elimination of SGBV and harmful practices through the creation of a broad partnership with government, private sector, media, among others; and, build a social movement of women, men, girls and boys as champions and agents of change at the national and community levels.

Issues covered in the training included abuse, children's rights, overcoming child marriages, the role and responsibilities of child protection staff. We are currently organizing projects that reinforce livelihood security in the face of COVID-19 pandemic impacts. Epworth is a community where the majority of people are in debt, more than 48 percent of households are food insecure, and almost a third of all children are stunted as a result of poor nutrition, according to an annual government of Zimbabwe commissioned urban vulnerability survey. As a result, Epworth was chosen to pilot an Urban Food Security and Resilience Cash Transfer initiative in June 2020. This cash transfer reaches 19,000 of Epworth's most vulnerable people. While Saving and Lending Associations and Enterprise Groups for economic empowerment activities are targeting women's groups for the technologies/value addition, system strengthening. This is because weak social security and safety nets for the predominantly informally employed Epworth community members. This has meant more vulnerability due to ongoing mandatory COVID-19 lockdowns.

In terms of community development this project is equipping community leaders and especially young people to become primary agents for the transformation of their communities alongside for example church leaders and political representatives. By equipping community leaders and young people to address their community's needs, the project planted the seeds for long-term and sustainable transformation.

To do this we used what we called the "Edu-tainment" approach encompassing blending civic education and entertainment as theater, music works well with young people. Messages on constitutional rights that communities hold and capacities that they possess through their numbers are disseminated through song, dance and drama to capture youth audiences' imagination. Moreover, giving a platform for young people on ELB's urban planning processes guaranteed that they feel genuinely valued and do not feel their involvement is tokenistic. This platform is enabling youth representatives' attendance of full ELB meetings whose agenda focus on amenities improvement and social development.

Achieving gender parity has been an ongoing challenge. This is because as some girls, owing to multiple gender-based roles as care and collecting water cannot always be available to participate in the community development project activities. This is despite the girl child focus of the project activities. Furthermore, navigating the various political and administrative hurdles in Epworth and Zimbabwe generally requires proactive planning as these can delay project initiation. It becomes crucial to have a critical mass of social capital for community members to easily buy in and have project ownership beforehand to minimize the impact of these hurdles.

Figure 5.2 Food sharing at the Pachamama Mamacocha Ayni event in August 2019 – Peru. Photo credit: Bernardo Alayza.

Case Study 2 – Peru
Sustainable Tourism in San Bartolo
By Ursula Harman and Bernardo Alayza

San Bartolo is one of the most popular beach towns in the south of Lima. The population increases considerably during the summer between January and March. Economic activities related to tourism – accommodation, food and local trade have a productive boom during the summer, but for the rest of the year decrease. Most of the year, the neighborhoods bordering poverty and social exclusion struggle to thrive economically. For this reason, the municipality and the local community consider it necessary to promote the benefits of tourism and to mitigate negative effects on community wellbeing. This case study looks at how community development practitioners can organize the community to promote a sustainable tourism approach taking account of current and future economic, social and environmental impacts.

In January 2019, San Bartolo municipality proposed to set up a Tourism Committee, as the result of the confluence between the priorities of the new district council of San Bartolo and the needs of the population. The Tourism Committee was divided in sub-committees chaired by residents from the five main sectors of the district. The joint work between the municipality and the different sectors represented an initiative of social inclusion and citizen participation in order to enable San Bartolo community to take collective action and increase their influence in the process of decision-making in tourism as a development strategy.

The Tourism Committee was led by the mayor, two district councilors and an administrative coordinator from the municipality, while the citizens participated in seven sub-committees. Community members volunteered to lead the sub-committees and to participate in them, but when there was more than one volunteer to lead, votes were taken. Once the sub-committees were constituted, they were responsible for proposing a working plan, including a general objective and activities to be accomplished in a period of time.

The Tourism Committee was in charge of organizing the meetings once a week, facilitating workshops with the sub-committees and monitoring the progress of the sub-committees' working plans. Also, a doctoral researcher was involved to help in the workshops and documenting all the process as part of his research project, based on the adaptive planning approach. This method and strategic perspective focus on rebuilding a better future, requiring multiple reconfigurations and adjustments to achieve the desired goals in a territory or system.

The purpose of the sub-committees was to enable people to work together and identify what they want to achieve. The aim of developing the working plans was to support the sub-committees to bring about positive change in the community, and influence decision makers to recognize the potential benefits of collective action and to build relationships with the citizens.

Despite the shared objectives of the initiative, there were different perspectives about community participation between the Tourism Committee members and the community representatives on the sub-committees. On one hand, the administrative coordinator from the municipality understood the role of the sub-committees as being primarily to do an inventory of the touristic resources, using guidelines from the Ministry of Exterior, Commerce and Tourism. For instance, the archaeology and history sub-committee would identify the archaeological sites in the district. On the other hand, the expectations of the sub-committees' members were creating initiatives to improve the district.

As a result, the community progressively lost interest in the sub-committees. and asked the district councilor and researcher for their advice and leadership. It was at this point, that the district councilor and the researcher then assumed the role of community development practitioners because they opened a close dialogue between community members through participative activities.

Rather than proposing rigid planning instruments, the community development practitioners promoted the creation of communication spaces such as face-to-face and virtual workshops, periodic meetings and roundtables. Communication spaces are physical or virtual places in which individuals can align their perspectives, desires, expectations, objectives with diverse unexpected occurrences.[27] In this view, the facilitation of such communication spaces was felt to bring new opportunities for change, understanding and configuring new discourses and actions. Creating communication spaces in a dialectical understanding, would allow the community actors to organize for change.

We present three examples of communication spaces in which different stakeholders have participated in the learning and decision-making processes for planning a more inclusive tourism in the district.

The first communication space allowed the community to express their ideas and values about the district. The community development practitioners facilitated various workshops that contributed to visualize San Bartolo as a district that can offer more than just beaches and surf (as it is usually recognized), because the community agreed that San Bartolo encompasses ancestral, cultural and nature values. In this vein, the community aspires to build opportunities in tourism upon these elements, addressing responsible behavior of tourists in terms of resource consumption and waste management.

Another unique communication space is called Pachamama Mamacocha Ayni, referring to motherland, sacred water and the reciprocity system in Quechua. The community development practitioners have been part of the organization of the event since 2018, together with other representative community members.

In this event, the community share knowledge, experiences and research regarding local problems and solutions. For example, participants perform recycling and home-made compost workshops, discuss their concern of marine contamination, present ideas to improve the management of community gardens and share historical reviews of the pre-Columbian vestiges around San Bartolo district. This event also includes sharing food with a Pachamanca, which is an ancestral underground cooking technique, Andean rituals and dances. In 2020, the event was celebrated online, but replicating the same dynamic of sharing ideas to tackle environmental concerns in order to develop a sustainable tourism that respects the traditional values of the territory.

The third communication space corresponds to the meetings of the Chamber of Tourism. Local tourism-related entrepreneurs, members of local associations and other citizens realized the importance of creating a formal organization to work collaboratively with the municipality and other actors, so they invited the community development practitioners to facilitate the process. In this process, the community development practitioners have invited experts from different universities and government agencies, and other recognized actors in the field, whose feedback has helped to improve and rethink the chamber's vision and actions.

For instance, a common concern among the members of the Chamber of Tourism is the protection and sustainability of San Bartolo Lomas (hills), which are areas of fog-watered vegetation in the coastal desert of Peru that had not been taken into account before as a tourist attraction in the district. Another interesting topic of discussion in the Chamber of Tourism meetings is the development of a district brand as a municipal management instrument that together with the Chamber of Tourism allowed them to certify business, restaurants, sports associations, tourism agencies, etc. with quality and environmental standards.

The current COVID-19 pandemic has negatively affected different economic sectors worldwide, especially tourism. At the same time, San Bartolo's permanent population has doubled from 7,500 inhabitants to approximately 15,000 because many families decided to spend the national lockdown in their summer houses. The increase of population has not only motivated the local entrepreneurs to reinvent their services, but also to work more collaboratively with their peers. For example, the members of the moto taxi drivers' associations and the restaurant owners (more than twenty-five businesses) are planning actions for the summer 2021, taking into consideration the restrictions of the pandemic.

Communication spaces have been extended and replicated among the entrepreneurs who have realized that collaboration is crucial to attend the local demand and for developing sustainable tourism in the long term. As well as these important advances in terms of collaborative actions, communication spaces challenged the community to strengthen their capabilities to effectively manage and address conflict, within and between community groups. Also, the community is extending their networks with universities, NGOs, government agencies and other actors to create more opportunities to address local needs, even more during the pandemic.

Although communication spaces do not guarantee the success of an initiative, they have reinforced San Bartolo community's sense of agency and self-organization in order to deal with the uncertainty of planning scenarios for the future. Therefore, the role of community development practitioners as facilitators of the communication spaces was critical for negotiation processes, building networks and platforms for dialogue, deliberation and critical reflection for organizing actions for change. We found that facilitating communication spaces was an effective strategy for community development.

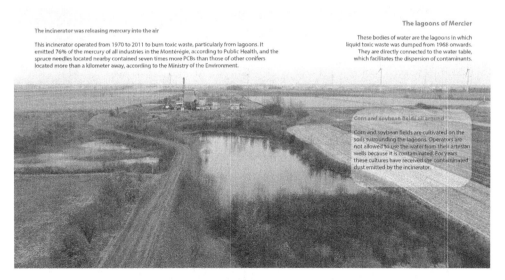

The incinerator was releasing mercury into the air

This incinerator operated from 1970 to 2011 to burn toxic waste, particularly from lagoons. It emitted 76% of the mercury of all industries in the Montérégie, according to Public Health, and the spruce needles located nearby contained seven times more PCBs than those of other conifers located more than a kilometer away, according to the Ministry of the Environment.

The lagoons of Mercier

These bodies of water are the lagoons in which liquid toxic waste was dumped from 1968 onwards. They are directly connected to the water table, which facilitates the dispersion of contaminants.

Corn and soybean fields all around

Corn and soybean fields are cultivated on the soils surrounding the lagoons. Operators are not allowed to use the water from their artesian wells because it is contaminated. For years these cultures have received the contaminated dust emitted by the incinerator.

Figure 5.3 Mercier Lagoon Community Action Campaign – Quebec. Copyright and photo credit: ArchivesMédiaQMI and Gilles Beauchamp.

Case Study 3 – Canada
Citizens Struggling Near the Lagoons of Mercier
By Jean-Denis Lefebvre, with input by Denis Bourque, translation by Gilles Beauchamp.

Community organizing as a specialization of social work has been part of the practice in Local Community Service Centers (CLSC) in Quebec province, Canada since the early 1970s. There are currently 400 professional community organizers (over two thirds women) as part of the basket of services offered to local communities.

Beyond this public network, social trends pushed the number of community organizers in Quebec province up to 2000: the rising importance (and visibility) of philanthropic foundations; new responsibilities of social development conferred to municipalities by the Quebec government; and a professionalization process in the non-profit sector, an effect (and partially a cause) of the long-term planning and financial support from state programs (provincial and federal).

Acknowledging the importance of social determinants of health, public health authorities recognize that most of the (thirty) years added to life expectancy in Western countries during the last century were the effect of actions on poverty, lifestyle habits, housing, quality of nutrition, education and environment. All actions that have been promoted and sustained by community organizing practices.

This local community case story looks at the support given by Jean-Denis Lefebvre, community organizer in a CLSC, to residents struggling near the lagoons of Mercier, Montérégie. It should be noted that community-based environmental interventions are still infrequent in Quebec province. Yet environmental problems often impact upon impoverished or less well-organized communities.

In early 1990, the water well in a mobile home park was contaminated. Some twenty families on the outskirts of Sainte-Martine (Quebec), were informed that their water was no longer safe to drink. I got a call from a worried citizen asking me to meet them. I was taking over an action that began back in the 1970s following an environmental disaster that had polluted the Mercier lagoons. The water table was contaminated by the burying of hazardous waste and the installation of an incinerator. Although new to this community, I wondered if there was again a link with the original contamination.

I met people who had never chosen to get involved as citizens in anything before, except that there they were directly affected. I told them that if they wanted to go further, they needed to organize, building upon their knowledge of the place and their contacts. In my meetings with the local community, I stressed that although I could help them build an action plan and strategies, we're going to become experts together. And it's going to change your lives! This was the beginning of Eau-Secours [*SOS Water*] citizen's action campaign. With my support, the community decided to make their voices heard at City Hall in a powerful and determined way. Their intervention was noticed as until then the city councilors had been unaware of the problem. It shook the city councilors who made a commitment to hold a public meeting with the Ministry of the Environment.

From there, we put the media in the game. The local people had never spoken to journalists in their lives, I supported them to prepare for this. The coverage of news items in the media about the new contamination and that the families were having respiratory problems attracted people who had been affected at the time of the earlier pollution of the lake. We were in the middle of a council election campaign and at the meeting we organized with officials from the Ministry of the Environment three hundred people attended. The meeting was covered by both local and national media.

The challenges I faced as a community organizer were to be attentive and take care of those people who are turning into activists. It meant taking the time to celebrate with them and reminding them of the opening sentence: "It's going to change your lives." In order to never lose sight of local roots while intervening at a national level, we put in our intervention the principle of maintaining strong links with the population, and we ran popular education activities so that people could understand the issues.

This small group of activists gave birth to the Mercier Decontamination Coalition, which brought together people with design, writing and research skills able to take the fight to the next level. We held national press conferences four to five times a year. My role as community organizer became that of coordinating, convening, and writing so that the local residents would take the lead in the various agreed actions. As a community organizer, we do have some leadership role and sometimes we are ahead and not just behind.

Political pressure led to the intervention of the BAPE (Bureau des audiences publiques en environment – *Office of Public Hearings on the Environment*). Former employees of the company that had originally polluted the lake came forward and spoke out and this led to a search of the site. We found things that were illegally buried. This led to criminal trials and conviction of those concerned. The citizen's group was represented throughout the trials and people concerned were sentenced to the maximum required by law at that time. At that time, we were influencing Canadian jurisprudence with this case.

When you get into that, you need to feel solidarity beyond the strict professional role. My employer always supported me, and I made sure to report regularly to my manager and colleagues on progress. The agency staff and administrators had a basic solidarity with the local community concerned. Supporting this citizens' struggle became an object of pride for the agency and for the staff. My employer allowed me to intervene on the issue because it recognized that it was indeed a public health issue. I was supporting victims whose lack of clean water was impacting on people's health. That the agency was supporting the residents was an important accreditation of citizens' actions, with my agency publicly endorsing the press conferences.

A group of third-generation citizens has since emerged from the community. They are more articulate and more skilled, often young people who organize themselves differently. There is still a group of citizens who are involved in the issue and doing a popular education project to share the archives of the campaign accessible on the Internet. At the same time, a joint citizens' committee with the municipality is pushing the issue on the political front since pollution in the lagoons remains a critical problem, one of the worst toxic waste sites in the country.

The various interventions carried out in this case study and in several others in the area have increased our expertise and knowledge as community development practitioners. In recent years we have created an environmental committee within the agency. It is producing an environmental impact assessment of all of the communities covered by the agency, intended to lead to community organizing support for other communities. We have also developed a close collaboration with the Environmental Health Program of the Montérégie's DSP (Public Health Director) and are using this case study in improving the community organizing expertise of public health officers in Montérégie.

Figure 5.4 Campaign against Buckfastleigh anti toxic waste dump – England. Photo credit: Simon Rines.

Case Study 4 – England

Anti Toxic Dump Campaign

By Julia Wilton

This is a David and Goliath story of confounding those who said, "It's a done deal." That's what everyone said; in the community, in the media, in the town hall.

Buckfastleigh is a small rural community of 1,300 households in Devon, southwest England. Nationally it has significant levels of deprivation, particularly so compared to neighboring communities. Its economy was largely built around wool mills, the last of which closed during the campaign. In 2010 a large German multi-national energy company (MVV), joined forces with a local company and proposed a significant industrial development in our small community. They sought permission to dump and/or mix incinerator bottom ash from their incinerator in the city of Plymouth in the exhausted Whitecleave quarry close to the town. This scheme was on course to be approved by the County Council planning committee.

This proposal involved 200 lorries a day carrying ash on an ordinary road, 50 metres from homes and the local primary school. While the companies concerned were assuring us that there was no danger to humans or wildlife from their proposals, local residents were worried. A previous plan to use Whitecleave quarry for industrial development had aroused concern and given rise to a committee to fight it, until that proposal's sudden withdrawal. This mineral quarry had been the source of considerable nuisance to the community in previous decades. Noise and dust, so much dust that the retired local doctor cited it as a contributory factor in the health difficulties of residents.

The County Council had granted permission for this on a planning "bargain" basis; the notional bargain being that while some generations of Buckfastleigh residents would endure the nuisance caused by the quarrying at Whitecleave, future generations would enjoy the benefits of the site "reverting to nature" once the quarry was worked out and no longer operational. The last quarrying firm left in the 1980s. A local demolition firm, Gilpin acquired the lease from the local landowner.

The new application for industrial development of the site sought to rip up this "bargain".

Gilpin, the local landowner and MVV stood to make a great deal of money. The only people that stood to lose were the residents of Buckfastleigh. They faced decades of further nuisance; lorries, more dust, damage to the environment and local wildlife that were already reclaiming the site. Most residents thought, sadly, that it was "a done deal".

Two residents, Julia Wilton, teacher and veteran of many political and trade union campaigns, and Neil Smith, disillusioned investment banker, fresh from the City of London led the campaign. In effect they became community development practitioners working together with the members of Buckfastleigh Community Forum, members of which had a range of expertise, including a retired professional community development practitioner. The campaign grew organically. It was very clear that there needed to be a public meeting to gauge the community's feelings and to get as many people involved as possible. It was clear from that meeting that there was considerable disquiet about the proposal and that a campaign might be built. Julia was aware from her previous campaigns of the importance of frequent meetings. This was enhanced by Neil's preference for a looser community structure for the campaign.

We quickly began meeting fortnightly/weekly depending on the level of current activity. The Community Forum was markedly different from the previous campaign's more formal committee. People could drop in and be part of the campaign when they could, with varying levels of activity as everyone was working their day jobs and living their lives! It worked in a small community because people felt accountable to their friends and neighbors and to the meeting. Over the three years of the campaign there was a core group for whom it was an additional part-time "job", placing demand on our families as well. We discovered a wide variety of skills and talents in our community that consistently fed the campaign, with specific useful knowledge in chemistry, health, transport, media, etc.

Strategically we ran a two-pronged campaign – political and planning.

The first thing we did was to start a petition. This had several functions. It launched a campaign based on activity, gave a focus for engaging people in discussion and people, who had never campaigned before, were knocking on neighborhood doors to collect signatures for the petition. Thus, we simultaneously built the confidence of our campaigners, learnt what the people in our community who hadn't come to a meeting were thinking, and therefore the arguments that we needed to win to build this campaign locally.

We:

- Convinced enough members of the County Council planning committee to reject the application, against all expectations.
- Raised £50,000 to fight Gilpin/MVV's appeal against this decision.
- Joined ourselves to the legal proceedings as an independent party thus maintaining our independence. Under English planning inquiry rules, a group such as ours is able to apply

to be an active participant in the Inquiry, so that then there are three parties in the legal argument not just two. Although the County Council planners and lawyers were going to be defending their own planning committee's decision to reject this proposal, we did not trust them to put the case properly. We wanted a seat at the table.

- Called witnesses and experts, put our case, and critiqued theirs, over a three-week planning inquiry. The other side spent approximately £1 million on this – twenty times as much as Buckfastleigh Community Forum spent.
- Were successful at the planning inquiry. Their application was conclusively rejected.

Communication was a key part of the success of this campaign. We hand delivered letters/newsletters to every home in the area on several occasions. We contributed to the regular local newsletter and we were proactive with the local media, issuing press releases and successfully challenging any misreporting. We went to neighboring councils and argued our case, mostly successfully. Over the three years we had approximately ten public meetings, (around important events like the County Council planning committee meeting) preparing for these with leafleting and postering. At every one we appealed for money and people gave so generously, even when 300 jobs were lost at the local mill during the campaign. At one meeting, by a show of hands, the community voted to raise the £50k to enter the appeal process. With jumble sales, a community auction of promises, club nights, local business support and an environmental grant, amazingly, this was achieved.

A crucial moment was a community poll, run exactly like an ordinary UK election. This was a couple of months before the planning committee vote. The local media showed voters queuing in the street for an hour just to cast their vote. With a high turnout of 50 percent of residents voting, 95 percent of residents voted "No". Everyone was talking to their friends and neighbors in the queue, many still fearing it was "a done deal". It was a turning point in the campaign. Overnight it was a safe topic of conversation as the overwhelming majority of people were against it. There was a huge feeling of unity in the town. This mobilization got the attention of our local and national politicians who suddenly found time to meet us.

We listened carefully to their advice, and the ever-supportive Green Party councilors and we did our own research. A group of us became well versed in national/local planning policy and law very quickly. We created an excellent detailed document, carefully countering each part of the planning application with objections rooted in fact, law and policy, e.g. the shortcomings of the Environmental Impact Assessment. We secured a barrister-cum-eco-warrior for the Inquiry and his advice was critical to our victory.

Following the planning inquiry, Community Forum members still had to monitor and challenge the activities of the operator which still sought to industrialize the site. Several members of the forum, however, decided to challenge the local parish or town council. (Outside English cities, there are County Councils, below that District Councils. Both of these run services and have planning powers. Below them are parish or town councils, which are essentially consultative bodies representing a local community.) A lack of candidates meant there had been no elections for more than 30 years, so volunteers were simply appointed, but very little was ever achieved. So, nine Community Forum members (or allies) stood and all were elected to the twelve-strong town council. Immediate actions included making town council meetings less formal and allowing the public to speak at any point, rather than simply allocating three minutes at the start. The town council also informally aligned itself to the independent movement known as "Flatpack Democracy", which is dedicated to empowering local people to make the best decisions for their community.

Realizing that the town council actually had very little money, it was decided to increase local taxes (for most residents it meant around £1 per week more on their bills) and invest in training to help local community groups to apply for much larger funding from government and charitable trusts. In total local groups received more than £400k in grant funding. This funding saved the local swimming pool and led to a major investment in children's play facilities, including a new skate park.

Other initiatives started by the new town council members include:

- Citizens Advice Bureau assisting people with legal and financial difficulties and to claim state benefits.
- Children's activity program offering at least one daily activity during holidays.
- Community cinema which came second in a national award.
- New floodlights at the football club, also serving as a night landing spot for the air ambulance.
- A part-time Town Ranger maintaining Council property, liaising with residents and reporting bigger problems to government authorities.
- Major schemes to assist cycling, protect wildlife and assist health/well-being.

Our town council Mayor said, "We have some very powerful people here in Buckfastleigh." She was right. What if every community does?

Figure 5.5 A brainstorming session in Ág, Hungary. Photo credit: Kitti Boda.

Case Study 5 – Hungary

The Story of Ág[28]

By Kitti Boda

We are in a small isolated and poor rural village called Ág in Baranya County, Hungary originally settled by Swabians and later by Roma. About 125 people live here. There are no public services. Due to the shortcomings of public transport health care is very difficult to access and jobs within commuting distance are completely inaccessible. This case study is about the process by which the village members came together, with the support of a community worker, to build its own future.

Main Stages of the Community Organizing in Ág

The original intention of the community development project, *PUBLIC-SPACE-NETWORK for Families* (PSN) was to try to find a way out for people living in areas with extreme poverty and despair by supporting local actions and initiating dialogue between different communities in the region. In 2013, as a result of conversations with community leaders in Ág, including the village mayor and the head of the Roma minority, it became clear that the joint action needed was to eradicate, or at least reduce, the poor quality of housing in the village. To realize this aim the community development worker proposed that a community cooperative be set up, with the village mayor as its president.

The second challenge was to support the co-op to raise funding for the raw materials needed for the renovation of the poor-quality houses in the village. Visiting builders' merchants in the area brought surprisingly good results. Thanks to their donations, several families were able to start the renovation of their homes, using traditional building methods. The success of this created exciting dynamics within the community. As they experienced the potential of local cooperation, helping and supporting each other started to become a more common practice in the village. Habitat for Humanity, who were looking for rural venues for their program, were identified by the PSN community worker as they were keen to support community housing projects. This enabled the co-op to obtain more building materials at a fraction of the market price for another twelve families to rebuild their houses.

At the end of 2016, the community development project was able to support the villagers of Ág again in cooperation with the Profilantrop Association and the ERSTE Foundation's Roma Partnership grant and financial support from Profilantrop's charity shop in Budapest (part of the profit from the shop was spent on this program). The culmination of the process was a conversation underneath a walnut tree in the summer of 2017, where it was decided what the co-op would do next. In the absence of an available technology to ensure that the homes were energy efficient and insulated, it was agreed to grow hemp as insulation material instead of hay, and an animal husbandry project started with three pairs of emus. This spawned the establishment of the Hemp-Emu Social Community Cooperative. Formed by the local community members, the cooperative keeps emus and grows hemp on a few acres of leased land.

Community Working Method

The steps in the process by which a local community living in extreme poverty creates resources and finds the faith for change with community development support has been described. The community development process as a result of the housing poverty need that had been locally identified, was the first step in creating motivation for involvement and subsequent engagement. It was a process where local knowledge and incoming experience were integrated at the level of day-to-day operation. The progress of the process, that is, the scale of change, must also take into account the dynamics of those involved. Practice demonstrated that the path to a decision was important as the decision itself. Taking responsibility was crucial and the local community needed to be involved not only in the action but also in all stages of planning. In Ág, regular joint community design events preceded each stage of development. This regularly allowed for community engagement, in some cases leading to thirty to forty people coming to the meetings, nearly a third of the village population. Collaborative planning enabled and encouraged everyone to get involved in brainstorming, exploration and collective decision-making. In Ág, this fell on very fertile soil.

However, this required facilitation by the community development professionals, to ensure that all participants became more and more comfortable with the situation. By creating a framework for community dialogue, not only could people share their ideas, but the final decision as to what to organize around was shared.

The villagers began to take ownership of processes, and this made real commitment achievable. The community came to appreciate that the community development professionals were also accountable, and that having differing opinions was alright. An exciting culmination of this process of becoming self-reliant can be seen in the composition of the leadership of the newly formed cooperative, in which the local community had a strong voice. Of course, this also required the professionals to take the initiative at the right moment, persistently asking questions gradually making the group realize their goals and the path to achieving them, and based on them, make their own commitments and become accountable. It was an exciting learning process for both the village participants and the project workers.

As a conclusion we feel it is important to also address aspects of the process in which the socio-economic context, that is, extreme poverty – may have played a role. Concrete and tangible results were needed, as a condition or motivation for participation. This was especially true in a local context where there had been a substantial loss of confidence in the community in relation to people willing to help them. In the past – in the absence of any meaningful involvement – interventions were opaque and top-down without any effect whatsoever.

The importance of tangible results was confirmed when the housing renovation process had to be "frozen" due to a shortage of resources. This set back the commitment to meetings and planning. From that point on, obtaining the necessary process-related resources became at least as important – and sometimes even more decisive – as empowering the community. Thus, the task of fundraising was a prerequisite for the community development program to be successful. Success in securing resources allowed visible change to take place. The villagers started to believe that things will only work out if they take part in shaping the process themselves.

The existence of the Hemp-Emu Community Social Cooperative today has seen an incredible change in local conditions. Today we see a local community whose representatives have left their defenselessness behind them, outstripping their own limits and courage and – having been reinforced in their self-esteem – sitting at the negotiating table with the leaders of the local authority and local agencies as equal partners. All this was further enhanced by the relationship with the charity shop in Budapest, through which new worlds have opened up to them. It is a relationship that can connect middle-class donors and volunteers and the inhabitants of a poor rural village in Baranya – almost two worlds apart.

The members of the cooperative are listing plans and taking into account the expected results of the coming years and the related activities – they are outlining a vision. A future. Many times, we may not even realize the significance of this. When it comes to "survival", people don't think about the future. However, in a seemingly hopeless situation, in which they are preoccupied with living from one day to another, it can also affect the survival of the local community if the people living there think about their future – as we see in the case of Ág.

Notes

1 F. Frank and A. Smith (1999) *The Community Development Handbook: A Tool to Build Community Capacity*. Human Resources Development, Canada.
2 F. Frank and A. Smith (1999) *The Community Development Handbook: A Tool to Build Community Capacity*. Human Resources Development, Canada.
3 C.L. Harper and K.T. Leicht (2016) *Exploring Social Change: America And the World*. 6th ed. Routledge, New York.
4 C.L. Harper and K.T. Leicht (2016) *Exploring Social Change: America And the World*. 6th ed. Routledge, New York.
5 S. Alinsky (1971) *Rules for radicals*. University of Chicago Press.
6 C. McConnell (1977) *The Community Worker as Politiciser of the Deprived*. Paisley.
7 C. McConnell (1977) *The Community Worker as Politiciser of the Deprived*. Paisley.
8 R. Zipfel (2019) *Community Organizing, Community Development Journal Thinkery*. Oxford University Press.
9 R. Zipfel (2019) *Community Organizing, Community Development Journal Thinkery*. Oxford University Press.
10 R. Hunjan and J. Pettit (2011) *Power: A Practical Guide for Facilitating Social Change*. Carnegie United Kingdom Trust.
11 R. Hunjan and J. Pettit (2011) *Power: A Practical Guide for Facilitating Social Change*. Carnegie United Kingdom Trust.
12 R. Meade, M. Shaw and S. Banks (2016) Politics, Power and Community Development: An Introductory Essay. In R. Meade, M. Shaw and Sarah Banks (2016) *Politics, Power and Community Development*. Bristol University Press; Policy Press.
13 R. Meade, M. Shaw and S. Banks (2016) Politics, Power and Community Development: An Introductory Essay. In R. Meade, M. Shaw and Sarah Banks (2016) *Politics, Power and Community Development*. Bristol University Press; Policy Press.
14 R. Phillips, S. Kenny and B. McGrath (2018) *The Routledge Handbook of Community Development: Perspectives from Around the Globe*. New York, NY: Routledge.
15 P. Chitere (1994) *Community Development: Its Theoretical Conceptions and Historical Background and Practice with Emphasis on Africa*. Gideon S. Were Press, Nairobi.
16 Center for Community Health and Development (2019) *The Community Tool Box*. University of Kansas.
17 D. Beck and R. Purcell (2013) *International Community Organizing*. Bristol University Press; Policy Press.
18 P. Ellis (2010) *Knight Soul of The Community* 2010. S. John and J. Knight Foundation. Gallup, Inc.
19 J. Ife (2013) *Community Development in An Uncertain World*. Port Melbourne: Cambridge University Press.
20 D. Beck and R. Purcell (2013) Developing Generative Themes for Community Action. In S. Curran, R. Harrison and D. Mackinnon (eds.) *Working with Young People* [2nd ed.]. Sage.
21 J. Neil (2009) *Stakeholder Engagement: A Road Map to Meaningful Engagement*. Fery Doughty Centre, Cranfield University.
22 L. Coser (1956) *The Functions of Social Conflict*. New York, The Free Press.
23 J. MacLeod and C. Byrne (2012) "It's Only A Garden" – A Journey from Community Building to Community and Back again. *New Community Quarterly*, Vol. 10, No. 2, Issue 38. University of Queensland.
24 M. Ledwith (2011) *Community Development: A Critical Approach* (3rd edn) Bristol University: The Policy Press.
25 M. Emery and C.B. Flora (2006) Spiraling-Up: Mapping Community Transformation with Community Capitals Framework. *Community Development: Journal of the Community Development Society*, 37: 19–35.
26 K. Freeman (1983) *Ancilla to Pre-Socratic Philosophers*. Harvard University Press, Cambridge, Massachusetts.
27 C. Leeuwis and N. Aarts (2011) Rethinking Communication in Innovation Processes: Creating Space for Change in Complex Systems. *The Journal of Agricultural Education and Extension*, 17(1): 21–36.
28 This is an abridged version of an article by K. Boda (2019) Még az Ág is húzza. Egy zsáktelepülés jövőt épít magának. Parola. *Journal of the Hungarian Association for Community Development*, 1: 30–34.

Chapter 6

Learning for Change

Kwok-kin Fung, Suet-lin Hung and Colin Ross

Introduction

This chapter looks at the educational role of the community development practitioner. In community development we think about education (and the learning that results from it) on the one hand, and organization (and the action that results from it) on the other, as two halves of the one whole. And we see the interaction between them as the driver of empowerment and change. Learning for change involves supporting individuals and organizations to learn together, facilitating their understanding, confidence and skills, and enabling them to reflect upon what they may need to learn about or do to bring about change. Community development practitioners require expertise in the use of educative approaches for working with individuals and community groups and with partner agencies at all stages of the development approach, from how you engage with a community, to how to organize, how to build up leadership skills, how to promote diversity and inclusion, how to facilitate participatory planning approaches and how to evaluate programmes and influence policy change.

Models of Learning in Community Development

Models for learning in community development have drawn on ideas of reflective and experiential learning, which emphasize learning by doing and the link between learning and doing, reflection and further action. Among the influential shapers of this approach was the Brazilian adult educator Paulo Freire who argued that *There's no such thing as neutral education. Education either functions as an instrument to bring about conformity or freedom.*[1,2]

DOI: 10.4324/9781003140498-6

Freire worked with poor rural communities in Brazil. In the community development field, Freire's "dialogical model" is among those commonly applied. He is critical of the traditional "banking" methods of education, which involve the depositing of pre-determined knowledge or skills in learners by their teacher, and contrasts this with "dialogical" methods, in which practitioner and learners are engaged in a joint process of discovering, reflecting and creating knowledge; and skills Freire calls this process "praxis". In other words, the dialogical approach is not a top-down process, but one that respects the knowledge and expertise that people in disadvantaged and vulnerable communities have, as well as seeing the introduction of new knowledge and skills by the practitioner.

The role of the practitioner is still an active one, but it treats the learners as creative and not passive and involves methods of intervention that start with a co-investigation of the problems, what he calls the "themes" that shape the lives of people in a community experiencing economic, social and/or cultural disadvantage and possible oppression. These themes are then reflected back to people by the educator, sometimes using a photo or other visual representation to enable them to see and discuss their situation more objectively, as though from the outside, rather than being submerged in it due to the pressures of day-to-day life of living in poverty. Here the practitioner begins to discuss issues of where power lies between the peasant and the landowner and who that landowner might be, for example some corporate agrobusiness. The consciousness-raising the practitioner co-creates with the participants is built upon people reflecting upon their lives and helping them to understand the forces shaping the problems they face, posing the question of how they might change through working collectively what has previously been experienced as unchangeable. In other words, as educators, community development practitioners focus on people's relationship to their lived experiences, exploration of the potential for action to change these, the resulting action, and reflection on this in order to empower them for future action. This process of linking learning, action and reflecting upon that action is seen as the key to raising the political consciousness of disadvantaged people.

Another important strand of thinking about learning in community development stems from the work of Saul Alinsky.[3,4] Alinsky worked with poor urban communities in the USA. His approach focused on strengthening communities through organizing collectively, in order to bring about concrete changes in the plans and services provided by for example local authorities or private corporations. Here a central part of the community development practitioner's role is to identify and recruit community leaders/activists, and work with them to identify, clarify and refine their strategies and tactics. The methodology is arguably less concerned than the dialogical model with the liberatory learning of participants; however, an educational role is implicit. Recognizing that every action is an opportunity for learning, which in turn informs the development of the next action, the community development practitioner must ensure that the learning opportunity is properly grasped, working with the experience of the people. "Talking the people's language", s/he works with them to further develop the leadership capacity of the community organization through reflection on the success or otherwise of their community action.

Both of the above approaches start with the premise that there is structural inequality in all societies. Other models that also start from this premise often used by community development practitioners include Anti-Oppressive Practice (AOP)[5] and the Structural Approach (SA);[6,7] These share concerns with improving the structural socio-economic and political position of disadvantaged communities. AOP originated in social work. It requires the practitioner to critically examine this power imbalance and focuses upon tackling oppression, racism, and other forms of discrimination. Here the practitioner works with community groups to explore issues of personal, cultural and institutional discrimination. SA theory regards society as composed of groups with conflicting interests who compete for resources and power, and the imposition by those with power of their ideological views. Here a practitioner focuses upon supporting the community group to demystify these ideologies and to thereby more clearly understand the structures and systems of oppression and discrimination in their lives. In all of these approaches, the community development practitioner works with disadvantaged groups in a process of facilitating their understanding of the structural causes of their disadvantages.

Then there are Asset Based Community Development (ABCD),[8],[9] and Collective Narrative Practice (CNP)[10] approaches. ABCD does not start with an inequalities analysis between haves and have nots, but upon identifying and building upon the strengths and resources that lie within all communities. This approach is critical of needs or problem-based approaches as assuming communities are deficient in some way. Rather practitioners work with community groups to help them identify the strengths and resources they already have to make change and if needs be to build upon those. It does not assume that communities require additional resources to realize their ambitions and tends to emphasize the pursuit of consensual strategies with outside bodies. CNP is an educative approach that has often been used with individuals and communities facing trauma, for example in a conflict situation or because of sexual violence. These two approaches focus on facilitating storytelling narratives by the community members and involve finding ways to share skills between different members by identifying their strengths and the sharing of their stories of success. Here community development practitioners might also use music and song in their work with individuals, groups and communities.

What all these community education approaches to adult learning share in common is an emphasis upon learning by doing, issue-based and action-oriented learning. Such approaches seek to support individuals and community groups, by providing a range of more or less structured learning support, run within the community outside a more formal adult education setting.[11] Notions such as "lecturer" and "classroom" are replaced by "community educator" and "out in the community". This is not to imply that the educational role of the community development practitioner is unprepared, nor that the learning required may not be rigorous. Once the issue or project has been identified with the community, the community development practitioner must do background preparation to ensure that their educative support is accurate, accessible and relevant, or if they do not have the necessary knowledge and skills required, to know where to source this. Whether building a well or organizing a campaign, the group will need the learning to be as effective as possible. This may require the need to introduce skills and knowledge the group does not have already, or if it does, needs drawing out and sharing. Here the community development practitioner's role is as much that of group work facilitator as it is an educator.

The Learning for Change theme within the IACD Standards is eclectic and encourages practitioners to draw upon the above approaches and others for supporting awareness raising and skills development in the community. The Standards do not promote a single model for promoting the learning, knowledge and skills within a community. And community development practitioners may find themselves using different approaches at different times dependent upon the situation, or a combination of methods. If the problem to be resolved facing the community is urgent, then Alinsky type methods may be appropriate. When engaging with external power the methods may focus more upon consensus building or more upon conflict, depending on specific circumstances, and the tactics used may change over time. When organizing a community festival ABCD approaches might be the more appropriate. When working in a community riven by conflict, the practitioner might adopt the CNP approach. From engaging with people in communities, to exploring their experiences and capacity with them, to reflecting upon and evaluating a project, community development practitioners should be looking for learning opportunities and activities in dialogue with individuals and groups, using a range of educational approaches, both informal and formal. Methods used, all of which support both individual and collective learning, include:

- "community gathering"[12] (through which members identify their commonly felt concerns for future action);
- open space workshops[13] (which create an environment for people to develop an agenda for action);
- "planning for real"[14] (in which a physical or virtual model of a neighbourhood is used as a focus for engaging residents in developing plans for the area);
- "asset mapping"[15] (which facilitates the community members to identify the collective resources possessed by the community);
- "community forum"[16] (in which members identify their collective identity through sharing stories about the history, struggles and strengths of the community).

The Framework for Practice

Before presenting the case studies, we will explore each of the community learning elements of the International Standards framework in a little more depth, relating them to some of the varied work contexts in which community development is practiced.

1. Using People's Experiences, Knowledge and Skills as the Starting Point for Community Development. And Why You May Need to Convince Your Agency of the Need to Invest Time in Doing This

This element guides the practitioner away from deciding in advance what people need to know, and delivering this to them, towards working with them to devise a participatory learning programme. This is important when engaging with a community for the first time, perhaps one where there is little history of formal organizations and people have little confidence that they can achieve change; or alternately when trying to identify with a group of experienced activists how they can build upon the knowledge and skills they have.

People will have huge local knowledge, skills and experience to bring to the development process. This must first be respected and identified. However, in communities that experience long-term disadvantage and marginalization, there may often be a feeling, born of past experience, that nothing changes, and they have no influence. They have become the "objects" rather than the "subjects" of change. So, as well as finding out what knowledge, skills and experience people have, community development practitioners need to explain that they are there to support them by sharing their professional expertise. Here it is important to explain what knowledge, skills and experience you have as a practitioner. It is usually helpful to use visuals rather than words to share examples of work you and your agency have done with other communities. Investing time in establishing this dialogue with the community leaders/activists and others is essential in order to find out more about the communities' capacity to take on a project. So, a community development practitioner will need time from their agency to do this. We cover this in more detail in the Engaging with the community chapter.

If the agency wishes to promote a specific educational campaign within the community, for example to do with child immunization, protection against coronavirus, or encouragement of new forms of more sustainable farming or forestry protection, these must be presented with sensitivity if they are to be adopted. The community development practitioner's role here might involve challenging local ways of doing things, customs and beliefs and wherever possible the practitioner should respect these and build upon them. In some cases, however, it may be local customs that are in fact part of the problem e.g. denying rights to girls through genital mutilation or damaging the environment. It is important to try to reach a point where people see such health or environmental education campaigns as being of real value to the whole community and that they will improve their situation. A well-tried approach is to train up a team of local people, often women, as paraprofessionals to help the agency roll out the programme. This "barefoot" approach has been widely adopted in China, India and other parts of the developing world.[17],[18]

2. Developing Learning Opportunities That People Feel Comfortable With and That Are Relevant to the Actions They Want to Take

The community development practitioner may be engaging with a community group or some individuals who have clear views about what they want to change. In this situation the practitioner needs to discuss with the group how best to bring about the change they seek, what it is they want to prevent or to create. As actions are identified the practitioner explores with them the knowledge and skills they need to realize their project effectively; these could range from design and construction skills to the business skills needed to run a community enterprise, or to learn how to be more effective at speaking in public or to the media. Some community members may already have the skills or knowledge required; and the task here is to share what they know or can do with each other. This can be simply done by together brainstorming the strengths and weaknesses of the group and its members, and the opportunities and threats presented. By doing this, the group identifies the learning it needs, as well as what may already exist within the community, and what may need to be sourced from outside. In should soon become clear what might be helpful for the group members, for example media training, and the job of the community development practitioner is to set these sessions up, bringing in an outside trainer if required, or using expertise that has been identified within the group.

It is important to understand what motivates people to want to learn new knowledge and skills:

- When the learning is related to solving a pressing need, resolving a problem or realizing a hope for something better;
- When the learning has relevance for their lives or of people close to them;
- When their beliefs and traditional ways of doing things seem no longer to be effective;
- When they recognize the need to acquire new knowledge and skills to set up and run a community project.

A common feature of disadvantaged communities, especially in developing countries, is that many people may have had little schooling. In developed countries they may have poor memories of formal education. In either context the practitioner needs to discuss with the group how they would like to acquire new knowledge and skills. Helping people to feel comfortable and confident is a key consideration. So are practicalities such as the timing to fit with other aspects of people's lives such as when they are working, childcare needs, access to technology, disability access and acceptance of the type of venues used. Most communities will have some sort of village or community hall where community learning sessions can take place.

The role of the practitioner will be to work with the people interested in co-designing the learning programme, identifying the venue and sourcing the people who can teach the skills needed and the funds to finance this. As people take action on a community project, one of the practitioner's key roles is to support them to take advantage of any opportunities for learning from the process as it develops. Use informal conversations, identifying while the experience is fresh in people's minds what worked or didn't. Periodically hold a more formal review meeting with the participants, taking stock of progress and agreeing next steps.

3. Using Effective Communication Skills Such as Active/ Empathetic Listening, and also Written and Visual Communication, Social Media, Film and Print Media and ICT – To Support Learning and Community Action

We all have different styles of communication, and most of us will be much more skilled in some modes of communication than others. The written word and visual imagery, using a wide variety of technologies, can be used to reflect people's own experience and introduce useful information and ideas that are unfamiliar. So, it is essential as a practitioner to identify your own particular styles and strengths as a communicator/educator, to develop and diversify them as much as possible, and to identify colleagues, community members, or outside "specialists" whose communication skills you can access and utilize, and perhaps aren't a part of your own skillset. In all cases use plain language and generally avoid any technical jargon.

There are a great many tools for communication and for education available these days that help adults learn. Generally, people like to learn from what another community has done. This might best be achieved by taking the community group you are supporting to meet with people in another community or bringing into your meetings speakers from other communities. If this is not possible then use films of communities who have achieved things in similar situations or if available, set up online zoom sessions so that people can ask questions and share experiences. There are dozens of practical community action manuals and tool kits that can be accessed, and ICT is becoming cheaper and more widely available in rural as well as urban areas.[19]

One communication skill that every community development practitioner needs to have and to use consistently is active and empathetic listening. Without this, the dialogue that should bring practice alive will be shallow and empty. Listening is the key to identifying the learning and the actions that will enable groups and individuals to realize their aspirations. There are several techniques that can be used here, starting with being aware that it is easy to make false assumptions about what the people you are working with mean by what they say, if they have very different worldviews and life experiences from you. There may be a need to check your understanding of what they say by summarizing your understanding of it and reflecting it back to them towards the end of a meeting, and asking questions focused on reaching an agreed understanding of what is being agreed.[20] In some contexts, you may not speak the language of the people you are working with and will need to take an interpreter with you. You also need to consider other forms of communicating when working with people with sight and hearing problems. In some communities, you may find that women are at first more reluctant to speak out and share their experiences and expertise than men, and in some cultures, you may need to bring in a female colleague to work with women and girls.

4. *Promoting Learning That Reflects the Values and Aims of Community Development*

One of the key values underpinning all community development practice, is a commitment to promoting social justice. As we have discussed in Chapters Two and Three, the community development practitioner's role is not just to enhance the expertise of existing community leaders/activists, but to reach out to the non-activists in the wider community, identifying their concerns and hopes and involving them too in shaping change; to listen to and engage the less articulated voices of people who are also affected by an issue but for one reason or another have not got involved.

As people engage with what they want to change in their lives, education may emerge as a key issue in itself, for example when working on a health project, you also identify low literacy levels or lack of educational opportunities for girls. Disadvantaged and vulnerable communities invariably face interlinked problems. While the community development agency may specialize in health work, you may discover related issues to do with people's educational opportunity or literacy levels. Here it is important to identify other agencies and disciplines that can be brought in.

Community development invariably involves an element of serendipity, with opportunities or challenges arising that were not at first foreseen by people within the community or by the practitioner. A key practice value required of any community development practitioner is to be open to the unexpected, and thereby encourage the individuals and groups you are working with to be flexible when planning a project. Problem solving needs creativity. There may be just one way of building a well, there is rarely one way of running a campaign. Alinsky told us to be creative and not to do what the "other side" expected.

5. Supporting Partner Organizations to Identify the Learning Needs of Their Staff in Relation to Community Development

Part of the role of all community development practitioners is building partnerships with other agencies and organizations who deliver services to, or make decisions affecting, the communities they work in, or who employ people from these communities. How these organizations relate to and engage with communities could be a major factor in enabling or blocking change. Even agencies and organizations that have clear aims and responsibilities for services that communities need such as town planners, the police or local economic development agencies may see people as passive recipients, or even as a problem if they do not "co-operate". Environmental, social, health, crime prevention or economic develop-ment agencies often have time and funding pressures that can lead them to tokenistic approaches to community engagement. They may not be skilled at participatory planning or used to working with service users as co-designers of their service. This is why for example footpaths and shopping centres are often designed in non-disability friendly ways. It is not because these agencies are consciously wanting to make disabled people's access more difficult. It is just because they have not experienced what it is like to be disabled or thought about inviting disabled people to advise on the design.

In many countries, legislation now requires public authorities and public service providers to consult local communities over how these services are planned and delivered. Part of the community development practitioner's educative role can be to help other agen-cies that impact upon communities to use participatory planning methods. Despite many disciplines employing staff who have had experience of working with communities in more participatory ways, and indeed employing staff with community development skills, there will be many staff working for housing, employment creation, planning, crime prevention, environmental protection and other services with little experience of co-design and co-plan-ning approaches with local communities. Experienced community development practition-ers can play an important role here supporting their continuing professional development. This will also provide opportunities to build closer multi-agency partnerships. The methods to use with other colleagues are similar to those outlined above working with community members.

Case Studies

The five case studies have been selected from around the world to illustrate the ways in which community development practitioners enable learning as part of the process through which communities bring about change. In the Hong Kong example, community develop-ment practitioners identified how "outdated" sewing skills could be community assets, shared as tools to support a community to understand the COVID-19 pandemic and fight back against its impact. The Nepal case study outlines how the community development agency use facilitation and empowerment methods to support poor communities across their region. The Scottish case focuses upon developing skills and knowledge to address health issues. The Mozambique case study looks at an isolated rural community affected by droughts, poor soil and disease, and how the practitioners introduced new nutritional and food production practices while respecting traditional values and beliefs. The final case study shows how community development practitioners from a range of disciplines, working in England and in Canada learned from each other, in order to improve their educative practice.

The case studies focus on:

- Using people's experiences, knowledge and skills as the starting point for community development.
- Developing learning opportunities that people feel comfortable with and that are relevant to the actions they want to take.
- Using effective communication skills such as active/empathetic listening, and also written and visual communication, social media, film and print media and ICT – to support collective learning and community action.
- Promoting change that reflects the values and aims of community development through community learning.
- Supporting partnering governmental, non-governmental and private sector organizations to identify the learning needs of their staff in relation to community development.

Figure 6.1   Together we sew – cloth face-mask workshop – a community hub – Hong Kong. Photo credit: Siu-wai Wong.

Case Study 1 – Hong Kong
Together We Sew, Fighting the Virus!
By Siu-wai Wong

Introduction

At the outbreak of COVID-19 in Hong Kong since early 2020, the severe shortage of face masks had greatly limited people's mobility, particularly the grassroots families living in subdivided flats who felt helplessness and isolated. A face-mask DIY sewing workshop was organized, and volunteers were mobilized, alongside education on public health and personal hygiene to empower people's mastery of their own fight against the pandemic. The project demonstrated that reconnection to the community and take action unitedly can make a difference to both the neighbourhood at large and underprivileged people themselves.

Context

In March 2020, a workshop and public health education campaign were held in ShamShuiPo district, an area highly crowded with subdivided flats, low-income families, new migrants, and elderly in Hong Kong. We invited the women skilled in sewing and making paper patterns, which are the assets to the community, to host the workshop and share their knowledge. "Learning to change" guided our project to equip people with the skillsets of face-mask-making, a tool they are familiar with to demonstrate the mastery of their own situation through knowledge practice, which ultimately led to a change of status quo and the understanding of can-do spirit.

The Project

The imminent needs for face masks had connected and engaged the community members across a broad array: women and men, ethnic minority groups, children and elderly, and flat owners and tenants. At the time of virus panic and a severe shortage of face-mask and anti-epidemic supplies, they were eager to know the available, accessible, feasible, and affordable alternatives.

The project involves bringing sewing machines and materials to the workshop instead of hand-making hundreds of face masks. The readiness of resources, both knowledge and materials familiar to the women participants, encouraged people to join the workshop in person. Such availability has turned a passive receiver into a participant and motivated them to learn for a change and the importance of mutual help in the community to make a difference.

The DIY workshop encouraged the residents to gather at the neighbourhood hub. The community members got "reconnected" to jointly handle the virus fear and understood they were not alone. At the workshop, the social workers served as community educators and organizers, shared empathetically, or through the language they were used to, the correct public health information.

Through on-site demonstration of face-mask DIY, the workers encouraged members of the community to make what they need for themselves and their family. To build on that they would help those people who could not make their own by creating special styles which represented their identities. All voices were heard in the group, and they would support with whatever resources the community could share to each other. That was a beauty of mixture of personalized need and shared resources.

After gaining the knowledge, they were also motivated to take care of their living environment, as they thought that their living environment could be different to get away from the virus. As such, the residents built up their creativity to take collective action to enhance hygiene of both personal and their living community by distributing the DIY face masks to the needy neighbourhoods; implementing cleaning campaign to clean up the public area and staircase of their buildings; and making the poster for hygienic tips.

At the time of the global shortage of surgical face masks, people questioned the usefulness and effectiveness of homemade face masks due to information chaos. We sought consultation from health professionals in Hong Kong and Taiwan. We also produced video clips and posted on social media to teach how to sew a cloth face mask with the filter to increase people's confidence.

The residents were noticed to have their fear and sense of helplessness reduced, and their everyday sense of health ownership regained. In addition, they acquired public health knowledge about protecting themselves against the virus transmission chain. All these echoed the aims of the project: regaining the sense of mastery.

Evaluation

To the social work team, the core value of "Learning for Change" is in rebuilding confidence in the participants' ability to influence change. The women volunteers were laid-off or retired garments factory workers whose skills and know-how were replaced by machines two decades ago. The workshop allowed them to regain their confidence in their talent and competence, connected them to the community through participation, and their contribution to the society was reaffirmed.

The workshop also contributed to the community hub for restoring community cohesiveness through reconnecting to the neighbourhood, facilitating the social interactions among community members in socially isolated condition, and empowering people's control over prevention of virus transmission.

In addition, this project can only work with both ends of the project synchronized: the women volunteers who are the hidden gem in the society and willing to share their know-how, and the community members who are eager to learn to make a change. This works well as both were facing a common pandemic situation, and both had experienced the challenge of shortage of the common goods (face masks). The scarcity of resources and the pursuit for a solution has been turned into a driving force. Shared experience had brought in rapport and understanding. At the time of COVID-19 pandemic, the offer of help and self-help is still possible when people are connected.

The project had shown that, though usually considered detached from the community, residents of the low-income families have the willingness to care about the wellbeing of the neighbourhood they are living in. People have gradually changed their concept about the community capacity for handling the public health issue like COVID-19. Subsequently, we have recruited them to form a "community concern group" to discuss and carry out collective action together, like cleaning the public space. Meanwhile, with public health knowledge enhanced, they had the understanding that any one person is indeed part of the community. As a result, the residents shifted their mindset of individual problems to a collective one, as they believed that everyone should contribute themselves to the wellbeing of both themselves and the community as a whole. The workshop had also facilitated a platform for sharing people's scared feelings and powerlessness to the pandemic, allowing them to voice it out and, more importantly, discuss openly and be listened to. It also made the community members realize that their collective participation is important to the community.

Figure 6.2 FEST – Constructing the community path – Nepal. Photo credit: Ammar Bahadur Air.

Case Study 2 – Nepal

Facilitation for Empowerment and Social Transformation (FEST)

By Ammar Bahadur Air

Sahakarmi Samaj is a Nepali social-change NGO (Non-Governmental Organization) which emerged from the United Mission to Nepal's Surkhet Project Awareness Raising Cycle (SPARC). SPARC succeeded in empowering poor communities; when funding came to an end in 1996, the staff sought funding and created their own independent NGO – Sahakarmi Samaj.

Prior to the SPARC and Sahakarmi Samaj, disadvantaged and marginalized families and communities lacked the awareness, skills, confidence and organization to address and overcome their poverty. They did not benefit from government and external donor projects and services. The FEST community development process, discussed below, developed by Sahakarmi Samaj addressed this disempowerment through a nine-year community empowerment process, using methods including the Freirean approach to enable poor people to organize themselves and act to improve their wellbeing. Through FEST, communities organized themselves into sustainable self-help groups and networks which successfully improved the quality of education and health services, increased their income from on-and off-farm livelihoods, accessed funding, materials and technical support from local government, and influenced local government policies, planning and implementation.

How FEST Works

Community members themselves are the most important drivers of the FEST process. The project provides no material or financial resources; its only inputs are community facilitators, who are recruited, trained, and hired to catalyze and support communities' analysis, reflection, and action. The aim of the process is the empowerment of the least empowered. FEST does not suggest what, if any, actions community members should do to first "start" development, e.g. literacy, savings, entrepreneurial schemes. Instead it recognizes community members' values and challenges and helps them analyse possible responses.

A core value of FEST is a humanistic recognition of the potential of human beings to learn and develop through critical analysis of their experience and ongoing praxis. And that those who are directly concerned are best (and most legitimately) placed to determine what is desirable and appropriate for their development. They can take effective steps to enhance their wellbeing if critically engaged and equipped with adequate self-esteem and skills.

Four Stages in the FEST Process

1. Issue Identification Through Listening and Observation

FEST serves marginalized and vulnerable people by listening to them, letting them set the agenda and increasing their capacity to change their livelihood and influence others. Together with commitment to social justice, the achievement of dignity, wellbeing, freedom and security for all, and to community members' imagination, creativity, resourcefulness, and interdependence to determine what is desirable and appropriate for their own progress and wellbeing, this results in increased trust and cohesion in the community.

The field team conducts Community Screening Process meetings, using participatory exercises, to identify and engage the most marginalized communities. They then visit every household in the selected communities several times to explain the purpose of the project, build relations and learn about the issues affecting each family. This "listening survey" is critical for trust and relationships to develop, and for these households to express themselves and feel heard.

2. Community Group Formation

During this stage, our community educators (CEs) explain the FEST process and ask communities if they wish to participate. CEs use participatory tools (including group concept, community vision, seasonal calendar, development trend analysis of past years, and resource analysis) to raise the communities' awareness. After several meetings, a "group contract" is agreed, which includes basic guidelines for effective group interaction, and CEs give regular feedback on the group's behaviour with reference to this. During this stage groups often ask for material support from the project; but after conducting a series of games and exercises, they come to understand their role as empowered actors, and of the project as facilitator.

3. Cycles of Planning, Action and Reflection

The FEST process is about empowering people to make their own decisions; it does not focus communities on one way to begin community development. Rather a plethora of community-sponsored activities arise from this process, depending on the strengths and challenges of each community.

The CEs conduct weekly group meetings, in which an issue (generative theme) is discussed using a problem-posing tool. This does not provide any answers but raises questions among the participants. Through discussion, the CE steers the group through the six steps of problem analysis in line with the Freirean method. The group members are encouraged to think through the problem, identify its root causes and come up with their own solutions.

CEs encourage groups to address small-scale problems, using locally available skills and resources. More ambitious projects may be initiated once the groups are confident with the process, although the emphasis remains on the creative utilization of local skills and resources. The CEs help the group to determine objectives. Pictures are used to represent these to make them accessible to those with limited or no literacy skills. CEs then assist the group to formulate an action plan and action/reflection cycle, which goes on as a regular schedule of the community.

This stage demands passion and skill from the CEs, who must have full trust in the approach to facilitate the groups to take action despite the pressure of people's expectations for material support from the project.

4. The Organizational Development of Self-Managed Organizations and Networks

Organizational sustainability must be central if progress is to continue after the cessation of facilitation support. It is developed through leadership training in the middle and end stages of the project, which covers: group work; participation; decision-making; roles and responsibilities; development theories; facilitation skills; leadership and meeting management; planning; record-keeping and financial management; group network formation; resource acquisition; and liaison with external agencies.

Groups learn to operate effectively without an external facilitator. Self-managing groups can choose to: affiliate with other groups, creating larger network institutions; develop linkages with government and non-government offices and agencies to secure appropriate resources; and advocate for necessary change. The ultimate role of project practitioners is to leave community groups fully interdependent internally and with healthy external linkages.

The project facilitates workshops to raise awareness among local representatives and officials regarding social injustice and good governance. Interaction meetings between local government and the groups are conducted to strengthen government service delivery process. Free organizational development consultancies are provided to these groups. Issue-related workshops among groups with similar issues are conducted to develop collective action plans. At the end of the project the CEs conduct participatory assessments of the group's capacity. Emerging group leaders visit the offices of resources organizations (government and NGO), and a workshop for group leaders is held to coordinate approaches to these offices. Project staff continue to be available after withdrawal for consultations providing encouragement and professional expertise. Groups have found it beneficial, after forming a network of groups, to hire their own facilitators to support groups and the network, after the project has withdrawn.

What Has Been Achieved

The FEST process has resulted in the communities being organized, informed, self-reliant and sustainable. Over 1,200 community development groups (CDG) have been formed, which have in turn formed twenty government-recognized Community-Based Network Organizations (CBNO). These CBNOs have formed a national umbrella federation.

CDGs and CBNOs have a strong presence and they advocate for enhancing groups' access to local government resources and services. Most of the local governments from FEST working areas appreciate the approach and have started a robust collaboration with CDGs, which has continued after the project withdrew. CDGs continued to run irrespective of the circumstances in Nepal (Maoist Insurgency (1997–2004); earthquake (2015); and other natural disasters like floods) and have become a useful infrastructure for effectively and transparently implementing local government programmes.

Challenges

Finding and retaining staff who have genuine empathy and respect for poor communities is always a challenge. Staff must believe in the value and abilities of disadvantaged and marginalized people and communities, who society often disrespects. Sahakarmi Samaj addresses this through rigorous two-week experiential training and recruitment workshops which identify those with the values and potential to be facilitators. Sahakarmi Samaj often draws recruits from close to the project area, so they are familiar with the local culture and language.

Learning and Future Plans

Sahakarmi Samaj has maintained its commitment to the values of the FEST approach, even at the cost of turning down funding opportunities that were oriented to service delivery rather than empowerment. This commitment has resulted in real sustained impact in terms of empowered communities improving their lives, while donor driven projects have come and gone with little impact. These results have in turn sustained Sahakarmi Samaj. Sahakarmi Samaj is successfully collaborating with a number of local government bodies which have seen the positive results of FEST on their constituents. These bodies are funding FEST projects in their areas. Now Sahakarmi Samaj is reaching out to other local governments, and central government, to expand the adoption of FEST. In order to more broadly disseminate cross-institutional learning, Sahakarmi Samaj is planning a training facility in Kohalpur in western Nepal. Sahakarmi Samaj expects learning and programmes resulting from the work of the centre will inform development interventions nationally.

Figure 6.3 Health Issues in the Community - Group in Douglas, Dundee, performing play –
Scotland. Photo credit: Andrew O'Brien.

Case Study 3 – Scotland

Health Issues in the Community
By Kate McHendry

Health Issues in the Community (HIIC)[21] is a course that helps people understand what affects their health and the health of their communities. HIIC supports people to develop the skills and knowledge to address health issues using community development approaches. HIIC was first introduced in 1997 and is still going strong today, delivered by tutors across Scotland. The Community Health Exchange, which is part of the Scottish Community Development Centre[22] trains and supports staff from across community organizations, health boards and local authorities to deliver the HIIC pack and then the tutors use the pack with groups in their communities. The course is based on supporting individuals to work collectively; extending participatory democracy; and social justice and equity.

The HIIC Course

This draws on a social model of health, viewing health and illness as having as much to do with economic and social factors as with individual behaviour. It:

* Promotes the value of equity in terms of equal access to health and challenges discrimination.

- Supports the right of people to participate in decision-making processes and to take a more active role in the planning and delivery of services.

Guiding Principles and Core Values Which Have Informed the Approach Are That

- The life experience and knowledge of participants are recognized as the starting point for analysis and discussion.
- One of the basic processes in learning is the opportunity to reflect on our ideas with other people.
- It is important for people to develop the skills of critical reflection on the determinants of health and ill health, and about themselves in relation to society.
- People should be enabled to participate in the political process as active citizens and helped to acquire the knowledge or confidence needed for this.
- Learning can be a creative, fulfilling and enjoyable activity.

Through the course participants gain a broad understanding of the social model of health, health inequalities, power and participation and community development approaches in health – and how they can use these to make change happen in their communities. When we reflect on the stories of participants and tutors, HIIC is a journey that participants and tutor go on together; it explores health inequalities, holding community development and popular education values and principles at its heart. HIIC is a toolbox that gives structure to the community development process. It gives it shape, direction and a clear purpose.

So How Does It Do This?

Central to the design of HIIC is that it calls on the person's experience to be the heart of the learning and uses people's experiences, knowledge and skills as the starting point for community development. Without people sharing their experiences HIIC will not work. For example, one of the first exercises is "what affects my health?" and "what affects the health of my community?", the start of a dialogical journey of action, reflection and co-creating of knowledge that reaches into the social model of health, and begins to unearth issues around poverty, power and inequality. HIIC is a consciousness-raising process, using the learning pack as a tool to encourage people to question and challenge what they may have seen as "it's always been like this". The aim of HIIC is to help participants identify things they want to change, identify the root causes of the issues, and work out ways to effect change in their communities.

HIIC is a journey away from the banking approach to education based on the transmission of information from teacher to pupil to one where all who take part are recognized as thinking, creative beings with the capacity for action. This is not always an easy journey for participants who have often been scarred by education and it takes a lot of skill and patience on the part of the HIIC tutors to support them through this unlearning process.

So an essential skill of the HIIC tutor is to listen deeply and empathically to the participants not only so that she can support them appropriately and grow in her understanding of how that person experiences life in their community and thus increase her own expertise as a community development practitioner; but also so that the participant can hear himself more, when other people listen to us we hear ourselves more and from that we may begin to hear solutions to the issues that we see in front of us.

HIIC tutors recruit from across the community (usually a marginalized and disadvantaged community) and draw in participants for many of whom it's the first time that they have been involved in community activity. So, it is an excellent tool for reaching out to non-activists in our communities; helping them to identify their concerns and hopes and supporting them in shaping change. HIIC asks participants to consider issues that they may not have thought about before but have been on the receiving end of. For instance, "who holds power in our society – who makes the decisions that affect your life?" Bringing this into participants' consciousness facilitates their understanding of the structural causes of their disadvantage and is an impetus to question and challenge. It is designed to help participants become critical, creative, free, active and responsible members of society. It is not neutral. While at first, the tutor holds this dialogical process and value base for the group, it becomes much more explicit as the participants move through the pack until in Unit 13 participants explore popular education principles, reflecting on their own experiences of education and trying out some Freirean methods such as decoding.

The group project is the magic ingredient of HIIC. This is where the group decides on a health issue that affects their community, research the issue and present their finding to an invited audience – elected representatives, agency workers, family, local community. This is more than a confidence building exercise: people see themselves differently, experience that they have something important to say and that other people will listen to them. They find their voice.

I will illustrate this by using the example of an amazing group of women from Douglas, one of the most deprived areas in Dundee. The group was brought together by a community development practitioner in the community health team. Meeting at Douglas Community Centre and going through the HIIC pack, the women delivered a group presentation on an issue close to their hearts: self-harm and suicide. They did this by writing and performing a play, "She Died Waiting", which depicts the story of a young woman who self-harms. This powerful piece of drama has been highlighted locally and nationally as an impactful piece of community learning and has been performed in conferences and events across Scotland, including Dundee University medical students. The group developed the play from lived experience, having dealt with issues around mental ill health, self-harm and addiction in their families.

The group have gained so much through doing this, their confidence has increased, and they feel empowered to bring change to their community. They have gone on to develop a local drop-in service for peer-to-peer support which they run as volunteers. They have also formed a self-reliant craft group to generate some income and help their own mental wellbeing. They have gone on to other training and have been asked to participate in Strategic Planning Groups, NHS inquiry and Health and Social Care Integration.

Looking to the future for HIIC, we hope to see HIIC groups active in their communities across Scotland. We are currently addressing the challenges raised by the COVID-19 pandemic. We were fortunate in that we had already made the HIIC learning materials digitally available via our online Tutor Hub. Prompted by tutors, we have developed a Moving HIIC Online Guide; an Induction Module that is split into several tech café style sessions to get participants used to the technology while giving them a good introduction to HIIC, their tutor and other participants. We have also adapted two of our Short Courses for delivery online. We have run ZOOM sessions to support tutors to deliver HIIC online, and we will continue to facilitate support via our online Tutor Support Network. It is not ideal, HIIC is best facilitated face to face, but we are supporting our tutors and participants as best we can through this challenging time.

I will end with the words of the Douglas Group:

We find it hard to believe the impact we are having locally with our drama, with volunteering and with our learning. We have had a government minister come to watch us, she took part in the lively debate that followed our play and pledged to do something about the terrible loss of young lives in Dundee particularly, but in Scotland as a whole. We have all loved meeting up, we benefit socially, mentally and physically from being involved in this learning and we want to continue. This whole experience has certainly been a life changer, we all love it and are so glad to be involved.

Figure 6.4 Lucia Narito giving testimony of the impact of the project – Mozambique. Photo credit: Eduarda Cipriano.

Case Study 4 – Mozambique

Preserving Through Change
By Eduarda Cipriano

NGUNI's work in Maciene draws from the community's self-established priorities to address basic needs such as access to potable water and food security.[23] Through facilitating structured conversations and directed technical assistance, NGUNI works with women to improve their crop yield and introduce new foods into their diet to improve their family's nutrition. In 2020, NGUNI helped increase the availability of staple food (maize and cassava) from four to six months, a significant increase for our subsistence farming families.

Context

The rural community of Maciene is in the Gaza province in the south of Mozambique. This province is prone to droughts and Maciene has poor, sandy lands that have been losing their productivity over the years due to overuse and climate change. Households have lost their capacity to produce enough food, and HIV/AIDS, malaria and waterborne diseases are rampant. Possession of animals (pigs, ducks, and chickens) is a form of demonstrating "wealth" more than a source of income or nutrition. There is paid employment for less than 100 people, in a community of around ten thousand. Most abled men move out to cities or to South Africa to work on farms.

NGUNI's Intervention Approach

NGUNI believes that to contribute to the improvement of people's lives, we must hold the beneficiaries' belief system, values and knowledge that grounds their choices and behaviours at the forefront of our mission. NGUNI does not seek to disrupt or destroy people's beliefs or values but, if needed, help them evolve. Hence, the *"Rodas de Conversa"* (conversation circles) approach is crafted to have dialogue without a "know-it-all" attitude and with the understanding of joint responsibility to identify hindering issues and share knowledge, suggest solutions.

The starting point of NGUNI's work in Maciene was consultation with community leadership groups (religious, traditional and government) to understand the challenges their constituency faces, and with potential beneficiaries. NGUNI also sought to understand the assets the community could contribute. Stakeholders were also questioned about their understanding of "vulnerability". The most frequent answers were taken to gender- and age-sensitive focus groups to be validated for use as criteria to identify and select the most vulnerable community members/households to participate in this project. Based on the agreed criteria, NGUNI visited each block of the Maciene community and, along with their leader, identified those who responded to the criteria, aiming to:

(a) Get a description of their wellbeing as individuals, households and communities.
(b) Identify what would be needed, in their perspective, to attain individual, household and community wellbeing.
(c) Identify the community's assets (human, natural and material).

The graphic below summarizes the results of the focus groups. This led to the development of NGUNI's Theory of Change (TOC), which is the basis for all community projects.

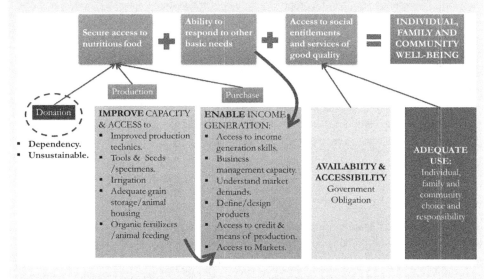

Figure 6.5 NGUNI Theory of Change. Image credit: Eduarda Cipriano.

The Sissimuka Project

From July 2019 to June 2020, in partnership with another NGO, Esperança, and with funding from the Ibis Foundation of Arizona, we implemented a project aimed at improving food security for the served households, complementing a water, sanitation, hygiene, and nutrition project. The Sissimuka (a Changana word, meaning "Persevere and rise") project's goal was to improve food security and access to nutritious food. We expected to increase the number of days staple food is available for vulnerable families, including increased yield of maize, cassava, beans, and vegetables in family plots; and to improve the quality of food storage, capacity of animal husbandry in selected households, and capacity to prepare nutritious meals. We expected to impact sixty households, approximately 300 people.

Besides providing improved agricultural practices and seeds, this project enabled families to increase the amount of land to be worked using the newly purchased micro-tractor. Some families have access to irrigation through NGUNI's small-scale irrigation system. NGUNI directly assisted 42 households and, as result of this effort, 21 families reported having increased their availability of staple food (maize and cassava) from four to six months. Demonstrations and dialogue are the two main approaches that NGUNI uses to implement this project.

Dialogue: Rodas de Conversa

NGUNI uses the Socratic method to guide the "Rodas de Conversa" and drive community members to link certain behaviours with their health status or crop yield. We have three conversation groups: one of the older women (grandmothers and mothers-in-law – it is more their role than age that counts in this culture); (2) those who are mothers/wives; (3) adolescent and young women.

These groups have separate sessions, but there are moments when two come together, or all of them participate in one single roda de conversa. When, for instance, we find that the experience of older women would benefit the younger ones we suggest and get agreement of joint conversation. Themes are selected based on the needs of the moment: a participant might want to share her visit to the hospital and the way she was treated or recommendations she was given that are disturbing her. She can put it out there and we discuss. Or if it is the rainy season and we know that malaria cases will be on the rise, each will talk about the causes and consequences of malaria and what to do to prevent it. The practitioner facilitates the conversation; makes sure people take turns expressing their thoughts and helps those who are less confident to contribute. We try to invite a nurse to be present when the issue is related to health; or an agriculture specialist if they express need to better understand an issue.

Demonstrations

Confucius' saying "I hear, and I forget. I see and I remember. I do and I understand" is the basis for our focus on demonstrations. Food preparation and feeding demonstrations as well as the establishment of demonstration farming plots (demo-plots) are central to our project. For instance, the introduction of new foods is done by carefully incorporating them into common dishes. Children are invited to "sample" the foods being prepared by their caregivers. Children tend to be less tied to "tradition" and are willing to try new things; when children take a liking to the different way of preparing their common foods, they will request their caregivers to cook that way at home. A different type of "demonstration" are the activists, who are community members selected among beneficiaries who model the teachings and are examples of possible change and improvement.

Challenges

The main challenges for this project are:

(a) <u>Traditional beliefs</u> – being afraid of witchcraft – and the consequent need to pay a "nyanga" (witchdoctor) to cleanse, treat and fend away evil spirits - are a major drain on a household's scarce resources. There is the belief that witches go after those who stand out, therefore, community members do not want to be that tall reed by sharing their success or being perceived as successful. NGUNI does not have the motivational value of showing that others in the community have done well as we cannot use successful members as an example of healthier choices or adoption of good practices.

(b) <u>Forgotten communities</u> –There are no minerals, gas, or oil and lands are prone to long droughts, therefore, communities like Maciene see no investment by the government, let alone the private sector. There is no effort to leverage these community assets and set in place a more sustainable food security strategy that goes beyond agriculture.

(c) <u>Short term funding</u> – Cultural, social, and behavioural change takes time. Strategies and plans for the desired change should be on medium to long-term (three to five years) basis, not yearly bursts of action.

Addressing the Challenges

The first challenge is addressed two ways: (a) by slowly bringing new elements into people's cosmology of knowledge through the "Rodas de Conversa". And (b) respecting community members' understanding of critical elements of wellbeing; thus, NGUNI performs all ceremonies deemed necessary to hold community's ancestral blessing and the rituals for cleansing and protection. The second and third challenges are interlinked as more and comprehensive funding would allow to design and implement transformational interventions in Maciene. Although annual "expected results" are being achieved, NGUNI does not take these as bringing long-term changes in the community as one cannot make commitments of technical and material support that is needed until beneficiaries are convinced, evidence is produced and behaviours are changed.

Lessons Learned

NGUNI's "Rodas de Conversa" have been successful because they allow for non-threatening conversations on participant's terms. Participants choose the topic for the following session and get to think about it, prepare and "bring some evidence" to sustain their position. Set rules help maintain a respectful and enriching environment for all participants.

Plans for the Future

NGUNI's motto, built by the first letter of our core values, is "CREMOS" – we believe/trust/ have confidence in ourselves and the communities we serve. Change is happening in Maciene. Those children who have learned to wash their hands, who eat fortified porridges and under-stand the value of health seeking behaviour will surely fare better than those who do not. It was said by Brigham Young "You educate a man, you educate a man. You educate a woman, you educate a generation."

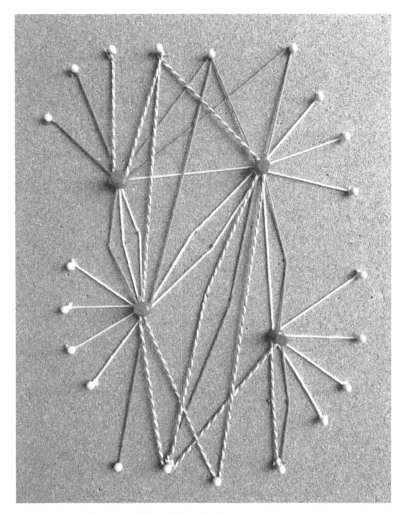

Figure 6.6 Illustration of the relationships built to share and learn about community development – Canada and England. Photo credit: Jen Wingate.

Case Study 5 – England/Canada

Building Relationships for Community Development Practice Learning and Sharing

By Jen Wingate

This case study draws on research that explored how some practitioners from Newcastle-up-on-Tyne and Suffolk in the UK, and Nova Scotia in Canada, have learnt about and shared their community development knowledge in everyday practice settings through networks of relationships. The research showed that these practitioners had a complex web of relationships through which they learnt and shared knowledge, so learning about practice was occurring alongside these practitioners' networking and community learning roles.

Background and the Project

This research project sought to understand how a selection of community development practitioners (in both paid and unpaid roles) had developed their knowledge and whether/how they
sought to share this knowledge with others. The project built on my experiences of supporting
practitioner learning through networks, workshops and online spaces. I was interested to find
out what other methods practitioners used and how these could be better supported. In the
experiences of these practitioners, practice learning occurred through everyday interactions as
well as in structured spaces. Each practitioner had their own story that formed a rich tapestry
of ongoing learning that occurred throughout their lives, with participants being influenced by,
and having an influence upon, the people they had contact with. While each experience was
individual, there were many common features that are explored below.

What Was Shared and Learnt? Who Were Practitioners Connected to in Their Learning Networks?

What study participants shared and learnt was dependent on the context, who was involved,
the purpose of the activities, as well as the knowledge and experiences each person brought.
Broadly these were strategic (why community development was done) and operational (how
to do community development). The strategic aspects included values and principles of community development that provided a framework for deciding what was right, as well as aims
and outcomes looking at the larger-scale and longer-term changes that were being sought. The
operational aspects included practitioner stances in relation to communities (such as working
with not upon), and approaches to community development. These approaches included activities (the things that were delivered through community development), objectives (shorter-term
changes that were sought through these activities) and practices (the ways of working, tools
and processes used). These were combined in different ways dependent on the situation and
varied from relationship to relationship. The flow of these different combinations is illustrated
below (see Figure 6.7); this diagram shows the response of some participants when asked to
name up to six people who they thought had learnt from them. The knowledge held by these
people was constantly evolving.

  Even within the confines of that question, it can be seen that participants were sharing with a range of people. The range of people expanded further when looking at their broader
learning network, by including responses to questions about who they had learnt from and
who they shared with more generally. The research found that the learning networks reached
beyond other community development practitioners to include the people that practitioners
met in work, volunteering and social settings.

  The types of people included in a practitioner's learning networks included: community development, youth, leisure, recreation, sports and arts workers; people working in housing, health, economic development, planning, regeneration, equalities, diversity and human
resources roles; locally elected representatives; colleagues, managers and fellow volunteers;
committee members, community members and groups, young people, clients, students; and
family members.

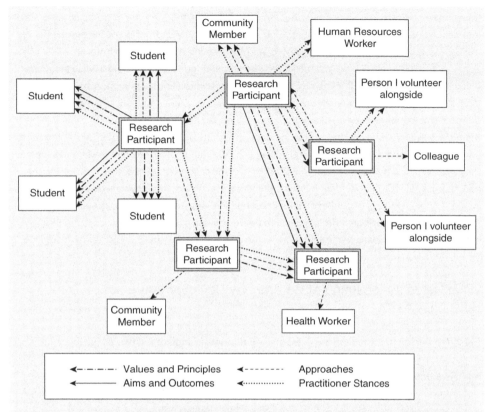

Figure 6.7 An illustration of what was shared to named individuals by some community development practitioners in Canada who participated in the research. Image credit: Jen Wingate.

Practitioners were giving and receiving through these connections, using their own and others' experience, knowledge and skills. Seeing practitioners as existing in a web of connections through which knowledge spreads suggests that this could be an additional networking role, specifically the building of relationships for practice sharing and learning. This could work alongside long-established community development networking roles that connect people within communities, build connections between communities and build partnerships with other organizations/practitioners.

How Was Practice Shared and Learnt?

Participants used a variety of methods for sharing and learning practice. These went beyond structured settings that were intentionally designed for learning, to include methods that were based on relationships and everyday interactions that happened as part of delivering community development. This formed a patchwork of methods, which were stitched together differently by practitioners in each relationship. The methods ranged from: structured learning opportunities (training courses, workshops, conferences and practice placements); through relationship-based learning (dialogue, networking, coaching and mentoring); to using everyday interactions (learning by doing, whether alone or supported by another practitioner; observing; modelling practice; and gradually absorbing learning through a process of osmosis).

While the structured and facilitated learning methods are familiar, less visible opportunities for practice learning in everyday actions and through relationships were also highlighted. One example was in Canada, where a practitioner had actively engaged in drawing learning opportunities out of everyday actions; this practitioner had designed moments for reflection into the project delivery. She combined "by doing with support" and "dialogue" methods to facilitate community members to individually and collectively note things that they had learnt and aspects they wanted to develop. Another practitioner in Newcastle-upon-Tyne described how they had "modelled" community development practices in a group they were involved in. In other instances, learning was occurring in these settings without the awareness of everyone in the relationship. A participant in Suffolk described how she would "observe" other practitioners, and if she spotted an approach that might work for her, she would then build it into her own practice.

What Helps the Learning of Community Development Practice Through Relationships?

Person-to-person practice learning was enabled through a range of factors, including:

- Awareness of the potential to share as well as to learn through relationships in these informal setting.
- Long lasting relationships with opportunities for repeated contact.
- Time to make new connections, to build and maintain relationships.
- Trust and respect for the existing knowledge and experiences of the people involved and using this as a starting point to tailor what is shared and how it is shared.
- Spaces for practice conversations with a range of people.
- Space and time for critical reflection, so that learning can be identified from everyday actions and so that values and principles (which may not be easily visible) can be perpetuated.

Barriers to Learning Community Development Practice Through Relationships

While many participants were able to talk freely about the different people they had learnt from, they were reluctant to claim that others might have learnt from them. One reason for this was that participants hadn't considered that others were learning from them. This lack of awareness could have been a barrier as it meant that enablers were less likely to be in place. The barrier could be overcome by recognizing that it is possible to give as well as receive through learning networks, as part of a mutual flow of knowledge.

Another barrier was being isolated from other practitioners. Some participants described how budget cuts and a lack of resources had created a sense of competition, which made collaboration more difficult. To overcome this there needs to be support from organizations and funders to recognize the value of practice learning through relationships.

Learning From This Project

Many practitioners already consider network building and community learning as practice roles. This project suggests that these two roles could be expanded further to include a focus on practice learning through networks. The following questions might help you to consider how you are already involved in relationships for community development practice learning and how you can build on this.

- Who are you connected to that you share practice with or learn from? (It may help to sketch this out.)
- What do you learn from other people who practice community development?
- What do you share with other people?
- How do you learn and share community development practice on a day-to-day basis? (You may want to consider the methods that came through in this study and see which of those you currently use.)
- Is there scope for growing your learning network? How can you make these new connections? Who from your existing network can help with this?
- How can you strengthen your existing connections so that they can be used for learning as well as for practice delivery?
- How can you create moments for critical reflection as part of your practice, either alone or with others?
- How could you empower others (such as volunteers or relatively isolated practitioners) to share their practice?
- How could your organization support you to share your knowledge and to learn through a network of relationships?

This project has shown that community development knowledge is held and shared by practitioners through a continually evolving intricate web of connections. Each participant was connected to people who had influenced their practice and those that they had influenced. How will you continue to weave connections in your own practice-learning web?

Notes

1 P. Freire (1996). *Pedagogy of the oppressed* (revised). New York: Continuum; P. Freire, (1985). *The Politics of Education: Culture, Power, and Liberation.* Greenwood Publishing Group; P. Freire (1972). *Conscientization: A Research.* INODEP; P. Westoby and G. Dowling (2013). *Theory and practice of dialogical community development: International perspectives.* Routledge.

2 P. Freire (1996). *Pedagogy of the oppressed* (revised). New York: Continuum; P. Freire, (1985). *The Politics of Education: Culture, Power, and Liberation.* Greenwood Publishing Group; P. Freire, P. (1972). *Conscientization: A Research.* INODEP; P. Westoby and G. Dowling (2013). *Theory and practice of dialogical community development: International perspectives.* Routledge.

3 S. Alinsky (1971). *Rules for radicals: A pragmatic primer for realistic radicals.* New York: Random House; S. Alinsky (2010). *Reveille for radicals.* Vintage.

4 S. Alinsky (1971). *Rules for radicals: A pragmatic primer for realistic radicals.* New York: Random House; S. Alinsky (2010). *Reveille for radicals.* Vintage.

5 L. Dominelli (1998). Anti-oppressive practice in context. In *Social Work* (pp. 3–22). Palgrave, London; D. Baines (ed.) (2011). *Doing anti-oppressive practice: Social justice social work.* Fernwood Pub; J. DeFilippis, R. Fisher and E. Shragge (2010). *Contesting community: The limits and potential of local organizing.* Rutgers University Press.

6 R. Mullaly (1997). *Structural social work: Ideology, theory, and practice.* Oxford University Press, USA; B. Mullaly and M. Dupré (2019). *The new structural social work: Ideology, theory, and practice.* Oxford University Press: S. Reitmanova and R. Henderson (2016). Aboriginal women and the Canadian criminal justice system: Examining the Aboriginal Justice Strategy through the lens of structural social work. *Critical Social Work*, 17(2), 1–19.

7 R. Mullaly (1997). *Structural social work: Ideology, theory, and practice.* Oxford University Press, USA; B. Mullaly and M. Dupré (2019). *The new structural social work: Ideology, theory, and practice.* Oxford University Press: S. Reitmanova and R. Henderson. (2016). Aboriginal women and the Canadian criminal justice system: Examining the Aboriginal Justice Strategy through the lens of structural social work. *Critical Social Work*, 17(2), 1–19.

8 J. McKnight (2017). *Asset-based community development: the essentials.* Chicago: Asset-Based Community Development Institute; R. Stan (2015). *What is Asset Based Community Development (ABCD)?* Collaborative of Neighbourhood Transformation. ABCD Institute.

9 J. McKnight (2017). *Asset-based community development: the essentials.* Chicago: Asset-Based Community Development Institute; R. Stan. (2015). *What is Asset Based Community Development (ABCD)?* Collaborative of Neighbourhood Transformation. ABCD Institute.

10 D. Denborough (2008). *Collective narrative practice.* Adelaide: Dulwich Centre Publications; L. Shevellar (2015). From bearers of problems to bearers of culture: developing community in the community development classroom. *International Journal of Qualitative Studies in Education*, 28(4), 457–475.

11 R. Moreland and T. Lovett (2006). *Lifelong learning and Community Development.* Taylor and Francis online

12 K. Popple (2015). *Analysing community work: theory and practice*, 2nd edition. Maidenhead, UK: Open University Press.

13 https://openspaceworld.org/wp2/what-is/

14 http://www.planningforreal.org.uk/

15 A. Haines (2009). Asset-based community development. *An Introduction to Community Development*, 38, 48.

16 D. Denborough, ibid.

17 See the work of the Barefoot College in India https://www.barefootcollege.org

18 See the work of the Barefoot College in India https://www.barefootcollege.org

19 See for example the excellent Barefoot Guides https://www.barefootguide.org/https://practicalactionpublishing.com/book-series/12/barefoot-guides

20 R. Chambers (1997). *Whose Reality Counts? Putting the First Last.* Practical Action Publishing.

21 https://www.hiic.org.uk/

22 Scottish Community Development Centre (2007). LEAP – A Manual for Learning, Evaluation and Planning in Community Learning and Development https://www.scdc.org.uk

23 This organization is named after the Nguni people, a group of Bantu ethnic groups that reside across Southern Africa.

Chapter 7

Promoting Diversity and Inclusion

Maryam Ahmadian and Holly Scheib

Introduction

This chapter is about the role of the community development practitioner and community development agencies in promoting inclusion and diversity and in creating socially inclusive, culturally diverse, equality-focused community structures, programs, and systems. As South African President Nelson Mandela so cogently said:

> It is not our diversity which divides us; it is not our ethnicity, or religion or culture that divides us. Since we have achieved our freedom, there can only be one division among us: between those who cherish democracy and those who do not.[1]

At its heart is the profession's longstanding commitment to tackling the social, cultural, political, and economic injustices and inequality (e.g. class, race, gender, sexuality, migration, age, disability) facing disadvantaged and vulnerable communities across the world. A concern with promoting inclusion and valuing diversity should be a central theme running through community development practice.

An inclusive community is one where all people, regardless of their abilities, disabilities, age or needs, have the right to be respected and appreciated as equal members, and the right to participate in decisions and activities regarding the wellbeing of the community and that is in their interest. A diverse community is one where individuals of different ages, ethnicity, religion, social class, language, geographical origin, ability/disability, gender,

DOI: 10.4324/9781003140498-7

or sexual orientation bring their lived experiences and interests for the benefit of the whole community.

An Inclusive and Diverse Community:

- Does everything that it can to respect all its members, giving them full access to resources, and promoting equal treatment and opportunity.
- Works to eliminate all forms of discrimination.
- Engages all its members in decision-making processes that affect their lives.
- Values diversity.
- Responds quickly to discriminating incidents.

Culturally diverse experiences, backgrounds and identities enrich community development perspectives. Population movement throughout the world is a modern reality, which challenges our concept of community as a fixed entity. Instead, it is more helpful to think of community as fluid, constantly changing, raising challenges for community development practitioners to adopt a wide range of approaches and skills. Community development practice is always political. Issues of power as well as the related issues of access to resources are key components of the work. Challenging xenophobia, discrimination, stereotyping and "labeling" are critical and enhances the challenges for community development practitioners.

The chapter investigates how community development practitioners can challenge such discrimination and work in inclusive ways across diverse communities, ensuring that methods of engagement foster inclusion and respect that diversity. Definitions of diversity and inclusion, while coming from a desire for social justice and equality, have often stopped short of challenging the hierarchies within community development practice itself. Talmage and Knopf have argued that diversity can be defined as a community resource, inclusion as a community process, and inclusiveness as a community outcome.[2] This chapter expands on that definition to include self-reflection, recognition of power hierarchies, and inequalities that might be promoted unintentionally by community development practitioners or agencies. It examines how social, political, economic, cultural, and environmental factors influence marginalized groups and how to adopt inclusive practices to overcome inequalities, including how to challenge discrimination by agencies working in communities and by community groups and leaders, how to support people who are excluded, marginalized, or discriminated against to participate fully and actively in activities and groups.

Community Development Thrives on Inclusion and Diversity; and Having Multi-Cultural, Inclusive, and Tolerant Values is Necessary for Work With Marginalized Groups

Community development practitioners have a moral responsibility to promote equality wherever possible. In many countries, this is a legal responsibility.[3] As we have seen in Chapter One our deepening understanding of social and economic injustice and inequality now appreciates its predominantly structural and systemic causes. This impact is profound, and further exacerbated by longstanding systemic racism, sexism, ablism, ageism, homophobia, heteronormativity, xenophobia, and other forms of cultural, social, or political discrimination. As the community development field has grown, it has come to recognize that much of this disadvantage and discrimination is created and maintained through failures to uphold human rights, address economic injustices, and ensure social and political inclusion. These failures are reflected within interpersonal systems, community systems, organizational systems, and regional, national, and international systems. Community development practice recognizes that addressing change within systems at all levels requires the inclusion of marginalized groups. They are part of the solution. Therefore, the inclusion of diverse groups, and honoring their experiences and knowledge as critical, should be an essential feature of community development practice, offering results that impact systems change from the small community level to larger national and international changes[4].

It is the appreciation of these primary causal affects and impacts that has led community development scholarship and practice to challenge "blame the victim" or individual/group inadequacy/pathology explanations for people's disadvantages.[5] Yet there remains in most countries a strand of state/NGO/donor and media thinking that has seen such communities as "problems" to be cured. In other words, disadvantaged, excluded, and discriminated people are seen as social problems. It is in such contexts that community development practitioners work. Unsurprisingly, years of discrimination among disadvantaged groups will mean that community development practitioners will also find both skepticism among discriminated communities that you are going to do any good, along with a warmth of welcome if you can demonstrate sincerity and early success. It is therefore vital to demonstrate respect, creating spaces that are safe for people with different views and perspectives, including indigenous ways of knowing and doing, in order to be able to participate fully in shaping change that reflects their ideas and interests. To be inclusive, you must reach out beyond more easily accessible community leaders and activists to those within any community who are less represented or more hesitant to engage.

As you will find in Chapter Eight on participative planning, there are many ways in which the community development practitioner can engage those who have been excluded and to listen and to value these people's ideas and opinions and ensure their involvement in co-designing solutions that better meet their needs. A simple example is the involvement of differently abled people in transport planning. The key is to design and deliver programs that recognize and respect diversity, promote inclusion, and work toward equality. Promoting the rights of and justice for discriminated and marginalized groups have become central objectives within community development practice, often through advocating for more involvement in community action from a more inclusive and diverse range of people[6] However, principled statements committing to rights have not always translated into inclusive practice. Current social and political movements, such as *Black Lives Matter*, emphasize the need for diversity and inclusion to not simply be prioritized as short-term efforts to increase participation, but rather, to be oriented to long-term equitable public policies and practices that result in greater and sustained diversity in representation and leadership throughout society.

Just as these political movements are bringing attention to longstanding, continued inequities, so too, community development practice needs to recognize and address inequities and lack of diversity within its own field of practice. This includes looking for that diversity (class, gender, race, sexuality, ethnicity, ability, age) in positions of power at the practitioner and agency level. A community development practitioner can represent privilege in socio-economic opportunities, education, nationality, or connections. Their professional education can distance them in terms of the language and methods they use. While community development practitioners who come from a particular disadvantaged or indigenous community may have themselves suffered discrimination and social exclusion. All practitioners require personal self-awareness, professional flexibility and humility, and the strength to challenge discriminatory cultures and systems within their own organizations that may unintentionally promote or protect discriminatory, anti-equality practices.

Therefore, community development agencies and practitioners must work with a larger world view and a self-awareness of how their own position may contribute to limitations in diversity and inclusion in the communities they support. Being self-aware of your own position as a professional and how you are perceived is key to a successful partnership and the co-creation of positive change. This requires community development practitioners to think on multiple levels simultaneously, looking at whole systems, even as they consider and work on individual issues, or as they initiate processes that engage as many people and viewpoints as possible.[7] Diversity and inclusion are built through activities working toward equality, and as such, it is not up to the community development practitioner to determine when diversity and inclusion have been met as a goal or set of targets. The community development practitioner must also be seeking insight on what equality means for people who are excluded, disadvantaged, or have experienced discrimination.

To assist the community development practitioner to design policies, deliver programs, and demonstrate practices that are inclusive, respect diversity, and work toward equality, the following list of practice skills are presented.

Practice Skills for Supporting Diversity and Inclusion for the Community Development Practitioner

1. **Community development practitioners must be aware of the conditions that shape an excluded group's experiences.** Seeking to understand the experience of individuals and groups, and looking through the lens of how that experience is shaped by local, societal and international factors is key in order for the practitioner and the group they are working with to understand the causes of their exclusion and the conditions for inclusion and change as opposed to exclusion and status quo. Community development practitioners will be more effective if they learn about the histories of the people they are working with, for example, legacies of colonialism, slavery, sexism, homophobia, being differently abled, restrictions resulting from discriminatory laws, social, or religious beliefs, and past and current movements for human rights. Practitioners should seek out media (research, ethnographies, novels, films, articles), particularly those produced by members of the community with whom they are working. In this sense, community development practitioners need to become "insiders", empathetic to experiences people face in their day to day lives. This "insider" role has an important function both in terms of defining the nature of practice but also in terms of the community development practitioner's sense of self.

2. **Community development practitioners must ensure that their methods of engagement, education and organization promote inclusion and respect diversity.** This includes creating the conditions for involvement, such as offering transportation arrangements to events, ensuring disability access, providing childcare, and creating meeting times that are suitable for low paid workers on shifts, etc. The educational and organizational methods used by community development practitioners should reflect the communication styles of the community, working in the local language (including sign language for those with hearing difficulties), using activities, storytelling, and artistic approaches familiar to the participants. Didactic classroom experiences with one standing speaker may be associated with negative connotations where schooling was restrictive or punitive. While at times you will run workshops and bring in expert speakers, it is preferable to use more informal approaches including new technologies and use of social media. This is covered in more detail in Chapter Three.

    Similarly, when helping a community group to organize more effectively to take on an issue, it is important to ensure that diverse voices are brought into the process. Here the practitioner needs to be aware of local power dynamics that can perpetuate lack of representation, inequality, and marginalization within any community. Community development practice while giving respect to local traditions, perhaps where men or elders are in leadership roles, may include encouraging women and young people to take on such roles and to be accepted by the community when doing so. Chapter Five on community organizing look at this in more detail.

3. **Community development practitioners should demonstrate cultural respect and create spaces that are safe for people with differing world views.** Practitioners need to recognize that the people they are working to support are in many ways the experts of their own lives. This includes for example, respecting local and indigenous ways of knowing and doing and how traditional teachings can be so central to people's understanding of how they should live in their community. Within any community the practitioner will also find prejudice and fear of difference. Community development work should foster engagement and inclusion of diverse voices, with clear attention to the power differentials that marginalize and minimize contributions. Practitioners need to be sensitive to the reality that for discriminated or marginal community members, there will be concerns with safety. A practitioner working with a LGBT+ community needs to be aware of where and how people gather and that it is illegal in some countries. Notwithstanding, the community development practitioner must offer safe spaces for people to meet that respect everyone's need for safety and security.

4. **Community development practitioners should support agencies and communities to adopt inclusive practices and respect diversity.** Governmental and non-governmental agencies working with disadvantaged communities to promote social and economic development and environmental protection, including community development agencies, often carry systemic racist, ageist, and sexist practices. Community development practitioners can run anti-discriminatory workshops and promoting inclusive practices that respect cultural, ethnic, and other diversities. As we have seen, community development practitioners can be found working across many disciplines and this provides opportunities for influencing several agencies working within a locality, such as health, social work, education. Increasingly these disciplines

have improved in efforts to address systemic discrimination and promote diversity within their operations and working culture.

5. **Community development practitioners may need to tackle conflict within communities of locality and between communities of identity.** People of different ethnicities, religions, and cultures increasingly live within the same localities in many countries. This includes situations where recent migrants or asylum seekers have moved or been moved by the state to live within what is already a disadvantaged, vulnerable neighborhood. Conflict between them may be unavoidable, indeed may be encouraged by power elites, if they don't understand or appreciate one another's cultures, have misinformed or negative stereotypes about one another, and/or compete with one another for resources and power. If this is the case, your educational and organizational challenge will be to help them to address their concerns in a constructive way and to develop people's willingness to work together. Some community development practitioners may have had training and experience in conflict resolution. If not, you may need to identify an outside conflict resolution facilitator who can work with you and the competing groups and their representatives to identify and address issues causing conflict and to work together to resolve these.

6. **Community development practitioners should support and build upon the strengths that diverse and inclusive communities can bring.** Multi-cultural, intergenerational and mixed ability communities bring diversity and a richness to people's lives. Any community development practitioner involved in organizing/ supporting a community festival will know the huge joy that food, storytelling, music, and dance from different cultures and abilities brings to everyone. Bringing people of all ages, abilities, ethnicities, gendered expressions, and personal diversities together in designing and running community projects and activities creates the sharing of experiences, ideas, and talents.

The following case studies are drawn from Ecuador, Georgia, England, Zimbabwe, and Australia. They have been selected from IACD members to illustrate in more detail the range of approaches that community development practitioners can use. The Ecuadorian example comes from a vulnerable rural community and focuses upon work with people with disabilities. With the support of community development practitioners, the community with disabled residents successfully campaigned for a local law that would enhance the voice and rights of the disabled. The Georgian case study is also concerned with disability and the emergence of a new community development and disability network across countries of the former USSR. The English case study looks at the work of community artists supporting people with mental health problems and with young people at risk in poor post-industrial urban communities. Here we see the power of art, music, festivals, and environmental projects in giving people a voice. The Zimbabwean case study puts a focus upon empowering women with the inspiring story of an activist who helped poor rural women form income generating cooperatives. The final Australian case study looks at community development work confronting the legacy of racism toward aboriginal people who through sharing their stories of discrimination successfully engaged with those who develop social policy toward aboriginal people in order to change it.

Each case study explores the role of the community development practitioner/s in:

- how to promote inclusion and diversity within communities
- how to challenge discrimination by agencies community groups and to help them to work in more inclusive ways
- how to support people who are excluded, marginalized, or discriminated against to participate fully and actively in development programs and community activities
- how to create spaces that are accessible and safe for people to participate fully
- how to demonstrate cultural humility, including working with indigenous ways of knowing and doing
- how to develop and advocate for policies, programs and practices that promote inclusion and diversity and the rights of excluded people.

Figure 7.1 Promotion of an affirmative action civic law in the town of Espindola, Ecuador.
Photo credit: CBM.

Case Study 1 – Ecuador

Promotion of an Affirmative Action Civic Law in the Town of Espíndola
By Karen Heinicke-Motsch and Olmedo Zambrano

Espíndola, Ecuador, is an agricultural community with 3,700 inhabitants in eight rural communities and a small urban center. In 2010 it had a poverty rate of 97%. People with disabilities were discriminated against, denied full participation in community life, had little access to services and a limited voice. From circumstances of marginalization, the people themselves achieved an affirmative action civic law. Working through the local political system and using the national legal system, people with disabilities in Espíndola improved their living conditions, their participation in community life and exercised their voice in claiming their rights. The community gained experience in engaging with the political system to implement national law and now benefits from the perspectives, experiences, and skills of people with disabilities.

Ecuadorian law requires municipalities to allocate a portion of their budget to vulnerable populations. In 2016 the municipality of Espíndola asked the NGO (non-governmental organization) "Discapacidad y Desarrollo" to undertake an investigation about people with disabilities with an aim to inform its budget process. The roles of community development practitioners from "Discapacidad y Desarrollo" included: designing and implementing the participatory situation analysis, listening to suggested solutions, promoting the first meetings, training and helping with the mid-term evaluation.

The investigation undertaken included focus group discussions with people with disabilities in Espíndola including members of the local Organization of Persons with Disabilities (OPD) "Venciendo Barreras" and others not affiliated with the OPD. The investigation uncovered many problems experienced by people with disabilities associated with discrimination and stigma, poverty, limited access to services, and low levels of empowerment. One focus group proposed the promulgation of a municipal law to protect the rights of people with disabilities. With support from the NGO, the OPD set to work on this aim.

The Community Development Project

In the past, local laws had always been proposed by councilors, the mayor or by the national government. In this community initiative, people with disabilities took the lead and participated in developing local laws. The key members engaged in the project were people with disabilities themselves and their families. Also involved were the councilors, the mayor, and municipal representatives of service units, particularly health, education, justice, and transport. The aim of the project was to model community participation of and with persons with disabilities in the elaboration of local laws and policies protecting the rights of people with disabilities. The law was developed, analyzed, and approved together. When the law was finalized, the local OPD defended it at the town council meeting and advocated its endorsement. The law includes provisions that protect the rights of persons with disabilities to a life in dignity and without discrimination, accessibility, access to services, and equal opportunities.

One year later, meetings took place to evaluate progress and after two years, representatives of the OPD began traveling to neighboring communities to promote replication. The evaluation showed persons with disabilities felt themselves less discriminated, had better access to health care, education, and transport, that more architectural accessibility existed and that the OPD was significantly empowered.

Project stages included:

- Situation analysis and investigation of needs
- Participatory elaboration of the local law
- Advocacy for its endorsement
- Explaining what the new law meant within the community
- Advocacy for its implementation
- Mid-term evaluation
- Replication in other localities

The community development processes used in the project included:

- Involvement of parties affected
- Joint advocacy
- Participatory evaluation

Core Values

Core community development values of respect for the participation of people directly affected and empowerment were essential to the process. The primary assets harnessed were the voices of disabled people who are excluded, time and capacity for joint activity, the desire for self-advocacy and social and political pressure and will for the realization of rights guaranteed under national legislation.

The project demonstrates it is possible to co-write, gain approval of and implement a local law as a proposition for community development. It was the pressure from the base to listen to the voices of people with disabilities in order to promote their empowerment and to ensure that meeting their needs and finding solutions proposed by the people affected can result in more effective and inclusive laws and policies.

What Worked Well

The things that worked well include:

- The spaces and fora created for participation and advocacy.
- The planning based on the felt needs of people with disabilities themselves and the mapping tool used to facilitate this process of investigation.
- The planning based on achieving a single goal.
- The leadership of people with disabilities themselves.

Challenges and Overcoming Them

In the first stages of the project, several people with disabilities thought this process would be a waste of time. They felt the municipality would not enforce a law elaborated in this manner or, if approved, would not implement it. It was not easy to address this challenge as the perception was deeply embedded in people's minds. The NGO found that similar laws had been developed in other municipalities without the involvement of people with disabilities. Sharing this information regarding developments in other municipalities motivated people and spurred their involvement. The challenge felt truly overcome after the law was passed and particularly when people with disabilities began to experience changes in their lives because of a law, they had been so central to realizing. This motivation will continue to bear fruit as people with disabilities hold their local government accountable for its continued implementation.

Learning and Future Plans

- Community development facilitated by national legal frameworks can be successful if there is a commitment to living the principles of participatory and locally driven action.

- Collectively focusing on a single principal goal can be a powerful way to strengthen and empower a local organization.
- Listening to and respecting the voices of excluded groups is an essential foundation of community development.

The NGO completed the project in 2019. The COVID-19 outbreak delayed the final evaluation, which will be carried out once restrictions ease. The local OPD will continue to work with nearby municipalities on similar processes with funds provided by the municipal government of Espíndola. Priority will be given to ensuring people with disabilities themselves replicate the processes used in this project. The NGO will continue to follow similar steps regarding participation and collective agreement in any future work they are involved in.

Figure 7.2 Inclusive practices team – Georgia. Photo credit: Inclusive Practices.

Case Study 2 – Georgia

Tackling Disability: The Inclusive Practices Network

By Anastasia Matvievskaya

Despite the fact that the former republics of the Soviet Union have diverged significantly, and they differ in the types of political regimes, other than the three Baltic States, which joined the E.U, for the remainder in cultural and social aspects – it is still a single space. Of the 295 million people living in the former Soviet Union, more than 30 million people have disabilities. And this is a low estimate, because many parents are afraid of the stigma of "disabled" for their child and try to manage on their own, without seeking state or medical support. In Soviet times, there was a well-established system of special institutions for disabled people with full state support, based upon a general policy of complete social isolation from the rest of society. The collapse of the Soviet Union in 1991 and the subsequent long economic and social crisis destroyed this well-established system of "support". In addition, families raising children with special needs lost guaranteed state medical and other care.

Paradoxically, in a state that for 74 years had declared communistic development values, community development as practice-based profession and an academic discipline had not been established. This in turn meant that there was virtually no availability of professional community development practitioners to promote community-based social inclusion models as opposed to institution-based social exclusion models of support for disabled people. So, the emergence of local community organizations working with people with disabilities were very new and very unstable, with these organizations citing lack of money, state support, and negative public reactions, but also constant stress and rapid emotional burnout of community members. Even the more successful organizations noted the level of depression among members and a frequent feeling of inner emptiness even after very successful social inclusion projects had been established.

It was against this context that The Inclusive Practices Network (IPN) was launched in 2008. The aim of IPN was to bring together community development and disability initiatives across the successor states of the former Soviet Union and to promote community development as practice-based profession. IPN was founded by a group of graduates of Moscow State University who completed training and internships in human resource development and social work, and who, inspired by their supervisor Dr. Vladimir Matvievskiy, had become active in the field of disability. The IPN was developed by the efforts of thirty to thirty-five volunteers and existed on private donations. IPN currently brings together more than 450 communities of people with disabilities and their families from eleven, mostly post-Soviet, countries.

A person with a disability constantly lives with the circumstances and consequences of their disability: limited mobility/behavioral capacity, dependence on others, fake and hostile reactions, the presence and possibility of pain, dissatisfaction, depression, loneliness, alienation. But it's also evident, that social isolation and lack of self-actualization significantly deteriorates the quality of life of a disabled person. At the same time, awesome strength of mind, mobilization, efficiency, sincerity, hypersensitivity ... are just some of the qualities that disability also brings when given the opportunity to become socially included within the wider society. With guidance, an ability to empathize, to feel another person, the willingness to help and be helpful can be highly developed in people with disabilities. Inclusive Practices see these potential strengths in all disabled people as the basis for our approach to training in community development.

The past thirteen years have demonstrated that an inclusive practices approach is the right one. Communities where people with disabilities and/or parents of disabled children learn and are encouraged to be active members within the wider community are much more sustainable. This kind of learning is about putting the valuing of inclusion and diversity into practice, supporting people with disabilities and their families to be active participants in designing and planning activities within the wider community. It is important to note that community development learning is much more than just a social or professional activity for a person with a disability and their family. It is an opportunity to feel needed, which immensely helps overcome depression and burnout of both the disabled themselves, their loved ones, and other people around them.

In January 2018, the IPN opened its head office and a training center in Ureki (Georgia). Now the IPN has four full-time stuff and more than seventy irreplaceable volunteers who have been involved in the IPN's projects for more than five years. IPN's main source of revenue comes from seminars, workshops, and other training support held at the center and around post-Soviet countries. Private contributions and donations also make up a significant part of the IPN's funding.

The following are some examples of how IPN supports community development practitioners working with disabled people.

Community Development Training

One of the IPN's projects was to inspire and assist in organizing the first associations of parents of children with autism in Russia and Kazakhstan. The idea of the project being to train the parents of children with disabilities to become community development practitioners. In doing this, IPN was supporting parents who for years had had to face a cultural attitude within their communities of "accept the inevitable, your child will never be like everyone else, there's no place for him/her in the 'normal' life; it's better to put him/her in an institution where he/she will be taken care of and feel safe". We wanted to give support to the parents in order to challenge these attitudes. As a result of this project, in 2013 the government of Kazakhstan supported the IPN by providing permanent funding for local inclusive communities in Kazakhstan. This created more than thirty paid jobs for mothers of disabled children to be community development practitioners.

Internship Programs

The purpose of this project is to offer short and long-term residential internship programs for future and actual community development practitioners working with disabled people. These programs are based in the Inclusive Practices village in Ureki, which was built by a community of parents of children with autism at their own expense not far from the IPN head office and training center. The idea of the internship is in immersion in everyday life of the community with its daily routine, together with special training through master classes. This allows a disabled person and his/her family to learn to deal with their stress and depression in a safe environment, allowing the disabled person to learn to control his/her psychological and emotional state and supporting the learning of the community development practitioners.

Inclusive Events

We pay great attention to the organization of international inclusive events such as the annual *Inclusive Practices Festival "Pushing the Limits" Inclusive Community Development Conference* and the *"Best Inclusive Practices"* competition. The first festival was held in October 2018, in Ureki. It was attended by non-governmental associations, representatives of universities, leaders, organizers, and participants from inclusive communities, as well as creative teams from countries across the post-Soviet space and Western Europe. The goal of the festival through plenary sessions and workshops, is to share the best international inclusive practices projects, as well as to facilitate full access to them by parents, specialists, organizers of inclusive communities and other interested parties. This festival was supported by the International Association for Community Development – IACD and we used the opportunity of this event to launch the Russian and Georgian language versions of the International Standards for Community Development Practice. This launch was not only useful for practitioners, but also pushed several universities in the post-Soviet region to introduce community development as an academic discipline. The IACD Standards have since been translated into six languages of post-Soviet countries.

The idea of an Inclusive Practices Festival has resonated with local communities in other countries. In 2018–2019, events of this kind took place in Armenia, Belarus, and Ukraine. The festival is intended to become an annual traditional event and despite the state borders being closed due to the COVID-19 pandemic, in 2020, it was held in virtual format as a week-long Inclusive Practices Marathon. The integration of two genres – festival and conference, in one inclusive event has proven to be quite successful. The cultural program of the festival demonstrates creative and sport achievements of inclusive communities, the strength of their spirit and the incredible victories of persons with disabilities. The opportunity to share their success with the audience inspires them and gives them incentive to move forward. At the same time, the conference program gives an opportunity for professional exchange and development of connections and cooperation among the participants of inclusive projects from different countries.

Virtual Support

One of IPN priorities is accessibility. and that is possible thanks to modern online technologies. In 2017, we launched the free online Inclusive Practices Catalog in three languages (Russian, English and Ukrainian). The Catalog is also accessible for visually impaired people. It is continuously updated and shares the experience of more than 450 inclusive communities in post-Soviet space countries. We videotape all the inclusive events held by the IPN and publish the videos in this online Catalog.

Figure 7.3 Mural arts project inspired by architectural archways of our town. Ways of seeing, using photography – England. Photo credit: Members of Ebeneezer Mental Health Center, Halifax.

Case Study 3 – England. UK
Using Community Arts for Inclusion: Red Water Arts
By Sue and Mike Pemsel

This case study shows how the arts made an important contribution to community development in an area affected by high levels of unemployment and poverty in the Calderdale valley in the north of England. The project described lasted for 14 years and was the first arts led community development initiative in this semi-rural valley of industrial towns and villages, including Todmorden, Hebden Bridge and Halifax.

It is a beautiful, yet scarred and largely deforested landscape, with steep-sided valleys which lent to the growth of the water and steam powered woollen and cotton mills and the creation of these industrial settlements in the eighteenth and nineteenth centuries, building upon earlier medieval villages. By the 1960s the mills had all but closed, leaving a legacy of high unemployment and poverty, together with row upon row of poor-quality Victorian working-class terraced housing, many "back to back", clinging to the hillsides. With the mill closures many families had to leave the valley for work elsewhere. Much of the housing, often without indoor sanitation, was demolished along with some of the huge mills leaving ugly gap sites.

The area had always been known for its dissent and non-conformity, with a long tradition of cooperative societies, the Workers' Educational Association, welfare, and social societies. Chapels were not only religious but educational, covertly political, and strong cultural centers for the community. Out of these sprung choirs, scientific and literary societies, drama societies, brass bands, social gatherings, Sunday schools, walking and cycle clubs. While the valley had a neglected, depressed look, there remained a strong sense of neighborliness and civic pride.

Sue and Michael Pemsel moved to Calderdale initially attracted by low-cost housing and land. Mike was an art and design teacher, Sue a musician and community arts worker. They purchased a semi-derelict farmhouse in the area, with three hectares of hill land, bordered by the fast-flowing river – Red Water. Their vision was to establish a charitable social enterprise which would contribute to community development through the arts. Red Water Arts (RWA) was conceived through grant aid they secured from the Council of Small Industries in Rural Areas (Cosira). A barn, a stable, and a piggery were converted for use as art/design and music workshop spaces, together with residential accommodation. RWA from the outset also had a commitment to outreach work across the valley towns.

The focus of RWA was initially upon support for the general community, but quickly specialized upon excluded groups with special needs particularly people with mental health problems or learning disabilities. Small groups with their specialist nurses and carers came to the RWA center for residential weekends. Much sensitivity, trust, and emotional intelligence was required. These proved successful projects and over the years many groups spent time at RWA, learning new skills and developing confidence. Environmental work developed with group courses, using the arts and the natural surroundings to foster an awareness of the impact of climate change. Through tree planting, straw bale building, and Yurt-making activities, RWA used what nature had to offer: earth, air, fire, and water. They also involved children, using self-devised music, theater, dance, and the visual arts. Clay was dug from the earth around; a Roman kiln was built, and pottery fired.

Artlink, a training organization, whose aim was to foster access to the arts in West Yorkshire, offered RWA funding to develop an arts project at the Ebenezer center in Halifax which caters for adults recovering from mental illness. Out of this, and preliminary artwork, grew a desire to produce a wall mural depicting the activities at the center. It was quite a challenge to draw and paint on such a large scale. This vibrant mural set high on the wall completely transformed what had been a bland area at the center and the group felt extremely proud of its achievement. On the strength of this success more funding was made available from the Local Health Authority and members of the Ebenezer center with RWA produced a mural for the local health center. This drew on images of canal barges, mills, and hills, all impressively symbolic of Calderdale. It was well received by both the Health Authority and the local community. RWA found that through working with excluded people who initially had little confidence and low self-esteem, the more the project developed the more the group developed cohesively, working and learning together, aiming for a high standard and they all rose to the challenges.

RWA organized several community festivals, involving and attracting hundreds of people young and old. The 4th Community Festival entitled "Peasants Revolt" was inspired by the then Conservative government which brought in a poll tax that particularly hit poor households hard. So, the community festival had a political theme but was created within an historical, multi-media community arts dimension, comparing it to the Peasants Revolt which arose out of a similar poll tax being forced upon the population of England six hundred years before. RWA worked with local primary schools, youth clubs and the local Anglican church. An historical re-enactment society portrayed in authentic costume and manner, the actual events leading up to the earlier Peasants Revolt. The anti-poll tax message was put across vividly throughout the five-day festival, using drama, dance, storytelling, medieval music, wall hangings and banners, a fayre and street theater, totally transforming the community center and the village. The local press responded with great interest and vigor.

In June 1992, we attended the International Community Education Association conference in Hungary. RWA made firm connections with the Hungarian Association for Community Development and from this seed the youth arts exchange emerged. The aim of the exchange was to share cultures and to develop the interpersonal skills of all the young people involved. Through Calderdale Youth and Community Services, RWA worked with the Ashenhurst Community Association in nearby Todmorden. The Ashenhurst estate had a challenging reputation, with socio-economic problems, "troubled" families, and a high petty crime rate: not the kind of kids usually interested in twinning or the arts. Two months were spent with the young people getting the group to gel through discussion and workshops, drama, song writing and art, addressing social issues of relationships, family problems, school, future expectations, and aspirations. The objective was to build self-confidence and strengthen group cohesion. We then took the group to meet a group of young people in Debrecen, Hungary for the first leg of the exchange.

The return visit by the Hungarian group the following year was a qualified success on certain levels. The drawback was that although the Hungarian group consisted of the same young people, whereas our group had changed, a year is a long time and their lives lacked stability. Some dropped out from the project, consequently this made cohesion much harder. Two youngsters from the local area broke into the RWA work buildings, stealing a video camera, TV monitor and two sets of minibus keys. At the conclusion of the project and on reflection, lessons were learned: community arts projects have their ups and downs. One offshoot of the project was the placement with RWA of a Hungarian community development student from Budapest, who worked with the young people at the Ashenhurst estate.

Conclusion

The running of RWA required hard work – raising funds, employing volunteers, and visiting artists, as well as forging partnerships with schools, health and social services and local community associations. Thousands of people over the fourteen years engaged in RWA's courses and festivals. Its philosophy was to make no division between so called "high art" and community art. All should be inclusive and participatory in different and complementary ways, helping vulnerable and often excluded people make sense of an increasingly complex and changing world. RWA's work and that of others in Calderdale, punched way above their weight in producing high quality art among people of all abilities. The whole community has, over the years, become a vibrant place for participatory arts organizations and is recognized nationally as having made a huge contribution to the regeneration of the area.

Hebden Bridge now holds an annual Arts festival and an International Piano Festival, which without strong community involvement could not exist. "Pushing Up Daisies", an annual community generated festival in Todmorden, uses a broad spectrum of the arts, to create conversations around the taboo subject of death, dying and bereavement. Out of the local wholefood and green movement grew "Incredible Edible" from Todmorden, where volunteers grow vegetables on street roundabouts and other previously neglected roadside land, to be picked free by anyone in the community. It has since been replicated in many parts of the world. And more of the Calderdale valley has been reforested.

These life affirming activities stemmed from local grassroot led arts initiatives. They would not have happened without the inspiration and talent of the people who live in these communities, many of whom have been involved with Red Water Arts.

Figure 7.4 Northern Products detergent making graduation ceremony – Zimbabwe. Photo credit: Nyarai Sabeka and Yvonne Phiri.

Case Study 4 – Zimbabwe

Taking Women Empowerment to a New Level in Hwange District

By Nyarai Sabeka and Yvonne Phiri

Women play a pivotal role in ensuring sustainable community development. Community development practitioners are realizing that the adoption of gender diversity and inclusion ensure shared responsibility which is key if tangible results and innovations are to be achieved. Policy on diversity and inclusion eliminates all barriers to sustainable community development that hinder the full participation of women. Current trends demand increased diversity and inclusion efforts thus most community development initiatives are adopting more inclusive approaches.

Patience Kashiri's community development initiative is an epitome of resilience and unbridled zeal. Born thirty-five years ago in Karoi, Zimbabwe, Patience, a single mother of three, is a victim of gender-based violence (GBV). Her personal life experience prompted her not to play victim but be an active agent against GBV and promote economic emancipation of women. Patience realized that women empowerment through increased diversity and an inclusive approach was crucial if gender equality and equity are to be achieved. As a result, she embarked on a plan of action in which she sought to empower women through various projects and training in Hwange District.

Patience sought to economically empower women by training them to make detergents, soap, petroleum jelly and production of juice with ingredients and materials sourced from Harare, the capital city of Zimbabwe and to set up cooperatives. Her target group consist mainly of all women regardless of their age, tribe, economic or social status. However, some men also undergo the training workshops without discrimination. To date she has trained approximately seven hundred women in Hwange and Binga Districts. Participants usually pay eighty Zimbabwean dollars for a two-day training workshop. In February 2019 she conducted a refresher course which saw eighty-six women in Victoria Falls being retrained. The training program was in partnership with an organization called Progressive African Youth Network (PAYN) and the government. Those women who have been trained sell their products to the public in line with the government's empowerment program meant to empower small to medium enterprises.

She encourages the women to register companies and assists them with knowledge on how to go about the process. So far only two women have managed to register companies. Unfortunately, costs required to register a company are out of reach for most of the women, so currently the majority opt to form cooperatives through which they pull resources together and sell products from their homes as there are no funds to rent shop space as yet. Some of the cooperatives that received training include Hands Together, Together as One, Women of Virtue and Golden Angels. However, Patience is faced with a myriad of challenges such as lack of funding, office space, illiteracy among women and failure for the products to penetrate the mainstream market.

Patience now hosts a talk show called "Patie's Talk Show" through the program "Lebeleka Nhukaji" (Speak Out Women), which focuses on enlightening people on GBV, HIV/AIDS, and child marriages. "Patie's Talk Show" has managed to bring together people of different tribes, social and economic background. Through her talkshow initiative women have managed to discuss issues affecting them openly and acquire knowledge and clarity on certain issues and misconceptions. The Hwange District Development Coordinator (DDC) acknowledged the positive results of Patience's initiative citing cases of domestic violence were slowly decreasing.

Community development practitioners play an important role in assisting Patience's initiatives to be a success. The DDC's office as the overseer of all development initiatives in the district have been supportive of Patience's initiatives and at times offer her their conference room as venue to conduct training sessions or host the talkshow. In addition, they also assist with topics that need awareness within the community and how to go about getting relevant trained personnel or professionals on the concerned topics. This has allowed Patience's talkshow to contain very rich and well-researched information. During graduation ceremonies for those who have successfully completed the detergent making training workshop, the DDC's office is always represented which gives credibility to Patience's initiative.

Meanwhile, the Ministry of Women Affairs, Community, Small and Medium Enterprises Development has also been instrumental in offering technical assistance and mobilization efforts. The community development practitioners help mobilize women for detergent making training workshops. Their emphasis is on diversity and inclusion of all women regardless of tribe, educational background, or societal standing among other discriminatory tendencies. The community development practitioners organize women into groups and encourage them to form mukando/stokvel savings clubs to pull resources together. This enables them to procure products for resale or for their own consumption or to pay for their training such that they start making their own detergents for resale. Furthermore, during the Hwange Agricultural Show usually held in August of every year, these cooperatives are given space by the Ministry to showcase and market their products.

The diversity and inclusion approach has resulted in a change of attitudes, understanding and attainment of skills for women who initially had no source of income nor skill and had to rely on their male counterparts for financial support. There are marked changes in the women's action and behavior as they now opt for cooperativeness and social responsibilities. The Ministry's community development practitioners' efforts have helped improve the economic, social, and cultural conditions of women and enabled them to contribute to the government's goal toward women empowerment. Women in the district are now seen as instrumental players within the household and the economic development of the community.

Community development practitioners from Basilizwi Trust mobilize women from Binga District for collective action through skills attainment and the Trust pays for their detergent making training expenses. These women are now empowered through a skill that has become a source of income for them. This has helped improve their quality of life. There is now increased participation of women in community development projects and the provision of technical and other services by both government and non-governmental organizations have encouraged self-help initiatives which are more effective in ensuring empowerment of women. Through training on self-help projects, solutions to community development are generated as now women no longer wait upon men to be the sole breadwinners.

Community development practitioners from Basilizwi Trust also help "Patie's Talk Show" to reach out to more women through cooperativeness and resource mobilization. However, the major hindrances are patriarchy and tribalism. The language barrier has affected "Patie's Talk Show" in the sense that it is shunned by members of society on the grounds that she does not hail from Hwange District in terms of birthplace and does not speak the local languages. As a result, she finds it difficult to penetrate the communities and discuss the issues in depth. On the other hand, due to patriarchal thinking and attitudes some men shun attending the talkshow citing they have nothing to learn from a woman, worse a single mother. However, Basilizwi Trust has been conducting awareness campaigns in communities highlighting that issues of GBV can only be effectively addressed through an inclusive approach as it affects everyone in the same way. The efforts are seeing changed attitudes as the number of males attending the talkshow are slowly rising and cases of GBV are decreasing.

A lot still needs to be done in Zimbabwe to fully achieve women empowerment and women emancipation. As the fight rages on there is another challenge in the form of imbalances between rural and urban women. The other factor is that there is lack of appreciation and acknowledgment of the many roles that women have to endure in the community on top of being entrepreneurs. Cultural stereotypes have resulted in lack of social acceptability for women. There is need for community-based networks which will be availed with resources that can assist women to support their projects.

Figure 7.5 Elders representing the Waka, Yagarabul, Biggera, Kao and Wangan Jaoialunga countries gather to support Sorry Day – Australia. Photo credit: Tina Lathouras and Dyann Ross.

Case Study 5 – Australia

Challenging Racism: The Case of Benarrawa Aboriginal and Torres Strait Islander Solidarity Group[8]

By Tina Lathouras and Dyann Ross

> Benarrawa is flowing. We dream that the people will listen to the land and to each other.
> Benarrawa Dreaming Statement

For 200 years, white colonists to Australia regarded Aboriginal groups as unworthy of regard as human beings. Aboriginal groups, supported by some (admittedly weak) legislation, have continued to organize, to develop a voice and act from the bottom up to confront this shameful history of ethnic cleansing, violence, abuse and expropriation of land and culture. This case study summarizes community development work with one Brisbane group to confront the ongoing legacy of racism. One of us (Tina) has had a very long association with the Benarrawa Solidarity Group (BSG) as a member and Board member. There was one community development worker supporting the group and three part-time workers employed by BSG.

Twenty-five years ago, members of the BSG came together to explore issues of racism and learn more about Aboriginal and Torres Strait Islander histories and culture. The Group, comprising Indigenous and non-Indigenous community members, has demonstrated long-term commitment to community development actions to promote justice and understanding between all people. BSG challenged racism through the adoption of a multifaceted structural analysis about the root causes of oppression which sought to address the issues at their source. BSG challenged this racism and sought to take collective action beyond the local level to effect wider systemic change. BSG learned in their work that racism has a functional value that serves some people – namely those powerful groups of white people who gain from the status quo. BSG wanted to engage with that system to create change, working to reduce the deleterious effects of racism as they critically analyse, vision, and take practical steps to bring that vision into reality.

Benarrawa takes its name from the land near where the organization is located. BSG members were aware that the non-Indigenous histories of the Benarrawa area were completely silent about its Indigenous past. Their hope in forming the BSG was to reclaim community consciousness of the Aboriginal history of their local area. Their local history project, for example, found surviving historical records and stories that revealed a level of very distressing overt racism and cruelty toward local Indigenous people. The project made members more aware of the historical lack of recognition and the importance of Australia's First Peoples' cultures and heritage. An important outcome of this work has been the building of strong ties with the Indigenous community.

As a community of interest for anti-racism work, the BSG emphasizes communication in forming "purposeful developmental relationships" laying the foundation for community action. Here, the community development worker works with community members who set the agenda; and make decisions about how the work will be undertaken and issues that affect them and their communities. The BSG informs themselves and the wider community about issues affecting the lives of indigenous peoples through regular gatherings and actions. These provide a range of opportunities for people to connect with others, build relationships and to work together.

These include:

- An Annual Sorry Day Ceremony providing the opportunity for local community members, both Indigenous and non-Indigenous, teachers and pupils, youth groups, clergy and church members, and politicians to join in the ceremony. This is a key annual event for the BSG to listen to the history of the "stolen children" and its intergenerational effect on the children's families' lives.
- On Survival Day (26th January), each year members meets to honor the strength and resilience of the First Peoples and the opportunity to reflect on the eighteenth century invasion by the British and consequent changes to their lives. The 26th of January is Australia's National Day that marks the anniversary of the 1788 arrival of the First Fleet of British Ships.
- The annual Mabo Day Celebration acknowledges the significance of "terra nullius", and Torres Strait Islander Eddie Koiki Mabo's challenge that his people's land was not legally theirs, and subsequent action that eventually led to the granting of Native Title legislation. The "invisibilization" of the Indigenous people allowed European settlers to claim the "empty" land for themselves.
- A Biennial Aboriginal and Torres Strait Islanders (A&TSI) Art Show and Cultural Festival, an event providing the wider public an opportunity for developing relationships with Indigenous peoples and opportunities for learning about each other's lives, culture, traditions, and art.

- A&TSI Awareness Workshops conducted by Indigenous cultural workers, are occasions where people share stories, histories, culture, knowledge, and protocols with the BSG and members of the wider community.
- The BSG's Elders' Lunches create spaces for personal sharing through dialogue, where members educate each other to the realities of racism and disadvantage and where a culture of self-interest is sacrificed for common interest. These lunches are held in non-formal spaces, such as Elders' own homes or community spaces. They foster respectful and egalitarian relationships, and although very sensitive sharing occurs, these are happy occasions with storytelling, and humor, creating a sense that people are on common ground.

The BSG's approach fosters a genuine mandate for community development that seeks to foster solidarity and instil a sense of hopefulness that members' private concerns can be addressed. The starting place for this is with people's stories about their experiences of who holds power and how it is exercised. Processes that raise the consciousness of a group regarding arbitrarily applied policies that overshadow their particular circumstances, can be empowering for group members, especially when they make decisions to act against such oppression. A vast array of social realities and their associated power inequalities are discussed in areas such as health, housing, education, income, employment, culture and the impact of racism and violence on family and community life, identity, and gender. This conscientization process can be viewed as analysis constituted by a matrix of lenses to examine social realities and disadvantage based on race, gender, class, geographical living situation and other indicators of structural disadvantage. This process helps to develop greater understanding and the skills needed to address these areas of disadvantage.

Members of BSG have opportunities to talk and to build relationships with government bureaucrats and others who represent diverse groups within the wider community. Members are working both horizontally and vertically, creating webs of connections within that system. What seems evident in the BSG story is that the quality of the relationships across the system is characterized by mutuality and reciprocity, where all participants are valued for the range of gifts, talents, skills and knowledge they bring to the table. Participation is key to BSGs strategy because it is seeking to educate a broad range of participants, including those who develop social policy within the remit of ATSIC (Aboriginal And Torres Strait Islander Commission), the Government department responsible for Australian indigenous affairs, regarding the deleterious effects of policies on community members. Critical reflection helps the group know if and how their practice is making a difference.

The final element of this jigsaw is a political community development framework which views practice as a space for citizens to participate in processes for democratic equality. The BSG's analysis about racism and the historical oppression of Australia's First Peoples provides a vehicle through which they are enacting their rights as citizens. In this regard community development practice is a form of citizenship-making, where citizen participation and engagement provide members with a voice for achieving democratic equality. These are the kind of politics in which people are not empowered by leaders but empower themselves when they develop skills and habits of collaborative action.

Power can be viewed as consciousness-raising, learning to perceive social, political, and economic contradictions, and to take action against the oppressive element of these realities.

Notes

1 N. Mandela (2011) *Conversations with Myself*. Pan Macmillan.
2 C. Talmage and R. Knopf (2017) Rethinking Diversity, Inclusion, And Inclusiveness: The Quest to Better Understand Indicators of Community Enrichment and Well-Being. In: P. Kraeger, S. Cloutier and C. Talmage (eds), *New Dimensions in Community Well-Being. Community Quality-Of-Life and Well-Being*. Springer, Cham.
3 N. Thompson (2017) *Promoting Equality: Working with Diversity and Difference*. Palgrave Macmillan.
4 P. Farmer (2005) *Pathologies of Power: Health, Human Rights, And the New War on The Poor*. Berkeley: University of California Press; J. Fergerson (1990) *The Anti-Politics Machine: "Development," Depoliticization, And Bureaucratic Power in Lesotho*. Cambridge University Press.
5 M. Shaw and M. Mayo (eds) (2016) *Class, Inequality and Community Development*. Bristol: Policy Press.
6 L. Shevellar and P. Westoby (eds) (2018) *Routledge Handbook of Community Development*. Routledge; B. Checkoway (2011) Community Development, Social Diversity and The New Metropolis, *Community Development Journal*, Vol. 46, Issue 2.
7 D. Western and C. Varley (2018) Preventing Violence Against Women: The Development and Evaluation of a Cald Community Family Violence Project, pp. 99–114; J. Gillespie (2018) Enhancing Aboriginal Child Welfare Through Multi-Sector Community Collaboration, pp. 181–194; and H. Scheib (2018) Hurricanes, Oil, And Rising Water: The Role and Work of Community Development in Coastal Louisiana in the Intersection of Disasters, Recovery, and Planning for The Future, pp. 267–282. In L. Shevellar and P. Westoby (eds) *Routledge Handbook of Community Development*. Routledge.
8 This case study is an adapted version of a longer article in G. Craig (ed.) (2017) *Community Organising against Racism: "Race", Ethnicity and Community Development*. Policy Press.

Chapter 8

Building Leadership and Infrastructure

Michelle Dunscombe and Ron Hustedde

Introduction

This chapter focuses on various dimensions of leadership and the building of an infrastructure for community development:

- It will explore the meaning and role of leadership in the field.
- It will outline the infrastructure that a community development practitioner needs to develop, strengthen and to support community development work.
- It will identify the challenges of community development leadership work.
- Lastly, it will examine case studies to illustrate how leadership anchors community development practice.

What Is Leadership?

Every community has leaders. These include formal leaders such as elected representatives or those in appointed positions in government or non-government organizations. These are positional leaders whose influence is determined by the formal positions they hold in the community. There are also informal leaders or opinion makers whose leadership is based upon their reputation and ability to influence thinking, behaviour and action. Some of these leaders serve narrow interests while others have broader concerns about the common good. Much of the community development literature tends to challenge elitist or

 DOI: 10.4324/9781003140498-8

hierarchical leadership models while emphasizing the kinds of leaders who are sensitive to the needs and visions of a community's diversity.[1]

A true leader has the ability to inspire, or as Gustav Nossal, a great Australian community leader put it: *"Community leadership is the courage, creativity and capacity to inspire participation, development and sustainability for strong communities."*[2] But leadership involves more than a select few. The UN Sustainable Development Goals include targets to "Ensure women's full and effective participation and equal opportunities for leadership at all levels of decision-making in political, economic and public life"[3] and to "empower and promote the social, economic and political inclusion of all, irrespective of age, sex, disability, race, ethnicity, origin, religion or economic or other status" respectively. [4]

This chapter focuses on those leaders who foster and support organizational development and infrastructure for promoting and empowering democratic and participatory practices that leads to creating lasting community change. Communities can generally identify the people they want to nurture in such leadership roles. It may not always be the positional leaders or those who label themselves as a leader. For any community development practice, it is important that formal and informal leaders be involved.

The Role of the Community Development Practitioner in Leadership and Infrastructure Building

While many local formal and informal leaders have their strengths, community development practitioners have an advantage because they are often outsiders without personal agendas. They can enhance the quality and capacity of local leaders and can encourage community groups to see how it is in their self-interest to have a succession planning mindset and a participatory style of government in which every voice is important. They have the freedom to ask difficult and probing questions which people may have not considered or have been afraid to explore. They know how to create safe spaces for people to listen to each other and move towards greater understanding of each other's perspectives.

They have the skills and knowledge to create community development infrastructures that are rooted in the values of democratic participation, inclusivity, self-help and self-determination. This infrastructure helps the community move towards a sense of solidarity and agency. It builds on the *International Standards for Community Development Practice* theme on leadership and infrastructure. [5]

How Do Community Development Practitioners Support Groups to Review Their Own Practices, Policies, External Opportunities and Challenges?

Understanding Power

Community development practitioners are agents of change who understand how to mobilize human and other resources. One of the places to begin is to understand the power of those who influence community action and decisions. Failure to appropriately involve these community power actors in the early stages could lead to opposition. That's why it's important to ask questions of representatives of key groups and organizations to understand the various dimensions of individual and organizational power. If a community issue has been identified, some questions to ask include:

1) Who has the authority, justification or license to define and act on this issue?
2) Who are the formal and informal influence makers who can oppose or support how this issue might be addressed?
3) Who has a stake in this issue and is most likely to be affected negatively or positively when decisions are made?
4) Who has resources inside and outside the community to address this issue?
5) Who else needs to be invited into the conversation to support broad community representation to co-create a solution to the issue?

The responses to these questions provide insights into the complexity and diversity of a community's power structure. Most likely, this power is not unified. Community power actors change from time to time and there may be a need to review and revise. It can be asserted that everyone has a dimension of power including those groups with limited economic resources or those whose voices have traditionally been ignored by elites. Some community development practitioners point to an invisible power which is about reimagining social and political culture to transform how people perceive themselves and their influence. [6]

Understanding the Issue(s)

After developing a list of key leaders and stakeholders that are part of the diverse power structure, the community development practitioner helps people to learn more about issues of concern from these influence makers or opinion leaders. These are some of the questions to clarify current practices and policies and new opportunities that sets the stage for an appropriate infrastructure:

1) How do you define the issue?
2) Who is defining the issue?
3) How do others define it? Are there differences in how it is defined?
4) Who needs to be involved in working on this issue? Why?
5) Who is most affected by this issue? Who is the least affected?
6) Who is likely to oppose and support work on this issue? Why?
7) How can safe and culturally appropriate spaces be created to collaborate on solutions and actions?
8) Who else needs to be involved to strengthen communication bridges in the community to address this issue?
9) What resources and assets exist locally to address the issue?
10) What additional resources from outside might be needed to address the issue?
11) What kind of technical expertise is needed to better understand the issue at hand? It may be an economist, a health expert or someone who understands ecology or the natural environment.
12) How will you measure the outcomes of action?

Most likely, there will be different responses to these questions. However, a community development practitioner creates a climate for a deeper understanding of the complexity of issues and for people to hear and learn from each other and to move towards greater clarity and a sense of common ground in order to make informed decisions. [7]

How Do Community Development Practitioners Support Groups to Plan Their Future Sustainability, and to Develop Strategic and Business Plans to Achieve Their Aims and Objectives?

Community development practitioners help people to build a framework, a type of infrastructure around which people are organized. This infrastructure involves questions about how participants are accepted, how leadership is chosen and how decisions are made. An infrastructure binds people together and gives clear guidelines on how to proceed. Many community development initiatives start with a loosely knit steering committee which can involve a diversity of people. These steering committees typically focus on defining the issues to be addressed, brainstorming, prioritization of issues, goal setting, strategic planning and implementation as well as monitoring and evaluation. These steering committees are designed to eventually dissolve as goals are accomplished.

There are other kinds of infrastructure for community development. Partnerships involve a coalition of key groups and organizations that are instrumental in addressing issues with rules for behaviour and decision-making. These partnerships may be informal or more formal in nature. They can be constructed to be short-term or long term; it depends on the issue, the urgency of the task and the time needed for implementation. Those issues that require a greater sense of urgency and significant involvement will most likely require a more formal structure with by-laws and legally acceptable structure while other partnerships may require more informality.

Some infrastructures are more permanent and are products of democratic participation and decision-making. For example, worker-owned cooperatives are businesses in which employees invest in the company, share in its profits and each person has one vote in decision-making. Consumer-owned cooperatives such as grocery stores or housing units are owned by people who invest to become members and are also involved in profit redistribution and in decisions. In some cases, community development leads to other kinds of permanent structures such as new governmental agencies, non-governmental organizations or other kinds of enterprises. Communities are also able to establish community level committees to address identified concerns. The community development practitioner can therefore serve as a guide in asking questions about structures that are most effective for the task and goals at hand.

In working with a variety of infrastructures, community development practitioners provide various forms of engagement to identify participants' many concerns and issues and to involve participants in ranking their concerns into priorities which become the basis for goals and action steps for implementation.[8]

After a goal has been established, participants can be guided through more deliberation:

- Who needs to be part of the implementation?
- What financial, political, technical expertise or other kinds of resources do we need to implement the goal(s)?
- What are the economic, political and cultural forces that will maintain the *status quo* or impede this goal?
- How can we minimize these negative forces?
- What are the forces that will support the goal?
- How can we build upon the strength of those forces?

In considering these forces, do the goals need to be altered? In answering these questions, participants' sense of agency or capacity building is strengthened.[9]

How Do Community Development Practitioners Support the Development of Capacities for Accountable and Democratic Leadership Within Communities?

Part of the community development process involves facilitation which is rooted in the Latin word, *facilis,* which means "to enable, to make easy." There are many tools that make it easier to work collaboratively. These include ground rules for behaviour such as "respect for everyone; no interruptions when someone is speaking; temporarily suspend judgement about ideas.", agreement on a process of decision-making and how conflict will be resolved. Community development practitioners train and mentor others to be facilitative and participatory community leaders with interpersonal skills of communication, problem solving, and addressing conflict constructively.[10]

How Do Community Development Practitioners Build Upon a Community's Strengths?

The community development practitioner seeks input from the diverse power influence makers in a community while also providing participatory tools such as the identification of the community's cultural, organizational and economic strengths and other assets for their development goals. The community learns more about participatory governance structures, project planning, evaluation practices and other processes for community involvement. Contemporary community development practices focus more on framing the problems or issues a community group wishes to tackle in terms of first building upon the assets and strengths any community has rather than deficits, because community groups can become mired in what they lack which leads to a sense of despondency and inability to think that things can change. When a community understands what exists within it, it can leverage these assets to get what they need. The focus upon community strengths is part of an asset based or community organizing approach that engages individuals across systems that emphasizes renewal and positive change. The emphasis here for the practitioner, is to build upon the positive, while at the same time not underplaying the challenges disadvantaged and vulnerable communities face are very real. The community development practitioner presents tools for the identification of a community's cultural, organizational and economic strengths and assets, together with advice on participatory governance structures, project planning, evaluation practices and other processes for organizational development that are appropriate.

How Do Community Development Practitioners Nurture and Encourage Local Community Leaders to Adopt Democratic, Participative and Inclusive Styles of Leadership for Working with Communities and in Partnerships That Seek to Involve Communities?

Some community leaders may be more inclined to deemphasize democratic and participative perspectives because they view these inclusionary practices as time consuming and inefficient. While it might be true in the short run, it can lead to less acceptance or opposition to goals and actions which does not ensure sustainability of the actions taken, or a feeling of ownership by the wider community. The role of the community development practitioner is to illuminate and support capacity building of participatory leadership skills within the community. This may include connecting local and emerging leaders with leadership programmes to support the development of skills and knowledge in this style of leadership. Those leaders who practice democratic, participative and inclusionary styles are likely to have more influence and acceptance because people feel that their input matters.

How Do Community Development Practitioners Support and Influence Organizations to Develop Work Systems That Promote Effective Community Development?

Top-down decision-making can be alienating for those who invest their lives in an organization because they feel they are incidental and don't matter. Groups and organizations that are open to adopting more democratic and inclusionary practices can become more effective and dynamic. Community development practitioners can provide ideas from other communities, practical tools and skills to make these organizations more vibrant. Community development practitioners work with a variety of infrastructural arrangements to build a more inclusive culture of participation that involves rules for behaviour, processes that use people's time effectively and maximizes participation, and expectations for decision-making.

There Are Some Key Principles Involved in Building a Deeper Sense of Democratic Participation That Come from Community Development Practice

Principle One

"Create a space where people can learn from each other and make their own changes." For example, well-intentioned white community activists in South Africa should not define the needs and aspirations of blacks. They could cooperate in creating a safe space for social transformation, not lead it. In such a space, people can explore options and trade-offs.

Principle Two

Foster dialogue. Essentially, dialogue helps people to learn from each other through peer-to-peer exchanges. It's not only helpful for learning but it helps to build a greater sense of solidarity.

Principle Three

Trust the process and let go of the outcome. Community development practitioners can help connect grassroots efforts through fostering dialogue and networking. However, they have to respect group outcomes and action plans and forfeit their favourite goals or antici-pated outcomes. The role is not to push a certain agenda or attempt to "fix" things, although it is to encourage discussion about the foreseen and unforeseen consequences of adopting a particular action plan.

Principle Four

Encourage participants to reflect and learn from their practice, action and thinking. Questions to ask: What worked well? What mistakes or omissions occurred? What needs to be changed for future action steps?[11]

Role of Community Development Practice in Addressing Conflict

In efforts to move towards a sense of purpose, clarity and cohesion, conflicts may emerge within communities and within community organizations. Not everyone in a community may be in conflict but if key individuals or groups perceive there are sharp differences expressed through bitterness, anger, fear, or an injustice then conflict exists. If this is the case, the community development practitioner can create a safe space where people can explore the essence of those differences without interruption, judgement or being bullied. In other situations, some of the community leaders may be reluctant to cooperate. If that is the case, it sets the stage for how community development efforts will continue. Some community groups may oppose power structures and use legal means, the power of per-suasion or non-violent protests to influence change and achieve their goals. However, others may find these approaches too divisive and will choose to work actively to resolve their perceived differences and find common ground. Whatever course of action emerges, the community development practitioner can create a greater sense of transparency, openness and understanding through ground rules, expectations and an organizational structure to anticipate differences, together with training tools in various approaches to conflict resolution.[12]

Exit Strategies for Community Development

Community development is about creating solidarity, capacity building and sustainability. That's why there is a need for community development practitioners to work with project participants to create an exit strategy from the outset. Exit is a harsh reality of community development because of funding and time limitations. The field often involves deep conversations and rich relationships, but it is not about creating a sense of dependency.

There are several steps involved in preparing an effective exit strategy. It is always gradual and never abrupt. It involves a plan with a focus on sustainability and frequent communication with partners and stakeholders. As projects gets underway and people feel greater sense of cohesiveness and agency, community development practitioners continue to ask how this work is sustainable and how to ensure that expertise and momentum for change is not lost. They can also help communities to plan for access to internal or external expertise, resources and partners for sustainability. The practitioners' eventual exit must not have a detrimental effect on the community initiative. Exits should not be sorrowful. It is important to celebrate successes and reflect on lessons learned along the way as the community development practitioner gradually leaves the project and moves on to other initiatives.[13]

Case Studies

Each of the following five case studies come from diverse regions across five countries - Senegal, USA, Australia, Hong Kong and Scotland. They have been selected to share experiences of community development practice in action and highlight their link to the leadership and infrastructure within IACD's International Standards for Community Development Practice. The case studies provide place-based examples of the standards in practice. While quite different, each of the case studies share a participatory, bottom-up approach to community development with insights about what worked and challenges. From Senegal we see an innovative grandmothers' leadership programme, highlighting the key but often under recognized role of grandmothers, for example in mobilizing communities to stop female genital mutilation. In Kentucky in the USA, the case study reflects on an entrepreneurs' leadership programme set up to support former small tobacco growers as this sector in the local economy declined. The Australian case study looks at how immigrants from the Indian sub-continent have organized community leadership programmes in order to better address issues impacting upon the Indian communities across the state of Victoria. From Hong Kong the case study focuses upon building leadership capacity among young people and supporting their participation in community development programmes, set against a context of growing distrust towards existing institutions. The final case study looks at the work of the Children's Parliament in Scotland, and the support infrastructure this has given to children to have a voice and to become the next generation of community leaders.

Each case study explores elements of the role of community development practitioner in:

1. Supporting groups to review their own practices and policies and external opportunities and threats.

2. Supporting groups to plan for their future sustainability, and to develop strategic and business plans to achieve their aims and objectives.

3. Supporting the development of capacities for accountable and democratic leadership within communities.

4. Knowing how to influence and advise on organizational structures, culture, policies, practices and behaviours to support community development within own and partner organizations.

5. Understanding the political context and the opportunities, challenges and risks arising from it; and support communities and partners to do so and to decide on strategies in that context.

6. Nurturing and encouraging local community leaders to adopt democratic, participative and inclusive styles of leadership for working with communities and in partnerships that seek to involve communities.

7. Supporting and influencing organizations to develop work systems that promote effective community development practice.

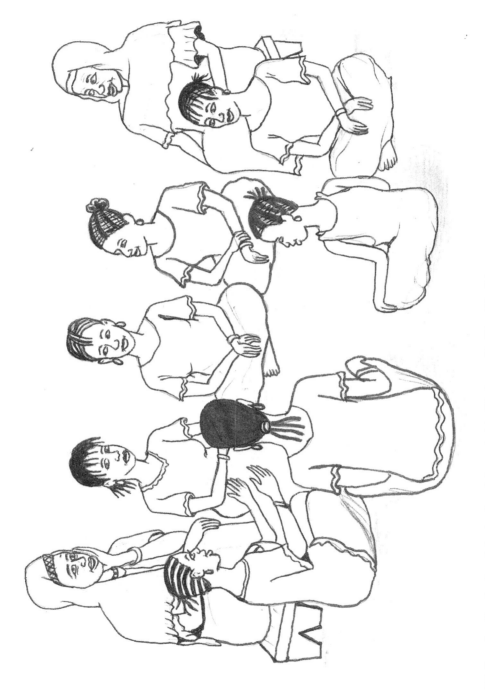

Figure 8.1 Grandmother leaders listening to adolescent girls. Photo credit: Aliou Mbathie.

Case Study 1 – Senegal

Grandmother Project – Change Through Culture

By Judi Aubel

Adolescent girls in southern Senegal face various challenges including limited family support for girls' education, child marriage and teen pregnancy. Numerous non-governmental organizations (NGOs) that address these issues focus only on girls and many have had limited impact. Girls alone cannot change entrenched social norms. A systemic approach is needed that involves those who have the power to change harmful norms that affect girls – parents and elders. Also, in African cultures, grandmothers and aunties are responsible for the socialization of adolescent girls but most programmes ignore the grandmother resource. Based on insights from community development, community psychology and behavioural sciences, the NGO, *Grandmother Project – Change through Culture* (GMP) taps into this abundant community asset, grandmothers, to support girls and promote change in harmful traditions that affect them. GMP discovered, furthermore, that in all communities there are *natural grandmother leaders* who can be empowered to collectively promote girls' wellbeing in families and communities.

In 2005, Dr. Judi Aubel, an American anthropologist and community health educator co-founded GMP with Australian journalist, Elisabeth Mealey. GMP is an American and Senegalese NGO committed to *Change through Culture* by developing community programmes that build on cultural roles and values. Many community programmes in the Global South, do not reflect local cultural realities and this can decrease both community motivation to participate and programme outcomes. A key feature of all non-western cultures is the influential and respected role of elders, and specifically of grandmothers in the lives of women, children and girls.

In 2008, GMP initiated an action research programme to develop a culturally grounded approach to promote Girls' Holistic Development (GHD). An initial participatory community assessment found: weak leadership and social cohesion; and serious breakdown in communication between generations. It also revealed the presence of natural grandmother leaders in all communities. This information informed development of the GHD programme whose goal is to increase capacity of community leaders and groups to promote girls' development by strengthening positive roles and values and changing harmful ones.

To build community-wide consensus for action to protect and promote girls, GHD involves: strengthening the knowledge and confidence of formal and informal community leaders; increasing communication between elders, parents and adolescents; and using adult education methods to catalyze dialogue between generations and between men and women to identify community actions to promote GHD. Participatory learning activities include: intergenerational forums; all women forums; under-the-tree participatory learning sessions with girls, mothers and grandmothers; grandmother-teacher workshops; and grandmother leadership training to optimize the *grandmother resource* for GHD. The IACD Standards theme on leadership and infrastructure was not developed until 2018, but GMP staff realized that collaboration with formal and informal community leaders is essential for any effort to improve community wellbeing.

Grandmother Leadership Training

According great importance to culture, elders and participatory learning, and recognizing grand-mothers' influential role in girls' upbringing, GMP developed an innovative training strategy to reinforce the role of natural grandmother leaders in communities. While the grandmothers involved are illiterate, they are respected and valued members of their communities. This initi-ative builds on this human resource through five interrelated objectives:

1) Strengthen grandmothers' self-confidence in their roles as community leaders.
2) Increase solidarity among grandmother leaders and with other grandmothers in the com-munity to support girls.
3) Strengthen grandmothers' knowledge of the changes that girls experience during adoles-cence.
4) Strength grandmothers' communication with girls using an approach based on listening and dialogue.
5) Increase grandmothers' collaboration with other community leaders to promote GHD.

Rather than conventional western leader–follower notions of leadership, the training promotes shared leadership, reflecting collectivist values of African cultures.

The training programme consists of four two-day-long sessions over 6 months. The training curriculum is based on adult education principles, catered to illiterate participants. It involves a variety of participatory learning activities using drawings, photos, stories, role plays and games. The training took place in twenty communities with 320 grandmother leaders. The trainers are female community development workers from the area who have strong relational, communication and facilitation skills. They challenge grandmothers to revisit traditional atti-tudes and norms and identify the best way to support girls in today's world.

Core Values

This initiative is anchored in an *assets-based approach* where grandmothers are recognized as a key cultural asset that has been underutilized in social change efforts. It builds on grandmoth-ers' wisdom, experience and societal respect to increase their understanding of adolescent development and encourage them to take individual and collective action to support girls. The training curriculum, rooted in the African concept of *Ubuntu*, promotes solidarity and interde-pendency among people. It involves community development principles of participatory dia-logue to strengthen communication among grandmothers, with the girls they mentor, with families and within the wider community.

What Works

Six months after the training, individual interviews were conducted with a sample of 103 grand-mother participants and in focus groups with adolescent girls. The data revealed very positive changes related to training objectives:

- 89% of grandmother leaders reported increased self-confidence as leaders.
- Most grandmothers stated that there is now increased solidarity among grandmothers. They share a common goal of protecting and supporting girls as their mentors.
- Grandmothers improved communication with girls. 100% of grandmothers stated that they changed their communication style with girls to use more listening and dialogue rather than scolding. Girls stated that grandmothers "are no longer giving us orders".
- Grandmothers are collaborating more with community leaders, including males, to address community problems. They have blocked child marriages planned by fathers, have promoted greater family support for girls' education and mobilized communities to stop female genital mutilation and cutting.

Grandmother Project is sharing its *Change through Culture* approach with other NGOs to encourage them to use grandmothers as agents of social change, in programmes on maternal and child health and nutrition, reproductive health, early childhood development, adolescent health, child marriage and teen pregnancy. Given the important role and influence of grandmothers in families and communities across the Global South and this positive experience empowering grandmother leaders in Senegal, we believe that this approach can be relevant in many contexts to address issues related not only to the wellbeing of women and children, but also to a variety of other community issues confronting communities. Strengthening leadership of men and of women of all generations provides the foundation for building solidarity, intergenerational relationships and social infrastructure in communities.

Challenges

Communities' response to GMP's Change through Culture approach is overwhelmingly positive. Challenges faced by GMP arise from extra-community factors:

Western Ageist Values and Bias Toward Youth in International Development

In spite of the fact that elders, and specifically grandmothers, are respected and play critical culturally designated roles within families and communities across the non-western world, western ageist biases contribute to the fact that usually they are not included as key actors in community development programmes. Unfortunately, not only programmes of international organizations, but also those of national governments and NGOs, often reflect ageist values, focusing on younger members of the population. This same critique can be levelled at scholars in the North and South, most of whom use Euro-American concepts and frameworks that ignore the role of elders within families and communities in non-western collectivist cultures.

Funding for Grandmother-Inclusive Programmes

A significant challenge for GMP, related to the previous one, is accessing funding to support Change through Culture, intergenerational and elder-inclusive work. Given the preference of foundations, western governments and individuals to support youth-focused programmes that reflect western youth culture that has been disseminated around the world, it is a challenge to mobilize financial support for GMP's programme. Unfortunately, youth-focused programmes that fail to involve elders actually contribute to further breaking down already weakened relationships between generations and social cohesion within communities.

Learning and Future Plans

There are several key learning points from the Grandmother Project

First, community development practice has discounted the role of elders in social change because of ageist biases and stereotypes. Grandmothers Project has learned that elders can be nurtured to become effective change agents and protagonists to promote change within communities to support families, children and especially adolescent girls in the Global South. Grandmothers are an abundant but underutilized cultural resource for programmes that aim to promote girls' education, reduce teen pregnancy, child marriage and female genital mutilation/cutting.

Second, leadership training for grandmothers has supported grandmothers to reclaim their culturally designated role in the community and has strengthened their sense of empowerment to become stronger community mobilizers to promote the wellbeing of girls, and children more broadly. Given cultural similarities in the role of elders across non-western societies in Africa, Asia and Latin America, it is hypothesized that this training approach would be well received by grandmother leaders across the three continents.

Third, grandmother leaders' collective action has had a significant impact on changing social norms regarding girls' education, child marriage and female genital mutilation and in increasing communication and support to girls to help them avoid teen pregnancy.

GMP aims to continue to share the Change through Culture approach with other NGOs, government departments and training schools. GMP pursues collaboration with universities and graduate students who are proficient in French and who have some prior experience in Africa.

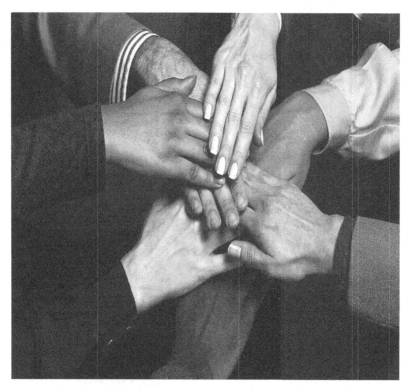

Figure 8.2 Crossing hands. Photo copyright: University of Kentucky Community & Leadership Development Department.

Case Study Two – USA
Kentucky Entrepreneurial Coaches Institute (KECI)
By Ron Hustedde

Tobacco farming has been an important source of income for many rural Kentucky families across generations. It is labor intensive and only involves a modest amount of acreage. However, U.S. federal policies about tobacco changed dramatically in 2002 and many families lost this source of dependable income. There did not appear to be many alternatives to the more lucrative tobacco market.

The question was raised in the tobacco-dependent region: How can we encourage people to become innovators and entrepreneurs to address the needs of others and provide new sources of income? The University of Kentucky community development faculty led focus groups and interviews in the region to explore this question. While there were some modest government small business services, they learned from people in the region that weren't even aware of these services nor did they have a culture or an infrastructure to promote innovation and entrepreneurship. They didn't have a community development infrastructure that involved imagination, listening to the needs or wants of others and exploring business and non-profit opportunities. The University of Kentucky team also learned that grassroots leaders in this tobacco-dependent region were essential in strengthening this potential. They were respected influence makers who did not necessarily hold public office. Their occupations covered a broad range: retail merchant, tobacco farmer, medical provider, clergy, nun, teacher, manufacturer, civic activist and entrepreneur.

Ron Hustedde and Larry Jones, faculty members at the University of Kentucky, worked with key leaders and tobacco farmers to develop a plan. Its major goal was to provide knowledge and tools to these people to strengthen their abilities as entrepreneurial leaders and advocates in the region. It was determined that they needed to learn how to coach potential or existing entrepreneurs in the areas of innovation, market research, competitive advantages, partnerships, marketing, finance and other aspects. Coaching is not about providing advice but asking probing questions to keep the entrepreneur focused on a holistic and healthy business plan. While entrepreneurial coaches do not provide answers to these questions, they can have networks to link entrepreneurs with small business service providers to provide further guidance and insights.

The Kentucky Entrepreneurial Coaches Institute emerged out of this planning effort. It was eventually determined that this tobacco-dependent region needed about 120 grassroots leaders who could learn how to advocate for entrepreneurship in the region and would be able to coach entrepreneurs.

Government funds were accessed to address the entrepreneurial need for tobacco income alternatives. Participants were selected through a competitive process involving interviews and recommendations. Over the course of 5 years, the entrepreneurial leadership programme involved four groups. Each group consisted of 30 people from a particular region. Individuals were selected that reflected a diversity of ages, gender, race, occupations, and various forms of civic engagement.

The eight educational goals that emerged through this effort involved participants, partners and organizers:

1. Build a network of entrepreneurial leaders who could support and encourage each other.
2. Develop knowledge and skills to host or lead events that promote imagination and entrepreneurship.
3. Understand how to work with others to strengthen the visibility and need for a stronger entrepreneurial culture in the region.
4. Learn how to coach budding or existing entrepreneurs.
5. Visit and learn from other rural areas that have fostered and promoted entrepreneurship, particularly agrarian entrepreneurship;
6. Work in small groups to foster entrepreneurship promotional events with youth and others;
7. Make a commitment to donate volunteer hours back to the region to foster greater awareness about the potential for entrepreneurship;
8. Build an exit strategy for sustainability after funding ended.

As the initiative got underway, the organizers decided to integrate the arts as a form of innovation and entrepreneurship in all the classes. For the most part, the artists that were featured came from the tobacco-dependent region; they could be viewed as a unique form of entrepreneurship. They included poets, visual artists, musicians, dancers, and others who brought a sense of delight to educational workshops. In addition, participants visited and learned from a diversity of entrepreneurs in the region. They represented the field of tourism, agriculture, manufacturing, retail, health and unique specialties that served regional, national or international needs. Such exchanges increased the awareness of the entrepreneurial strengths and potential.

Workshops were led by those with expertise from inside and outside the region. They covered topics such as building partnerships to influence change, entrepreneurial coaching tools, various approaches to rural leadership, power and policy-making, youth entrepreneurship, new forms of agrarian and rural entrepreneurship and other related topics. Typically, the workshops relied on principles of adult learning engagement which included small group work, facilitated dialogues, storytelling and the use of art and physical movement to illustrate important concepts. The participants learned how to apply community development principles of community and democratic participation, self-help and self-determination. They were also guided in the problems and limitations of top-down leadership approaches.

After each class of 30 participants completed the 16-month programme, they were required to participate in alumni events for the next two years. These learning events focused on participant accomplishments and shared struggles in their community work. They included "show and tell" events that highlighted a diversity of local entrepreneurs, artists, and pro-entrepreneurship policies and cultural shifts in entrepreneurship awareness and behaviour. These events also strengthened the sense of solidarity among the participants and others about the importance of an entrepreneurial culture.

External evaluators set up an evaluation process with the first 60 participants and University of Kentucky programme leaders to measure impacts such as number of entrepreneurs who were coached, presentations about entrepreneurship to the community and contact with network providers. [14]When alumni gathered, we learned more about the impact of business start-ups and expansions and other initiatives such as youth entrepreneurship contests, entrepreneurial showcases and community-wide programmes about entrepreneurship. The impacts were not immediate. In many cases, workshop participants had more impact when they completed the programme. Based on participant feedback, this initiative led to the creation of over 500 new business starts and expansions. It also provided the DNA for unexpected impacts. For example, one of the participants was instrumental in attracting one million U.S. dollars in federal grants to bring youth entrepreneurship into elementary, middle school and high schools in the region.

Teachers worked with students to prepare them to launch businesses that sold products and services. In another case, a community college in the region launched an entrepreneurial programme and hired one of the participants who did not have a business background to lead this effort. Some participants ran for local office on a pro-entrepreneurship platform or they fostered local government policies that encouraged entrepreneurship and innovation. Some participants concentrated their efforts in local libraries to have exhibits and books to encourage entrepreneurial awareness and the potential for business start-ups. Local newspapers featured the work of participants who fostered "entrepreneurship awareness days" that focused on local business and non-profit entrepreneurs and the potential for untapped markets. These efforts stimulated an appreciation for community economic development efforts in entrepreneurship. One participant claimed, "It takes a whole village to raise an entrepreneur."

While initial funding for the Kentucky Entrepreneurial Coaches Institute was generous, it was clear from the inception that there needed to be an exit strategy when funding would eventually end after the 120 participants were trained and concluded their two-year volunteer commitment. Consequently, the programme organizers stressed to the grassroots leader participants that they had the tools, knowledge, network and mutual support to influence major shifts towards an entrepreneurial culture in the region. The overall goal was sustaining the momentum that started with this effort.

After funding concluded, there weren't any resources for extensive programme evaluation. However, the University of Kentucky programme organizers continued communication efforts to encourage sustainability. The momentum has continued in unexpected ways. The programme has fostered spin-offs for efforts including youth entrepreneurship programmes and contests. Schools in the region are including entrepreneurship into their curricula including social sciences, the arts, business and vocational training. In addition, the local press and business groups have highlighted the work of local entrepreneurs. The programme has had significant impact because it integrated community development leadership principles of democratic participation, and self-determination with the tools and knowledge to build sustainable community and regional infrastructures that foster entrepreneurship.

Figure 8.3 Board members and General Manager of IndianCare – Australia. Photo credit: Harpreet Singh.

Case Study Three – Australia

IndianCare
By Jaya Manchikanti

During the last twenty years, the Indian-born population has increased dramatically in the state of Victoria, Australia. In the main, Indian migrants have settled well in Australia. However, like any other community, there are difficult issues to deal with, such as family violence, intergenerational conflict and struggles of international students, just to name a few. These issues have not been addressed adequately in the past, due to a number of reasons. Therefore, a group of concerned people in the Indian community set up IndianCare to bridge a gap in the service system. This case study is an example of how community leadership and community development infrastructure has led to IndianCare becoming an established and reputable service aiming to achieve better outcomes for people of Indian origin in Victoria.

IndianCare set up as a legally constituted organization in November 2013. This was after a year of deep conversations with key informants in the Indian community and many informal conversations with diverse groups in the Indian community. Meetings were also held with mainstream agencies, such as health services, and government officials. Support and encouragement were provided by the Victorian Multicultural Commission (VMC). The VMC is an independent body that acts as the main link between multicultural communities and the government. In recognition of a gap in the service system, VMC provided seed funding for the formation of IndianCare.

The vision of IndianCare is to enable people of Indian origin in Victoria to achieve their full potential and contribute positively to society. IndianCare has a growing membership base and a structure that includes a Board of Management of eight people, a staff of ten people and a dozen volunteers. Together, the team reflects to a certain degree the vast language, cultural, age and gender diversity within the Indian community. The Board of Management created four subcommittees that report at the bi-monthly Board meetings. These subcommittees are – 1) Policy and Risk Management 2) Finance and Fundraising 3) IT and communications and 4) Human Resources. Strategic planning and evaluation are undertaken regularly, and policies and procedures guide the organization's work. IndianCare is currently working on projects to prevent family violence, reduce harm from alcohol, support international students, provide emergency relief, promote health messages and support during the pandemic, as well as a broader information and referral service.

Community development processes have been maintained throughout the journey of IndianCare. That is, decisions are made by people from the community for the benefit of the community. Feedback is consistently sought from relevant stakeholders. Participative democratic decision-making processes are upheld. For example, many of the projects are guided by steering committees that comprise of relevant community and partner agency representatives. IndianCare applies a strengths-based community leadership approach and a structure that is inclusive, transparent and accountable. A trained community development worker leads the Board of Management in a voluntary capacity and has ensured that community development principles and practices are followed. A trained social worker has been recruited to ensure that welfare services are delivered to quality standard.

The community development practitioner leads by example and works with people's strengths, thereby increasing the involvement and confidence of others to progress the work. The strategic planning sessions and training sessions have enabled participants to grow and improve community development praxis. The community development practitioner is working on a succession plan by mentoring potential leaders and providing them leadership opportunities wherever possible. The enables smooth transition to a new leadership and contributes to sustainability of the organization. The strong mix of community development and social work skill sets, along with the range of other skill sets such as financial, IT, risk and human resources management, policy development, and cultural and linguistic understandings has led to the success of IndianCare thus far. A recent positive comment received was that "IndianCare is a benchmark for its community".

The core values of IndianCare are the following: empowerment; culturally responsive; connection; care; honesty; discretion (i.e. being flexible); professional; dependable; ethical and responsive. The primary assets that have been harnessed are the cultural and linguistic understandings by team members and the deep connections to the large and diverse Indian community in Victoria (approximately 209,000 people of Indian origin). Additionally, the other professional skill sets mentioned above are important in ensuring a good standard of work. IndianCare has enabled people to break away from unhelpful stigma and shame that are huge barriers in the community. IndianCare also works towards building the capacity of mainstream services to better respond to people of Indian origin.

The main strength of IndianCare is the commitment of the team and the passion to work with the community and partner agencies to achieve better outcomes. A lot of effort is placed on supporting and caring for each other. Establishing a robust structure enables IndianCare to be strong and sustainable. IndianCare now receives significant funding from the Victorian government as well as other funding bodies.

The ongoing challenge for IndianCare is to maintain adequate resources to undertake the necessary work and to not be everything for everyone. This challenge is managed as best as possible by forward planning, careful leadership and always staying true to its values and vision.

The key learning from the journey so far is to carefully select people into the community leadership team. Make sure they have the right values and some required skill sets. Additionally, it is important to spend time in planning and reflecting and not being constantly caught up in day-to-day activities. Strategic thinking and robust structures are necessary for good governance, management and sustainability. Finally, never forget to have some joy along the way, as that is the magic ingredient.

Figure 8.4 Tuenmununity formed by a group of youth leaders concerned with primary care of the elderly in Hong Kong. They establish close community relationships by organizing weekly fitness class with the local elderly – Hong Kong. Photo credit: Jackie Ho.

Case Study 4 – Hong Kong, China
Tuen Mun District Council Yan Oi Tong Youth Space
By Kim Cheung

Overall Synopsis

Socio-political conditions and the closing of social systems in Hong Kong have discouraged young people from being involved in community affairs. As a consequence, their social trust and stability in formal institutions is declining. They tend to participate in community affairs outside of formal institutions, such as online forums, concern groups, and social movements. In the long run, the divergence between the youth and the formal institutions becomes larger and consequently, social trust and stability decline.

Social Innovation Incubation Scheme aims to build social networks among youth in the community. It goes beyond the duality of formal and informal community participation. Making good use of advantages of our service units (the social connections of different groups, and institutions in the community), we want to nurture the motivation of community participation among youth in the community through a deeper understanding, proactive action, and personal growth to create meaning and principles of community participation. The goal of this project is to build leadership among youth in the community and develop the infrastructure for the leadership nurturing communities/groups, which emphasizes a constructive and friendly environment.

Background

This project launched in Tuen Mun (the northwest Hong Kong) in 2017 focuses upon youth interested in community work in Tuen Mun. Tuen Mun district council chose Yan Oi Tong to be the partner organization of *Signature Project Scheme: Promotion of Youth Development in Tuen Mun*. Therefore, the district council helped to establish a social innovation centre for youth community participation in Tseng Choi Street Government Services Complex. The project staff consists of social workers, corporate communication personnel, youth workers, and clerks.

In the formulation of this project idea, we realized that the youth in Tuen Mun district are increasingly paying more attention to community affairs. They are willing to express their concerns and participate in change. However, we also noticed the district lacked an infrastructure for them to participate or to recognize their voices. At that time, the district did not have many service units that noticed the desire and motivation of youth interests in community change. This meant that the social services units could not effectively address their needs for community participation through systematic learning, organization, and development. As a consequence, the community missed out an opportunity to co-develop youth leadership and involvement. It led to youth frustration in the community and a sense of powerlessness. This project provides a community development infrastructure for youth between the ages of 15 to 29. It is also structured for the community to provide sufficient support and resources to nurture young people's motivation and capacity of meaningful community participation.

The project goal is to nurture youth community leadership and a culture of proactive community participation. To support participation, we connected different youth lived experience with community issues, nurturing their capacity to pinpoint the policy gaps and provide feasible bottom-up solutions from young people, especially those from marginalized groups. We believe that the birth of community leaders is rooted in a friendly atmosphere for a developmental and sustainable infrastructure of community participation.

The Project

This project brought the youth into the community context. Through the design thinking methods, we encourage the youth to think "out of the box" about the community issues and needs. We employed design thinking, a method in social innovation. It involves five processes:

1) empathy;
2) define (the problem);
3) ideation (design process focuses on idea generation);
4) prototype implementation (from idea to action); and
5) test.

For example, the youth started interviewing the community members to learn more about their social conditions. Based on the interview data, the youth identified the most important community issues and developed potential ways to address these issues with community feedback.

Through their participation, young people learned the meaning of research, community responsibility and community leadership. They learned how to create momentum about community issues and how to identify and mobilize resources. This project served as an incubation hub for youth leadership and community development by providing resources, venues, social trust, promotion, and networks to reduce the barriers for meaningful youth participation. Moreover, this project proactively connected and communicated with youth and the district council's Home Affairs department, and community organizations to implement their community development planning.

Since 2017, we have successfully nurtured 31 teams of between three and ten youth to address the community needs and organize for change. They successfully accumulate useful and practical community experiences through their direction connection with community members. Through participation and constructive feedback, they build positive self- images as community advocates and activists. For example, the team "Tuenmununity" learned that older persons did not have sufficient social life and exercise. The team collaborated with physical therapists to explore using public space to hold community exercises once a week. Regular social gathering, aimed to raise the awareness of fall risk at home, they collected food products, and daily necessities to distribute to older people in the community.

Another team, "HobbyHK", realized that a group of youth in the community had hobbies, with knowledge to mentor others. The project provided a platform for youth to pass down their value, skills, and knowledge about the hobbies to the younger youth. The youth become hobby mentors in primary and secondary schools in the community. They promoted the importance of hobbies for holistic youth development beyond school studies.

Youth and social workers learn from each other to collaborate to maximize the social impact of the change in the community. In the process, youth are encouraged to "own" their initiatives. The social workers support them to go through the design thinking process towards the prototypes. Social workers in this project motivate youth to make use of the prototypes to advocate the structural change about their initiatives. During the process, the social workers provide space, resource, and support to the youth from design of the prototypes to the advocacy. The project aims to develop a youth voice in the community and encourages participation for youth to drive their own initiatives.

Project Values

We firmly believe that the community has their capacity to address any community problems. also. These community problems are often rooted in social system conflicts, such as the inequality of resource access and the lack of participation and power among marginalized groups.

The most important core value was for a bottom-up change, and for young people to build a clear goal for their life from the experience. Moreover, the project staff provided sufficient resource and opportunities for the young people to keep testing their prototypes. With this resource and emotional support, they finally could grow and be confident in overcoming challenges and failures.

To practice the value of social equality, we believe that young people having a creative and alternative mind, play a vital role in social change. We firmly believe that social organization could be a solution to facilitate the community participation through systematic organization to reduce the social isolation and barriers and build up a pathway to participate. We believe that an obvious structural change towards social equality is based on the effort of simple changes in everyday life.

What Worked

This project successfully provided the physical and social space for the youth to experience community capacity building. We emphasized the project as a social innovation experiment. We believe these experiences, regardless of success or failures, help the youth learn the practical insights on how to influence community development.

Through youth feedback, we learned that the project staff played a vital role in accompanying and providing emotional support when youth were facing challenges in their project. Through their mentoring, the project staff reminded the young people that "failure teaches success".

We successfully built the infrastructure which is beneficial for community youth development. We strove to build up a supportive and resourceful collaboration and communication platform to support community collaboration and synergy. We successfully connected with different formal and informal organizations and institutions in the community.

Lastly, we successfully built up the youth community in Tuen Mun community. While the project participants joined the project with similar values and beliefs, the peer group becomes a strong social and emotional backup to every participant. For example, the social network in the group can help the participant line up with different people quickly and keep up the momentum in the learning.

Challenges

The current socio-political unrest in Hong Kong, weakens participant motivation and confidence in creating social change in the community, especially among young people who have limited community development experiences. The project organized support groups to share the sense of powerlessness in the current socio-political situation. We kept the participation channels and the connection work in the community to show "there is life, there is hope" to youth.

The second challenge is the sustainability of the project, while this 6-year project is funded by the Tuen Mun district council. We worry there will not be sufficient resource to maintain a similar infrastructure after this project.

Our Learnings

We learned how to trust the motivation, potential, and capacity of each young person in the community. We learned that supportive platforms for individual and collective idea generation are essential for stimulating a sense of solidarity and build capacity for community change.

We learned project participants are agents for change, instead of being recipients of one-way services. With appropriate support for equal participation, respect, shared spaces and resource, and frameworks for collaboration, young people in the community become community leaders. Community members have an important role to accompany the young people throughout this transformation.

In conclusion, as a youth social service unit, we deeply believe that youth are the future of our society. We need to nurture them by providing them with more exposure to community issues and change rather than de-skill them by overprotecting them. This fundamental value will be emphasized in our future service planning.

Figure 8.5 Members of Children's Parliament in Scotland celebrating 30 years of the United Nations Convention on the Rights of the Child (UNCRC). Photo credit Children's Parliament. 2019.

Case Study 5 – Scotland, UK
Children's Parliament
By Katie Reid

> Rights impact upon your life because they keep us safe, healthy and happy. They're there to help us grow as human beings.
>
> *Member of Children's Parliament, aged 11*

In Scotland, the Children's Parliament provides the leadership and civic infrastructure for children to influence positive changes in communities of place and of interest. This community development initiative supports the Scottish Government and other public bodies to fulfil their legal obligations to protect and promote children's human rights. 1,500 children from diverse backgrounds and a mix of rural and urban settings across Scotland are involved each year. Through the Children's Parliament's human-rights-based approach, children influence policy, practice, legislative, behavioural and cultural changes in state and local government, schools and communities.

Background

Scotland's Children's Parliament was established in 1996. It was founded with the dream that children grow up in a world of love, happiness and understanding. It inspires greater understanding about children's human rights and supports the implementation of the United National Convention on the Rights of the Child (UNCRC). These rights include children's safety, access to education and the right to express opinions and to be heard. Reflecting the IACD International Standards for Community Development on leadership and infrastructure, Children's Parliament provides a structure to support children to express their views, experiences and ideas and to shape their schools, communities, and local and national governments. Children also learn about democratic participation, and their own power as children and to better understand how to work together to make change.

The Programmes

Each year, Children's Parliament works in partnership with schools, social workers and community groups to engage children aged 8–14 in creative, participatory programmes that demonstrate the power of a children's human-rights-based approach in different settings. At a local, community level, children participate in projects and "investigations" exploring rights-based issues children are experiencing and developing "calls to action" to adult leaders who can bring about the necessary changes. For example, the "Imagineers" work in Aberdeen saw children working closely with Aberdeen City Council in the design, delivery and monitoring of services to ensure that Aberdeen is a Child-Friendly City and a Rights-Respecting City.

At a national level, Children's Parliament supports children to participate in government consultations, and legislative, policy and practice developments. Each year, 7 children meet with the First Minister and the Scottish Cabinet to highlight the key issues and recommendations raised by Members of Children's Parliament in the previous year. In 2020, the children's three key issues were: a childhood free from the impact of alcohol; food security; and children's human dignity issues in school.

Core Values

Children's Parliament is committed to forming strong relationships and an infrastructure that provides opportunities for children to exercise their right to have a say, to be listened to and taken seriously.

Children's Parliament is not about advocating on behalf of children but rather about children advocating on behalf of themselves in a positive environment for listening and cooperation. When children come together at Children's Parliament, they are asked to bring their own knowledge, ideas and opinions and explore their differences and commonalities. Children work together to learn to take responsibility and to work in self-directed groups. They also develop friendships, social resilience, confidence and gain new insights from their peers.

> I couldn't communicate before, I couldn't say if I was struggling, but since coming to Children's Parliament, now, I can talk to people, I feel like Children's Parliament really changed me.
>
> *Member of Children's Parliament*

When adults come into the space, they are asked to bring their commitment to listen and welcome children's opinions, and accept the diversity of children's experiences, talents and abilities. When adults and children work together, they can form relationships involving mutual trust, honesty and responsibility in which they can learn from each other. Like adults, children's experiences and perspectives are diverse; they do not speak with, or share, one voice. Involvement in democratic processes supports children and adults to reflect on, and empathize with, their shared and differential lived experiences and perspectives.

While this initiative places a high value on preparing children to become the adults of tomorrow, it places its emphasis on children as citizens of today. When these children's experiences are defined by respect, empathy and human dignity, they become more confident as individuals, citizens, learners and leaders.

What Works Well

According to a 2019 Scottish Government evaluation report,[15] Children's Parliament is effective because it builds relationships that allow children to voice their concerns and opinions about the social and political landscape. It supports early interventions to help children understand their human rights and participate in democratic process while increasing public bodies' understanding and fulfilment of their human-rights obligations to children.

> It's really important that younger children can take part in something like Children's Parliament because they [decision-makers] see things from a children's perspective. It shouldn't just be young people or adults who have a voice. Children should be included too!
>
> *Member of Children's Parliament, aged 11*

Children's Parliament recognizes and values the power of relational, partnership working, and this is clear from its well-established relationships with schools, communities, governmental and non-governmental organizations, and international human-rights committees and networks. Such relationships have supported the organization to demonstrate and amplify its outreach and impact more effectively.

Children's Parliament incorporates play, creativity, intergenerational learning and education into their work. The COVID-19 pandemic crisis has led to more digital involvement to address the geographic isolation of many children in Scotland's remote islands and rural areas.

Challenges

Although there is a growing awareness and understanding of children's human rights in Scotland, there continues to be prominent cultural barriers to accepting and valuing children. There continues to be common perceptions of children as "innocent," "vulnerable," "cute," "naughty," and "unruly," to lacking in knowledge, rationality or experience. All too often, this results in children's contributions to society being dismissed, devalued, or overlooked.

> *I want to be treated more than just a child who plays games and watches TV. I want to be treated as someone who has a voice. I want to be listened to and taken seriously.*
>
> *Member of Children's Parliament, aged 12*

Children's participation, while becoming increasingly recognized as integral to ensuring decisions impacting children's lives reflect and are shaped by the views and experiences of children themselves, continues to be susceptible to becoming a tick-box, tokenistic exercise if not properly understood.

Meaningful participation is all about relationships and this takes time to achieve. Like many organizations, funding continues to be an ongoing concern for Children's Parliament. Some funders want relatively quick results while the nature of this work, which is fundamentally about nurturing a cultural and systemic change towards realizing children's human rights, takes time for involvement and to document outcomes.

Learning and Future Plans

Children's voices are often marginalized or neglected in mainstream community development work. However, Scotland's Children's Parliament demonstrates the pivotal role of children in this field. With similar initiatives taking place in other countries, there is a clear opportunity for international learning and partnership work. While there is rich existing evidence and research about children's meaningful participation in democratic processes more broadly, there is interest in, and a need for, further research exploring and highlighting the intrinsic links between children's human rights and community development.

As the Scottish Government looks to incorporate the UNCRC into domestic legislation in the coming year, it is an exciting, significant time for children's human rights in Scotland. Children's Parliament recognizes that cultural and behavioural change is needed to accompany this legislative change. Children and adults need to understand what respecting children's human rights looks and feels like for children at home, in schools and in communities. Children's Parliament will therefore continue to work with children and adults at the community level, as well as influencing the national agenda, to make sure that children continue to have meaningful opportunities to express their opinions and to be listened to.

Notes

1   L. Botes and D. Van Rensburg (2000) Community Participation in Development: Nine Plagues and Twelve Commandments. *Community Development Journal*, 35(1), 41–58.
2   G. Nossal (2003) quoted in Qualities of good leadership. What is community leadership? Ourcommunity. com.au
3   United Nations High Commissioner of Refugees, The Sustainable Development Goals and Addressing Statelessness, Goal 5: Achieve Gender Equality and Empower All Women and Girls, March 2017. Retrieved on September 10, 2020. https://www.Un.Org/Sustainabledevelopment/Gender-Equality
4   United Nations High Commissioner of Refugees, The Sustainable Development Goals and Addressing Statelessness, Goal 10: Reduce Inequality Within and Among Countries, March 2017. Retrieved on September 10, 2020. https://www.Un.Org/Sustainabledevelopment/Inequality
5   *Towards Shared International Standards for Community Development Practice.* (2018) International Association for Community Development. http://www.Iacdglobal.Org/Wp-Content/Uploads/2018/06/Iacd-Standards-Guidance-May-2018_Web.Pdf
6   L. Veneklasen and V. Miller (2002) *A New Weave of Power, People & Politics: The Action Guide for Advocacy and Citizen Participation.* Oklahoma City, Ok: World Neighbors, pp. 39–58.
7   J. Ife (2016) *Community Development in An Uncertain World: Vision, Analysis and Practice.* 2nd edition. Melbourne, Australia: Cambridge University Press.
8   Community Tool Box (n.d.) Chapter 9, Section 1, Organizing Structure: An Overview. Retrieved on September 1, 2020 from https://Ctb.Ku.Edu/En/Table-Of-Contents/Structure/Organizational-Structure/ Overview/Main
9   R. Hustedde and M. Score (1995) Force-Field Analysis: Incorporating Critical Thinking in Goal Setting, Community Development Practice Issue 4. *Community Development Society.* Retrieved on September 1, 2020 from https://www.Comm-Dev.Org/Images/Pdf/Forcefieldanalysis.Pdf
10 S. Kaner (2014) *Facilitator's Guide to Participatory Decision-Making.* 3rd edition. San Francisco, Ca: Jossey-Bass
11 P.A. Wilson (2019) *The Heart of Community Engagement: Practitioner Stories from Across the Globe.* New York: Routledge Press, pp. 93–120.
12 J.W. Robinson and S.L. Smutko (2011) The Role of Conflict in Community Development. In J.W. Robinson and G.P. Green (eds) *Introduction to Community Development: Theory, Practice and Service Learning* (pp. 101–118). Thousand Oaks, Ca: Sage Publications.
13 R. Hayman, J. R. Popplewell and S. Lewis (2016) Exit Strategies and Sustainability: Lessons for Practitioners. Special Series Paper No. 1. Oxford: Intrac.
14 D. Markley, J. Gruidl, T. Bradshaw and J. Calvin (2007) An Evaluation of The Kentucky Entrepreneurial Coaches Institute: Insights and Recommendations. Rupri Center for Rural Entrepreneurship. https:// citeseerx.ist.psu.edu/Viewdoc/Download?Doi=10.1.1.169.8769&Rep=Rep1&Type=Pdf
15 Evaluation of The Children, Young People and Families Early Intervention and Adult Learning and Empowering Communities Fund: Interim Report, (March 2019) Appendix 2 – Case Study Scottish Government, Social Research Series, pp. 36–37. Issn 2045–6964

Chapter 9

Evaluating and Improving Policy and Practice

Jo Ferrie and Paul Lachapelle

Introduction

Community development is about change.[1,2] This chapter aims to capture how community development practitioners and community groups produce inclusive and participatory methods that are in turn, considered robust enough to produce evidence that triggers impact beyond delivering an individual project goal.

> *We make our own history. The course of history is directed by the choices we make and our choices grow out of the ideas, the beliefs, the values, the dreams of the people. It is not so much the powerful leaders that determine our destiny as the much more powerful influence of the combined voice of the people themselves.*
>
> *Eleanor Roosevelt[3]*

Earlier chapters in this volume allow you to learn about engaging fully with a community to ensure all members are represented: see Chapter Four and the definition of "grassroots" as well as Chapter Five regarding the various methods of change and why they are important. Indeed, much of this book has focused on the local community, for this is where development must start. This chapter begins with the skills required to monitor and evaluate progress toward a community goal. It then moves from this local perspective, to consider how evaluation can inform strategic and operational practice, and in turn lead to wider regional and global impact. The focus moves from activities that center on "having a voice" to mediating with those in power to ensure voices are "heard" and acted upon.

DOI: 10.4324/9781003140498-9

This chapter focuses on methods, and considers specifically participatory action research (PAR), as a toolkit for not only reaching hidden voices, but as a systematic framework by which community voices can be captured and accessed by stakeholders. Stakeholders have been defined in Chapter Four as those who can affect or are affected by a decision, particularly those who are separate from the community because of the power, status, geography or education that they hold. For example, how can success in one community, delivering clean drinking water, supporting a local school, or ensuring adequate housing: help other communities deliver their activities and goals? Fundamentally, a change of policy should trigger impact for many communities. The best way for policies to work, is if they are thoroughly informed by the communities who experience the problem. It is not just the problem, but also the solution that should emerge from the grassroots level.[4],[5] This provides a vital role for community development agencies and practitioners and points once again to the two-way nature of practice. It is about supporting the local community, but also encouraging wider systemic and structural changes by other stakeholders such as local or federal/national authorities, and shared learning through program evaluation with other vulnerable communities seeking to address similar challenges.

Community development practitioners often have a mediation role. Community action is required because those in power (politicians, policy makers, dominant media) often perpetuate, if not increase, inequalities, and simultaneously delegitimize groups who experience exclusion and marginalization.[6],[7] To better support communities, it takes economic investment and in turn, a political commitment to the redistribution of wealth.[8] Redistribution is something that leaders on the left of politics tend to support and those on the political right tend to resist. Even those that support redistribution, may struggle to affect change as they can be constrained by tax law and available revenue, a welfare system that is in crisis management (which is expensive and leaves no resources for investment), or they work in a country without a welfare system (no resource at all).

Community development practitioners then, should develop an understanding of the local and regional governance, and the freedoms and potential to influence positive change. The term ownership in both process and outcome has been presented as one way to frame and promote empowerment in community development efforts.[9],[10] Applying the concept of ownership can determine how the strategic interests and actions of individuals or organizations contribute to community development efforts. It can help evaluate whose voice is heard, who has influence over decisions, and who is affected by the process and outcome.

Evaluating Progress

Two core areas of competence required of all community development practitioners are 1. the ability to evaluate progress within the community development programs they support, and 2. the ability to then present the findings back to project stakeholders, including funders, to the community and to public policy makers.

Program evaluation is simply about trying to measure any changes that have come about as a result of your agency's work with the community. For example, if the focus is about community economic development you could measure the number of jobs and local enterprises created each year or over five years. If the focus is upon an adult literacy or a public health campaign you could measure the number of adults now literate or the reduction in child mortality rates. This type of evaluation is quantitative. It is about measuring "hard" numbers. But in community development practice we are also concerned with qualitative evaluation. For example, the extent to which people involved in a community action campaign feel more empowered. Or the extent to which a minority group feel more included within the wider community. This "softer" information can be collected through individual and group interviews, or anonymously through questionnaire.

Evaluation as a tool is most helpful to a community development program when it is both formative, i.e. ongoing, where you are measuring progress and feeding that back to all involved in order to improve the success of project or activity; and summative, i.e. undertaken at the end of the project or activity, where you require both quantitative data and qualitative information as part of a report to present to funders or government for example.

A community development approach to evaluation lays emphasis upon engaging the community groups you are working with in the evaluation process. The term used here is participatory action research and models of this are explored below. The question to ask here is why would disadvantaged and vulnerable people be interested in getting involved in project evaluation when they are so busy either getting on with their lives or focusing upon getting things done? The reason is that they then "own" the evaluation. In order to engage them to participate in this process, you must be minded as to what support needs they may have in order to spare the time. This is particularly the case when trying to involve those who may not be community leaders and activists within the project, but who are impacted by the issues it is trying to address. Here you will need to address access issues for women in some traditional communities, or for those with disabilities, or low levels of literacy.

All community development programs are required to produce annual reports of their activities for their management committees of funders. Quantitative and qualitative evaluation information generally are at the heart of such reports. This is also a way of reporting back to the community information as to how the project/activity/campaign is going, not least to demonstrate that it has been worth their involvement. Such information can then be used to inform work plans and the setting of new goals for the year ahead.

Evaluation for large programs may require the contracting of external consultants to help with the process. This has the advantage of giving an additional sense of independence over the findings. But when appointing outside consultants it is important that they have experience of working with communities in a participative way. Consultants can be an expensive cost for any community development agency and the community being supported need to have confidence that this money is well spent. External consultants, if they have a recognized brand name can also help open the door to external policy makers. Such consultancy companies or academic institutes may also have public affairs expertise that can advise the community and the development agency on how best to get their evaluation report noticed in the media and that it lands on the right government or corporate desks. Public affairs expertise may already lie within your agency for example if you are part of a well-resourced NGO such as Oxfam or a Community Development Corporation.

By getting this right, those with power are more likely to hear what is coming out of the project and its achievements. This may in turn convince them to give further financial support or to make some policy change as a result of the findings. Presentation of findings is important. Few community members, journalists, grant makers or policy advisers can be bothered to read long turgid reports. Here journalistic type skills can be powerful in engaging the reader: presenting a strong storyline that contains key quantitative facts and qualitative stories. Evaluation reports should always contain images such as graphs that simply show the figures, and photos of the people involved and the problems being addressed. All community development projects should collect visual images throughout the project journey, to include in the report and subsequent presentation. These may be of polluted water supply or the fact that there is only one well in the refugee camp for hundreds of families. If you can get the media to pick up on your story, politicians, funders and others will be more likely to be briefed on the project evaluation.

Hearing Voices of Communities Through Participatory Action Research

As most community development practitioners know, terms like "hidden" or "silent" voices are a misnomer. Community activists call out the inequalities and injustices they face. The failure in communication is most often played out at a privileged level, by voters who champion individual rights and freedoms; policy makers prioritizing issues "popular with voters" to retain power; and private corporate entities who focus on regional targets dominated by economic growth and capital accumulation.[11],[12]

Community development practitioners are required, in part, because community groups who are challenging an injustice and/or long-term inequality also face stigma. This is the institutional marginalizing of their community. This form of discrimination may be intentional, or not. In either case, those in power may have rehearsed, even to the point of believing in, a range of assumptions that delegitimize the community's voice, and by extension their cause. It is harder for policy makers to resist hearing and recognizing community voices, if the voice is a collective one. Many of the chapters in this book will help community development practitioners work with communities to produce this collective voice, and Chapter Seven on diversity and inclusion is a useful resource in particular.

Participatory action research (PAR) is a range of tools used to hear and represent communities. It aims to deliver a high standard of robust data analysis and can be used with different kinds of data collection to optimize usefulness for each community. At its foundation, PAR encourages changing practices with an emphasis on democratic involvement, challenging hierarchies and power imbalances, and critically addressing real-life community-level problems. A PAR orientation places an emphasis on collaboration with the local community.

For marginalized groups, even a fully accessible process may be difficult to engage with, as they have not "practiced" what they wish to say. This is due to the stigma they may have experienced[13] and the extent to which they have internalized this stigma, and feel that change is not possible. Community development practitioners then have a role in ensuring that there is diverse and inclusive participation. The time spent in and with communities is a key investment in order to build trust, skills and ownership.

Data is understood here as evidence of the life experienced by the community (simply put: identifying barriers) and what they want to change (solution). As well as traditional interviews or focus groups, using photographs, making documentaries, or art and craft projects[14] can be used as a way to engage all members of a community regardless of age, communication ease, confidence or education. A single PAR project may use more than one method of data collection in order to allow different parts of the community to engage optimally. Often, the kind of data collection selected, is chosen with the community,[15],[16] and thus all decisions are made collectively. This approach will aid a community development practitioner to make engagement accessible and hear the broadest range of voices. Transparency in process and outcome is also imperative to ensure trust and positive relationships moving forward. In practice, this means that PAR works at two levels: repeated actions; and repeated periods of reflexivity, also known, as critical evaluation.

After each action, a period of reflection allows the community with the development practitioner to consider: what was gained; what should be achieved next; whether the goal can still be reached; or if planned activities need to evolve. This phase may also consider if the data collection used should still be applied to hear more people, or whether it should be modified to hear different groups of people. The next agreed action is performed, and then another period of reflective working happens and so the pattern continues until the goal is reached (see Figure 9.1): this process could take weeks or years depending on the size of the community and the ambition of the project. It is vital, that the community are as involved in this phase, as with the action-work to produce inclusive and organic development of activities.[17],[18]

Community development practitioners have a key role in monitoring both these types of progress. It is not just the action that should be recorded and monitored to help gauge progress toward the goal, but the reflective work to evaluate how cohesively the community is working together, and how well members are represented.

If successful, PAR is a toolkit that can synthesize the concerns of a community into a collective voice and "findings" or outputs that are recognized as "legitimate" to policy makers. Findings should not be passed over to those in power, however but trigger opportunities for those in positions of power to work directly and in collaboration with community activists and community development practitioners on what happens next.

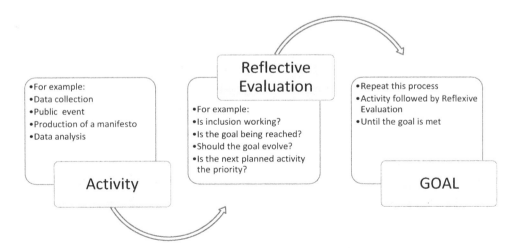

Figure 9.1 The dynamic flow of activity and reflexivity toward community goals.

Thinking Globally: Sustainable Development Goals as an Impetus for Change

Community groups that have faced stigma, inequality and injustice will arguably need more support to adjust their messages and community development practitioners must work with this difficult tension of retaining authenticity and producing an argument that policy makers will engage with. It is not just the community or grassroots that must re-skill for impact to occur, those in power must also learn new ways of working and there are many open to this.

There is increasing pressure on policy makers to work with communities. As outlined in Chapter One, the climate crisis and increasing gaps between the richest and poorest have led to the development of the Sustainable Development Goals (SDGs). As a global initiative, this strategy was distinct in how it collaborated with community groups as well as engaging with those in power (economic and political) to agree the goals. The SDGs have been adopted by most nations, at least partially and in addition to meeting the goals themselves, these nations have also committed to embracing inclusive practices[19] as they develop new policies generally. In this way, there is a "top-down" force upon policy makers who need to engage meaningfully with community groups in order to demonstrate their commitment to the SDGs. There is opportunity here, and community development practitioners who can demonstrate the link between fairly generic-termed SDGs and the specific goals[20] as set out by a community group, will be well-placed to harness it.

In moving to activities that can have impact beyond the community (for example, create regional policy), community development practitioners must recognize their role in reminding those in power, that to deliver against global progress targets such as SDGs, then policy must be informed by communities (bottom-up pressure). Thus, while the framework exists for communities to impact on policy, those in power must be held to account for this to be delivered in practice.

Collective Impact: A Potential Framework for Engaging Those in Power

Inclusive working, and dismantling of traditional, hierarchical ways of working, requires a commitment from policy makers to engage in new ways moving from a management role to an ally role, and one framework that could help is Collective Impact (CI) .[21,22] This framework is useful if community activists remain central to all activities, and progress toward their goal is monitored. CI requires five conditions to be met:

1. a common agenda;
2. a shared measurement system;
3. mutually reinforcing activities;
4. continuous communication; and
5. a backbone of support organization.

To impact policy, the conditions should co-exist and be mutually beneficial, rather than be seen as distinct and individual achievements on the pathway to impact. The final condition "a backbone" may be understood as the role played by community development practitioners, who are dedicated professionals working with the other actors toward a defined goal, and thus acting as a resource that all others can utilize.

For this "structure of practice" to work in community development may require practitioners to not only mediate, but translate, apply method (such as PAR to deliver measurement, the second condition) and draw links between community-level local goals and activities, and global level goals and activities, for example the SDGs. Thus, the community development practitioner translates (communication, the fourth condition in the list above) bottom-up pressure from communities, and top-down influence of SDGs (reinforcing activities, the third condition) to help those in power produce new, useful, and inclusive policies (a common agenda, the first condition).[23],[24]

It is important to establish that all allies (from the community to those in power) are enthusiastic about the common agenda.[25],[26] This may seem common sense, but for the community activists their goal will feel essential, and so the community development practitioner could have a role in helping the community choose their allies as they move their activities toward wider impact. That is, to work with those in professional and leadership positions, who are committed to reforming policy.

Even if the five conditions are met, impact on policy is not guaranteed.[27] To imagine the role of a policy maker with relative status and power: they need do little to join the table created by the CI structure of practice. Rather a great deal of re-skilling and learning terminology is required of the activist, and similarly the community development practitioner is given responsibility for the labor and success becoming the "catalyst" (though potentially with others) of any action. In this way "risk" lies with the community activist and practitioner, but not with the policy maker. One argument to help policy makers invest their time, is that by generating the solution at the local level using community experts, then any investment is likely to be successful, and cheaper in the long run (versus long-term investment which does not really solve the problem). In one of the first academic reviews of this approach, Mayan, Pauchulo et al. conclude that where it has worked, CI has been used to develop a "common language"[28] around the goal, and commitment to the series of activities required to deliver the goal. For community practitioners then, CI is a framework in the sense that it can help deliver the building blocks toward social change, but requires other tools, such as PAR to ensure that the goal and work toward the goal are driven by activists.

To explore these themes usefully, a series of case studies follow. Derived from real-life projects, the case studies focus on six key areas toward impacting beyond a community goal:

a. Review and evaluate community development activities and practice using participatory methods.
b. Support community groups to use monitoring and evaluation to reflect on progress, learn from experience, evidence impact and inform future action.
c. Assess the evidence from evaluations of community development activities and analysis of the wider social, political, economic and environmental context to inform the development of policy and practice.
d. Incorporate critical reflection processes into our work, in order to identify and apply learnings, and continually improve our practice.

e. Prepare accountability and evaluation reports for one's agency, funders and other stakeholders, including impact measures.

f. Work alongside community groups as engagement with policy makers increases to ensure activists are central to decisions.

The first of five case studies focuses upon the establishment of the community development learning and evaluation framework within Scotland by which community development practitioners can evaluate their own practice and the success they can build with community groups. This case study champions the significance of transparency around community engagement, and strong evaluation of how inclusion, participation and democracy were achieved within any activity. The second case study, located in Montana, USA illuminates the "catalyst" elements and considers the significance of funding and status in protecting and legitimizing the activities of practitioners. Further the study emphasizes the need for critical evaluation of practices and full and careful inclusion of the community. The third case study takes us to Canada, and demonstrates with a focus on poverty alleviation, the value of evaluation and the resulting evidence-base to influence decision making across several cities. The fourth, re-centralizes activities of communities by introducing a case study from Cameroon that covers environmental progress, combats lived poverty and harnesses the power of inclusive conferencing to aid reflection and trigger new action. The final case study reflects on an ongoing project in Hong Kong, as it focuses on multi-dimensional barriers that are facing disadvantaged communities as they optimize health during the covid-19 pandemic. This allows us to see the importance of grounding action in community concerns and realities, and also highlights the significance of delivering change even where there is not time to manage lasting policy shifts.

Figure 9.2 Outcome-led participatory planning workshop in progress – Scotland. Photo credit: Stuart Hashagen.

Case Study 1 – Scotland, UK

Supporting Best Practice in Community Development

By Alan Barr and Stuart Hashagen

The 1970s saw a fast-growing interest in community work as a strategy in social and public policy in the west of Scotland with a cohort of over 400 community workers and portfolio of community projects established in virtually all disadvantaged neighborhoods. By 1990 it might have appeared that the existing high level of investment in community development and the emergent trend toward more participatory and accountable public services would not be fertile ground for another new initiative.

However, research into the social work department of Strathclyde region,[29] had identified many examples of positive work but overall a lack of clarity about the role of community development practitioners, systematic performance measurement and clearly defined outcomes, and means to share learning and apply lessons. Literature offering critical analysis was also largely absent. Strathclyde's own assessment of the broader community development approach that they hoped would be adopted by all staff showed a lack of understanding of what this might mean in practice. This general uncertainty about more accountable public service provision was echoed elsewhere in Scotland notably in health and community education. Some form of initiative was needed to address these concerns. The Scottish Community Development Centre (SCDC) was established in 1994 as a partnership between the University of Glasgow and the Community Development Foundation, adopting the strapline to represent its core purpose – "Supporting Best Practice in Community Development".

But what is best practice and how can it be promoted? The SCDC sought to define this and to develop strategies to cement it across practitioners, employers (especially in the public sector) and in communities. Here we set out the SCDC understanding of what best practice entails and how this was supported and encouraged.

The starting point for SCDC resources and programs was always rigorous research, grounded in participatory action research, into the need or issue of concern. The first commissioned study[30] of the contribution of community education to community development in Scotland reinforced the need for clarity about the purposes of community development and more rigorous planning and evaluation. Early work therefore focused on these issues. The core elements of community development practice were later codified in the Achieving Better Community Development (ABCD) model (see Figure 9.3).

SCDC also took the view that communities would be much better able to argue their case if they were able to provide sound evidence from participatory action research into local experience of key issues, and to use this evidence constructively in negotiations with responsible bodies. SCDC supported a large number of community organizations in this way through the SCARF (Scottish Community Action Research Fund) program and successors up to the present day with the Knowledge is Power program.

Working out what "best practice" signifies requires a framework that identifies the core components of community development (and also what it isn't). The ABCD model emerged from extensive discussions with experienced practitioners (funded by government agencies across all nations of the UK and Ireland) which led to a model that proposed that the highest-level purpose of community development (CD) was to enable communities to be "sustainable, livable and equitable". Pursuing this outcome, the model proposed that community whether of place, interest or identity; development needs to pay equal attention to:

- Learning – personal development of confidence, skills and understanding
- Social justice – positive action on prejudice, discrimination, disadvantage and powerlessness
- Organization – supporting and sustaining independent service providing and campaigning community-led organizations
- Influence – seeking to change the policies and actions of governmental and any other interest detrimental to the interest of the community

All four would need to be evident for any agency to describe its role as community development. Specialist and non-CD agencies would be encouraged to adopt these principles.

The model (see Figure 9.3) then set out the various domains where the aspects of organization and influence would have a positive impact in communities. These included community economic development (a working community), community health and care (a caring community), community environmental action (a safe and healthy community), community arts and recreation (a creative community) and engagement with governance (a citizens' community). With significant progress in these five domains the overall goal of livability, sustainability and equitability could be attained.

The ABCD Handbook was the first key resource published by the SCDC. It was shortly followed up with LEAP (Learning Evaluation and Planning) .[31] This took the

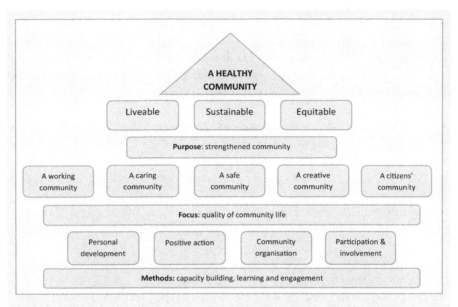

Figure 9.3 The ABCD model: a framework toward a healthy community[32]

essence of the ABCD model and incorporated it into an outcome-led planning and evaluation framework.

SCDC had always argued that clear purpose and thoughtful planning were
the core of good practice. The LEAP framework provided an integrated planning and
evaluation cycle that started with evidence of need and the definition of the desired
outcomes - how things would be if the need was addressed. The next step was agreeing on outcome indicators - the ways in which the initiative would be able to understand whether the outcome was being achieved. All stages of the process would be
discussed and agreed among the key interests in the project or program. Attention
would then turn to the resources that would be needed (inputs), the methods that
would be used (processes) and what would actually be done, by whom and when (outputs). Consideration would also be given to the motivation, opportunity and capacity
of each participant to assist or hinder the process. This would form the action plan;
progress would be reviewed at regular intervals (monitoring), and, using the evidence
gathered, periodically work would be evaluated against the outcomes. If the needs had
not been fully addressed the cycle would re-start, with revised or refined outcomes
in place.

The third element in the practice development suite was the National Standards for Community Engagement, commissioned following a Ministerial Review of community empowerment. As with ABCD and LEAP, this was designed through extensive
engagement with practitioners and their employers in local government, health, police
and a number of third sector organizations. The Standards set out ten areas in which
the relationship between community organizations and their members or constituency,
and the relationship between public bodies and community bodies could be assessed,
and where the characteristics of a "good" relationship could be understood and worked
toward. The standards sought to ensure: equalities, respectful dialogue, effective

planning, and many other areas. Again, as with ABCD and LEAP extensive training and support was built into the dissemination strategy, and the Standards benefited from being endorsed by a wide range of government and service agencies and community and third sector bodies.

The SCDC subsequently published further practice development resources building on the ideas in the three key elements described. These included:

- VOiCE (Visioning Outcomes in Community Engagement) which combined LEAP and the National Standards in a digital form
- LEAP online, which like VOiCE could be used across projects and programs digitally
- LEAP for Health, which adopted a social model of health improvement and linked it to the LEAP model
- Building Stronger Communities, which drilled down into ABCD to provide a resource for strengthening community organizations

The SCDC always gave priority to enabling organizations and staff to support and learn from each other by hosting networks of common interest. The first of these was CHEX, the Community Health Exchange which supports community-led health initiatives across Scotland. More recently similar networks on co-production and participatory budgeting are in place.

As already indicated, ongoing training and support for best practice was central. Several programs were designed to include a funded program of training, planning and learning events. Aside from those already discussed, the CHEX, for example, runs a Health Issues in the Community program, designed to give local activists a basic grounding in community work, delivered by practitioners who have been through the training.

Both before and after Scottish devolution, the SCDC has been fortunate to work in a political and policy environment broadly supportive of community participation. The programs discussed above were all funded directly or indirectly by government in Scotland (and more widely in the case of ABCD). Since 1994 the level of direct funding to community work in local authorities has reduced but government policy retains a high level of commitment to community participation in public services. Community development is now predominantly delivered by a wide range of local or national organizations primarily in the community/voluntary sector: health, housing, environment, economic development and equalities among many others. This has led to some dilution of the capacity building elements of community development and suggests a need to encourage more coherence and collective endeavor across this wider, but potentially more influential sector.

Figure 9.4 One Valley Community Foundation, Montana, USA. Photo credit: Armstrong Marketing, Bridget Wilkinson and Macleod Photography.

Case Study 2 – USA

Critical Reflection of Community Philanthropy

By Paul Lachapelle

Critical reflection of the role of community philanthropy can provide insights into persistent community development problems. Evaluating community philanthropy is often initiated with metrics and measures of how much capital is raised and where the funds are allocated. However, there are other measures of community success and the potential to advance community policy and practice. Community foundations are one way that communities can reflect on and act in a way that is inclusive, participatory and that builds not only community capital but also community capacity. Evaluating this capacity building potential is critical to ensuring that current policy initiatives are successful, and that future actions will be planned and implemented. This case study outlines the importance of measuring community philanthropy impacts through community capacity building of leadership, trust and relationships in one small community, Bozeman, Montana in the western United States.

With a dry continental climate and 300 days of annual sunshine, proximity to natural amenities (100 miles from Yellowstone National Park), low crime rate, and technology and healthcare industry boom, the town often makes Top 10 lists; for example, Outside Magazine named Bozeman a Top 10 finalist in its "Best Towns Ever" competition.[33] Bozeman was listed on Bloomberg Businessweek's list of "The Best Places to Raise Your Kids 2012".[34] In short, the secret is out, and many are flocking to this community that locals refer to as "that university town with a ski problem."

The area has long been recognized as a unique destination. In the mid-1800s, Colonel Robert G. Ingersoll, a civil war veteran and accomplished attorney was cresting Bozeman Pass in southwest Montana, in the United States and noticed the brilliant lush fields of green and gold below. He turned to the stagecoach driver to ask the location; "that sir, is the Gallatin Valley" by which Ingersoll replied, "Ah, it is a dimple on the fair cheek of nature.".[35] Bozeman, Montana has become a popular destination for residents and visitors alike since settlers first came to the area generations ago. With approximately 40,000 permanent residents, the area is now the fastest growing city in Montana; population in the area is expected to grow by an additional 30,000 residents by 2050.[36]

Rapid growth presents unique challenges for those concerned with equity, vitality and prosperity. Among the relevant questions for a community experiencing this type of growth are: what are the best methods for policy planning and implementation of community and economic development projects? How are housing and cost of living issues best addressed? In what ways can the public and private sector address growth issues? What is the role of philanthropy in promoting community development? How can community philanthropy play a role in community development policy implementation?

Defined as community savings banks, community foundations are emerging as an important and effective method of promoting community dialogue about present needs and future priorities. Community foundations are non-profit public charities that manage endowed funds for individuals, families, corporations, and non-profit organizations and grant money back to a community or region. These foundations are run by a board of directors who are typically volunteers from the community serving the role of providing collective oversight of the investment and distribution of community funds. In this spirit, the community foundation is in essence, the *community's* foundation. Perhaps more importantly, community foundations allow for community members to engage in critical conversations and reflections about the present and future vision of the community, determine leadership capacities, strengthen relationships and build trust, and work to prioritize the needs and aspirations of the community. In short, community foundations hold great potential as spaces for citizens to engage in the development of their community to advance from survival to prosperity.

Serving an estimated 86% of the US population, there are over 700 community foundations in the US with over $50 billion in permanently-endowed funds; they provide almost $4 billion in grants to communities each year.[37] Yet, the potential for community foundations to influence not only fundraising for local non-profits as well as their endowments is great. Perhaps just as significant is their ability to galvanize support for community policy change.

Since 1999 the One Valley Community Foundation has served the Bozeman area and grown its assets to nearly $1 million and distributed more than $300,000 in grants to more than 100 local non-profit organizations. In 2014, the foundation nearly doubled its giving from 2013 by distributing $20,000 through a competitive grants cycle to twenty-five local non-profit organizations. The mission of the foundation is to enhance the present and future quality of living in our community through innovative charitable activities that provide leadership, identify charitable needs, and galvanize resources.

The current board of directors are made up local volunteers from the area who set policy, determine strategic direction, and oversee operations. In 2013, the foundation hired their first Executive Director, Bridget Wilkinson. The board evaluates its success by being open to all citizens in the area with active recruitment of a diverse and representative membership while at the same time recognizing the necessity to provide the public an opportunity to participate and be directly engaged in activities and decision making.

The board also measures success by ensuring the grant making process is open to the community who can actively participate and contribute to decision making regarding how funds are distributed. Community members are actively recruited and invited to participate in the process of selecting projects and amounts. In this way, the foundation espouses a participatory approach to decision making about community issues. The many grantee stories detail narratives of active community participation; where the donor interacts with local non-profit organizations through community members and volunteers and the foundation serves as a catalyst for community participation, relationship building and decision making. In addition, community foundations are becoming credible organizations for engaging a community in critical conversations about the future direction of development in a community as well as a method of raising significant capital for community projects.

The foundation also measures success by actively promoting leadership development particularly focusing on a younger generation of leaders. Wilkinson argues that community foundations serve to provide and develop leadership in a community:

> We can function at that catalytic level, by providing the space and the opportunity for leadership in the community to be developed. The foundation provides opportunities in the non-profit sector. We can help inspire leadership and provide opportunities to act. For example, members of non-profits can present at the monthly forums we host to share information, network, and better coordinate work of mutual interest.

The foundation also develops youth leadership through events. Wilkinson adds, "We can develop leadership through our youth giving project which creates goals for youth in terms of learning budgeting and public speaking." She adds that her personal leadership skills have evolved as a result of her position in the foundation:

> What I've realized is that my leadership style is leading from behind – by empowering others to lead and step up. I've learned the value of listening as a leader. When people feel listened to, they feel trusted, and work gets done.

The foundation also measures success by serving as a catalyst for cooperative community spirit and trust building. Currently, the foundation is exploring partnerships with the local university and school districts. Ideas include developing opportunities for students to learn about board governance, investment options, and financial planning. Through these partnerships come new relationships, increased trust and a renewed sense of cooperation and collective spirit. For Wilkinson,

> *trust is our greatest growth opportunity. Two years ago, people were skeptical of the foundation because they didn't know us. My first few months, my goal was to build that trust and for the community to know that we are providing a value-added service to community. We need the community to know that we are going to invest in this place and you can trust us to be an ally.*

Wilkinson has been busy meeting with stakeholders, non-profits, and city and county officials talking about the role the foundation can play in the community, adding, "it took time, but we are starting to see the fruits of those relationships. People think of us now when they think of philanthropy." Yet, she further explains:

> *Part of the work we do is stewarding community assets for today and tomorrow, and those assets are critical in terms of our future. But the role of community foundations is to impact the community in a variety of ways, not just financially.*

In Bozeman, this sector of community philanthropy is providing a critical response to the issue of growth and planning. The community is better informed of the potential growth of the transfer of wealth sector and in turn is better engaged in conversations of community investment. Perhaps more importantly, community foundations are illustrations of a community's capacity to promote leadership in youth and adults, to strengthen relationships and built trust, and to work to prioritize the needs and aspirations of the community to transition from survival to success. For this community foundation, measuring how and where funds are distributed is just as critical as assessing the development of community capacity around leadership, trust and relationships.

Figure 9.5 Evaluating Communities – Canada: Image credit: Laura Zikovic in collaboration with Bastian Publishing Services Ltd.

Case Study 3 – Canada
Vibrant Communities[38]
Tamarack Institute[39]

In April 2002, leaders from the non-profit sector, people with first-hand experience of poverty, civil servants and private sector representatives from thirteen Canadian cities met in Guelph, Ontario. They gathered because they were "relentlessly dissatisfied" with existing efforts to reduce poverty and were eager to explore new ways of tackling the problem. During these sessions, they developed the Vibrant Communities (VC) initiative, a pan-Canadian network committed to substantially reducing poverty through cross-sector collaboration and compre- hensive local action. Tamarack – an Institute for Community Engagement, the Caledon Institute of Social Policy, and the J.W. McConnell Family Foundation provided matching grants, policy and research support, cross-community learning opportunities, and coaching in exchange for the communities' commitment to rigorously document and share their learnings so others in the network could benefit from their experience.

Rather than a model to be replicated throughout the country, VC was developed as a set of core principles adapted to various local settings, plus a set of national supports to facilitate these efforts. To generate significant reductions in poverty, sponsors and participating communities developed five core principles:

- Poverty reduction
- Comprehensive thinking and action
- Multisectoral collaboration
- Community asset building
- Community learning and change.

The underlying theory was that, guided by these five principles, and assisted by extra program supports provided by national sponsors, local organizations and leaders could revitalize poverty reduction efforts in their communities and generate significantly improved outcomes.[40]

The Vibrant Communities project targeted people from the thirteen trail-builder communities who were experiencing poverty first-hand. The outcomes and findings of the VC initiative have been documented in a number of ways over the nine years. Trail-builder community staff prepared statistical reports of the initiative every six months. VC staff and communities prepared a series of mid-term assessments between 2004 and 2007. C.A.C International completed two interim evaluations on the impact of national supports to the project. The Caledon Institute wrote several reflective reports. VC completed a two-phase evaluation report at the end of the nine-year Vibrant Communities experiment. The conclusions presented in the report were developed and refined through a user-oriented process. Priority questions were identified in consultation with internal and external stakeholders. Key representatives from the participating communities and national sponsors participated in a process of analysis and interpretation facilitated and supported by an external, independent evaluator. As a formal research project, Vibrant Communities was completed at the end of 2011.[41]

The outcomes-based evaluation and planning methodology that was examined in the literature review on community development evaluation commissioned by Community Waitakere, are evident across much of the VC evaluation work, including participant community reporting, mid-term assessments and end-of-evaluation reports.

The philosophy of Appreciative Enquiry and Asset-Based Community Development are also evident in the VC evaluation work, where the strengths and assets of communities are the core focus and starting point for program development. Aspects of this kind of thinking is evident in the adoption of the Sustainable Livelihoods Framework.

Across the evaluation projects, a range of qualitative evaluation tools are being used, such as focus groups and interviews with evaluation stakeholders, which were used to generate questions to guide evaluation work.

The Sustainable Livelihood Framework is an evaluation method and tool in its own right, applicable to various levels of details and utilized in both program planning and evaluation.

Table 9.1 Details of the evaluation work undertaken over the course of the Vibrant Communities project.

Evaluation Activity	What Is Measured
In 2004 VC staff completed Reflections on Vibrant Communities, which reports on The Face-to-Face forum held in September 2003. The forum provided participant communities with an opportunity to reflect on some of the key lessons and observations from the first eighteen months of the program in order to refine their strategies.[42]	What is the added value of these initiatives? What is the primary target household level outcomes or community-level change?
In 2005 C.A.C. International was externally commissioned to complete *Mid-Term Assessment of the Vibrant Communities Initiative*, which focused on VC's learning initiatives (Pan-Canadian Learning Community) and involved detailed questionnaires and follow-up interviews with representative of each of the participating communities.[43]	Measure effectiveness of the Pan-Canadian Learning Community initiatives and put forward recommendations for change.
In 2006 VC staff completed *Understanding the Potential and Practice of Multisectoral, Comprehensive Efforts to Reduce Poverty: The Preliminary Experiences of the Vibrant Communities Trail Builders.*[44]	Explores how the VC principles have been applied by the communities.
In 2006 VC staff completed *In from the Field: Exploring the First Poverty Reduction Strategies Undertaken by Trail-Builder in the Vibrant Communities Initiative.*[45]	Describes specific strategies implemented by communities. Identifies unifying themes and patterns.
In 2007 VC staff completed *Reflecting on Vibrant Communities 2002–2006.*[46]	What is VC? How did it come to be? What difference is it making?
In 2007 the learning and evaluation process for trail-builder communities was upgraded to incorporate the Sustainable Livelihoods framework, which was adapted from a model developed by the UK's Department for International Development and adjusted for use in Canada. It is a holistic, asset-based framework for understanding poverty and the work of poverty reduction. It can be applied to various levels of detail – as a broad conceptual framework or as a practical tool for designing programs and evaluation strategies.[47]	The individual and household outcomes achieved by each project and community.
In 2010 Imprint Consulting was commissioned to work with VC staff to produce phase one of the end-of-campaign evaluation Evaluating Vibrant Communities (2002–2010).[48]	What constitutes the VC model? What is the performance of the VC approach with respect to poverty reduction? What is the experience of applying the VC approach in different communities?

Through a process of continuous evaluation, VC were able to set targets and measure outcomes throughout the project. Some of the key numbers reported by the 13 communities over nine years include:

- 322,698 poverty reducing benefits to 170,903 households in Canada
- 164 poverty-reducing initiatives completed or in progress by local trail-builders
- $19.5 million invested in local trail-builder activity
- 1690 organizations partnering in trail-builder communities
- An additional 1,080 individuals serving as partners, including 573 people living in poverty
- Thirty-five substantive government policy changes[49]

The Vibrant Communities (2002–2010) Evaluation Report was published and distributed on the completion of the project. A more comprehensive summary of findings was published in a book edited by Paul Born.[50]

The primary audience of VC evaluation is the staff and board members of sponsoring organizations, the key volunteers, staff and organizational partners and the funders and institutional partners that have made significant contributions. The secondary audience for the evaluation is composed of other people and organizations that might be usefully informed by the experience of VC.

Throughout the project, the thirteen participating communities provided feedback on their outcomes and learnings with national sponsors and their peer communities. Every six months, they provided an update on key statistics related to their local work; annually they also provided a report that explored their progress, challenges and learning in more depth.

Figure 9.6 Soulédé, a village in the Mayo-Tsanaga division in northern Cameroon. Photo credit: Moussa Bongoyok.

Case Study 4 – Cameroon

Empowering Partnerships and Supporting Communities in Francophone Africa

By Moussa Bongoyok

The abject poverty in which many African citizens live calls for policy action. Higher education institutions can play a critical role. This case study focuses on African French-speaking nations as they occupy a strategic place in Africa with over thirty countries having French as one of their official languages or widely using French in the educational system and business.

Although most universities in the French-speaking context focus on the education of the elite of the society, the *Institut Universitaire de Développement International* (IUDI), based in Cameroon, and serving all the French-speaking nations, has opted for a different approach. It educates students up to the Ph.D. level while at the same time connecting them with the members of the society who were not fortunate enough to pursue studies at college, high school and primary school levels. Since 2012 a strategy at the IUDI is to connect students and faculty to communities so they can collectively pursue policy actions to achieve sustainable holistic development.

One method used to advance policy goals is the use of community development conferences that bring together community leaders from various French-speaking nations for up to two weeks in Cameroon. During these interactions, university professors and practitioners present papers on different facets of the central theme through the lenses of an interdisciplinary policy approach. Adequate time is set aside for workshops, small group discussions, and visits to relevant communities or projects. Before the end of the conference, participants write and submit an action plan so that the training yields results in communities. A follow-up system is put into place to maintain communication with all participants reviewing progress on the action plans.

Another method of policy action is the initiation of model community projects with the active participation of members of the most impoverished villages. One such project is the Moringa Project initiated in several villages of the Mayo-Tsanaga division in northern Cameroon. This project was conceived after careful field research using interviews, participant observation, and focus groups. According to Cameroon's ministry of public health, 42.7% of children under five are malnourished in this part of the country, while 8.6% suffer from acute malnutrition. One of the identified causes of this child malnourishment is the low quality and quantity of food intake and lack of knowledge about and access to nutritious crops. The climate in this area is of a Sudano-Sahelian type, with temperatures ranging from 20°C to 40°C during the dry season. In addition, this area as well as other localities in northern Cameroon face severe land degradation due to the harmful use of chemical fertilizer, overuse of farmland, and deforestation due to the uncontrollable destruction of trees for firewood. This IUDI project consists of working with local villages to determine policy actions. One approach has been the planting of several moringa (moringa oleifera) species of trees in farms. Each farm has an average of one thousand trees. Due to its tropical climate, the area can produce abundant moringa trees since it is a fast-growing, drought-resistant, and low soil-tolerant tree. These qualities of the plant will adapt to the local climate with its low soil quality. Moringa has been named a "miracle tree" by some because of its nutrient-dense food source. Local villagers use leaves as a food source, but very few people are aware that it is a high-quality food supplement, being rich in minerals, protein, amino acids, and some vitamins, as well as the leaves and seeds having pharmaceutical value. Through this interaction and learning, local villagers have come to understand the value of the leaves, seeds, and other products derived from the moringa trees, while earning additional income in the process.

In this endeavor, IUDI pays special attention to orphans, widows, and the society's poorest members. The idea is that if the condition of people who hurt the most changes in a society because of positive policies, it will inspire the rest of the community members. The model consists of involving local villagers in every aspect of the project including identification of needs and objectives, constitution of a leadership team, planting a model farm, training community members, and technical support so that they can start and manage their farms. Consultants from the university are always available for technical support and regular evaluation. For the long-term sustainability of the project, IUDI has also started to train community development practitioners, so that villagers will have people within their communities to collaborate with to enhance their living conditions. The only thing IUDI requires from a village is to adopt another village, share the knowledge and skills acquired with its leaders, and help them to start a moringa farm or any other sustainable project that is relevant in their context.

The IUDI's commitment to turn education into community development practice through policy changes benefits students, professors and local villagers alike. This type of community development work can address policy change at the village level while enhancing learning and building relationships. This way, education contributes to launch a movement of positive transformation in the world, one village at a time.

An essential element of this case study was the interaction between communities, as one village is charged with sharing their knowledge with the next to be involved in planting moringa trees. It also usefully demonstrates the "backbone" and "catalyst" roles of the community development practitioner as they facilitate bottom-up community work with top-down professional activities.

Jo Ferrie, Paul Lachapelle

Figure 9.7 Sealing off residents of Hong Kong Jordan neighborhood in January 2021 – Hong Kong. Photo credit: Yu-cheung Chan.

Case Study 5 – Hong Kong, China
Evaluating Community Work Amid COVID-19
By Kwok-kin Fung, Suet-lin Hung, King-lai Wong, Yu-cheung Chan, Juxiong Feng

Evaluating community development work is a prerequisite for positive learning, information sharing, and further program refinement. The sharing and evaluating of methods and outcomes among community development practitioners was seen as critical to support disadvantaged communities from the outbreak of Covid-19 pandemic in Hong Kong. Collective wisdom of community development practitioners in Hong Kong in response to Covid-19 was shared in a formal conference titled "Community Work amid Covid-19 Pandemic in Hong Kong" that was conducted in the spring of 2020. It was co-organized by the International Association for Community Development; Community Development Initiatives, Social Work Practice and Mental Health Centre, Department of Social Work; and Faculty Niche Research Areas (Population), Faculty of Social Sciences. The conference involved community workers from thirteen NGOs as speakers and more than 160 participants.

Among the many topics discussed were the regulations and infrastructure overseen by the Hong Kong Special Administrative Region of the People's Republic of China's (SAR) government to protect the public from the contagious disease. Specifically, discussion was centered on the social distancing regulations, the lack of health protection facilities, the inflation of consumption goods (particularly health-related products), and the continual rise of unemployment of disadvantaged groups. It was recognized that the impact is particularly severe for

248

communities in poverty in Hong Kong. In addition, the requirement of social distancing severely affected the ability of many NGOs to provide social services to disadvantaged groups. Nevertheless, different NGOs, civil and philanthropic associations of various kinds have been initiating support measures to deal with the challenges. Community workers have had a strong desire to learn from this experience and share among themselves their different approaches of reaching out to the disadvantaged groups.

During the conference, the following key themes were raised because of the deep discussions and introspection of the situation that are summarized as follows:

Innovative measures were initiated by different NGOs to balance the need of social distancing but still reaching out to disadvantaged groups. The techniques involved continuing face-to-face contacts between community development practitioners and disadvantaged populations, for example by arranging meeting points at the entrance of buildings where the disadvantaged populations reside, distributing resources of health protection facilities at the building entrance, setting up meeting spots outside in the streets where the users live, inviting disadvantaged populations to use online platforms at community centers for small group meetings, setting up physical activities in community centers, and the active re-arrangement of service hours and physical settings to suit the social distancing requirement while offering service delivery. These kinds of special arrangements were highly appreciated by disadvantaged populations during lockdown particularly in Hong Kong communities with a concentration of subdivided flats that are tiny in space and with poor ventilation.

Active use of **information and communication technologies** in particular digital devices to reach out to disadvantaged populations and delivery services including individual counselling, group meetings, training and tutorial sessions for children and adults, and designing games and activities for users of different backgrounds. In addition, telephone applications were used to arrange for face-to-face meetings. There were cases reporting how community workers have actively explored the different resources via Google searches to develop training materials for easy consumption of the disadvantaged populations.

Mobilization of community resources to cater to the needs of disadvantaged groups. Different community development practitioners highlighted their experience of linking resources from philanthropic/charity associations to their disadvantaged populations. There were NGOs actively utilizing social capital within the community by bridging with disadvantaged groups; and circulating health-related information among the disadvantaged populations through community networks. In addition, there were NGOs lending digital devices and distributing SIM cards to disadvantaged populations to mitigate the impact of digital divide. This is particular critical in view of the widespread adoption of digital devices for maintaining community contacts.

Linking the disadvantaged populations with different consulting professionals. This was found to be critical, as the knowledge relating to Covid-19 has not been well understood by the public and particularly by disadvantaged groups. Difficulties in accessing health protection facilities, knowledge relating to appropriate use of facilities, rumor and myths around the local strategies for healing those infected were among the controversies that stirred up panic. The high density of living among disadvantaged groups has aggravated tensions among disadvantaged populations living nearby. Different NGOs have been active in attempts to bridge disadvantaged populations with professionals including medical doctors, mental health professionals, and nurses of different specialties and were found to be effective in easing the tension of disadvantaged populations.

Development of collective capacity and empowerment of disadvantaged populations in different ways. There were community development practitioners who facilitated disadvantaged populations to form groups for negotiating with suppliers for affordable prices when purchasing daily necessities that were often price-inflated. In addition, community development practitioners facilitated disadvantaged populations to utilize their knowledge and skills when visiting health protection facilities to acquire items such as hand-made face masks. Further, there was assistance provided in organizing cleaning campaigns, distributing health items to needy families, and volunteering to take care of young children at the centers. All these moves were found to be empowering during the time when disadvantaged groups experienced stress and isolation.

In addition to evaluating programs, exchanging experiences and offering innovative measures of service delivery, there were different challenges identified that were encountered by the community development practitioners who themselves are in need of support. They include:

1. Problems relating to **communicating with disadvantaged groups**. As there is often, insufficient possession/ownership of digital devices by the disadvantaged groups, and community development practitioners noticed that there is seldom even one digital device per family member. Community development practitioners noted that resources are lacking beyond digital devices: also, for digital learning. Utilization of online classes for students have generated problems relating to supervising children. In addition, there was inadequate infrastructure, like Wi-Fi within high-density residential communities, supporting the digital devices. The sudden halt of nearly all public services by the government due to the lockdown has aggravated this problem further. Disadvantaged populations did not possess adequate knowledge of digital platforms.

2. **Community development practitioners were often overwhelmed** with the various challenges among disadvantaged populations, including unemployment, difficulties in accessing social services, and family conflicts at home. In addition, because of the SAR government refusal to provide unemployment benefits and the low social assistance support, community workers felt overpowered to address these compounding problems.

3. **Sustainability of ad hoc support** to the disadvantaged communities was another issue identified by community development practitioners. Even though there were different kinds of resource support mobilized through the efforts of NGOs, philanthropic associations and civic groups, the resources are still not enough for the disadvantaged groups as a whole and cannot be sustained in the long run. Advocating for support from government was an action that was greatly advocated.

4. **Struggling to fulfill different "key performance indicators"** (KPIs) requested by funders. Since the ongoing services of NGOs have KPIs to be met, the additional increase of workload in response to short term support to the disadvantaged communities has generated different problems to these active NGOs. Struggling with the limited resources to meet the original KPIs is a concern.

Evaluation is the key to learning from any past experience or situation. The conference environment allowed participants the opportunity to evaluate past performance and share lessons learned. Most importantly, the results show both improved service delivery and better networking and practice from the community development practitioners.

The final case study demonstrates the vital role community development practitioners have in ensuring that policies made, in this case, a response to the Covid-19 pandemic, were useful and responding both for the community and for policy makers to impact toward positive change. As well as solving digital access, the practitioners here use KPIs, to demonstrate how policy makers need reform if they are to meet their own targets. This case study also points to a key issue yet to be discussed: the risk of burn-out. Earlier in the chapter when discussing Collective Impact (CI), the community development practitioner was described as a "backbone", a resource and/or catalyst that cohesively binds a project and the multiple actors. This can place an enormous stress on individuals. Professional frameworks, can help practitioners place parameters around what they do, and what they are responsible for which could help them employ self-care strategies that reduce the risk of burn-out.

Jo Ferrie, Paul Lachapelle

Notes

1 Towards Shared International Standards for Community Development Practice. (2018). International Association of Community Development. iacdcglobal.org http://www.iacdglobal.org/Wp-Content/Uploads/2018/06/Iacd-Standards-Guidance-May-2018_Web.pdf (Accessed 30 July 2020.)
2 Towards Shared International Standards for Community Development Practice. (2018). International Association of Community Development. iacdcglobal.org http://www.iacdglobal.org/Wp-Content/Uploads/2018/06/Iacd-Standards-Guidance-May-2018_Web.pdf (Accessed 30 July 2020.)
3 E. Roosevelt (2012) *Tomorrow Is Now: It Is Today That We Create the World of The Future.* (Reprint Edition) Penguin Classics, London.
4 J. Ferrie and A. Hosie (2018) Methodological Challenges in Developing an Evidence Base, And Realizing Rights. *International Journal of Human Rights*, 22(1) Doi:10.1080/13642987.2017.1390300
5 J. Ferrie and A. Hosie (2018) Methodological Challenges in Developing an Evidence Base, And Realizing Rights. *International Journal of Human Rights*, 22(1) Doi:10.1080/13642987.2017.1390300
6 H. Jones, Y. Gunaratnam, G. Bhattacharyya et al. (2017) *Go Home? The Politics of Immigration Controversies.* Manchester University Press, Manchester.
7 H. Jones, Y. Gunaratnam, G. Bhattacharyya et al. (2017) *Go Home? The Politics of Immigration Controversies.* Manchester University Press, Manchester.
8 N. Fraser and A. Honneth (2004) *Redistribution or Recognition? A Political-Philosophical Exchange.* Verso, London. ISBN-10: 1859844928 provides a strong exploration of this theme.
9 L. Simpson, L. Wood, L. and L. Daws (2003) Community Capacity Building: Starting with People Not Projects. *Community Development Journal*, 38, 277–286; K. Bessant, (2005) Community Development Corporations as Vehicles of Community Economic Development: The Case of Rural Manitoba. *Journal of The Community Development Society*, 36(2), 52–72; P.R. Lachapelle (2008) A Sense of Ownership in Community Development: Understanding the Potential for Participation in Community Planning Efforts. *Community Development: Journal of The Community Development Society*, 39(2): 52–59.
10 L. Simpson, L. Wood, L and L. Daws (2003) Community Capacity Building: Starting with People Not Projects. *Community Development Journal*, 38, 277–286; K. Bessant, (2005) Community Development Corporations as Vehicles of Community Economic Development: The Case of Rural Manitoba. *Journal of The Community Development Society*, 36(2), 52–72; P.R. Lachapelle (2008) A Sense of Ownership in Community Development: Understanding the Potential for Participation in Community Planning Efforts. *Community Development: Journal of The Community Development Society*, 39(2): 52–59.
11 K. Raworth (2017) *Doughnut Economics: Seven Ways to Think Like A 21st-Century Economist.* Penguin: London, for a compelling account of economic growth as a global phenomenon.
12 K. Raworth (2017) *Doughnut Economics: Seven Ways to Think Like A 21st-Century Economist.* Penguin: London, for a compelling account of economic growth as a global phenomenon.
13 B. Baumberg, K. Bell, D. Gaffney et al. (2012) Benefits Stigma in Britain, Turn2us. https://wwwturn2us-2938. Cdn.Hybridcloudspan.Com/T2uwebsite/Media/Documents/Benefits-Stigma-In-Britain.Pdf (Accessed 29 July 2020)
14 J.S. Hirsch and M.M. Philbin (2016) The Heroines of Their Own Stories: Insights from The Use of Life History Drawings in Research with A Transnational Migrant Community. *Global Public Health*, 11(5–6): 762–782; and J. Wheeler, J. Shaw and J. Howard (2020) Politics and Practices of Inclusion: Intersectional Participatory Action Research. *Community Development Journal*, 55(1): 45–63.
15 D. Donovan (2016) How Children Represent Sustainable Consumption Through Participatory Action Research and Co-Design of Visual Narratives. *International Journal of Consumer Studies*, 40(5): 562–574.
16 D. Donovan (2016) How Children Represent Sustainable Consumption Through Participatory Action Research and Co-Design of Visual Narratives. *International Journal of Consumer Studies*, 40(5): 562–574.
17 M. Rios and P.R. Lachapelle (2017) Community Development and Democratic Practice: Pas De Deux or Distinct and Different? In: P.R. Lachapelle and M. Rios. (eds) *Community Development and Democratic Practice.* New York: Routledge.
18 M. Rios and P.R. Lachapelle (2017) Community Development and Democratic Practice: Pas De Deux or Distinct and Different? In: P.R. Lachapelle and M. Rios (eds.) *Community Development and Democratic Practice.* New York: Routledge.
19 J. Howard and J. Wheeler (2015) What Community Development and Citizen Participation Should Contribute to the New Global Framework for Sustainable Development. *Community Development Journal*, 50(4): 552–570.
20 P. Narayanan, V. Gayathri Sarangan and S. Bharadwaj (2015) Charting New Territory: Community Participation at The Centre Of Global Policy Making. *Community Development Journal*, 50(4): 608–623 for an overview of the challenges where community development meets policy-making forums.
21 J. Kania and M. Kramer (2011) Collective Impact. Stanford Social Innovation Review. https://ssir.Org/Articles/Entry/Collective_Impact. (Accessed 26 July 2020.)
22 J. Kania and M. Kramer (2011) Collective Impact. Stanford Social Innovation Review. https://ssir.Org/Articles/Entry/Collective_Impact. (Accessed 26 July 2020.)
23 K. Prange, J.A. Allen and R. Reiter-Palmon (2016) Collective Impact Versus Collaboration: Sides of The Same Coin or Different Phenomenon? *Metropolitan Universities*, 27(1): 86–96; and L. Weaver (2016) Possible: Transformational Change in Collective Impact. *Community Development*, 47(2): 274–283.

24 K. Prange, J.A. Allen and R. Reiter-Palmon (2016) Collective Impact Versus Collaboration: Sides of The Same Coin or Different Phenomenon? *Metropolitan Universities*, 27(1): 86–96; and L. Weaver (2016) Possible: Transformational Change in Collective Impact. *Community Development*, 47(2): 274–283.

25 M. Cabaj and L. Weaver (2016) *Collective Impact 3.0: An Evolving Framework for Community Change.* Tamarack Institute: Community Change Series 2016. http://www.Tamarackcommunity.Ca/Library/Collective-Impact-3.0-An-Evolving-Framework-For-Community-Change (Accessed 29 July 2020.)

26 M. Cabaj and L. Weaver (2016) *Collective Impact 3.0: An Evolving Framework for Community Change.* Tamarack Institute: Community Change Series 2016. http://www.Tamarackcommunity.Ca/Library/Collective-Impact-3.0-An-Evolving-Framework-For-Community-Change (Accessed 29 July 2020.)

27 R. J. Gillam, J.M. Counts and T.A. Garstka (2016) Collective Impact Facilitators: How Contextual and Procedural Factors Influence Collaboration. *Community Development*, 47(2): 209–224.

28 M. Mayan, A.L. Pauchulo, D. Gillespie, D. Misita and T. Majia (2020) The Promise of Collective Impact Partnerships. *Community Development Journal*, 55(3): 515–532 at page 521.

29 A. Barr (1991) *Practising Community Development.* Community Development Foundation London: London.

30 A. Barr and S. Hashagen (2000) *Achieving Better Community Development.* Community Development Foundation London.

31 More detail on the LEAP resource and on a revised version of the national standards can be found at the SCDC website.

32 A. Barr and S. Hashagen (2000) *ABCD* Handbook: A Framework For Evaluating Community Development. Community Development Foundation London.

33 A. Ricker (2013) Bozeman in the Running for Title of "Best Town Ever". *Bozeman Daily Chronicle.*

34 Bloomberg Businessweek. (2011). Available at: http://www.bloomberg.com/News/Photo-Essays/2011-11-23/The-Best-Places-To-Raise-Your-Kids-2012#Slide27 (Accessed 14 August 2016.)

35 P. Smith (1996) *Bozeman And the Gallatin Valley: A History.* Helena, Mt: Two Dot Publishing.

36 Montana Census & Economic Information Center (2016) Montana County Total Population by Gender and Age Group, 1990–2060. Available at: http://ceic.mt.gov/Population/Popprojectionstitlepage.aspx (Accessed 14 August 2016.)

37 Council on Foundations (2010) Centennial Plan: Strategies for a Strong Community Foundation Field 2011–2014. Arlington, VA: Council on Foundations.

38 This case study is reprinted with permission from the Tamarack Institute.

39 tamarack@tamarackcommunity.ca

40 J. Gamble (2011) *Evaluating Vibrant Communities 2002–2010.* Tamarack – An Institute for Community Engagement: Waterloo, Ontario.

41 This case study is reprinted with permission from the Tamarack Institute.

42 E. Leviten-Reid (2004) *Reflections on Vibrant Communities.* Caledon Institute of Social Policy: Ottawa.

43 C.A.C. International (2005) Mid-Term Assessment of The Vibrant Communities Initiative: Final Report.

44 M. Cabaj and E. Leviten-Reid (2006) *Understanding the Potential and Practice of Comprehensive, Multisectoral Efforts to Reduce Poverty: The Preliminary Experiences of The Vibrant Communities Trail Builders.* Unpublished manuscript, Tamarack – An Institute for Community Engagement, Waterloo, Ontario, Canada.

45 M. Cabaj, A. Makhoul and E. Leviten-Reid (2006) *In from The Field: Exploring the First Poverty-Reduction Strategies Undertaken by Trail Builders in The Vibrant Communities Initiative.* Unpublished manuscript, Tamarack – An Institute for Community Engagement, Waterloo, Ontario, Canada.

46 E. Leviten-Red (2007). *Reflecting on Vibrant Communities (2002–2006).* Caledon Institute of Social Policy: Ottawa.

47 The Sustainable Livelihoods Framework: An Overview http://tamarackcommunity.ca/Downloads/Vc/Sustainable_Livelihoods.pdf

48 J. Gamble (2011) *Evaluating Vibrant Communities 2002–2010.* Tamarack – An Institute for Community Engagement: Waterloo.

49 J. Gamble, ibid.

50 P. Born (ed.) (2008) *Creating Vibrant Communities: How Individuals and Organizations from Diverse Sectors of Society Are Coming Together to Reduce Poverty in Canada.* BPS Books: Toronto.

Chapter 10

The Way Forward

Charlie McConnell, Daniel Muia and Anna Clarke

Introduction

What are the key challenges that community development practice faces in the next decade and beyond? António Guterres, UN Secretary General highlights some – growing poverty and inequality, conflict, climate change. There are definitely many more and more will emerge. In the same speech to the UN Guterres stated: "*We have the tools and wealth to overcome these challenges. All we need is the will.*"[1]

As this book goes to print, the horrendous impacts of the coronavirus global pandemic have and continue to take their toll on individuals, communities and the societies of which we are all a part. These impacts have been both indiscriminate and highly discriminatory at the same time, affecting all levels of society yet affecting some far more than others. With an estimated three billion people across the world without access to clean water, little access to adequate healthcare and living in overcrowded conditions or refugee camps where social isolation was impossible, it was obvious that the poorest and most disadvantaged communities would be the worst hit by the pandemic. Communities in conflict areas or experiencing a humanitarian crisis were especially susceptible to conditions that spread the virus.[2] In economically developed countries it was still the poorest and more vulnerable who were at greatest risk.

The pandemic has shone a very bright light on the structural inequality and systemic discrimination that exists, and which long predated the arrival of the virus. And through the lens of the pandemic, the very complex and interconnected nature of the issues that affect people's lives, and what should be the core concerns of community development practice have been exposed.

DOI: 10.4324/9781003140498-10

In far too many cases governmental and non-governmental public health and social service delivery systems failed to protect the most disadvantaged people and vulnerable communities, even in the most developed economies. Yet, at the same time, community groups as well as community development organizations and practitioners, with limited and largely non-governmental resources, acted swiftly and decisively to mobilize mass programmes of support targeting those most in need – a testimony to the ingenuity and resourcefulness of community development practice, examples of which we have included in this book.

At the same time, many community development agencies and practitioners have continued lobbying, campaigning, and raising awareness of the extent to which inequality and disadvantage, racism, xenophobia and gender discrimination continue to be endemic within societies and at all levels and have been reinforced by the pandemic. Examples here include the increased rates of gender-based and domestic violence against girls and women; lack of human rights for those in refugee camps and displaced communities; the ongoing issues of racial discrimination; and the disproportionate impact upon older people, people living with disabilities and those with underlying health issues, often linked to poverty.

Alongside the global pandemic, economic recession and climate change and the rise of the extremist far right and its challenge to democracy and professional "experts" have compounded the already huge pressures upon disadvantaged and vulnerable communities trying to take action around grassroots concerns, as well as being exposed to unexpected and extreme events.[3]

This is more so when looked at from the aspiration of the first UN Sustainable Development Goal – to "end poverty in all its forms everywhere".[4] While global extreme poverty rates have fallen over recent decades, they are now rising again as the health, social and economic impacts of the pandemic compound other shocks, such as conflict and climate.[5] The World Bank estimates that in 2021 150 million more people will be faced with extreme poverty and the associated disadvantages that will bring and this figure will grow.

Community development agencies and practitioners have never claimed they alone could abolish poverty, end discrimination, and create a just and sustainable future. But through the support of community development agencies and practitioners, across a range of disciplines, the experiences of people in countless communities around the world, have improved. The chapters in this book indicate that with organizational, educational, and other technical and resource support communities can take collective action to build fairer, stronger, more resilient, and sustainable futures. What is needed now is a scaling up of community development support over the coming hugely challenging decade for disadvantaged and vulnerable communities as such communities grow in number.

This will require investment in more community development staff and a growth in the number of such staff being trained to enter the workforce over the coming years, alongside the continuing professional development of existing practitioners so that they are equipped to take on the challenges of change as effectively and professionally as possible.

This calls for an expanding of the frontiers of community development practice.[6] We propose six priority areas here

1. The need to place more emphasis upon strategies and programmes that tackle inequality.

2. The need to place more emphasis upon strategies and programmes that address climate change and biodiversity loss.

3. The need for national governments and local authorities to play a more pro-active role embedding community development approaches and practice within policy, strategy and service delivery.

4. The need to increase the community development workforce and to invest in its professional development.

5. The need to harness the opportunities for community development practice presented by digital technologies.

6. The need to improve the exchange of research, evaluation and learning across all aspects of community development practice.

The Need to Place More Emphasis Upon Strategies and Programmes That Tackle Inequality

Despite the fact that women and girls represent half the world's population, there is a long way to go to achieve full gender equality, socially, economically and politically. Yet this is precisely what the UN Secretary General António Guterres has referred to as the unfinished business of our time.[7] It is therefore critical that community development practice puts gender equality (end to gender-based violence, equal access to health and education services and resources and employment opportunities, the right to self-determination and participation in political life and decision-making at all levels) front and centre of all activity.

Equally, racism, discrimination and xenophobia continue to maintain, reinforce, and perpetuate global inequality and disadvantage across all levels of society, structurally, institutionally and individually. While dominant groups with power and influence benefit, those discriminated against experience cumulatively negative outcomes. The pervasive nature of structural and systemic racism in particular reinforces and replicates old forms of racism while simultaneously producing new forms that impact all areas of life. As with gender, addressing racial inequality must be a fundamental focus of community development practice. In this context it is critical to acknowledge the intersectional nature of inequality, particularly in the context of working with the most disadvantaged and vulnerable communities, whose lives, experiences, and voices are marginalized and ignored.

In economic terms also, there is growing awareness of the levels of inequality between the small percentage of the rich globally and the huge and growing numbers of the poor around the world. Redistributive processes are needed, in which governments adopt more progressive and redistributive tax regimes, encompassing wealth as well as income, in order to invest in addressing pressing global poverty as well as the other SDGs. At the micro level, there is a need to expand investment in community economic development strategies and projects that promote job creation and community entrepreneurship in areas that bring positive social benefits founded on values of inclusion, shared wealth and community ownership and control.[8] Such projects should also seek to empower women's and youth engagement in areas of economic leadership as well as ensuring sustainable models of economic development.

While this book demonstrates that community development practice has played a significant role on the ground in promoting social equity as evidenced by support for those experiencing racism, gender inequality, disability, and other forms of discrimination, growing levels of xenophobia, and human rights abuses indicate that much more work is still needed. The Black Lives Matter movement has been seminal in this regard and brought to the fore of public attention again, that racism and xenophobia towards black and minority ethnic groups is not far under the surface across all countries.

It is also a reminder that promoting social justice must remain the central guiding principle in our work and that community development agencies and practitioners must enhance programmes tackling all forms of exclusion and inequality.

In order to support disadvantaged and vulnerable communities to deal with the challenges of the coming decade, community development programmes and practitioners should target support towards those communities experiencing the greatest levels of socio-economic inequality, discrimination and injustice.

The Need to Place More Emphasis Upon Strategies and Programmes That Address Climate Change and Biodiversity Loss

Without community development there is no sustainable development – it is increasingly becoming evident that sustainable development is not an option for humankind, it is a prerequisite. The UN, national governments, local authorities, NGOs (Non-Governmental Organizations), and other players must scale up the capacity of disadvantaged and vulnerable communities to become stronger, more connected, and resilient. The main focus of community development in the past has been around social and economic issues. In the last three decades, however, we have seen a growing interest among environmental organizations and governments in how to educate and mobilize communities to be players in climate action, adaptation, and mitigation measures locally and to protect and enhance biodiversity.

Climate change and biodiversity loss is happening at an increasing pace with dire implications for coastal, highland and desert communities. Climate change scientists tell us that the coming decade is a critical one. Environmental NGOs need to be employing more staff with community development practice knowledge and skills. Existing social and economically oriented community development agencies need to be working much more closely with environmental organizations.

Climate change is an existential challenge as it is a social challenge, a health challenge, an urban design challenge, a migration challenge, an agricultural, water management and land use challenge, a jobs challenge, a conflict reduction challenge. It is also a huge opportunity for realizing a "Green New Deal"[9] transition to a low carbon future, where large numbers of jobs are created through local energy renewable projects, creating more energy efficient housing, building low-cost housing more sustainably, growing food locally and in ways that do not damage soil quality, cause cruelty to animals or damage biodiversity.

In order to support disadvantaged and vulnerable communities to deal with the challenges of the coming decade, community development programmes and practitioners must focus more attention upon supporting communities to deal with the challenges and opportunities presented by climate change and biodiversity loss and to play their role in the greening of the economy and in protecting biodiversity.

Charlie McConnell, Daniel Muia, Anna Clarke

The Need for National Governments and Local Authorities to Play a More Pro-Active Role Embedding Community Development Approaches and Practice Within Policy, Strategy and Service Delivery

In recent years we have witnessed the rolling back of much state support around the world often couched in the rhetoric of localism and self-help. Localism and self-help cannot overcome challenges of poverty, conflict, inequality, and climate change. The reality facing all societies is that the dismantling of state support has reinforced disadvantage and made communities less resilient and less capable of dealing with change. Governments and local authorities must enhance investment in and support for community development programmes.

In order to address the critical challenges that communities and societies face highlighted above, there is an ever-growing need for collaborative inter-agency strategies and multi-disciplinary approaches that also include local communities at the heart of such processes.

Over the past six decades since the UN started promoting community development programmes, its agencies such as the World Health Organization, UNDP, UNESCO, World Bank, UN-Habitat and the World Food Programme have consistently encouraged governments, NGOs, foundations and the corporate sector to support such approaches. Community development practice, when adopted by a wide range of disciplines working closely together, has proven to make a major contribution in supporting and facilitating the kind of change that is needed.

We need a greatly enhanced role being played by local authorities in all countries. Local authorities need to support community development strategically and to embed this approach into the mainstream of their planning, policy, and service delivery and in providing support for communities to become active partners. This book has illustrated examples of where democratically elected local authorities have introduced community development strategies, employed community development practitioners, and worked in a community planning and delivery partnership with NGOs, CBOs, the business sector and community organizations.

In order to support disadvantaged and vulnerable communities to deal with the challenges of the coming decade, governments and local authorities need to support and embed community development practice and approaches as a key part of their sustainable development strategies and programmes to tackle inequalities and discrimination.

The Need to Increase the Community Development Workforce and to Invest in Its Professional Development

In recent years we have witnessed a significant reduction in community development posts in most countries, as resourcing for programmes and initiatives have been withdrawn, due to budget cuts and the rolling back of state support. In their place less experienced and untrained staff have been taken on to give some back up assistance or more likely no support has been provided at all. This is not sufficient to the challenge.

The issues disadvantaged and vulnerable communities are faced with require experienced and often specialized technical support. The provision of professional community development support for disadvantaged and vulnerable communities is patchy across the world and needs to be increased. To address the increasing challenges such communities face over this decade, more skilled community development practitioners need to be employed by governmental and non-governmental agencies and CBOs.

In many countries the availability of initial and continuing professional education and training necessary to create a professional workforce skilled in community development practice is non-existent. In this regard we urge UN agencies, governments, employers, and higher education institutes and other training organizations in all countries to use IACD's International Standards for Community Development Practice to inform the design and delivery of professional community development education for the range of practitioners required. This book provides examples of how this can be done.

In order to support disadvantaged and vulnerable communities to deal with the challenges of the coming decade, governments and NGOs will need to increase the number of staff skilled in community development practice. This in turn will necessitate governments and employers working with HEIs to enhance the number of programmes training community development practitioners.

The Need to Harness the Opportunities for Community Development Practice Presented by Digital Technologies

The digital revolution is transforming all aspects of our lives. This has been clearly evidenced throughout the pandemic. Those who were able to access digital devices and broadband connectivity secured some of their needs online. At the same time, it brought the issue of digital exclusion to the fore. Almost 4.57 billion people were active internet users as of July 2020, encompassing 59 per cent of the global population.[10] But less economically developed countries as well as disadvantaged and vulnerable communities in all countries are far behind this percentage in terms of access to digital technology.[11]

Digital technologies have been used to enhance methods of community engagement, organizing, educating, reaching out to excluded groups, involving communities in participatory planning and design, and in project evaluation. The same also applies to professional community development training as teaching and learning has migrated in part to online platforms. Although this virtual environment will never replace the need or desire for face-to-face contact and relationship building between practitioners and the communities they support, digital community development practice will certainly become more commonplace. Indeed, in a global context, it offers much opportunity for networking, learning, and sharing of practice and experience.

Recent concerns in relation to the use of digital technologies to disseminate "fake news" and misinform, for example in relation to the Covid-19 vaccines, and claims of voter fraud in the US Presidential election has also led community development academics and practitioners to examine how to counter this through community educational and organizational work on the ground.[12] This is likely to be an area of increasingly important focus to counter and challenge populist politics that furthers division.

Charlie McConnell, Daniel Muia, Anna Clarke

In order to support disadvantaged and vulnerable communities to deal with the challenges of the coming decade, community development practitioners must become ever more skilled at using digital technologies and solutions as well as working to address digital exclusion.

The Need to Improve the Exchange of Research, Evaluation and Learning Across All Aspects of Community Development Practice

Historically, the short-term nature of support for community development has often included an emphasis on project and programme delivery and overlooked the importance of research, evaluation, and the sharing of learning. Community development practitioners and organizations have frequently found themselves in cycles of delivery with little time to reflect. This is not conducive to good practice. Similarly, policy makers and funders of community development programmes all too often fail to learn from past experiences and programmes. Excellent work as a result can be lost, and the design of new programmes can be impeded by a failure to document and share the lessons learned.

The nature of community development practice working at the grassroots, requires responding to issues of concern raised by communities themselves as well as the agendas of those agencies that invest in community development programmes. While each community is different, what this book demonstrates is that there are also many similarities between communities around the world and the issues they experience. With the challenges we face today, there is no time for reinventing wheels or losing valuable learning. Governments (national and local), state agencies and non-governmental organizations need to ensure appropriate resourcing is allocated to support research and evaluation that informs existing and future practice, and which supports the participation of all those involved in the process. Over many years the journals and institutes in our field have documented thousands of community development programmes, but we need to share this in a less academic form, more accessible to communities, practitioners, funders, and policy advisers. This sharing of programme learning is ever more vital in order that practice that works and is effective is built upon.

We are keen to see enhanced sharing and exchange of programme learning and research between the various disciplines adopting community development approaches, and between communities and agencies seeking to address often common problems.

IACD is keen to play its part, advocating for this six-point agenda at the UN, at its conferences, through its membership and by working with national professional associations, employers, HEIs and others in the field. Our priorities are to advocate for the values and methods of community development and to support community development programmes and practitioners, irrespective of their discipline, in their work with disadvantaged and vulnerable communities. The decade ahead and beyond could not be more critical for these communities.

Wherever you are around the world people will generally have a shared understanding of what a doctor, a teacher or an engineer does. IACD has championed the need for a clearer global understanding of what a community development practitioner does. And as with doctors, teachers, engineers, for all community development practitioners to be professionally trained and competent in their work, underpinned by shared values and professional ethics. This book and the International Standards for Community Development Practice that informed the chapters and the illustrative case studies will help development agencies, practitioners, educators, and students around the world appreciate more fully, that irrespective of the country or the context the approaches used are similar, should be easy to articulate and understood by all involved, not least the communities with which we work.

Notes

1   A. Guterres (2017) Make ' "We the Peoples' " Reality by Transcending Differences to Overcome Increasing Conflicts, Inequality, Secretary-General Says in Message for United Nations Day, https://www.un.org/press/en/2017/sgsm18754.doc.htm
2   Oxfam (2020) How the coronavirus pandemic exploits the worst aspects of extreme inequality. (2020) Oxfam.
3   K. Joice and K. Joseph et al. (2020) Community resilience mechanism in an unexpected extreme weather event: An analysis of the Kerala floods of 2018, India. *International Journal of Disaster Risk Reduction*, - Volume 49, October, 101741, Elsevier ScienceDirect.
4   United Nations (2015) Resolution adopted by the General Assembly on 25 September 2015, Transforming our world: the 2030 Agenda for Sustainable Development (A/RES/70/1).
5   The World Bank Group (2020) Poverty and Shared Prosperity 2020: Reversals of Fortune. International Bank for Reconstruction and Development/The World Bank. doi: 10.1596/978–1-4648–1602–4
6   R. Hustedde (2019) On Community Development Education. In Issue 12, Practice Insights – see http://www.iacdglobal.org/wp-content/uploads/2019/02/Practice-Insights-12-b.pdf
7   A. Guterres (2018) Secretary-General Declares ' "Time Is Now' " for Gender Equality, Women's Empowerment, in Remarks on International Day, https://www.un.org/press/en/2018/sgsm18928.doc.htm
8   M. Fortunato and T. Alter (2015). Community entrepreneurship development: an introduction. *Community Development*, 46(5), 444—455. https://doi.org/10.1080/15575330.2015.1080742
9   The Green New Deal is a movement gaining traction internationally, building upon the government-led New Deal movement in the USA.
10   https://www.statista.com/statistics/617136/digital-population-worldwide/
11   Carnegie UK Trust (2020) Learning from lockdown: 12 steps to eliminate digital exclusion https://d1ssu070pg2v9i.cloudfront.net/pex/carnegie_uk_trust/2020/10/14161948/Carnegie-Learning-from-lockdown-Report-FINAL.pdf
12   S. Kenny, J. Ife and P. Westoby (2020) *Populism, Democracy and Community Development*. Policy Press.

Towards Shared International Standards for Community Development Practice

Summary Guide

International Association for Community Development
Association Internationale de Développement et D'Action Communautaires

WITHOUT COMMUNITY DEVELOPMENT
THERE IS NO SUSTAINABLE DEVELOPMENT

After adopting its global definition of community development in 2016, the IACD began work to produce guidance for community development practice. The IACD worked with the Community Learning and Development Standards Council Scotland and, following an extensive consultation process with colleagues, practitioners and members from all over the world, the IACD launched the Shared International Standards for Community Development Practice at the IACD International Conference at Maynooth in June 2018.

IACD, as the international professional association, believe that it is important to encourage practitioners, paid and unpaid, to adopt a shared understanding of the purpose of community development, built upon shared values. The IACD aims to support high standards of practice based upon an agreed collective view of what practice is. While it values relevant qualifications, it does not equate professionalism with being qualified.

Community Development Practice

Community Development practice is carried out by people in different roles and context who seek to apply community development values and adopt community development methods: by people called professional community workers (and people taking on the same role but with a different job title); by professionals in other occupations such as social work, adult education, youth work, health disciplines, environmental education, local economic development, urban planning, regeneration, or architecture; and by people active in their own communities. We refer to them all as 'community development practitioners' and use this as an overarching term that includes also 'community workers'.

The IACD Definition of Community Development

"Community Development is a practice-based profession and an academic discipline that promotes participative democracy, sustainable development, rights, economic opportunity, equality and social justice, through the organisation, education and empowerment of people within their communities, whether these be of locality, identity or interest, in urban and rural settings."

This definition embodies a set of underpinning values, a purpose and a set of methods for work.

A. Underpinning values

The definition expresses values that should underpin practice:

Commitment to rights, solidarity, democracy, equality, environmental and social justice. It positions professional practice as working according to ethical standards applied in various contexts, working with people and organisations with different agendas.

B. The purpose

Within the definition is a statement about the purpose of community development:

'To work with communities to achieve participative democracy, sustainable development, rights, economic opportunity, equality and social justice.'

This high-level purpose statement can be used as a template against which to measure both the journey and the destination.

C. The central methods and processes

Within the definition there is a clear statement of the methods and processes adopted by community development practitioners: "(the) organisation, education and empowerment of people within their communities...".

D. Participants

The IACD definition refers to people within their communities, whether these are of locality, identity or interest. These are the primary groups of people community development practitioners will be working with. They will also engage with public agencies, NGOs and businesses in support of the values and purpose of community development.

Themes and Key Areas

Eight themes that are common across practice in community development. These are outlined below together with the eight Key Areas. Each of the Key Areas have a range of statements about practice that provide guidelines for community development practitioners. More information is available within the full Standards document.

Theme Title	Theme Description	Key Areas
Theme 1: **Values into practice**	This theme focuses on understanding of the values that underpin community development practice in all contexts, the processes on which it is based and the outcomes that result from it; and the application of this understanding in the practitioner's own context	Understand the values, processes and outcomes of community development and apply these to practice in all the other key areas
Theme 2: **Engaging with communities**	This theme focuses on getting to know the communities the practitioner works with, understanding the issues that impact on them and developing the relationships that provide the basis for working for positive change	Understand and engage with communities, building and maintain relationships with individuals and groups
Theme 3: **Ensuring participatory planning**	This theme focuses on developing community participation and empowering partnerships and supporting communities and agencies to develop the skills to sustain these	Develop and support collaborative working and community participation
Theme 4: **Organising for change**	This theme focuses on enabling communities to take collective action and to develop the skills needed for this; and on developing a context where their collective action is sustained and supported as a positive force for change.	Enable communities to take collective action, increase their influence and if appropriate their ability to access, manage and control resources and services
Theme 5: **Learning for change**	This theme focuses on facilitating the learning of people in communities and practitioners working with them in support of their priorities for change and development	Support people and organisations to learn together and to raise understanding, confidence and the skills needed for social change.
Theme 6: **Promoting diversity and inclusion**	This theme focuses on recognising diversity and supporting inclusion as core aspects of practice.	Design and deliver practices, policies, structures and programmes that recognise and respect diversity and promote inclusion.
Theme 7: **Building leadership and infrastructure**	This theme focuses on developing empowering leadership in and with communities and developing the infrastructure for community development and sustainable change.	Facilitate and support organisational development and infrastructure for community development, promoting and providing empowering leadership
Theme 8: **Developing and improving policy and practice**	This theme focuses on using evidence from participatory evaluation, and from analysis of relevant external factors, to inform and develop policy and practice.	Develop, evaluate and inform practice and policy for community development, using participatory evaluation to inform and improve strategic and operational practice

How might the International Standards be used?

The Standards can be used as a guide to help collectively identify the destination (outcomes) and shape the journey (process). They can also be used to critically reflect on both the journey and the destination. In other words, they can be used to plan, implement and review action and support learning from the process. As such they can be used by all community development practitioners in many ways to:

- build shared awareness and understanding of what community development is

- promote the values upon which community development is based

- enhance practice

- inform theory and policy

- shape academic and practice-based learning

We hope that they will be embraced by community development practitioners and used in a complementary manner in countries where national standards and frameworks already exist, and as a guiding resource in those countries where no national standards have been developed. As part of our consultation process on the draft Standards, we asked for specific ideas on how the Standards might be used. We have included these ideas below:

- To generate discussion on the purpose, values and key areas of community development in global and local contexts, within and between communities and between different agencies and organisations

- To develop resources that help to demonstrate how different contexts impact on shared areas of practice within different countries/communities

- To support international networking and sharing of practice examples and experiences

- To build shared understanding within communities and within organisations about the key purpose and values of community development

- To support discussions around participatory planning and community ownership that build collective action and empowerment

- To inform the design of pre and in-service education and training of community development practitioners

- To develop reflective practice self-assessment learning tools

- To support the development of stories from the 'field' sharing examples of how the Standards are being used to support practice development – perhaps around each of the Key Areas – international examples around common/ shared themes

- To develop international resources for inclusion in programmes of education and training – drawing out the contestations and sensitivities associated with practice

- To inform the IACD Global Community Development Exchange (GCDEX) repository of teaching and learning resources

- To provide a 'common base' upon which to develop international research and scholarship exploring aspects of community development practice

For more information on the IACD or a full copy of the Shared International Standards, please contact us:

t:+44 141 248 1924 e: info@iacdglobal.org | www.iacdglobal.org

facebook.com/IACDglobal/ @IACD_global @IACDglobal

International Association for Community Development

For details of how to become a member of IACD please visit:

www.iacdglobal.org/join-us/

Index

Figures are indexed in *Italic* page numbers, Tables in **Bold** page numbers.

ABCD *see* Asset Based Community Development
abductions 81–2
Aberdeen (Child-Friendly City) 221
Aboriginal and Torres Strait Islander Commission 192
Aboriginal and Torres Strait Islanders 190–1
Aboriginal groups 174, 190
Aboriginal history 191
Abu Samah, Asnarulkhadi 85–92
abuse 45, 111, 121–2, 190
Achieving Better Community Development model 234
actions 10, 26–7, 30–3, 40–2, 60–5, 115–19, 124–9, 134–5, 137–44, 146–9, 151–2, 164–6, 191–2, 194–7, 199–201, 204–5, 226–9, 231–2, 234–5, 245–7; affirmative 176; charting 31; collaborative 56, 126, 192; environmental 234; global 32; local 241; plans 105, 128, 152, 200, 235, 246; prioritizing 27; and reflection cycle 152; research 41, 121, 204, 226–8, 234, 252; social 6, 10, 20, 63
activists 3, 10, 40, 42, 56, 58–62, 89–91, 115, 128, 171, 174, 227, 231–2; civic 209; civil society 20; consumer 13; local 15, 88, 236
administrative coordinators 124–5
ADRA *see* Adventist Development & Relief Agency
adult education 6, 204
Adventist Development & Relief Agency 72–4
Africa 4, 7, 18, 21, 26, 137, 207, 245
Ág, Hungary *134*
ageist biases 206–7
agencies 1–4, 6, 10, 30–1, 34, 56, 58–62, 86, 88, 118, 129, 141–2, 144–5, 170, 258–60; external 46, 60, 152; local 136; mainstream 212; non-governmental 106, 173, 259; partner 138, 213; service 236

agriculture 66, 72, 110, 161, 210; climate resilient 65; industrial scale 16; organic 75; specialist 160
agronomists 74
Agunya Project 46–8
Ahmadian, Maryam 169–76
AIDS/HIV 18, 121, 158, 188
Air, Ammar Bahadur 150–3
Alayza, Bernardo 124–6
alcohol 120, 213, 221
Alinsky, Saul 5, 113–14, 139, 141, 144
America *see* United States
American Community Development Society 7, 17
Anti-Oppressive Practice 139, 168n5
anti-racism 190–1
Anti-Terror Police Unit 81
anti-toxic dump campaign 130
AOP *see* Anti-Oppressive Practice
architects 5–6, 9, 97
architectural archways *184*
architecture 98
arts *see* community arts
Arnstein, Sherry 5, 86, *87*
Ashenhurst Community Association 186
Asia 4, 7, 18, 207
assessment 45, 73, 75, 89, 107, 233; comprehensive community 105; environmental impact 129, 132; fair 30; initial participatory community 204; joint 122; mid-term 242–3, 253; participatory 152; skill 66
Asset Based Community Development 12, 100–2, *109*, 110–12, 140, 168, 234, *235*, 236; approach 12; community 101; method 101, 109–10, 112, 168, 242; model 234–5; limitations of 12; practitioners 109; principles 102, 111; process 110; proponents 12; successful 109

assets 12, 26–7, 56, 61, 64–5, 89, 103,
107, 109–11, 196, 198–9, 239–40, 242;
community 69, 102, 106, 109, 145, 159,
161, 204; cultural 205; environmental 64;
individual's 102–3; local 12, 89–90, 111;
mapping 141; national 11; primary 98, 110,
178, 213
Association of Volunteers for Community
Development 69–70
asylum seekers 174
ATPU see Anti-Terror Police Unit
ATSIC see Aboriginal and Torres Strait
Islander Commission
Aubel, Judi 204–7
Australia 7, 17, 34, 46, 102, 174, 190, 201,
212; community leaders 195; First
Peoples 191–2; indigenous affairs 192;
National Day 191
autism 181–2
AVODEC see Association of Volunteers for
Community Development

Bakwena Platinum Toll Concessionaire Pty
109, 110
balance of power 113
Baltic States 180
Bangladesh 11–12, 16
bank accounts 65
Banks, Sarah 35–8
Bantu ethnic groups 168
"barefoot" approach 66, 142
barefoot engineers 65–7
Barr, Alan 233–6
barriers 56–7, 85–6, 91, 166, 187,
217–18; and challenges in participatory
planning 91; cultural 222; identifying
228; intersectional 247; language 189;
multidimensional 232
Basilizwi Trust 189
beekeepers 74–5
Beethoven, Ludwig van 2
beliefs 4, 33, 46, 61, 63, 96, 116, 142–3, 146,
218, 225; guiding 30; neo-con ideology
10–11, 26; passionate 5; people's 159;
religious 172
Benarrawa Solidarity Group 190–2
beneficiaries 45, 88, 159, 161; existing 45;
new 45; potential 45, 159; prioritized 122
Berlin Wall 14
Bhattacharyya, G. 31
Binga District 188–9
biodiversity 19–20, 32, 257; global 20; loss
16, 20, 22, 257; protecting 257; urban 79
Black Lives Matter 171, 257
Blair, Tony (British Prime Minister) 18
Boal, Augusto 10
board members xx, 190, 212, 244
Boda, K. 137n28
Bongoyok, Moussa 245–7
Born, Paul 244
Bosnia 15, 92–3

"bottom-up" (community development) 86,
190
Bozeman (Montana) 238–40, 253
brainstorming 134, 135, 142, 197
Bretton Woods 10
British Community Development Foundation
12
Brooks, Dee 85, 85–92
Brundtland World Commission on
Environment and Development Report 20
BSG see Benarrawa Solidarity Group
Buckfastleigh anti toxic waste dump 130
Buckfastleigh Community Forum 131–2
Budapest Declaration 14
building 44, 66, 206; construction
46; developers 89; leadership and
infrastructure 6, 194–223; materials 135;
methods 134; partnerships 118, 145, 210
bureaucracies 9, 114
business and community development 33,
89, 116, 139–40, 142, 144, 171, 199, 228

Caledon Institute of Social Policy 241
Cameroon 17, 232, 245–6
campaigning 16, 121, 131, 234, 255
campaigns 18, 52, 129, 130, 131–2, 140, 144;
citizen's action 128; community action
6; council election 128; environmental
education 142; literacy education 10;
organizing cleaning 148, 250; public health
147, 227; trade union 131
Canada 17, 118, 127, 146, 163, 165, 166,
232, 241, 243
capacity building 45, 74, 103, 198, 201, 235,
237; elements of community development
236; experiencing community 218;
opportunities 71; workshops 121
capitalism 11, 14
CAPS see Potable Water and Sanitation
Committee
carbon footprint 19–20, 77, 257
caregivers 161
Caribbean 4, 10
caring 78, 107, 117, 213, 235
Carnegie Trust 12, 16
Carter, President. Jimmy 12
case studies 34–5, 43, 92–3, 101, 108–9,
118–20, 124, 129–30, 134, 175–6, 184,
190, 193–4, 201, 212, 231–3, 245, 247–8,
251, 253
cassava 158, 160
caste system 34–5, 37–8
castes 35–7
catalyst 64, 111, 231–2, 239, 247, 251
Catholic priests 10
CBNOs see Community-Based Network
Organizations
CBOs see Community-Based Organizations
CDCs see Community Development
Corporations
CDGs see Community Development Groups

CDJ *see* Community Development Journal
CDL *see* Community Learning and
  Development
Centeno, Victorino 69–71
central government 18, 78, 121, 153
ceremonies 187–8
Cerro Verde del Milagro, Peru *76*, 78
Chan, Yu-cheung 248–51
change 24, 32–3, 37–8, 45, 54, 59–60,
  66–7, 112–19, 121–67, 198–9, 204–7,
  216–19, 221, 225–6, 228, 242–3, 246–7,
  258; community work and social 12, 26;
  processes 44, 116–17; structural 217–18,
  226; sustainable 56, 63
chapels 184
charitable trusts 133
Charles Stewart Mott Foundation 12
CHASE *see* Community Health Assessment
  Sustainable Education
chemical fertilizers 246
Cheung, Kim 215–19
CHEX *see* Community Health Exchange
child 15, 180, 182, 221, 223; health 206;
  immunization 142; malnourishment 246;
  marriages 122, 188, 204, 206–7; mortality
  rates 227
childcare 143, 173
children 15, 30, 36–7, 44, 121–2, 161–2, 201,
  204, 206–7, 220–4, 246, 249; disabled
  181–2; experiences of 222; families
  raising 180; parents of 182; rights-based
  issues 221; stolen 191; working
  221–2
Children's Parliament of Scotland 220–3
Chile 17
China (PRC) 4, 14, 17–18, 72, 97, 142, 215, 248
chronic traumatic disorders 93
churches 44
CI *see* Collective Impact
Cipriano, Eduarda 158–9
city planners 92, *97*, 98
civil rights movement 5
Clarke, Anna 29–34, 254–61
CLD *see* Community Learning and
  Development
climate 197, 246, 255; action 257; change
  xx, 3, 16, 18, 20, 22, 66, 114, 118, 254–5,
  257–8; continental 238; crisis 230; justice
  32, 48, 256; local 246; tropical 246
cloth face-mask workshop, Hong Kong *147*
CNP *see* Collective Narrative Practice
co-ops 12, 14, 16, 18, 134–5
codes 34, 50–3, 74; draft 50; of ethics 49–53;
  for practitioners 34
Cold War 4, 8, 14–15
collaboration 40, 47–8, 80, 90, 118,
  126, 204–5, 207, 219, 228–9,
  252–3; close 129; cross-community
  21; cross-sector 241; resourceful
  218; robust 153; supporting the
  community 218

collective action 1–2, 32, 48, 64, 70–1,
  115, 148–9, 189, 191, 205, 207; and
  participation 48; potential benefits by
  communities 119; potential benefits of
  119, 125
Collective Impact 230, 251
Collective Narrative Practice 140–1, 168
collectives 65–6
colonialism 4, 34
colonization 46, 190
Combined European Bureau 8
communication 57, 99, 105, 132, 143, 191,
  198, 204–5, 213, 228, 231; continuous
  230; efforts 211; frequent 201; improved
  206; increasing 204, 207; platforms 98–9,
  218; reciprocal 99; responsive 107; skills
  62, 143–4, 146; spaces 125–6; styles 173,
  206; technologies 249; visual 143, 146
communism 5, 11, 14, 26, 180
communist governments 4, 18
communities 1–3, 21–4, 29–34, 39–47,
  55–83, 85–99, 106–11, 113–22, 124–45,
  147–56, 169–77, 180–2, 188–9, 194–202,
  204–7, 212–13, 215–23, 225–32, 234–51,
  254–61; affluent 2, 113; and agencies 86,
  260; agricultural 176; architects 6, 58–9,
  91; artists 174, 186, 234; and the arts 10,
  184, 186; beneficiary 73; capitals 61, 84,
  118, 137, 237; centers 6, 52, 185, 249;
  coastal 16, 114; controlled 12; deprived
  10, 18; developing 168; disadvantaged
  9–10, 12–13, 113, 118, 139, 143, 156,
  173, 248, 250, 254; discriminated 30,
  171; diverse 169–70; and economic
  development projects 238; education 4,
  6, 12, 21, 47, 114, 233–4; educators 6,
  117, 140, 148, 151; empowered 86, 94,
  153; empowerment 46, 235; foundations
  12–13, 237–40; health care 106, 108,
  204; health workers 6, 59; inclusive
  169, 174, 182–3; minority 15; mobilizing
  62, 102, 201, 206, 257; multicultural
  212; organizations 10–11, 47–8, 59, 81,
  139, 154, 180, 200, 217, 234–6, 258;
  organizers 114, 118, 127–8; ownership 61,
  70, 82, 110, 256; peri-urban 77; planning
  solutions 98–9; post-conflict 95–6;
  projects 60, 69, 143, 159, 174, 233, 239;
  screening processes 151; selected 65,
  109, 151; sensitization forums *80*; small
  118, 130–1, 238; social workers 6, 9, 13,
  18, 24–5, 91, 93, 148, 213, 216–17, 221;
  stakeholders 107, 116; support groups
  36–8; sustainable 12, 211; traditional 60,
  227; trail-builder 242–3; vibrant 241–3;
  work 4, 6, 12, 25–6, 54, 168, 210, 216,
  233, 236, 247–8; workers 6, 24, 26, 58,
  134–5, 137, 233, 248–50
community, definitions of 2
community activists 1–3, 42, 116, 228–31;
  and community development practitioners

Index

42, 229; and community leaders 1;
passionate 33; unpaid 23; well-intentioned
white 199
community arts 10
Community-Based Network Organizations 1,
3, 6, 11, 13–14, 56, 58, 64–6, 81, 88, 153,
258–9
community development 3–10, 12–14,
16–19, 21–7, 31, 34, 54, 84–6, 93–6,
137–8, 144–6, 163–5, 178–82, 184–5,
192–4, 201, 223–5, 233–4, 252–3,
260–1; academics 10, 259; actions 191;
activities 2, 55–6, 231; agencies 2, 55–6,
62, 89, 91, 144, 169, 172–3, 226–7,
255, 257; approaches 6, 9, 13, 25, 32,
88, 154–5, 227, 233; definitions 2, 31;
groups 153; infrastructure 195, 208, 212,
216; initiatives 13, 184, 187, 220, 248;
integrated 15; new 174; non-governmental
14; participatory 36; practice 3, 5, 8–10,
14–15, 19–25, 27–32, 34, 54–5, 60–1,
112, 116–17, 169–71, 195, 199–201, 252,
254–6, 258–61; practitioners 1–5, 14–17,
20–1, 24–5, 31–4, 56–8, 68, 105–6,
113–19, 124–6, 138–42, 144–6, 165,
169–74, 181–2, 187–9, 194–201, 225–6,
228–33, 247–51, 260–1; professional 5,
113; programmes 4–5, 9, 13, 15, 19, 23,
201, 206, 226–7, 257–8, 260; projects
12–13, 15–16, 21, 38, 57, 72, 87, 92,
106, 134–5, 177; promoting 238; rural
12; supporting 8, 12, 27; sustainable 187;
workers 38, 134, 190–1, 205, 213
Community Development Corporations 13,
16, 26, 56, 227, 252
Community Development Foundation 179,
234
Community Development Journal 7, 17,
25–7, 193, 224, 252–3
community groups 115–17, 119, 138, 140,
142–3, 170, 173, 195, 198, 200, 225,
227–8, 230, 232; local 133; and networks
103; supporting 231
Community Health Assessment 105–6, 108
Community Health Exchange 154, 236
community leaders 1, 55, 58, 60, 64, 69, 74,
120, 122, 199–201, 204–6, 216, 219;
accessible 171; and activists 58–60,
89–91, 227; existing 62; informal 204;
local 78, 202; participatory 198; volunteer
69
community leadership 102, 195, 212, 217,
224; groups 159; nurturing youth 216;
roles 8; structures 110; teams 214
Community Learning and Development
Standards Council, Scotland 50, 52–4, 168
community participation 86, 89–90, 125,
215–16, 218, 236, 239, 252; active 239;
informal 215; meaningful 216; proactive
216
Community Reinvestment Act 12

Community Service Centers 127
companies 3, 7, 110, 114, 118, 128, 130,
188, 197; armament 11; construction 77;
consultancy 227; German energy 130;
multi-national 118; oil 115; private 79;
public benefit 77
competencies 22–5, 96; see also core
competencies
confidentiality 44, 51, 83
conflict 14–17, 22, 53, 58, 73, 117, 119, 141,
174, 198, 200, 254–5, 258; family 250;
inter-racial/religious 15; intergenerational
212; potential 34; reduction 257;
resolution 56, 174, 200; social system
217; wartime 94; zones 15
consciousness-raising workers 38, 139, 192
consensus 60, 88, 99, 112, 117, 141, 204
conservatives 4
contamination 126, 128
core competencies 25; for community
development practice 17, 21; required of
all community development practitioners
24
core values 44, 46, 102, 106, 110, 149, 151,
155, 162, 213, 217, 221
Coronavirus pandemic 43, 92, 142, 254, 261
Council of Europe 14, 27, 124–5
countries 3–12, 14–15, 17–27, 29, 32–3,
89, 101, 103, 170–1, 173–4, 181–3,
223–4, 226, 245–6, 257–9; democratic
13; developed 4, 7, 11, 16, 91, 143,
254, 259; industrial 11; oil-producing
11; poorer 18, 30; post-Soviet 181–2;
wealthiest 18
COVID-19 43, 45, 48, 107, 110, 122, 126,
145, 147, 149, 179, 247–9, 251; see also
Coronavirus pandemic
Craig, Gary 9
Crickley, Anastasia 17, 29–34
crime 121, 238
criminal gangs 81
critical analysis 151, 233
critical evaluation 229, 232
Croatia 92–4
crops 16, 158, 160, 246
crossing hands 208
CSG see community support group
Cuba 4, 10–11, 17
culture 31, 33, 85, 91, 94, 103–4, 107–8,
168–9, 174, 190–2, 202, 204–6, 208;
entrepreneurial 209–11; inclusive 199;
non-western 204; political 196; and power
85; of proactive community participation
216; working 174

data collection 228–9
DDC see District Development Coordinator
decision-making 15, 40–2, 45, 48, 53, 85–7,
90, 121, 124–5, 152, 155, 195, 197–9
decoding 156
Delors, Jacques 14

democracy 11, 19, 21–2, 30–1, 42, 64, 91, 112, 169, 255, 261
democratic participation 31, 195, 197, 199, 210–11, 221
democratic processes 222–3
demonstration projects 8
Department for International Development (previously called Ministry of Overseas Development) 4, 14, 26, 94, 206, 243
depression 181–2
developers 87
development, definitions of 2
development agencies 13, 19, 55–7, 72, 145, 227, 261; community 257; economic 145; international 4
development initiatives 19, 187–8
development practitioners 1, 20, 22, 86, 91, 180, 229, 246, 259; community 6, 10, 21, 106, 131, 258–9; economic 12; trained 24
development programmes 8, 15, 25, 59, 115, 175; domestic community 18; funding community 1, 15; international 9; peacebuilding community 15; public sector community 13; state-funded community 11; supporting rural community 4
development projects 4, 6, 94; economic 26, 47, 238; evaluating 6; expensive top-down 11; new community 61; promoting social 9; supporting community 13
devolution 236
dialogical model 139
digital devices 249–50, 259
digital divide 21, 91, 249
digital technologies 21, 256, 259–60
dignity 32, 36, 65–6, 73, 95, 151, 176–7, 222
disabilities 2, 15, 21, 27, 30–1, 95, 169, 174, 176–83, 255, 257
disabled persons 143, 173–4, 181–2
disadvantage 9, 18, 33, 58, 88, 115, 140, 156, 171, 192, 255–6; cultural 139; groups 86, 140, 171, 248–50; inter-related 18; long-term 141; people's 33, 171; populations 249–50; reinforced 258; structural 9, 192
"Discapacidad y Desarrollo" 176
disciplines 3, 6–9, 13, 17, 21, 24–5, 32–4, 86, 91, 144–6, 173, 255, 260; academic 1, 22, 31, 180, 182; new 6; occupational 22; professional 6; specialist 25
discrimination 3, 32, 34, 36–8, 44, 48, 53, 121–2, 140, 170–2, 174–5, 177, 255–8; caste-based 36–7; entrenched institutionalized 34, 38; experienced 172; institutional 112, 140; political 171; systemic 3, 174, 254; transphobic 15
disorders, traumatic 93
diversity 30, 32–4, 48, 50, 56, 61, 164, 169–75, 181, 189, 193, 196–7, 209–10; community's 195; cultural 106; gender 187, 213; and inclusion 24, 138, 170–2, 188, 228; personal 174; skill-based 47; sustained 171

Donnelly, Dessie xix, 39, 39–42
Dundee 154, 156–7
Dunscombe, Michelle 101, 194–202

Eastern Europe 8, 14–15
ecocide 19
ecology 19, 66, 196
economic development 12, 24, 30, 59, 164, 173, 189, 226, 234, 236, 256
Ecuador 174, 176
Edinburgh Tenants Federation 40–2
education 1, 4, 9–11, 35–6, 106–7, 138–9, 143–4, 155–6, 168, 172–3, 177, 204, 206–7, 221–2, 245–7; accessing 38; adult 6, 204; civic 122; community 4, 6, 12, 21, 47, 114, 233–4; and empowerment 22, 31; environmental 78; formal 143; goals 209; professional community development 259; services 256
educators 8, 16–17, 33, 60, 139–40, 261
Egypt 5
ELB see Epworth Local Board
elders 46–8, 173, 190, 192, 204–7;; role of 206–7
employees 7–8, 197
employers 3, 7–8, 23–5, 28–9, 42, 52–3, 114, 128–9, 234–5, 259–60; non-governmental 30, 32; and practitioners 23
empowerment 15, 17, 22, 31, 38, 40, 48, 50–1, 105–7, 110, 120–1, 150–1, 153, 177–8, 206–7; economic 93–4; methods 145; process 48; profession 1–25, 27; social 78; sustainable long-term 109
engagement 41–2, 55–7, 61–6, 73–4, 81–2, 84, 90, 110–12, 135, 137, 173, 209–10, 232, 234–6, 253; active 64, 66; adult learning 210; civic 209; early 73; and inclusion of diverse voices 173; local participatory 73; long-term 63; meaningful 81, 90, 137; process 61–2; strong 41
engineers 67, 260–1
entrepreneurs 126, 189, 201, 208–10
environment 6, 19–20, 27, 58, 127–8, 131, 141–2, 236; hostile 42; issues 6, 23; policies 14; problems 9; unhealthy 16
environmentalism 20
Epworth, Zimbabwe 120–3
equality 30–2, 38, 50, 121, 164, 170–2, 224, 235–6; democratic 192; and human rights 32, 38; of opportunity 30; promoting 193; social 218; and social justice 22, 31, 39
equity 36, 46, 51, 154, 187, 238, 256; commitment to 46; and human rights 48; social justice and 154; value of 154
Espindola, Ecuador 176, 177, 179
ETF see Edinburgh Tenants Federation
ethics 29–54, 82; and community development practice 29; and human rights principles 82; professional 24, 34, 50, 116, 261; and professionalism 50; and values 24, 29

Index

ethnic minorities 9, 148
ethnicity 21, 30–1, 56, 169, 172, 174, 195
Europe 5, 8, 14, 27, 54
European Union 8, 14
evaluating communities 241
evaluation 83, 193, 197, 224–5, 227, 229,
    231–2, 234, 242, 244, 250, 256, 260;
    continuous 243; critical 229, 232; cycle
    235; framework 232, 235; interim 242;
    methods 242; mid-term 177; outcomes-
    based 242; participatory 17, 177;
    practices 198–9; processes 210, 227,
    243; programme 211; projects 242;
    qualitative 227; regular 246; reports
    227–8, 232, 242, 244; stakeholders
    242; strategies 243; strong 232; work
    242, **243**
evidence 5, 8, 15, 23, 30, 78, 161–2, 225,
    228, 231, 234–5; empirical 121; existing
    223; photo 41; scientific 25
exchange 14, 24, 186, 210, 241, 256, 260;
    encouraged learning 8; farmer 65; peer-to-
    peer 200; professional 183; of viewpoints
    98; youth arts 185
exclusion 44–5, 111, 172, 257; digital 259–61;
    experience of 226; social 32, 48, 95, 172,
    180
exit strategies 201
expertise 2, 6, 20, 23, 56–61, 114, 116,
    129, 131, 138–9, 142, 144; balanced 7;
    external 201; financial management 13;
    organizational 8, 129; professional 142,
    152; public affairs 227; specialist 9
experts 50, 56–7, 59, 71, 73–4, 90, 94–5,
    117, 126, 128, 132
extra-judicial killings 81–2

facilitators 126, 151, 153
families 43, 45, 126, 128, 131, 134–5,
    148, 151, 156, 160, 181–2, 184, 204–6,
    208; enabled 160; low-income 147,
    149; marginalized 150; needy 250;
    troubled 186; upper caste 37;
    vulnerable 160
family violence 212–13
Far Right ideology 25, 255
farmers 18, 65–6, 74, 193
Feng, Juxiong 248–51
Ferrie, Jo 225–32
films 10, 41, 143, 146, 172
First Peoples 191
focus groups 73, 86, 90, 159, 177, 205, 208,
    228, 242, 246
food 19–20, 66, 72–3, 108, 122, 124, 158,
    161, 174; banks 108; baskets 72; boxes
    105; diversity 74; poverty 107–8; sharing
    124
Ford Foundation 5, 12
France 12
Freire, Paulo 10, 26, 33, 54, 139, 150, 152,
    156, 168

Fung, Kwok-kin 138–46, 248–51
furniture (from felled trees) 46

garment workers 34–7; districts 35; in India
    34; potential 36; sensitizing 35
Gavaa, Tsetsgee 72–5
GBV see gender-based violence
GCDEX see Global Community Development
    Exchange
Gemmell, Kirsty 49–53
gender 30–1, 36, 56, 58, 60, 66, 121, 159, 169,
    172, 192; based violence 43, 121–2, 187–9,
    256; based violence, see also sexual
    gender-based violence; discrimination 8,
    255; diversity 187, 213; equality 66, 187,
    256, 261; inclusiveness 65
general managers 212
Georgia 17, 174, 180–2
Germany 9
GHD see Girls' Holistic Development
Gibson, Huston 85–92
Gilpin (demolition company) 131
girls 19, 43–5, 121–3, 142, 144, 204–7,
    224, 255–6; adolescent 35, 203–5,
    207; experiencing marginalization 43;
    supporting 206; young 120, 122
Girls' Holistic Development 204–5
glasnost reforms 14
Global Community Development Exchange 17
global pandemic 101, 254–5
global warming 18, 25, 64
globalization 14, 17, 64
Gorbachev, President 14
governments 4–5, 8–15, 17–18, 20–1, 24–5,
    44, 56, 58, 150, 152, 188–9, 194–5, 236,
    250, 256–60; agencies 16, 126, 234;
    authoritarian 19; central 18, 78, 121, 153;
    communist 4, 18; Conservative 185;
    elected 19; and local authorities 58, 258;
    municipal 78, 179; national 17, 25, 177,
    206, 221, 256–8; western 5, 206
graduation ceremonies 187–8
Grameen Bank 12
grandmother leaders 203, 205–7
Grandmother Project 204, 206–7
grandmothers 160, 201, 204–7
graphic harvest of the ABCD (un)conference 100
grassroots xix–xx, 63–4, 66, 69, 81, 86,
    91, 208–9, 211, 255, 260; approach 63;
    development 91; groups 86
Green Belt 77–8
"Green New Deal" 257
Grieg, Andy 46–8
Gulbenkian Foundation 12
Guterres, António 254

hamlets 35–7
Harman, Ursula 124–6
Hashagen, Stuart 233–6
health 4, 6, 26, 69, 72, 106–7, 142, 154–5,
    160, 162, 164, 192–3, 232–3, 235–6,

255–7; adolescent 206; care 19, 105, 107, 134, 177, 247; crisis 66; delivery 88; disparities 106, 108; education 26, 69, 91; experts 117, 196; inequalities 155; initiatives 71, 236; issues 129, 145, 149, 154, 156, 236, 255; mental 41, 107–8; outcomes 105, 108; physical 107; professionals 6, 249; programmes 11; reproductive 206; services 39, 107, 150, 212; workers 3, 9, 13, 24–5, 91, 144, 165
Health Issues in the Community 154–7, 236
healthcare 6, 30, 56, 96, 106–7, 238, 254
Heinicke-Motsch, Karen 176–9
HEIs see Higher Education Institutes
Herzegovina 92–3
Higher Education Institutes 3, 7, 15, 23, 259–60
HIIC see Health Issues in the Community
HIV/AIDS 18, 121, 158, 188
holistic approaches 3, 8, 106, 209, 217, 243
Hong Kong 18, 97–8, 147–8, 201, 215, 218, 232, 247–9
horticultural industries 43
housing 4, 7, 13, 40, 46, 119, 127, 134, 184, 236, 238; poverty 135; problems 41; projects 47, 135; workers 9; working-class terraced 184
Housing Rights in Practice 40–1
HRBA see human rights-based approach
Hrvatska Kostajnica City and Una region, Croatia 93
human resources 64, 67, 164–5, 205, 213
human rights 15, 27, 30, 32–3, 37–42, 46, 48, 80–1, 171–2, 220–3, 252, 255; abuses 9, 15, 22, 41, 257; approach 39–40, 42; awareness 121; commitments 41; and community development 223; obligations 222; promoting 21; protecting 82; recognizing 32; standards 41–2; traditional 40; universal 39; work 40, 82
Human Rights Agenda 80–3
Hung, Suet-lin 138–46, 248–51
Hungary xxi, 14, 17, 118–19, 134, 185–6
HURIA see Human Rights Agenda
HURIA Executive Director addressing community members 80
Hustedde, Ron 194–202
Hwange Agricultural Show 189
Hwange District Development Coordinator 188

IACD see International Association for Community Development
ill health 8, 118, 155–6
Illich, Ivan 5
inclusion 50, 57, 81, 85, 93–6, 110, 116, 169–73, 175–93, 228–9, 232, 252, 256; and accountability 50; and diversity 175, 181; of marginalized groups 171; political 21, 171, 195; promoting 169; and respect 170, 173; social 17, 124

Inclusive Practices Festival 182
Inclusive Practices Network 180–3
India 8, 11, 13, 17, 26, 34–5, 62–3, 65, 142, 261
IndianCare 212, 213–14
Indigenous 3, 16, 46, 191–2; communities 10–11, 16, 19, 34, 46, 64, 66, 172, 191; peoples 191; young men 191
inequalities 9, 30, 32, 41, 48, 169–70, 173, 226, 228, 230, 254–8, 261; economic 16; entrenched 39; extreme 261; global 256; internal 96; long-term 228; racial 256; reducing 11, 20; socio-economic 16, 18, 257; systemic 13
information and communications technology 21
infrastructure 24, 69, 71, 103, 111, 153, 194–223; administrative 70; basic 94; civic 220; for community development 194, 197; projects 4, 18; regional 211; social development 4, 206; sustainable 216; transport 5
injustices 80, 200, 228, 230, 257; economic 169–71; social 32, 38, 152
Institut Universitaire de Développement International 245–6
institutes 8, 100–1, 260; higher education 3, 259; national support 8; regional 8
integrity 30, 32
interests 17–18, 22, 24, 31–3, 37–8, 40–1, 51, 55–6, 86, 115–17, 169–71, 220, 223, 234; community's 85; conflicts of 30, 86, 88; growing 5–6, 74, 233, 257; lost 125; mutual 239; narrow 194; public 30; strategic 226
International Association for Community Development 1, 3, 6, 8–9, 15–17, 21–4, 26–8, 31, 34, 112, 182, 252, 260
International Community Education Association 185
international days 45
International Standards for Community Development Practice 24–5, 27, 34, 141, 182, 195, 261
IPN see Inclusive Practices Network
Ireland 14, 17, 24, 33–4, 39, 234
Israel 5, 17
issues 33–4, 36–7, 41–2, 44–5, 56–62, 73–4, 88–91, 114–18, 121–2, 128–9, 139–40, 144, 151–2, 155–6, 160, 173–4, 188–9, 191, 196–8, 259–61; of conduct 53; of power 170; of racism 190; of violent extremism 82
IUDI see Institut Universitaire de Développement International

jargon 59, 143
Jennings, Anne 46–8
jobs 2–3, 5, 13, 18, 23, 49, 52, 56, 131–2, 134, 257; community development type 15, 114; good quality 56, 96; and local

enterprises 226; lost 72; for mothers of disabled children 182
Jordan (neighborhood of Hong Kong) *248*
journals 7, 137, 252, 260
justice 94, 171, 177, 191

Kazakhstan 26, 181–2
Kentucky Entrepreneurial Coaches Institute 208–9, 211, 224
Kenya 17, 34, *43*, 44, 62, 80–1
key performance indicators 250–1
Keynesian interventionist policies 11
Knezić, Dragana 93–6
Knopf, R 170
knowledge 55–6, 65–6, 128–9, 139–42, 145–8, 154–5, 164–7, 188, 192, 204–5, 209, 211, 217, 246–7, 249–50; creating 139; existing 61, 166; new 95, 139, 142–3; of participants 155; pre-determined 139; shared 163; technical 99
KPIs *see* key performance indicators
Kwai Fong District 97–8
Kwok, Kate 98

Lachapelle, Paul 225–32
"ladder of participation" 86, *87*
landowners 114, 131, 139
languages 24, 90, 144, 148, 153, 169, 172, 182–3, 213
Lathouras, Tina 190–2
Latin America 4, 7, 10, 18–20, 27, 207
laws 80, 128, 132, 177–8; civic 176; discriminatory 172; inclusive 178; international 40; local 174, 177–8; municipal 177; national 176
lawyers 40, 117, 132
LBSI *see* Life Bloom Services International
leaders 56, 61, 70–1, 78, 115–17, 192, 194–5, 199, 222, 225–6, 239, 241–2, 246; adult 221; business 13, 61; emerging 44, 199; entrepreneurial 209; faith 9, 61; informal 194–5; opinion 196; political 14; potential 213; religious 9, 114; western 205
leadership 65, 67, 71, 171, 194–5, 197, 199, 201–2, 204–6, 214, 216, 220–1, 238–40; capacities 139, 238; democratic 198, 202; economic 256; effective 66; and infrastructure 24, 194–5, 201, 204, 221; inspiring 239; programmes 199, 201, 209; roles 44, 60, 66, 70, 117, 128, 173, 195; rural 210; shared 205; skills 138, 239; training 152, 204–5, 207; weak 80, 204
LEAP *see* Learning, Evaluation and Planning
learning 33–4, 40, 48, 103–4, 111, 138–40, 142–6, 153, 155, 157, 165–8, 181–2, 185, 191–2, 218, 234–5, 242–4, 246–7, 259–61; action-oriented 140; adult 50; collective 141, 146; cross-institutional 153; digital 250; intergenerational 222; international 223; liberatory 139; ongoing 164; organizational 17; participatory 27, 205; positive 248; professional xix, 51, 53; programmes 143, 260; relationship-based 166; shared 226; systematic 216
Learning, Evaluation and Planning 234–6
learning networks 164, 166–7
Ledwith, Margaret. 32
Lefebvre, Jean-Denis 127–9
Leith, Scotland *39*
liberal democrats 4–5, 11
Life Bloom Services International 43–5
local authorities 3, 9, 15, 18, 40, 42, 88–90, 94–6, 136, 139, 256–8; *see also* local communities
local communities 6, 9, 16, 18–19, 73, 77, 83, 92, 94, 96, 127–9, 135–6, 145, 225–6, 228
local government 1, 5, 13–14, 70, 73–5, 81, 114, 150, 152–3, 210, 220
local laws 174, 177–8
local organizations 95, 105, 177, 179, 242
Lomas de Zamora 76–7

Mabo, Eddie Koiki 191
MacGillivray, Clare 39–42
Maciene 158–9, 161–2
Madziwa, Bongani 120, 123
magazines 4, 17, 238
maize 158, 160
Manchikanti, Jaya 212–14
Mandela, President. Nelson 15, 169
Mann, Samuel 105–8
marginalized groups 73, 170–1, 216–17, 228
marine contamination 126
markets 97–8, 189, 210
Marques, Taícia 76–9
Matvievskaya, Anastasia 180–3
Matvievskiy, Vladimir 181
Mayan, M. 231
Mayo, M. 32, 193n5
McConnell, Charlie 1–29, 55–63, 113–19, 254–261
McConnell Family Foundation 241
McHendry, Kate 154–7
McKnight, J. 89
MDGs *see* Millennium Development Goals
Mealey, Elisabeth 204
media 11, 58, 114, 122, 128, 130–2, 142, 146, 172, 227–8
meetings 58–60, 65, 69, 85–6, 91, 101, 104, 124, 126, 128, 131–2, 135–6, 177–8; consultative 17; face-to-face 69, 249; introductory 60; neighborhood 87; organized 73; public 41, 86, 128, 131–2; virtual 78
mega cities 16
Members of Children's Parliament in Scotland *220*
membership 27, 50, 260; encouraged 16; fees 7; representative 239

MENA *see* Middle East and North Africa
mental health 41, 107–8
Micheni, Meriba Mwende 43–5
Middle East 4, 18–19
Millennium Development Goals 17–18
Ministry of Exterior Commerce and Tourism 125
Ministry of the Environment 128
Ministry of Women Affairs 121, 188
minorities 9, 23, 86, 148, 257; ethnic 9, 148; religious 2
mobilization 74, 77, 95, 111, 120–1, 132, 181, 188, 249
models 19, 33, 41, 44, 64, 77, 138–9, 227, 234, 242–3, 246; of community health care 106; dialogical 139; emerging research 106; empowerment 122; existing 42; gender transformation 122; hierarchical leadership 195; for learning in community development 138; limited 106; physical 141; research 105; single crop contract farming 66; social entrepreneurship 66; sustainable 256; traditional 42; visual 98
Mondragon (co-operative) 12
money 6, 12–14, 43, 52, 61, 72, 89–90, 96, 117, 131–3, 180
Mongolia 62, *72*, 74–5
monitoring 64, 66, 79, 83, 90, 124, 197, 221, 229, 231, 235
Montana, USA 232, 238
Moringa Project 246
Mozambique 11, 145, *158*
Muia, Daniel 113–19, 254–61
mural arts project *184*
Mwatsefu, Yusuf Lule 80–3

Naivasha, Kenya 43–4
Narayan, Pradeep 35–8
Narito, Lucia *158*
National Counter Terror Centre 81
national governments 17, 25, 177, 206, 221, 256–8
National Institutes of Community Development 8
The National Standards for Community Engagement *57*, 84n5, 84n6, 235
nationalists 25
Nature-based Solutions 77–8
NCTC *see* National Counter Terror Centre
Needs-Based Community Development Approaches 112n12
neighborhoods 14, 44–5, 124, 141, 147, 149; disadvantaged 9, 233; urban 10, 88; vulnerable 174
neighbourhoods, needy 148
"neo-cons" (neo-conservatives) 10–11, 24
Nepal 17, 145, 150, 153
networking 7, 21, 80, 95, 107–8, 118, 163, 165–6, 200, 250, 259

networks 102–3, 110–11, 150, 152–3, 163–4, 167, 209, 211, 217, 222, 236, 239, 242; active support 42; community-based 189; comprehensive 69; developed 109; existing 167; hosting 236; international 10; issue-based 66; national 15; planning groups 103; public 127; of relationships 163, 167; and resources 102; social 215, 218; well-developed 95
New Zealand 17, 22, 92, 105–6
Ng Kwan-lim, Kenny 97–9
Ng Mee-kam, Prof. 98
NGOs *see* non-governmental organizations
NGUNI 158, *159*, 160–2, 168
Nhapi, Tatenda 120–3
Nicaragua 62, 68–9
Nixon, President. Richard 10
non-governmental organizations 1, 3, 5–7, 11, 13, 35–6, 56, 77–80, 88, 150, 176–9, 204, 206–7, 248–50, 257–60
non-indigenous community members 191
non-profit organizations 238
Nordic countries 14
North Africa 4, 18–19
Northern Ireland 12, 15
Northern Products detergent making graduation ceremony *187*
nurses 106, 160, 249

Obama, President. Barack 18
OECD *see* Organization for Economic Co-operation and Development
One Valley Community Foundation *237*
Opačić, Anna 93–6
OPD *see* Organization of Persons with Disabilities
OPEC 11
open space practice discussion *49*
open space workshops 141
oppression 140, 191–2
organic agriculture development 74
organic agriculture programme 74
organic agriculture training 74
Organization for Economic Co-operation and Development 14
Organization of Persons with Disabilities 177, 179
Organizational Development of Self-Managed Organizations and Networks 152
organizations 21–2, 31, 33–4, 51, 53, 56–7, 62–5, 80–1, 117, 138, 145, 172–3, 196–7, 199, 222–3, 234; community-based 1, 26, 56, 65–6, 81, 88, 121, 234; environmental 257; formal 126, 141; funded 42; informal 218; international 94–5, 206; national 236; non-government 94, 103, 194; partner 202, 216; social 61, 218; sponsoring 244; successful 181; systematic 218; voluntary 63
Ortiz, Anna C. 69–71
"Our Kwai Fong Circuit" city-planning workshop *97*

outcomes 32, 34, 44–5, 47, 69–70, 88, 90–2, 95, 103, 164–5, 212–13, 226, 234–5, 242, 244; accidental 41; anticipated 200; creative 48; household 243; intended 41; and learnings 244; measure 243; negative 256; programme 204; refined 235

P/CVE *see* prevention and countering of violent extremism
Pachamama Mamacocha Ayni event, Peru *124*
Page, Daphne 105–8
Pan-Canadian Learning Community 243
Pan Himalayan Grassroots Development Foundation 63
pandemic 45, 55, 101, 107–8, 126, 147, 149, 156, 213, 254–5, 259
PAR *see* participatory action research
parents 180–2, 204
participants 47–8, 50, 52, 139, 148–9, 155–7, 160–2, 164–7, 182–3, 192, 197–8, 200, 209–11, 246, 248; active 132, 181; grandmother 205; illiterate 205; and practitioners 34; trained 47; and tutors 155; workshop 210
participation 45, 48, 57, 77, 80, 85–8, 91, 109–10, 149, 176, 178–9, 199, 201, 217, 252; citizen 5, 19, 26, 86, 112, 124, 192, 224, 252; collective 149; democratic 31, 195, 197, 199, 210–11, 221; diverse 91; effective 195; equal 74, 219; increased 189; of local communities 77; meaningful 217, 223; public 15, 27, 85, 98
Participation and the Practice of Rights 40
participatory action research 41, 226–8, 234
Participatory Guarantee System 65, 74
participatory planning 24, 61, 85–111, 138, 145, 259; in community development 86; effective 89; methods 145; practices 85; processes 89, 98
Partners in Change 36–8
Partnership for Organic Agriculture 74
partnerships 17–18, 21, 23, 40, 42, 69–70, 80–1, 83, 86–7, 94–6, 105, 110, 197, 221–2, 239–40; creating 45; empowering 85, 245; forging 186; funded 18; multi-agency 145; public/private/NGO 13
Paterson, Maggie 49–53
Patie's Talk Show 188–9
Pauchulo, A.L. 231
Paul: Anita 55–83; Kalyan 55–83
PAYN *see* Progressive African Youth Network
peace and reconciliation projects 15, 81–2, 94
Peace Corps 4
Pemsel, Michael 184
Pemsel, Sue 184
perestroika reforms 14
PGS *see* Participatory Guarantee System
philanthropic foundations 21
Philippines 4, 7, 17
Phiri, Yvonne 187–9

PiC *see* Partners in Change
planners 6, 27, 87, 101, 112
planning 4, 6, 85, 87–8, 90, 97–8, 101, 103, 131, 135–6, 144–5, 150, 152–3, 178, 234–6; activities 181; committee's decisions 132; decentralized 64; effective 30; financial 240; forward 214; groups 103; integrated 235; long-term 127; outcome-led 235; participative 17, 171; physical 98; proactive 123; process 88–91, 98–9, 122; programmes 65; service 219; strategic 86, 95, 197, 213; top-down 6, 14; transport 171
plans 41, 48, 98, 101, 108, 111, 161–2, 197, 201–2, 207, 209; annual government development 44; business 197, 202, 209; community post-COVID-19 recovery 108; comprehensive 112; developing 141; forestation 78; succession 213; working 124–5
PO *see* program officer
POA *see* Partnership for Organic Agriculture
policies 4–5, 8, 17, 175, 177–8, 180, 192, 195–6, 201–2, 213, 226, 230–1, 234, 256, 258; inclusive 231; new 230; planning 238; positive 246; regional 230
policy makers 66, 226–32, 251, 260
political 4, 9–11, 20–2, 24–5, 54, 85–6, 106, 110–11, 113–14, 122–3, 128–9, 131, 169–71, 176, 184–5, 192, 195–6, 198, 218, 226; education 106; processes 86, 113–14, 155; systems 9, 176
politicization 10
politicians 32, 41, 114, 191, 226, 228; benign 16; local 13; national 132; syphoning funds 13
poll tax 185
Popper, Karl 3, 25n5, 33, 54n15
popular education 128–9, 156
population 2, 44, 72, 76, 86, 93–5, 124, 126, 128, 238, 248
population: groups 107; growth 97; world's 16, 256
populism 261
Potable Water and Sanitation Committee 69–71
poverty 2, 5, 8–9, 11, 18–19, 43, 45, 48, 124, 127, 184, 241–3, 255, 258, 261; abject 245; alleviation 64, 232; amelioration 9; causes of 12; extreme 39, 134–6, 255; global 256; levels 19; reducing 241; reduction 11, 18–19, 242–3
poverty rate 176
poverty reduction 18
power 10–11, 13, 40–2, 85–7, 113–14, 137, 139–40, 155–6, 168, 170, 174, 192–3, 195–6, 221–2, 224–32; citizens 87, 90; consumer spending 103; differentials 173; dynamics 2, 173; economic 16; imbalances 39, 90, 140, 228; inequalities of 34, 39; invisible 196; organizational

196; people's 32; positions of 172, 229;
structures 42, 66, 85, 200
PPR *see* Participation and the Practice of
Rights
Practice Insights (magazine) 3–4, 17
practice learning 163–7
practitioners 3, 5–8, 10–11, 22–5, 28–34,
39–42, 44–5, 50, 52–3, 55–6, 89–91,
101–2, 139–45, 163–7, 172–3, 231–2,
234–6, 255, 257, 259–61; and academics
7, 32; active 107; and activists 40, 42;
articulating 51; black 8; civil/human rights
30; and educators 17; isolated 167;
like-minded 92; professional 10; skilled
25; unpaid 16; in Western and Eastern
countries 14
"praxis" process 42, 139, 151, 213
prevention and countering of violent
extremism 81–3
priests 9–10
primary care of the elderly, Hong Kong *215*
privatization 11
problem solving 3, 25, 33, 88, 143–4, 198,
251
problems 2–3, 9, 12–13, 55–6, 58–61, 89,
113, 115–16, 119, 139–40, 142–5, 168,
226, 228, 250; chronic 40; common 77,
260; compounding 250; environmental
127; family 186; identified 31; individual
149; interlinked 144; local 125; multiple
11; respiratory 128; shared 88; social 171;
socio-economic 186
professional development 2, 8, 23, 25, 34, 49,
145, 255–6, 258
professionalism 5, 23, 50, 52
programmes 5–6, 8–9, 14, 19, 35–6, 47–8,
65–6, 72–4, 94–5, 135, 171–2, 206–7,
210–11, 234–6, 255–8; aid 14; ambitious
20; anti-poverty 14; awareness-raising
36; community arts 10; comprehensive
74; cultural 183; entrepreneurial 210;
environmental 16, 62; evaluating 250;
funded 236; government's empowerment
188; international professional
development 17; local government
153; long-term residential internship
182; officer 36–7; participatory 221;
regeneration 6; sensitization 36; state-
funded 4; youth entrepreneurship 206–7,
211
Progressive African Youth Network 188
projects 13–14, 40–2, 44–8, 69–71, 73–4,
81–3, 94–9, 106–11, 120–2, 140–2,
147–9, 151–3, 158–61, 177–9, 181–2,
184–7, 216–18, 227, 242–4, 246;
community-initiated 88; craft 228;
environmental 174; group 156; inclusive
93, 183; and networks 111; planning 83,
91, 198–9; and programs 89, 236; staff
152, 216–18; teams 40, 98–9
public health 127, 147–9, 246, 255

public/private/NGO partnerships 13
public services 76, 108, 134, 233, 236, 250

Quebec government 127
Quebec province 127
Quebrada Verde community 77

racism 7, 9, 26, 34, 140, 171, 174, 190–3,
255–7; overt 191; systemic 9, 171, 256
racist ideologies 25
radicals 4
reciprocity cycle *78*
reconciliation projects 15, 81–2, 94
recycled industrial material *46*
Red Water Arts 184–6
refugee camps 228, 254–5
Regan, President. Ronald 14
Reid, Katie 220–3
relationships 30, 52, 56–7, 61–2, 86, 99, 136,
163–7, 191–2, 222–3, 235, 238, 240;
close 107; community 215; developmental
191; egalitarian 192; empowering 86, 106;
established 103; inter-generational 206;
inter-personal 40; strengthened 103, 118,
238, 240
religious minorities 2
research 8–9, 12, 56, 58, 62, 81–2, 105–6,
108, 163–5, 168, 172, 223, 260; action 41,
121, 204, 226–8, 234, 252; background
55, 58; baseline 82; exercises 81; market
209; methods 86, 105–6; partnerships
108; preliminary 58–9; projects 125, 164,
242; rigorous 234
residents 2, 5, 36, 40–2, 69–71, 97–9, 119,
124, 127, 129–33, 148–9, 238; community
92; disabled 174; engaging 70, 141; local
14, 118, 128, 130; permanent 238; rural 105
residents voting 132
resources 13–14, 32, 51–2, 57–8, 60–2, 87,
90, 94–6, 107–8, 118, 135–6, 140, 148–9,
152, 170, 195–6, 216–17, 226, 235–6,
249–51; allocated 96; channeling 63;
collective 40, 141; critical 67; developing
107; distributing 249; evidence-based
105; financial 151; grandmother 204;
inadequate 33; linking 249; mobilizing 65,
217; natural 64–5, 74; non-governmental
255; sufficient 217–18
"Rodas de Conversa" (conversation circles)
159, 161
Roosevelt, Eleanor 39, 225
Ross, Colin 138–46
Ross, Dyann 190–2
Ross, Jean 105–8
rural communities 5, 24, 56, 69, 86, 92,
105–6, 158, 176; isolated 119, 145; local
92–3; poorer 4, 139; small 130; vulnerable
174
Russia 27, 72, 181–3
RWA *see* Red Water Arts
Rwanda 15

Index

Sabeka, Nyarai 187–9
Saemaul Undong movement (South Korea) 4
San Isidro 69
Sánchez, Yamile 76–9
SCDC *see* Scottish Community Development
    Centre
SCEC *see* Scottish Community Education
    Council
Scheib, Holly Ann 169–76
schools 27, 36, 43, 61, 82, 94–6, 186, 211,
    220–3; closures *43*; community 6; high
    210, 245; local 226; middle 210; primary
    130, 185; secondary 217; summer 40;
    training 207
Schumacher, Ernst 19, 27n66
Scotland xix, xxii, 16–17, 39–42, 49–50, 54,
    154, 156–7, 201, 220, 222–3, 232–4, 236
Scottish Community Development Centre 57,
    84, 154, 233–6, 253
Scottish Community Education Council
    16–17, 27
Scottish devolution 236
Scottish Human Rights Commission 40, 54
SDGs *see* Sustainable Development Goals
Second World War 4–5
self-confidence 115, 186, 205–6
self-help groups 44, 63, 65, 73, 150
Sen, Amartya. 54n7
Senegal 201, 204, 206
sexual gender-based violence 43, 121–2
Shaker, Siena 109–11
shared interests 113
Shauri, Halimu Suleiman 80–3
SHGs *see* self-help groups
Sissimuka Project 160
skills 47–8, 50, 55, 57, 61, 65–6, 74, 101–3,
    117–18, 138–43, 149–52, 154–5,
    189, 192, 199; attainment 189; basic
    56; business 142; developing 145;
    development 46, 140; informal 110;
    interpersonal 186, 198; literacy 152; local
    152; new 185; social 122; technical 69
social change 5, 12, 26, 29, 34, 39, 48, 95,
    205–7, 218, 231
social democrats 11, 18
social development 17, 27, 123, 127
social justice 19, 22, 26, 30–1, *35*, 38–9, 42,
    106, 151, 154, 168, 170
social media 21, 25, 41, 58, 110–11, 143,
    146, 148, 173
social model of health 154–5, 236
social work 3, 6–7, 26, 30, 127, 139, 149,
    168, 173, 181, 248
social workers 6, 9, 13, 24–5, 91, 93, 148,
    213, 216–17, 221
Sorry Day Ceremony 190–1
"soul of the community" 116
South Africa 15–16, 26–7, 33, 92, 109, 159,
    199
spinning mills 35, 37

stakeholders 44, 75, 77, 81, 85, 88–9,
    92, 94, 96, *97*, 98–9, 105–6, 226;
    and accountability 81; analysis 83;
    engagement 137; external 95, 242; local
    94–5; strategic 44
standards 22–3, 25, 27, 30–1, 33–4, 40–1,
    53, 82, 88, 140, 235–6
Standards Council 50–3
state support 180, 258
stigma 44, 177, 180, 213, 228, 230
strategies 47–8, 78, 81, 85, 88–90, 118,
    121, 230, 233–4, 243, 245, 253, 255–7;
    collaborative inter-agency 258; community
    engagement 70; conflict resolution
    15; consensual 140; developing 40;
    dissemination 236; holistic intervention
    65; innovative training 205; local 249; and
    methods 85, 89–90; and programmes
    255–7; self-care 251; sustainable food
    security 161
Strathclyde 26, 233
strength-based approach 89
structural inequality 9, 139, 254
students *43*
study materials *43*
Saemaul Undong 4
support communities 119, 151, 202, 226
survival 70, 109, 136, 238, 240
Survival Day 191
sustainability 106, 110, 195, 197, 199, 201–2,
    209, 211, 213–14, 218, 224, 246, 250
sustainable change *63*
sustainable development 19–22, 31, 33, 39,
    64, 66, 252, 256–7, 261
Sustainable Development Goals *20*, 21, 30,
    195, 224, 230–1, 255–6
Syria 19
systemic discrimination 3, 174, 254
systemic racism 9, 171, 256

Talmage, Craig. 170
Tamarack Institute 101, 241
Tamil Nadu, India *35*
technical jargon 59, 143
technology, information and communications
    21
Theory of Change 80, 159
Thomas, David 5
Tongfeng Community, Wuhan 27
toolkits 7, 12, 144, 226, 229
top-down reconstruction and development
    5, 19
Torres Strait Islanders 190–1
training schools 207
transparency 30, 51, 64, 90, 200, 229, 232
tree-planting *76*
trust 30, 56, 59, 77–8, 82, 94, 151–2, 185,
    189, 228–9, 238, 240; community's 71;
    developing 64; establishing 83; increased
    151, 240; mutual 31, 52, 92–3, 222; and

relationships 151, 238, 240; social 215, 217
"tuenmununity" *215*

Ujamaa movement 4
UK 7–8, 17, 23, 26, 33, 49, 105–6, 118, 163, 168, 233–4; and Europe 5; government 28
UN-Habitat 258
UNCRC *see* United Nations Convention on the Rights of the Child
UNDP *see* United Nations Development Programme
UNESCO 10, 26, 258
United Kingdom *see* UK
United Nations 1, 26, 261
United Nations Convention on the Rights of the Child *220*, 221, 223
United Nations Convention on the Elimination of All Forms of Racial Discrimination 7
United Nations Convention on the elimination of all forms discrimination against women 8
United Nations Regional and Community Development Division and Division of Social Affairs 4
United Nations Convention on the Rights of Persons with Disabilities 15
United Nations Development Programme 4, 20, 258
United States 4, 10, 14, 17–20, 94, 204, 206–7, 238
University of Glasgow 233–4
US Agency for International Development 4, 94
USAID *see* US Agency for International Development
USSR 4, 11, 14, 72, 174

values 22, 24, 29–53, 64, 66, 114, 116–17, 144, 146, 151, 153–4, 159, 165–6, 204, 217–18; aesthetical 78; ageist 206; collectivist 205; cultural 56; functional 191; fundamental 219; indigenous 33; motivational 161; pharmaceutical 246; traditional 126, 146
Vibrant Communities (2002–2010) Evaluation Report 244
Vibrant Communities Project **243**
Victorian Multicultural Commission 212
violence 15, 120–2, 190, 192; domestic 188, 255; sexual 3, 118, 122, 140
VMC *see* Victorian Multicultural Commission

Vuković, Dijana 93–6
vulnerable communities 1–2, 9, 11–14, 18–19, 21–2, 25, 113–14, 118, 139, 144, 255–60

Wanjohi, Catherine 43–5
water nozzle *68*
water system *68*
WCDC *see* World Community Development Conference
Whiddon, Keith 105–8
white colonists 190
WHO *see* World Health Organization
Wilkinson, Bridget 239–40
Wilton, Julia 130–3
Wing Fong Street Market, Hong Kong *97*
Wingate, Jen 163–7
women and community development 15, 17, 44
Women's Community Development 27
Wong, King-lai 248–51
Wong, Siu-wai 147–9
workers 12, 30, 35, 43, 59, 148, 165, 173; community support 7; consciousness-raising 38, 139, 192; cultural 10, 24, 192; empowering women 36; environmental 24–5; health 3, 9, 13, 24–5, 91, 144, 165; mill 37; rural 16; youth 6, 216
workshops 78, 98–9, 121, 124–5, 147–9, 152, 164–5, 173, 181–2, 186, 210
World Bank 11, 13, 18, 26–7, 58, 112, 255, 258
World Community Development Conference 24
World Food Programme 258
World Health Organization 26, 258

xenophobia 22, 170–1, 255–7

YASC *see* Youth Alliance for Safer Cities
Young, Brigham 162
youth 6, 65–6, 120–3, 185, 188, 191, 206–7, 209–11, 215–19, 239–40, 245
Youth Alliance for Safer Cities 120–1
Youth and Community Services 186
youth leaders *215*
youth workers 6, 216

Zambrano, Olmedo 176–9
Zimbabwe 118, 120, 122–3, 174, 187–9
Zimbabwe Republic Police 121
Zucchetti, Anna 76–9

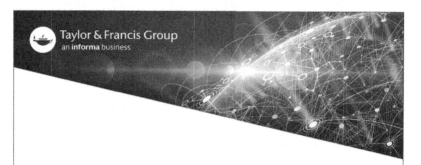

Made in the USA
Las Vegas, NV
29 July 2022

52320295R00171